$22.⁹⁵

A Collectors Identification
and Value Guide

LUCKEY'S
HUMMEL® FIGURINES
& PLATES
Tenth Edition

by Carl F. Luckey

ISBN 0-89689-100-3

DEDICATED
To

Sister Maria Innocentia (Berta Hummel)
1909-1946
for her legacy of joy.

Millions of people around the world have delighted in the artistic genius and love of this extraordinary woman.

ACKNOWLEDGEMENTS

In the Sixteen years I have been writing about *M.I. Hummel* collectibles, I have met an enormous number of very helpful people in the ongoing process of gathering data. So many, it's not practical to attempt naming them all. There are some, however, that have given me so much, including their friendship, that it would be an egregious error not to mention their names along with my heartfelt thanks.

Extra special thanks to Rue Dee and Judy Marker and Pat and Carol Arbenz for their most unselfish sharing, patience and hospitality over all these years.

Thank you Don Stephens and the Village of Rosemont, Illinois for allowing me to photograph your extraordinary collection for this book. A special thanks with a laurel wreath goes to Betty Rossi, director of the museum housing that collection, for putting up with me, a bunch of equipment, a photographer and my publisher on more than one occasion cluttering up the place and generally being an inconvenient intruder.

Others that directly contributed to this Tenth Edition in some way are Dan Alexander, Florence, Alabama; Marci Karales of Schmid, Inc., Randolph, Massachusetts; Jacques Nauer and Beatrix Laurent of Ars AG, Zug, Switzerland; Bill LaFevor, Nashville, Tennessee; Cathy Crist Talcott of the Hummel Museum, New Braunfels, Texas; and Gwen Toma of the *M.I. Hummel* Club, Pennington, New Jersey.

TABLE OF CONTENTS

AUTHOR'S NOTE TO THE COLLECTOR

It's hard for me to believe that I have been writing about *M.I. Hummel* figurines and related items for sixteen years now, and that this is the tenth edition of a book I had trouble selling to a publisher when I first proposed writing it back in 1976. That first edition was 300 pages long and by the time the ninth edition came out in 1992, it had grown to 450 pages; a full fifty percent! Because I am writing this long in advance of the release of this edition, I have no idea of its page length but suspect if it were to be reduced to the old 5" x 8½" format, it would exceed the ninth edition by a significant percentage. There has been that kind of increase in knowledge with regard to the hobby over the years. I have attempted with each new edition, to correct any misconceptions and mistakes in the previous edition and to present you with any additional information that had been uncovered since its release. There was little written about *M.I. Hummel* collectibles prior to the first edition of this book and some of what written guidance was available was either erroneous or misleading. This was not due to any attempt to profit through the presentation of spurious data, but simply due to the very little and study of the available limited resources at the time. I, and the majority of the other writers and collectors who have joined the ranks, have steadfastly tried to ferret out all the correct data possible and present it to you, the collector, so that you may enjoy the world of *Hummel* through the fun and excitement of new finds and additions to your collections. While we are on the subject of information, I urge you to read the next section. It will tell you how to use this book to your best advantage. If you use the book without reading how to use it, you may be led astray and make mistakes. It is sort of like trying to put the bicycle together on Christmas eve without referring to the directions.

Over my years of research and travel photographing collections and rare finds and picking the brains of dealers and collectors, I have noticed that there are many collectible items related to *Hummel* figurines, plates, etc., that make interesting additions to a *Hummel* collection. I have also noticed a growing interest in these items and therefore have expanded the books purview to include a selection of them.

Much of the information over the years has come directly from those of you who buy, read and use this book. You have been an important part in making the book the resounding success it has been over the years. I hope you will continue to help me as you have in the past. In addition to hearing from thousands of collectors and dealers through the years I also frequently hear from estate appraisers who have found a cache of *Hummel* items and people who discover that they have a *Hummel* item or two as a result of seeing my book. Consequently I have been able to uncover new(old) pieces and add much good new data to my bulging research files. I can never have enough so keep it coming. Good quality photos are preferred, but snapshots are welcome. Please see page 415 for directions on describing and photographing *Hummel* items before writing.

Please do not ask me to appraise from lists or photographs. I used to try to do them all, but time no longer allows me that luxury.

If you choose to write, I can't promise to acknowledge every single letter, but I will attempt to do so in time, as numbers allow. **Please, no telephone calls** and do remember to enclose a self-addressed stamped envelope (SASE) with your letter. That will go a long way toward helping to assure a response.

Happy Collecting!

Carl F. Luckey
Lingerlost
Route 4, Box 301
Killen, AL   35645

INTRODUCTION
TO THE TENTH EDITION

There is a continuing and unprecedented interest in Hummel figurines with every passing year. Of course, there have been collectors of Hummel figurines and related articles since very soon after they were first offered by Goebel at the Leipzig Trade Fair in March of 1935, but there has been an incredibly enormous surge of interest in the past fifteen or so years.

Values skyrocketed for the first ten or twelve of those years, but have settled down in the past few years, to a less spectacular but still mostly positive rate. Indeed some values have decreased, but these are the exception rather than the rule.

The book is for anyone having an interest in The world of *Hummel* art; the dealer, the collector or anyone owning just one or two figurines or may be contemplating beginning a collection. It is important to state that even though every effort is made to insure its completeness and accuracy, this book nor any other can make a claim at being the absolute authoritative work at this time. There is still too much unknown for any to make that claim just yet. There are too many diverse opinions, too many unknown circumstances surrounding the history of the development, production and marketing of the early *Hummel* pieces, new variations still being found, too many pieces not yet uncovered but known to have been produced at least in prototype, and last but not least, unquestionably genuine *M.I. Hummel* figurines showing up, never believed to have existed before.

This is a collector's guide, just that, a *guide*, to be used in conjunction with every bit of other information you may be able to obtain. To that end I not only recommend that you obtain all the other books and publications you can, but list the titles and brief descriptions of them and where possible, an address where you might obtain them.

The information in this book was obtained from many of the same sources the collector dealer and other writers have available. It is a compendium of information gleaned from the historians, old company and dealer pamphlets, brochures and publications, the dealers and the collectors themselves, shows and conventions, the distributors and the writers, all of which has been drawn together for all of their use.

The book also contains a short history of W. Goebel Porzellanfabrik, the company that makes the pieces, a biographical sketch of Sister Maria Innocentia Hummel (the artist from whose works virtually all the designs are taken), an explanation of the trademark system and other markings found on the figures, a glossary of terminology, a description of production techniques and most important of all, a comprehensive listing of all the pieces themselves. In this tenth edition the listings have been considerably expanded including much information not included in past editions. Each listing contains at least one photograph of each piece, detailed descriptions of color and mold variations and photos of them when available, current production status, sizes found and available, other remarks of interest, cross references when of interest a current market value range and the Goebel factory recommended retail price list at the back of the book.

THE HUMMEL MUSEUM

This is a beautiful new facility that opened in 1992, in New Braunfels, Texas, just north of San Antonio. It houses, among other things, an approximately 350 piece collection of original paintings and drawings by Sr. M.I. Hummel, from which about 50 have never been published. The collection is on loan from the Nauer family of Switzerland. The Nauer association (today in the 4th generation) with Sr. M.I. Hummel goes back to her days at the convent when their publishing company ArsEdition was first contacted by the convent regarding the publishing of all of Sister Maria Innocentia's works.

The Hummel Museum houses the world's largest collection of Sister M.I. Hummel's artwork, more than 350 original paintings and drawings. There is also an exhibit of current *M.I. Hummel* figurines and 2-D Hummel products.

To try to define the artist, the Museum has recreated her studios and other aspects of her convent life. There is also a children's artroom, where the children are encouraged to draw what they have seen in the Museum. This is an appropriate and living memorial to her love of children.

The Hummel Museum is a non-profit corporation, accepting donations, such as money or whole collections of *M.I. Hummel* figurines, which for the donator are tax deductible at its full today's market value.

Any lover of things *Hummel* must pay a visit to the Hummel Museum. The address is 199 Main Plaza, New Braunfels, Texas 78131. The museum hours are 10 a.m., to 5 p.m., Monday through Saturday and 12 p.m., to 5 p.m. on Sundays. There is a toll-free "Bee Line" that provides information about on-going museum activities, 1-800-456-HUMM or if you wish to talk to someone there, the office number is (210) 625-5636.

Interior views of the Hummel Museum, New Braunfels, Texas

Architectural rendering of the Goebel and *M.I. Hummel* Gallery.

THE DONALD E. STEPHENS MUSEUM
Goebel and M.I. Hummel® Gallery

The reason for the two names above is that at present there is the Donald E. Stephens Museum only. Goebel announced in the Spring 1993 (Vol. 16, No. 4) of the *M.I. Hummel* Club newsletter, *INSIGHTS,* that the new Goebel and *M.I. Hummel* Gallery will be located on the grounds of the Exposition Center in the Village Rosemont, Illinois, a suburb of Chicago, only five minutes from O'Hare International Airport.

In 1986 the Donald E. Stephens Museum was opened in the Exposition Center. Stephens, long-time Mayor of the Village of Rosemont had donated his magnificent collection of Hummel figurines amassed over more than twenty years of collecting in 1984 for the purpose of establishing a museum. The collection is probably the largest public display of both the current production *M.I. Hummel* figurines and old and rare pieces in the world. Additions to the collection did not stop with Stephens' donation. The museum has a board and with his expert consulting, they continue to seek out old and rare pieces to add to the collection.

The new 15,000 square foot building will be large enough to accommodate the Stephens collection as well as a display of all current *M.I. Hummel* products a facsimile Goebel factory that demonstrates the fashioning of the figurines, a display of other Goebel figurines, special exhibits and shows, a retail store and an auditorium. It is slated to open in early 1994.

The Stephens Museum, is open. The address is Rosemont/O'Hare Exposition Center, South Lobby, 5555 North River Road, Rosemont, Illinois. Museum hours are 9 am to 5 pm Monday through Friday and 10 am to 2 pm on Saturdays. It would be best to call first: (312) 692-4000. With the construction and transition, hours may ha to be modified.

Exterior view of the Donald E. Stephens Museum at Rosemont, Illinois.

Interior view of the museum.

M.J.Hummel®

SISTER MARIA INNOCENTIA (Berta Hummel)
1909-1946
Sister of the Third Order of Saint Francis.
Siessen Convent. Saulgau, Germany.

The story of the Hummel Figurines is very unique and full of interest for all lovers of the arts.

The charming but simple figurines of little boys and girls capture the heart of all who love children. In them we are, perhaps, our son or daughter, or even ourselves when we were racing along the path of happy childhood. These endearing figurines will take you back to your own school days so vividly portrayed in the "Schoolboy" or "Schoolgirl" figurine to the time when you perhaps purloined your first apple from a tree in the neighbor's garden and were promptly set upon by his dog, as shown in the "Culprits" figure.

You will delight in the beauty of the "Flower Madonna" or the "Little Shepherd". Yes, you will love them all with their little round faces and big questioning eyes. You will want to collect them. Then, you might ask yourself, who is this artist, the creator of beauty and simplicity?

Her name is Berta Hummel, and she was a Franciscan sister called Sister Maria Innocentia.

Berta Hummel was born on May 21, 1909, at Massing in lower Bavaria about forty miles northeast of Munich. She grew in a family of two brothers and three sisters in a home where music and art were a part of everyday life. It is, therefore, easy to assume that her talent for drawing and coloring was nourished and fostered by her parents.

The years between 1916 and 1921 were spent at a Primary School in Massing and we note that her imagination was vivid even at this early age. She painted delightful little cards and printed verses for family celebrations, birthdays, anniversaries and Christmas. The subjects of her art were always the simple objects with which she was so familiar: flowers, birds, animals and her little school friends. In this child's world in which she lived, Berta Hummel could see only the beautiful things around her. After that, however, it was necessary to give her great talent a wider scope for development. In 1921 she joined the Girls' Finishing School at Simbach. Here again her drawing and coloring found such acclaim that a further cultivation was found advisable. There was only one place in which her talent and, by now, her desire for art and its translation into everyday life, could be satisfied. It was Munich, the town of arts on the Isar. In 1927, after completing her elementary and secondary education, Berta Hummel, now a budding artist, moved to Munich, where she entered the Academy of Fine and Applied Arts. There she lived the life of the artist of her day, made friends, and painted to her heart's content. Here she acquired full mastery of art theory and method and it is here that she met two Franciscan sisters who, like her, attended the Academy.

It is an old adage that art and religion go together. In Berta Hummel's case this was no exception. Her desire to serve humanity became so great that she decided to join the two sisters in their pilgrimage for art and God. So we find her for a time dividing her talent for drawing and her great love for her fellow men between hours of devotion and worship. The first step into a new life, a life of sacrifice and love, was taken. For Berta Hummel, there was no turning back. After completing her Novitiate, she took her first vows in the Convent of Siessen on August 30, 1934.

While Berta Hummel, now Sister Maria Innocentia, gave her life unselfishly to an idea which she thought greater than anything else, the world became the recipient of her great works. Within the walls and beautiful surroundings of this centuries-old convent she created the pictures which were to make her name famous throughout the world. Within this sacred confine, she could give her desire unbounded impetus. There she made the sketches for the "Hummel Cards" and "Hummel Figurines". These little images were, after all, her childhood friends as she remembered them and one by one they appeared before her eyes until she had immortalized those who made her early life "Heaven on Earth".

Little did her superiors dream that this modest blue-eyed artist, who had joined their community, would someday win world-wide renown and realize enough from her art work to give her beloved convent a telling financial assistance.

By the end of World War II, in 1945, after the French had occupied the region, the noble minded artist's state of health was broken. On November 6, 1946, despite all the self-sacrificing care taken of her, God summoned her to His eternal home, leaving in deep mourning all her fellow nuns.

Today the Hummel figurines are known all over the world. They are the messengers of the art created by *M.I. Hummel* to give pleasure to so many people.

W. GOEBEL PORZELLANFABRIK
A Short History of the Company and How the Figurines Came to Be

The company was founded in 1871 by Franz Detlev Goebel with his son Friedrich William Goebel in an area very near Coberg in northern Bavaria. Once known as Oeslau, the village is now known as Rodental. Initially the company manufactured blackboards, pencils and marbles, but by 1872 the company was well into the production of porcelain dinnerware and beer steins. By the mid-1910's 1920's a third generation, Max Louis Goebel had taken the helm of the company and they were manufacturing fine earthenware products. His son Franz Ernst Goebel was now active in the company and the two of them had developed a line of porcelain figurines that had been well accepted on the international market. Upon Max Louis' death 1926 Franz took over the running of the company with his brother-in-law Eugen. Stocke, who was the manager of the financial side of the operation.

By the early 1930's Goebel had gained considerable experience and expertise in fashioning products of porcelain and fine earthenware. Sister Maria Innocentia's art came to the attention of Franz in December of 1933 in Munich in the form of religious note cards for the Christmas and New Year seasons. What is remarkable about this is that these cards were brand new publications of her art by Ars Sacra Josef Mueller Verlag, the predecessor to the Ars Edition company of today. They, as a result of a long association hold the rights to much of her artwork. It was just the previous March of the same year that the Siessen Convent had made an unsolicited inquiry of them regarding the possibility and cost of the reproduction of Hummel art.

Upon seeing the cards Franz conceived the idea of translating the children of Berta Hummel (*M.I. Hummel* into three dimensions; figurines). It took about a year after they gained permission from *M.I. Hummel* and the Siessen Convent, to model the first figurines, make the first molds, experiment with porcelain and ceramics, make the final decision to make them in earthenware and present the first models at the Leipzig Trade Fair. By the end of 1935 they had forty-six models in the line.

Production of *Hummel* figurines and practically everything else in the Goebel line slowly dwindled during the years of WWII and by the end of the war production had ceased altogether. During the American occupation, the United States Military Occupation Government allowed Goebel to resume operation. During this period of time the *Hummel* figurines became quite popular among U.S. servicemen and upon returning to the States their interest in them engendered a new popularity for the pieces. Today the company maintains a large factory complex in Roedental manufacturing, among many other things, *Hummel* figurines and related articles. They maintain a visitor center and welcome collectors. A film is shown and a short tour to show how the pieces are manufactured is conducted.

PITFALLS YOU MAY ENCOUNTER AND
SOME INSTRUCTIONAL CAUTIONS
Determining Whether it is a Genuine Hummel Item

The determination as to whether or not the piece in question is authentic is easy in the greatest majority of instances. If you have no reason to suspect it of being a fake or forgery and it bears the incised *M.I. Hummel* signature somewhere on it, it is genuine. There are a few instances where the piece is simply too small for the incised signature to be placed on it anywhere, or without defacing it. Under these circumstances the company usually places a paper or foil sticker where it is least obtrusive. Often these are lost from the piece over the years, but these small items are few in number and usually readily identifiable by the use of the incised mold number and trademark.

A careful study of the section on how Goebel utilizes mold numbers on the *M.I. Hummel* pieces will give you much more insight into correctly identifying them.

Be ever alert to the trademarks found on the pieces and how to interpret them (see pages 20-24). It is a complicated and sometimes confusing system and you must know how they are used and what they mean in order to know what you are buying.

Variations are rampant (see individual listings) in both size, coloration and mold variations, and you may think you are buying one thing and you'll be getting something quite different.

Concerning the value of broken but expertly restored pieces, they are generally worth one-half or less than the going current value of the unbroken, "mint" ones. This value is entirely dependent upon the availability of other "mint" pieces bearing the same mold number, size designator, and trademark. In the case of a rare piece, however, many times it is worth almost as much as the mint piece, if expertly restored, due simply to its scarcity. (See pages 34-36 for a list of some restorers.)

Detecting Restored Pieces

Even the most expertly restored *Hummel* figurines or articles are detectable, but it is sometimes difficult or impossible for the average collector. The two most reliable methods are examination by (1) *long-wave* ultraviolet light and (2) examination by X-ray. Until very recently one could rely almost 100% on ultraviolet light examination, but some restorative techniques have been developed in the past few years, that are undetectable except by X-ray examination.

Examination by X-ray

Access to X-ray equipment might prove difficult, but if you have a good friend who is a doctor or dentist with their own equipment, you might be able to get your X-ray by reimbursing expenses. You may be able to discern a crack where the piece has been restored otherwise invisible to the naked eye. If it does exhibit such, it is safe to assume it is a restored piece. There are some, however, that may not show up so it is not foolproof. The latter represents the state of the art of restoration.

Examination by Long-wave Ultraviolet Light

When an undamaged piece is exposed to this light, it will appear uniformly light purple in color, the value of the purple will vary with color on the piece. A crack or fracture with glue in it will appear a lighter color (usually orange or pink), patches will appear almost white, and most new paint will appear a much, much darker purple.

Non-Hummel Items Made by Goebel

You need to be aware that from 1871, when the company was founded, until 1991, Goebel used the same trademarking system on just about all of its products. In 1991, they changed the system so that now there is a special trademark that is used exclusively on *M.I. Hummel* items. The older Goebel trademark found on an item is, therefore, not necessarily an indication that it is a *Hummel* design, only that it *might be.* For further identification use the guidelines described above. You would not believe how many letters I get from folks who think they have a rare *Hummel* item only to find that they have another of Goebel's many other products.

With Goebel's *M.I. Hummel* products it is the rule that letter prefixes are not used. When a letter or letters are used they are almost invariably a suffix, placed **after** the incised mold number.

When Goebel marks a non-Hummel item the mold number usually has a one, two or three letter prefix associated. A few examples of the many prefixes are and what they mean follows:

Byj - Taken from designs by Charlot Byj
Dis - Take from Walt Disney characters
FF - Free standing figure
HM - Madonna
HX - Religious figurine
KF - Whimsical figure
Rob - Taken from designs by Janet Robson
Rock - Taken from Norman Rockwell art
Spo - Taken from designs by Maria Spotl

There are many more than listed here, and the pieces are just as well made as are the Hummel items and, are themselves eminently collectible. They are not Hummel art, however, so be sure before you buy.

There seems to be a developing market for some of the non-Hummel Goebel products such as the Charlot Byj "Red Heads" as they are known and the Little Monk or "Friar Tuck" pieces. There is already a well-developed secondary market for the Norman Rockwell and Walt Disney character figurines.

The reason for including this tea cup here is two-fold: One to illustrate the diversity of the products Goebel has produced and continues to produce. The other is to illustrate how the company has, until 1991, used the same trademarks on all of their products. In 1991 they developed a special trademark to be used exclusively on Hummel items from then on.

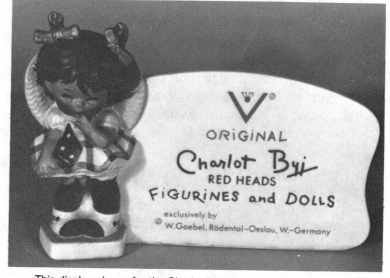

This display plaque for the Charlot Byi Red Head series from Goebel bears the mold number Byi 47, the Three-Line (TMK-4) mark, a 1966 MID and measures 4⅝" high.

Display plaque for the Goebel Friar Tuck series. The mold number WZ 2 is incised and inked in indicating it is a Mother Mold Piece. It bears the Stylized Bee (TMK-3) mark, a 1959 MID and measures 4¾" x 3⅞".

A Norman Rockwell piece from Goebel. It bears the ROCK 217 mold number, the Three-Line (TMK-4) mark and measures 3⅝'' x 5½''.

The Seven Dwarfs from the Walt Disney series by Goebel, Snow White and the Seven Dwarfs. They bear various trademarks from Stylized (TMK-3) through the Last Bee (TMK-5) and measure from 2¾'' to 3''.

Two examples of Shrine by Janet Robson. Each bears the Three-Line (TMK-4) mark, mold number ROB 422 incised and inked in indicating there are Mother Mold Pieces. Both have the incised 1961 MID and measure 5¼''.

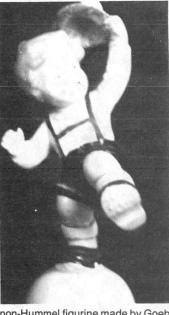

A non-Hummel figurine made by Goebel. Base markings: "FF 124/1 with a Full Bee trademark and Black Germany.

A non-Hummel figuring made by Goebel. Base markings: Crown and Full Bee trademarks, "FF 124/1 B"

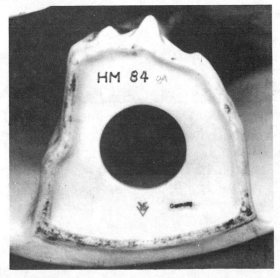

Base marking found on a non-Hummel Madonna made by Goebel. Note the "HM" letter prefix (enhanced for reproduction with pen and ink).

5

Fakes, Forgeries, Imitations and Copies

Fakes and forgeries

As far as I have been able to determine, there are not yet many blatant forgeries on the market, but, as noted earlier, we must be ever aware of their possibility and their nature.

Unfortunately there have been a few rather obvious alterations to the trademarks and to the figurines themselves to make them appear older or different from the norm therefore more valuable. There have been additions or deletions of small pieces (i.e. birds, flowers, etc.) to a figure and worse, one or two unscrupulous individuals have been reglazing colored figurines and other articles with a white overglaze to make them appear to be the relatively uncommon to rare, all-white pieces. These can be detected but it is left to the experts. Should you purchase a piece that is ultimately proven to be one of these, I know of no reputable dealer who wouldn't replace your figure if possible. At the very least, he would refund your money.

Imitations, Copies and Reproductions of Original Hummel Pieces

For anyone interested in these, called "Hummel Copycats" by Lawrence L. Wonsch in his book of the same name, should get a copy of this excellent book (Source listed on page 37) He has shown that the collecting of copycat *M.I. Hummels* can be fascinating and fun.

There are many reproductions and imitations of the original Hummel pieces, some better than others, but so far all are easily detectable upon the most casual examination if one is reasonably knowledgeable about what constitutes an original.

The most common of these imitations are those produced in Japan, similar in design motif but obviously not original when one applies the simplest of rules. (See discussion of Trademarks and other markings found on original pieces, pages 20-24.)

Plastic imitation of Hum 201, Retreat to Safety. Made in Hong Kong, it appears that this piece was taken directly from the genuine Hummel figurine.

Take note the photo of the "Retreat to Safety", Hum 201. To look at the photo is disconcerting in that it appears to be so real. When you hold this particular copy, however, it is easy to see that it is inferior and feel very light in your hand. Beneath the base is the phrase "Made in Hong Kong" I purchased this plastic copy in a truck stop gift shop in a midwestern state in 1979 for $3.95. It was probably worth about fifty cents at the time. Though I have not seen any others, I am told there is a whole series of these plastic copies.

I have seen many other figurines and articles that are obvious attempts at copying the exact design of the genuine article. In every single instance it was immediately detectable as being made of materials and paints severely inferior to the quality exhibited by the real thing. Most are manufactured form a material similar to the plaster or plaster-like substance used in the manufacture of the various prizes one wins at the carnival game booth. Some of these actually bear a sticker proclaiming that they are genuine, authentic or original Hummel pieces.

A 7" imitation "Strolling Along".

This 3" imitation appears to be a combination of "Easter Time" and "Playmates". No markings.

This pair of 4¼" figures is made of plastic and are decidedly inferior. No markings found

Six Herbert Dubler Figures.

The Dubler Figures

During World War II the Nazi government did not allow the Goebel company to carry on production of Hummel figurines. During this period a New York firm known as Ars Sacra (a subsidiary of today's ArsEdition in Munich) produced a small collection of figurines very much like the original designs and others in the *Hummel* style, but not copying any particular design. Those that were *Hummel* copies usually bore a ⅝" x 1" foil sticker as reproduced

here. They often also had "B. Hummel" and either "ARS SACRA" or "Herbert Dubler, Inc." associated with the signature. Either version was usually incised into the top or side of the base of the figurine. Frequently a copyright date also appears in the same area. Lawrence L. Wonsh's guide **HUMMEL COPYCATS**, pictures over 20 of these Dubler figures and his research indicates the possibility of sixty-one of them were designed and perhaps made.

Most Dubler pieces were made of a chalk-like or plaster-of-Paris type substance, but a few were rendered in bronze and even some have been found in silver.

Large and heavy bronze figures on marble bases. Left measures 7" and the other 6½". Incised at the rear of the figures is "Copyright 1942 Herbert Dubler, Inc."

These rather pitiful Hummel-like figures bear the inscription: "Copyright© 1947 Decorative Figurines Corp., Dubler's Company.

The English or Beswick Pieces

These interesting pieces are intriguing in that some mystery surrounds their origin. They are usually known collectively as "The English Pieces" by collectors. There has been some speculation in the past that they have some claim to legitimacy, but there has never been any hard evidence found that would support that claim. The backstamp "BESWICK-ENGLAND" indicates they were made by an old and respected English porcelain manufacturer that was later bought out by Royal Doulton. Inquiries to Royal Doulton were fruitless for they could find no reference to the pieces in what records of Beswick that were obtained when they bought the company.

There have been twelve different designs identified with or without the Beswick backstamp, *M.I. Hummel* incised signature and other markings. The mold numbers are 903 through 914. See following list:

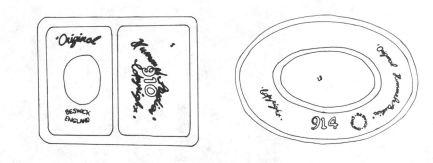

903 TRUMPET BOY
904 BOOKWORM
905 GOOSE GIRL
906 STROLLING ALONG
907 PUPPY LOVE
908 STORMY WEATHER
909 LITTLE FIDDLER
910 MEDITATION
911 MAX AND MORITZ
912 FARM BOY
913 GLOBE TROTTER
914 SHEPHERD'S BOY

The figurines are shiny and brightly colored in the faience tradition. Most of them bear the inscription "Original Hummel Studios Copyright" in script letters (see drawings above) and some version of the Beswick backstamp. Most, but not all, also bear an incised *M.I. Hummel* signature along with the base inscriptions described above and there have been some found with no markings at all. All are sought eagerly by many serious collectors. The collector value range of those bearing the signature is $800-1,000.00.

English/Beswick pieces. Left to right with their incised mold numbers: Meditation, 910; Trumpet Boy, 903; Little Fiddler, 909.

English/Beswick Strolling Along, 906.

English/Beswick Shepherd's Boy, 914.

English/Beswick Farm Boy, 912.

The Glass Goose Girl

Many collectors are familiar with this interesting piece, but before Lawrence Wonsch's guide "Hummel Copycats" few if any knew the history behind them. He goes into great detail about the historical background and the company, L.E. Smith Glass company, that originated them and still is producing them. The first were made in 1937. Inspired by the *M.I. Hummel* Goose Girl this hollow figure can be found in thirty-three distinct variations according to color, size, base variations and some other characteristics you will have to by Wonsch's book to discover. I will tell you that those with a plain glass base are pre-1970 vintage and those with the textured, wheat straw base as in the accompanying photograph are produced from 1970 on. Some of the colors are amber, blue, and green. There are others. The collector value range runs from $25.00 to $75.00. In 1992 Goebel began producing and marketing a line of crystal *M.I. Hummel* figurines. See page 36 for further information.

An example of the glass Goose Girl candy container. This is the 6''
version in clear glass with the textured base.

NOTES ON BUYING AND SELLING
FOR THE COLLECTOR AND WOULD-BE COLLECTOR

Finding and Buying *M.I. Hummel* Collectibles

The one most important factor in any collecting discipline is knowledge. Before you spend your hard-earned funds to start or expand a collection it is incumbent upon you to arm yourself with it. You have bought this book so you have made a good start. Now you must study it, learn from it and refer to it often when you're on your hunt. Don't stop there. Elsewhere in the book is a list of other books and publications dealing with the subject. Some are out of print and no longer readily available, but others are easy to obtain. Get them and study them as well. Be sure that what you do get is the latest edition.

In today's market there are many sources, some quite productive and some not so productive, as is true of any collectible, and times change the sources. Supply and demand is a very important factor in the world of *Hummel* collecting. We have been through some extraordinary times. Twenty years ago I owned a retail business that sold among other things *Hummel* figurines and plates. I had a very difficult time obtaining them in any quantity, never had a choice of pieces and often went for weeks with none in stock. As I remember, we had to order an assortment and there were three monetary levels of assortments. In addition it was often two to three months between ordering them and taking delivery. This was true of almost every retail dealer in the country. While the rule is still generally no choice, production increases have improved over the years to where the number you have to select from at your dealer is usually pretty good.

While I was a small dealer, I was known to local collectors and when my small shipment arrived it was usually gone in a matter of days. There was a time in the late 1970's and early 1980's that dealers not only couldn't meet collectors' demands, they kept lists of collectors and what each collector was looking for. The result was most of their stock was pre-sold. What was left would sometimes literally be fought over.

As many of you know, I try to attend most of the shows and conventions that feature *Hummel.* I will never forget the crowds in those early years of the surge in *Hummel* popularity. Frequently the dealers would literally be cleaned out before half the show was over leaving booths empty of all but tables and display fixtures. Even my book was snatched up so rapidly at one show, I was left with none to sell after the first day.

Our economic times have changed all that, but the good news is that the collector now has many sources from which to choose. This is particularly true if you are not specializing in the older trademark pieces. These can be readily found variously in gift shops, jewelry stores and galleries and shops specializing in collectibles. Even the popular new TV shopping programs feature *Hummel* figurine sales from time to time. They are also available by mail-order from various dealers around the country, many of whom also deal in the old mark pieces. The best way to find them is by looking in the various antique and collectible publications (names and addresses of these are listed elsewhere in the book). Many of them have a classified ad section where dealers and collectors alike advertise *Hummel* figurines and related pieces such as plates as being for sale or wanted. The most productive source, if you can travel to them, is one of the large annual gatherings of dealers and collectors held around the country. The productivity of those shows is probably more true with regard to finding the older marked pieces than the new ones. Don't let that stop you collectors of the new pieces because above all else they are fun and a good learning experience usually offering lectures and seminars by experts and dealers, all of which are subject to much "brain-picking" if you can get through the crowds of other collectors with the same thing in mind. There is also the opportunity to meet other collectors and learn from them. Just be sure to pick the ones with this book under their arm because we think they are, of course, the smartest!

Another source for the old trademark pieces, other than the shows and mail order, are those shops that sell both new and old pieces. There are a few around the country. With the increased awareness of the value of the older mark pieces it is very unlikely, but still possible that some smaller, uninformed shops could have a few pieces bearing older trademarks, bought some years ago for sale at whatever the current retail price is for the newer ones.

Bargains? Yes, there are bargains to be found. Sometimes you get lucky at auctions if no one else is looking for the particular figurine you have picked out. That would be a rare occurrence at an all-Hummel auction. Estate auctions and sales and country auctions would be your best bet. By far the best source for bargains are flea markets (especially in Europe), junk shops, attics, basements, relatives, friends, acquaintances and neighbors. In short, anywhere one might find curious, old gifts, castaways, etc. As a good example, a few years ago I discovered that one of my neighbors has eight older pieces bearing the Full Bee trademark.

These engaging little figurines have for over fifty years now, been considered a wonderful gift or souvenir because there are so many motifs, one can almost always find one that fits a friend's or relative's particular personality, profession or avocation. Until recent years they were also a relatively inexpensive gift. So "bone up", and start looking and asking. You may find a real treasure.

The Price to Pay

The province of this book is primarily *Hummel* figurines and related articles. The greatest preponderance of these collectibles are made by W. Goebel Porzellanfabrik (hereinafter called Goebel) and the ones covered here are primarily those that bear trademarks other than the one currently being used by the company. It is always nice to have a listing of what is currently being produced by Goebel along with the suggested retail prices. There is one printed in the back of the book, but a more portable version, printed by Goebel should be available at your nearest dealer.

There are several factors that can and do influence the actual selling price of the old and the new. The suggested retail price list released by the company periodically is for those pieces bearing the current production trademark. Each time the list is released it reflects changes in the retail price. These changes (usually increases) are due primarily to the basic principle of supply and demand, economic influences of the world money market, ever increasing material and production costs, the American market demand and last, but certainly not least, an expanding interest in Germany and the rest of the European market.

The list does not necessarily reflect the actual price you may have to pay. Highly popular pieces in limited supply can go higher and some of the less popular pieces can go for less. This has been the case more in the recent past that now, but the phenomenon still occurs.

The value of *Hummel* figurines, plates, etc. bearing trademarks other than the one currently being used in production is influenced by some of the same factors discussed above, to a greater or lesser extent. The law of supply and demand comes into even more prominent light with regard to pieces bearing the older trademarks, simply because they are no longer being made and the number on the market is finite. More simply, there are more collectors desiring them than there are available pieces. Generally speaking the older the trademark, the more valuable or desirable the piece to some collectors. One must realize, however, that this is not a hard and fast rule. There are many instances where there are larger numbers available of some pieces bearing an older mark than that of others bearing later trademarks. If the latter is a more desirable figure, and is in much shorter supply, it is perfectly reasonable for it to be more valuable.

There is another factor that must be considered. The initial find of the rare International Figurines (see page 73) saw values shoot up as high as $20,000 for each of them. At first they were thought to exist in just eight designs and in only one or two prototypes of each. Over the years several more designs and multiples of the figurines have been found. While they are still quite rare, most bring less than one half that original value. So you see, values can fall as a result of increase in supply of a rare or uncommon piece. This can be brought about artificially as well. If someone secretly buys up and hoards a large number of a popular piece for a period of time, the short supply will drive the value up. After he dumps them the market goes down. This has happened more than once in the past, but not so much now.

Yet another circumstance that *may* influence a fall is the re-issue of a piece previously thought by collectors to be permanently out of production. This has happened because of collectors' past confusion over company terminology with regard to whether a piece was permanently or temporarily withdrawn from production. Many collectors wish to possess a particular item simply because they like it and have no interest in an older trademark version. These collectors will buy the newer piece simply because they can purchase it for less. It follows naturally, that demand for the older trademark version will lessen under those circumstances.

You may find surprising the fact that many of the values in the old trademark listing are less than the values reflected in the current Goebel suggested retail price list. You have to realize that serious collectors of old mark Hummel collectibles have very little interest in the price of, or the collecting of those pieces currently being produced except where the list has an influence on the pricing structure of the secondary market. That is not to say that the current production pieces are not valuable. Quite the contrary. They will be collectible on the secondary market eventually. Time must pass. Make no bones about it, with the changing of the trademarks will come the logical step into the secondary market. The principal market for the last two trademarks is found in the general public, not the seasoned collector. The heaviest trading in the collector market in the past couple of years has been in the Crown and Full Bee trademark pieces. The Stylized Bee and Three Line trademark pieces are presently remaining stable and the Last Bee trademark pieces are experiencing a stagnant market presently.

Selling M.I. Hummel Collectibles

There is an old saying in the antique and collectibles world that goes like this: "You buy at retail and sell at wholesale". While this is true in some cases, it is most assuredly (and thankfully) not the rule. Where the axiom can be true is if you *must* sell and the only ready buyer is a dealer whose percent discount equals or exceeds the amount your item has appreciated in value. This can also be true if you have consigned your piece to an auction although auctions usually allow you to set a reserve. A reserve is the lowest price you will sell. If bidding doesn't reach your reserve you still owe the auctioneer his fee, but you get your item back. The same comments regarding auctions in previous paragraphs apply here also.

There are several other methods of selling, each of which has its own set of advantages and disadvantages.

Selling to a Dealer

The have-to-sell scenario above is an obvious disadvantage, but sales to a dealer will in most cases be a painless experience. If you have been fortunate in your acquisitions and the collection has appreciated considerably, it may also be a profitable encounter as well. If you are not near the dealer and have to ship, then you also run the risk of damage or loss.

Running Sales Ads in your Local Newspaper

Selling to another collector in your local area is probably the easiest and most profitable way to dispose of your piece(s). There is the advantage of personal examination and no shipping risks.

Running Sales Ads in Collector Publications

This is probably the other best way to get best price, as long as the sale is to another collector. The same shipping risks exist here also, and you do have to consider the cost of the ad.

Answer Wanted Ads in Collector Publications

The only risk beyond the usual shipping risks is the possibility of the buyer being disappointed and wishing to return for a refund.

Local Dealers

If you are fortunate enough to have a dealer near you, they may take consignments for a percentage.

Utilize the Club Services.

The *M.I. HUMMEL* CLUB has what it calls its Collector's Market for members where they register items wanted and items for sale and computer match them. There is no charge beyond membership dues for this service. The address is Dept. CM, *M.I. Hummel* Club, Goebel Plaza, P.O. Box 11, Pennington, NJ 08534. You must be a member, so if you need the enrollment forms call 1-800-666-2582 or use the membership form in the back of this book.

The HUMMEL COLLECTOR'S CLUB publishes a quarterly newsletter in which they publish, free of charge to members, sales and wanted ads. You respond to these ads by mailing your response to the club. They then forward the response, unopened, to the individuals running the ad. The address for membership is Hummel Collector's Club, P.O. Box 257, Yardley, PA 19067-2857. If you need a membership application write to them or call (215) 493-6705.

GLOSSARY

Following is an alphabetical listing of terms and phrases you will encounter in this book as well as other related books, references and literature during the course of collecting Hummel items. In some cases they are specific and unique to Hummel collecting and others are generic in nature, applying to other earthenware and ceramic and porcelain as well. Refer to this glossary whenever you read or hear something you don't understand. Frequent use of it will enable you to become well versed in collecting Hummel figurines and other related articles.

Air Holes - Small holes under the arms or other unobtrusive locations to vent the hollow figures during the firing stage of production to prevent them from exploding as the air expands due to intense heat. Many pieces have these tiny little holes, but often they are difficult to locate.

Anniversary Plate - In 1975 a 10" plate bearing the Stormy Weather motif was released. Subsequent anniversary plates were released at 5 year intervals. 1985 saw the 3rd and last in the series released.

Annual Plate - Beginning in 1971 the W. Goebel firm began producing an annual Hummel plate. Each plate contains a bas-relief reproducing one of the Hummel motifs. The first was originally released to the Goebel factory workers in 1971, commemorating the hundredth anniversary of the firm. This original release was inscribed, thanking the workers.

ARS - Latin word for "ART"

ARS AG - ARS AG, Zug, Switzerland, holds the two-dimensional rights of original *M.I. Hummel* drawings as well as the two-dimensional rights for reproductions of *M.I. Hummel* products made by Goebel. Owner: 50% Goebel Art GmbH, 50% Ars Holding Partners, CIO Jacques Nauer.

ArsEdition - Ars Edition was formerly known as Ars Sacra Josef Mueller Verlag, a German publising house, selling postcards, postcard-calendars and prints of *M.I. Hummel*, which first published the *Hummel Art*. Today ArsEdition GmbH is the exclusive licensee for publising *Hummel* (books, calendars, cards, stationery, etc.) Owner: Mr. Marcel Nauer (grandson of Dr. Herbert Dubler).

Ars Sacra - Trademark on a gold foil label sometimes found on Hummel-like figurines produced by Herbert Dubler, a New York firm, during the years of WWII when Goebel was not allowed to produce *Hummel* items by the Nazi government. Ars Sacra is also the original name of the Ars Edition firm in Munich (Dr. Herbert Dubler was a son-in-law of Mr. and Mrs. Mueller, the owners of ArsEdition formerly Ars Sacra, Munich). Although there was some corporate connection for a very short time between Mueller and Dubler there is no connection between the Mueller Ars Sacra firm and the Hummel-like figurines produced by Dubler under the name "House of Ars Sacra" or the statement "Produced by Ars Sacra". Please see the discussion on the Dubler figures elsewhere in this volume.

Artist's Painting Sample - See Master Sample.

Baby Bee - Describes the trademark of the factory used in 1958. A small bee flying in a V.

Backstamp - Backstamp is usually the trademark and any associated special markings on the underside of the base or the reverse side of an item.

Basic Size - The term, *as used in this book only,* is generally synonymous with STANDARD SIZE. However, because the sizes listed in this book are not substantiated initial factory released sizes, it was felt that it would be misleading to label them "STANDARD". BASIC SIZE was chosen to denote only an *approximate* standard size.

Bas-relief - A raised or sculpted design as on the Annual Bells and the Annual Plates, as opposed to a two-dimensional painted design.

Bee - A symbol used since about 1940, in various forms, as a part of or along with the factory trademark on Hummel pieces until 1979 when the Bee was dropped.

Bisque - A fired but unglazed condition. Usually white but sometimes colored.

Black Germany - Term used to describe one of the various wordings found along with the Hummel trademarks on the underside of the pieces. It refers to the color used to stamp the word 'Germany'. There have been many colors used for the trademarks and associated marks, but black generally indicates the figure is an older mode; however, this is not a reliable indicator.

Bookends - Throughout the collection of Goebel-made Hummel items are bookends. Some are the regular figurines merely attached to wooden bookends with some type of adhesive, but some, however, are different. The latter are made without the customary base and then attached. The regular pieces, when removed from the wood have the traditional markings where those without the base may or may not exhibit those markings.

Candle Holder - Some Hummel figurines have been produced with provisions to place candles in them.

Candy Bowl - See CANDY BOX

Candy Box - Small covered cylindrical box with a Hummel figurine on the top. There have been design changes in the shape of the box or bowl over the years, as well as the manner in which the cover rests upon the bowl. See individual listings.

Candy Dish - See CANDY BOX

CE - See Closed Edition

CN - See Closed Number

Closed Edition (CE) - A term used by the Goebel factory to indicate that a particular item is no longer produced and will not be placed in production again.

Closed Number (CN) - A term used by the Goebel factory to indicate that a particular number in the Hummel Mold Number sequence has never been used to identify an item and never will by used. A caution here: Several unquestionably genuine pieces have been found recently bearing these so-called Closed Numbers.

Collector's Plaque - Same as the Dealer Plaque except it does not state "authorized dealer", as most later Dealer Plaques do. Frequently used for display with private collections (see DEALER PLAQUE).

Crown Mark (CM) - One of the early W. Goebel firm trademarks. Has not been used on Hummel figurines and related pieces since sometime around 1949-50.

Current Mark - For many years this was a term describing the trademark being used at the present time. It has become a somewhat confusing term, for what is current today may not be tomorrow. Most collectors and dealers have come to use a descriptive term such as the "Crown Mark" or the use of trademark number designations such as Trademark #1 for the Crown Mark for instance. The number designation is usually shortened to "Trademark One" when spoken or "TMK-1" when written.

Current Production - Term describing figurines, plates, candy boxes, etc. supposedly being produced at the present time. They are not necessarily readily available, because the factory maintains the molds but doesn't always produce the figure with regularity.

Dealer Plaque - A plaque made and distributed by the Goebel firm to retailers for the purpose of advertising the fact that they are dealers in Hummel figurines. Always has the "Merry Wanderer" incorporated into it. Earlier models had a Bumblebee perched on the top edge (see COLLECTOR'S PLAQUE).

Decimal Designator - Many earlier Goebel Hummel figurines exhibit a decimal point after the mold number, ie: "154". This is ostensibly to mean the same thing as the "slash" mark (/). The use of the slash mark means that there is another, smaller size of the piece either in existence, planned or at least in prototype. Their is another theory that the decimal is to make it easier to clarify the incised mold numbers and to help determine whether a number is, for instance, a 66 rather than a 99. The decimal is not always found alone with the number. Some examples the author has observed are 49./0., 51./0. and 84./5.

Display Plaque - see COLLECTOR'S PLAQUE & DEALER PLAQUE

Doll Face - See Faience.

Donut (Doughnut) Base - Describes a type of base used with some figures. Looking at the bottom of the base, the outer margin of the base forms a circle or oval, and a smaller circle or oval within makes the base appear donut-like.

Donut (Doughnut) Halo - The only figures on which these appear are the Madonnas. They are formed as a solid cap type, or molded so that the figure's hair protrudes through slightly. The latter are called Donut Halos.

Double Crown - From 1934 to 1938 there were many figures produced with two Crown WG marks. This is known as the Double Crown. One of the crowns may be a stamped crown and the other incised. Pieces have been found with both trademarks incised (see page 25). Thereafter only a single Crown Mark is found.

Embossed - An erroneous term used to describe INCISED (see INCISED).

Faience (Doll Face) - Faience is defined as brilliantly glazed, bright colored fine earthenware in the dictionaries. More commonly called "Doll Face" pieces by collectors, this describes the few Hummel figurines that were made by Goebel in the early days of paint and finish experimentation. Several have made it into collectors hands. Refer to the color section for illustrations of a few.

Fink, Emil - Emil Fink Verlag, Stuttgart, Germany, is a publisher of a limited number of post cards and greeting cards bearing the art of *M.I. Hummel.* All US-Copyrights of cards published by Fink Verlag are owned by ARS AG, Zug, Switzerland.

Font - A number of pieces have been produced with a provision for holding a small portion of holy water. They can be hung on the wall. Often referred to as Holy Water Fonts.

Full Bee - About 1940 the W. Goebel firm began using a Bee as part of their trademark. The FULL BEE trademark has been found along with the Crown trademark. The FULL BEE is the first and largest bee to be utilized. There were many versions of the Full Bee trademark. The first Full Bee is sometimes found with (R) stamped somewhere on the base.

Germany - (W. GERMANY, West Germany, Western Germany) - All have appeared with the trademark in several different colors.

Goebelite - This is the name the Goebel firm gives to the patented mixture of materials used to form the slip used in the pouring and fashioning the earthenware Hummel figurines and other related Hummel pieces. Not often heard.

High Bee - A variation of the early Bee trademarks wherein the Bee is smaller than the original Bee used in the mark and flies with its wings slightly higher than the top of the V.

Hollow Base - A base variation. Some bases for figures are solid and some are hollowed out and open into a hollow figure.

Hollow Mold - An erroneous term actually meaning Hollow Base, as above. All Hummel pieces are at least partially hollow in finished form.

Holy Water Font - See FONT above.

Hummel Mark (TMK-7) - This mark was introduced in 1991. It is the first trademark to be used exclusively on Goebel products utilizing M.I. Hummel art for its design.

Hummel Number or Mold Number - A number or numbers incised into the base or bottom of the piece, used to identify the mold motif and sometimes the size of the figure or article. This designation is sometimes inadvertently omitted, but rarely.

Incised - Describes a mark or wording which has actually been pressed into the piece rather than printed or stamped on the surface.

Indented - See INCISED above.

Jumbo - Sometimes used to describe the few Hummel figurines which have been produced in a substantially larger size than the normal range. Usually around 30". (See Hum Nos. 7, 141, 142.)

Light Stamp - (See M.I. HUMMEL below) It is thought that every Hummel figurine has Sister M.I. Hummel's signature stamped somewhere on it; however, some apparently have no signature. In some cases the signature may have been stamped so lightly that in subsequent painting and glazing all but unidentifiable traces are obliterated. In other cases the signature may have been omitted altogether. The latter case is rare. The same may happen to the mold number.

Limited Edition - An item that is limited in production to a specified number or limited to the number produced in a defined period of time.

Malmuster - See Master Sample below.

Master Sample - This is a figurine or other item that is the model from which Goebel artists paint the newly fasioned piece. The Master Sample figurines usually have a red line painted around the flat vertical portion of the base. It is known variously in German as the Malmufter, (from the) Master Zimmer or Muster Zimmer or Originalmuster.

Master Zimmer - See Master Sample above.

Muster Zimmer - See Master Sample above.

M.I. Hummel (Maria Innocentia Hummel) - This signature, illustrated below, is supposed to be applied to every Hummel article produced. However, as in LIGHT STAMP above, it may not be evident. It is also reasonable to assume that because of the design of a particular piece or its extreme small size, it may not have been practical to place it on the piece. In these cases a small sticker is used in its place. It is possible that these stickers become loose and are lost over the years. The signature has been found painted on in some instances but rarely. It is also possible to find the signature in decal form, brown in color. Around the late 1950's to early 1960's Goebel experimented with placing the signature on the figurines by the decal method but abandoned the idea. A few of the pieces they tried it on somehow found their way into the market.

Collectors should also take note of the fact that sometimes the signature appears as "Hummel" without the initials.

Mel - There are a few older Hummel figurines made by Goebel that bear this incised three-letter group along with a number. It is supposed that they were prototype pieces that were never placed in production, but at least three were. Please turn to the description of the Mel pieces elsewhere in this volume for an in-depth discussion.

MID - See Mold Induction Date

Missing Bee Mark - In mid-1980 the Goebel company changed the trademark by removing the familiar "bee" mark collectors had grown accustomed to associating with *M.I. Hummel* items. It came to be known as the "Missing Bee" mark (TMK-6).

Model Number - See Mold Number.

Mold Growth - There have been many theories in the past to explain the differences in sizes of figurines marked the same and with no significant differences other than size. The explanation from Goebel is that in the earlier years of molding, the molds were made of plaster of paris and had a tendency to wash out and crode with use. Therefore successive use would produce pieces each being slightly larger than the last. Another possible explanation is that the firm has been known to use more than one mold simultaneously in the production of the same figure and marketing them with the same mold number. The company developed a synthetic resin to use instead of plaster of paris in 1954. While this is a vast improvement, the new material still has the same tendencies but to a significantly smaller degree.

Mold Induction Date (MID) - The actual year the original mold was made. Often the mold is made but figures are not produced for several years afterward. The MID is sometimes found along with other marks, on older pieces but not always. All pieces currently being produced bear an MID.

Mold Number - the official mold number use by Goebel unique to each Hummel item or motif used. See section on the explanation of the mold number system elsewhere in this volume for an in-depth discussion.

Mother Mold Piece - When Goebel proposes a new figurine the piece is modeled, a mold made, and usually three to six prototype figures are produced and then painted by one of Goebel's master painters. These are for the convent and others to examine and either approve for production or suggest changes. Sometimes the final approved models are marked with a red line and placed into service as a Master Sample for the artists. Although the Mother Mold Pieces do not necessarily have the red line, they are identifiable by the black ink within the incised mold number.

Muster Zimmer - See Master Sample.

Narrow Crown - Trademark used by the W. Goebel firm from 1937 to the early 1940's. To date this trademark has never been found on an original Hummel piece.

One-Line Mark - See STYLIZED BEE.

Open Edition - Designates the Hummel figurines presently in production or in planning. It does not mean all are in production, only that it is 'open' for production, not necessarily available.

Open Number - A number in the numerical sequence of factory designators HUMMEL MODEL NUMBER which has not been used to identify a piece but may be used when a new design is released.

Out of Production - A confusing term sometimes used to indicate that an item is not of current production but may be placed back in production at some later date. The confusion results from the fact that some with this designation have been declared Closed Editions others have been returned to production thus leaving all the others in the classification in limbo.

Oversize - A term sometimes used to describe a Hummel piece which is larger than that which is currently being produced. These variations could be due to mold growth (see MOLD GROWTH).

Painter's Sample - See Master Sample.

PFE (Possible Future Edition) - A term applied to Hummel mold design that does exist, but is not yet released.

Prototype - This is a proposed figurine or other item that must be approved by those with the authority to do so. See Mother Mold Piece.

Quartered Base - As it sounds this is descriptive of the underside of the base of a piece being divided into four more or less equal parts.

Red Line - A red line around the outside edge of the base of a figurine means that the piece once served as the model for the painters.

Reinstated - A piece that has placed back in production after having been previously placed in a non-production status for some length of time.

Sample Model - A prototype piece modeled for the approving authorities. May or may not have gained approval. See Mother Mold Piece.

Secondary Market - When an item has been bought and sold after the initial purchase as new, it is said to be traded on the secondary market.

Size Designator - Method of identifying the size of a figure. It is found in conjunction with Hummel Mold Number on the bottom of the figure.

Slash Marked - From time to time a figure or a piece will be found with a slash or cut through the trademark. There are two theories as to their origin. One, that it is used to indicate a figure with some flaw or imperfection, but several have appeared with a slash mark which are, upon close examination, found to be in excellent, unflawed condition. The other theory is that some are slash-marked to indicate that the piece was given to or sold at a bargain price to factory workers, and marked so to prevent resale.

Small Bee - A variation of the early Full Bee trademark wherein the Bee is about one-half the size of the original Bee.

Split Base - When viewing the bottom of the base of a piece it appears to be split into sections. Generally refers to a base split into two sections, but could be used to describe more than two sections.

Stamped - A method of placing marks on the bottom of a figure wherein the data is placed on the surface rather than pressed into it (see INCISED).

Standard Size - As pointed out in the section on Size Designators, this is a general term used to describe the size of the first figure to be produced, when there are more sizes of the same figure to be found. It is not the largest nor the smallest, only the first. Over the years, as a result of mold design changes and, possibly, mold growth, all figures marked as standard are not necessarily the same size (see BASIC SIZE above).

Stylized Bee (TMK-3) - About 1955 the traditional BEE design in the trademark was changed to reflect a more modern "stylized" version. Also called the "One-Line Mark".

Temporarily Withdrawn - Similar to Out of Production, but in this case it would be reasonable to assume that the piece so described will be put back into production at some future date.

Terra Cotta - Literally translated from the Latin it means "baked earth". A naturally brownish-orange earthenware.

Three Line Mark (TMK-4) - A trademark variation used in the 1960's and 1970's.

Underglaze - A term describing anything that is found underneath the glaze as opposed to being placed after the glazing.

U.S. Zone or **U.S. Zone Germany** - During the American occupation of Germany after World War II the Goebel company was required to apply these words to their products. After the country was divided into East and West Germany in 1948 they began using "West Germany" or "Western Germany". The various configurations in which these words are found are illustrated on page ---.

White Overglaze - When a piece has been formed, a clear glaze applied and fired it results in a shiny, all-white finish.

A HISTORY AND EXPLANATION OF THE PROGRESSION OF TRADEMARKS FOUND ON GOEBEL PRODUCED M.I. HUMMEL® FIGURINES

Since 1934-35 there has been a series of changes in the trademarks placed on *M.I. Hummel* items by the Goebel company. In later years of production each new trademark design merely replaced the old one, but in the earlier years frequently the new design trademark would be placed on a figurine that already bore the older style trademark. In some cases a change from an incised trademark to a surface stamped version of the same mark would result in both appearing on the figure. The former represents a transition period from older to newer and the latter resulted in what are called "Double Crown". This section is meant to give you an illustrated guide to the major trademarks and their evolution to the Trademark presently used on Goebel produced *M.I. Hummel* items.

There are many subtle differences that will not be covered for they serve no useful purpose in identifying the era in which an item was produced. There are, however, a few that do help to date a piece. These will be discussed and illustrated. The dates of the early trademark changes are approximate in some cases, but probably accurate to within five years or so. Please bear in mind that the dates, although mostly derived from company records are not necessarily as definite as they appear. There are documented examples where there are variations from the stated years both earlier and later. There are a number of words and phrases found associated with various of the trademarks that can in some cases help to date a piece also. (See page 24.)

NOTE: It is imperative that you understand that the various trademarks illustrated and discussed here have been used by Goebel on *all* of their products and not limited to *Hummel* items alone, until about mid-1991 when a new mark for exclusive use on *M.I. Hummel* was put into use.

Incised Crown Mark

Stamped Crown Mark

THE CROWN MARK (TMK-1)
1934-1950

The Crown Mark, TMK-1 or CM, is referred to as the "Crown-WG" in some references was in use by Goebel on all of its products when *M.I. Hummel* figurines were first offered on the market in 1935. Subtle variations have been noted but the illustration above is all you need to identify the trademark. Those subtle differences are of no significance to the collector. The letters WG below the crown in the mark are the initials of William Goebel, one of the founders of the company. The crown signifies his loyalty to the imperial family of Germany at the time of the mark's design around 1900. The mark is sometimes found in an incised circle. There is another Crown type mark that is sometimes confusing to collectors. Some references refer to it as the "Narrow Crown" and others the "Wide Ducal Crown".

This mark was introduced by Goebel in 1937 and used on many of their products. They call it the Wide Ducal Crown mark so we should adopt this name as well to alleviate the name confusion. To date most dealers and collectors have thought this mark was never found on a *M.I. Hummel* piece. The author certainly has never heard of its occurance. Goebel, however, in their newsletter *Insights* (Vol. 14, No. 3, pg. 8) states that the mark was used "...rarely on figurines" so we will defer to them and assume there might be some out there somewhere.

Often, as stated earlier, the Crown Mark will appear twice on the same piece, more often one mark incised and the other stamped. This is, as we know, the "Double Crown".

When World War II ended and the United States Occupation Forces allowed Goebel to begin exporting, the pieces were marked as having been made in the occupied zone. The various forms and phrases to be found in this regard are illustrated here:

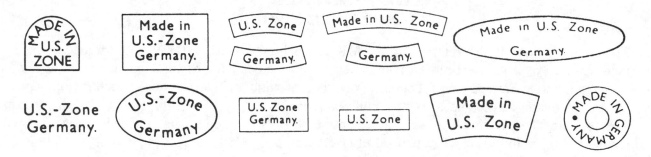

These marks were applied over the years 1946-1948. They were sometimes applied under the glaze and often over the glaze. The latter were easily lost over the years through wear and cleaning if the owner was not careful. About 1948-49 the U.S. Zone mark requirement was dropped and the word "Germany" took its place and with the partitioning of Germany into East and West, "W. Germany", "West Germany" or "Western Germany" began to appear most of the time instead.

Up until the early 1950's the company occasionally used a WG or a WG to the right of the incised *M.I. Hummel* signature.

$$M.I. Hümmel © W$$

When found it is usually when the signature is placed on the edge of or the vertical edge of the base. Some have been known to confuse this as being a Crown Mark (TMK-1) when in fact it is not.

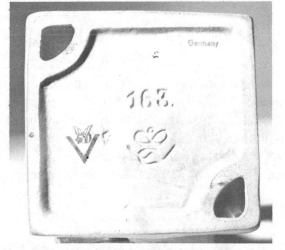

The base of Hum 163 illustrating the Incised Crown Mark and the stamped Full Bee trademark. Note also the use of the decimal designator with the incised mold number.

THE BEE MARKS
1950-1979

In 1950 the Goebel company made a major change in their trademark. They incorporated a bee in a V. It is thought that the bumblebee part of the mark was derived from a childhood nickname of Sister Maria Innocentia Hummel, meaning bumblebee. The bee flies in a V which is the first letter of the German word for distributing company, *Verkaufsgesellschaft.*. The mark was to honor M.I. Hummel who had died in 1946.

There are actually twelve variations of the Bee marks to be found on Goebel produced *M.I. Hummel* items, but some are grouped together as the differences between them are not considered particularly significant. They will be detailed as a matter of interest.

The Incised Full Bee

The Stamped Full Bee

THE FULL BEE (TMK-2)
1940-1959

The Full Bee mark is also referred to as TMK-2 or abbreviated FB is the first of the Bee marks to appear. The mark evolved over the next almost twenty years until the company began to modernize it so to speak. It is sometimes found in an incised circle. The history of the transition and illustrations of each major change follows. Each of them are still considered to be the Full Bee (TMK-2).

The very large bee flying in the V remained until around 1956 when the bee was reduced in size and lowered into the V. It can be found incised, stamped in black, stamped in blue in that order of its evolution.

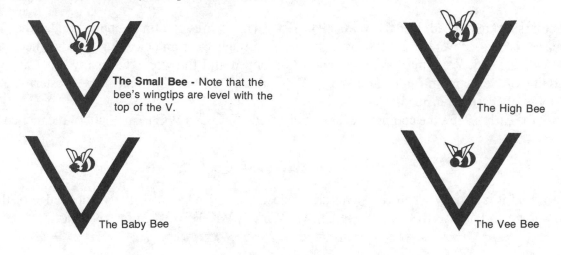

The Small Bee - Note that the bee's wingtips are level with the top of the V.

The High Bee

The Baby Bee

The Vee Bee

THE STYLIZED BEE (TMK-3)
1960-1972

A major change in the way the bee is rendered in the trademark made its appearance in 1960. The Stylized Bee (TMK-3), sometimes abbreviated as Sty Bee when written, as the major component of the trademark appeared in three basic forms through 1972. The first two are both classified as the Stylized Bee (TMK-3), but the third is considered a fourth step in the evolution, the Three Line Mark (TMK-4). It might be of interest to you to know that Goebel re-used the Crown-WG backstamp from 1969 until 1972. It is not always there, but when it shows it is a small blue decal application. This was done to protect Geobel's copyright of the mark. It otherwise would have run out.

Large Stylized Bee

The Large Stylized Bee was used primarily from 1960 through 1963. Notice in the illustration that the W. Germany is placed to the right of the bottom of the V. The color of the mark will be black or blue. It is sometimes found inside an incised circle. When you find the Large Stylized Bee mark, you will normally find a stamped West or Western Germany in black elsewhere on the base, but not always.

W. Germany

The Small Stylized Bee is also considered to be TMK-3. It was used concurrently with the Large Stylized Bee from about 1960, but continued in use until about 1972. Note in the illustration the W. Germany appears centered beneath the V and Bee. The mark is usually rendered in blue and it too is often accompanied by a stamped black West or Western Germany. The mark is sometimes referred to by collectors and dealers as the One Line Mark.

The Three Line Mark (TMK-4) is sometimes abbreviated 3-line or 3LM in print. The trademark used the same stylized V and Bee as the others, but also included three line of lines of wording beside it as you can see. This major change appeared in blue color.

THE GOEBEL BEE or THE LAST BEE MARK (TMK-5)
1972-1979

Actually developed and occasionally used as early as 1970, this major change is known by some collectors as the Last Bee mark because the next change in the trademark no longer incorporated any form of the V and the Bee. The mark was used until about mid-1979 when they began to phase it out, completing the transition to the new trademark in 1980. There are three minor variations in the mark shown in the illustration. Generally the mark was placed under the glaze from 1972-1976 and is found placed over the glaze 1976-1979.

THE MISSING BEE MARK (TMK-5)
1979-1991

Goebel®
W. Germany

The transition to this trademark began in 1979 and was complete by mid-1980. As you can see Goebel remove the V and Bee from the mark altogether. Many dealers and collectors lamented the passing of the tradition stylized V and bee and for a while called the mark the Missing Bee. In conjunction with this change, the company instituted the practice of the artist adding the date of finishing the painting of the piece to the traditional artist's mark. Because the white overglaze pieces are not usually painted, it would be reasonable to assume that the date is omitted on them.

THE HUMMEL MARK (TMK-7)
1991-Present

In 1991 Goebel made a move of historical import. They change the trademark once again. This time the change was not only symbolic of the reunification of the two Germanys by removal of the "West" from the mark, but very significant in another way. Until then, they used the same trademark on virtually *all* of their products. The mark illustrated here is for exclusive use on Goebel products made from the paintings and drawings of *M.I. Hummel*. Other Goebel products will bear a different mark than that used on Hummel pieces.

OTHER MARKS ASSOCIATED WITH THE TRADEMARKS

There are marks in addition to the U.S. Zone marks already covered that are to be found on the bases and backs of Goebel Hummel items.

First of all there are several colors of marks that you may encounter. The colors found to date are:

Black
Purple
Red
Brown
Green
Blue

The color blue has been exclusively since 1972. There also have been several combinations of colors found.

The following list contains various words and marks found associated with the trademarks. There are probably more to be discovered, but these are representative.

W. Germany - © by W. Goebel (in script)
W. Germany - © W. Goebel (in script) © W.Goebel
GERMANY - Copr. W. Goebel
Germany - © by W. Goebel, Oeslau 1957
WEST GERMANY - *II Gbl. 1948
West Germany - OCCUPIED GERMANY
WESTERN GERMANY - Western Germany

First Issue and Final Issue

Starting in 1990 Goebel began making any newly issued piece with the words "FIRST ISSUE" during the first year of production only. In 1991 they began doing the same thing for the last year before retiring a piece by marking each with the words "FINAL ISSUE". The words are also accompanied by the appropriate year date. The stamps are illustrated for you here. The first piece to bear the FINAL ISSUE backstamp was Hum 203, Signs of Spring, in both sizes. The final issue pieces will also be sold with a commemorative retirement medallion hung around it.

EXPLANATION OF THE GOEBEL MOLD NUMBER
AND SIZE DESIGNATOR SYSTEM

Mold Numbers

All Goebel-made *Hummel* items are made by the use of molds and each, unique mold is assigned a number. The number is part of the mold and it, along with the size designator becomes a part of the finished piece. It generally appears incised on the underside of the base, but for practical reasons may appear elsewhere on the item.

Until around the mid 1980's it was thought by most collectors that the highest mold number normally used in production was in the mid-400's. Extensive research by writers, dealers and serious collectors revealed, among other things, that the number in the Goebel design pool may actually exceed one thousand. A great many of these have not yet been put into production and are designated Possible Future Editions (PFE) by Goebel. A few of these (presumably in prototype) have somehow found their way into the collector market, but the occurrence is exceedingly rare. When a PFE becomes a production piece, the earlier PFE example almost always bears an earlier trademark than the mark found on the production piece. It, therefore, retains its unique status. Of the remaining designs, some may be PFE's and some may never make it into the collection.

Before we get into the explanation of the mold number system let's eliminate the source of one area of confusion. Some price lists (including the one from Goebel) have an odd letter or number preceded by a slash mark occasionally associated with the *Hummel* mold number. Example: Flower Madonna, 10/I/W. The "W" and the slash are *price list* indications that this piece is finished in all white. The actual mold number found incised on the piece is "10/I" only. The "/W" meaning white overglaze finish and the "/11" or "/6" meaning the normal color finish are the decor indicators found in some of todays price lists. Remember that they are not part of the mold number.

The Size Designator Portion of the Mold Number

While the mold number as discussed above was treated as separate from the size designator system, in reality the two comprise what is sometimes called the Hummel Number (Hum number), but more commonly, the Mold Number. It seems complicated, but isn't really if you factor out Goebel's occasional departure from the rules.

The system has changed little over the years, but has been modified once or twice.

Beginning with the first piece in 1934-35 and continuing to about 1952, the first size of a particular piece produced was considered by the factory to be the "standard" size. If plans were to produce a smaller or larger version, the factory would place an 'O' or a decimal point after the model or mold number. Frequently, but not always, the 'O' would be separated from the mold number by the placing of a slash mark (/) between them. There are many cases where the 'O' or decimal point do not appear. Apparently this signified that at the time there were no plans to produce other sizes of the same piece. In the case, of Hum #1, "Puppy Love", there exists only one "standard" size and no size designator has ever been found on the figure. It is reasonable to assume, however, that subsequent changes in production plans would result in other sizes being produced. Therefore the absence of the 'O' or decimal point is not a reliable indicator that there exists only one "standard" size of the particular piece. *In fact, there are some instances where later versions of a piece have been found bearing the "slash O", decimal point, and even a "slash I", which are smaller than the "standard" for that piece. In some cases the decimal point appears along with the slash mark. I have seen the figurine, Hum 51, Village Boy marked thusly: "51./0.". It could be that when they changed to the slash designator, they just didn't remove the decimal from the mold, but how do you explain the decimal point following the "O"?

The factory used Roman numerals or Arabic numbers in conjunction with the mold numbers to indicate larger or smaller sizes than the "standard".

The best way for the collector to understand the system is by example. The figure "Village Boy" Hum #51, has been produced in 4 different sizes.

EXAMPLE: 51/0

The number 51 tells us that this is the figurine "Village Boy" and the "slash O" indicates that it is the first size produced, therefore the "standard" size. In this case the size of the piece is roughly 6". The presence of the "slash O" (or of decimal point) is also an indication that the figure was produced sometime prior to 1952.

---

*After the mold for Hum 218, "Birthday Serenade", the use of the "slash O" size designator was eliminated.

As discussed earlier, not all the figures produced prior to 1952 were designated with the "slash O" or decimal point, but if present it is a great help in beginning to date a figure. The one exception in present knowledge, is the discontinuance of the use of the "slash O" designator on Hum #353, "Spring Dance". It was produced with the 353/0 mold and size designator about 1963, taken out of current production later and recently reinstated once more.

By checking the reference for mold #51, you will note there exist three more sizes, Hum 51/1/0, Hum 51/3/0 and Hum 51/I. Roman numerals are normally used to denote sizes larger than the "standard" and Arabic numbers indicate sizes smaller than the "standard". When utilized in the normal manner, the Arabic number is always found to the left of the 'O' designator. There are two exceptions to this norm, one specific, the other general. The specific, known exception is "Heavenly Angel", Hum mold number 21/0/2. This is one of only two known instances of the use of a fractional size designator. The last two numbers are read as one-half (½). The general exception is the occasional use of an Arabic number in the same manner as the Roman numeral. The Roman numeral size indicator is never used with the 'O' designator present, and the Arabic number is never normally used without the 'O' designator; therefore, if you were to find a mold number *51/2, you would know to read it *51/II and that it represents a piece larger than the "standard".

Continuing with our example, we will take Hum 51/I.

EXAMPLE: 51/I

As before the number 51 identifies the piece for us. The addition of the "slash I" tells us that this is larger figure than the standard. In this case it is about one inch larger.

EXAMPLE: 51/2/0 and 51/3/0

Once again we know the identity of the piece is #51, "Village Boy". In both cases there is an Arabic number, the mold number and the "slash O", therefore we can assume both are smaller than the "standard". The 51/2/0 is smaller than 5" and the 51/3/0 is even smaller still.

Since the 'O' and decimal point size designators are no longer in use and, keeping in mind the cited exceptions, we can usually assume that a figure with the model number and no accompanying Arabic or Roman numerals is the "standard" size for that model. If the model number is accompanied by Roman numerals, the figure is a larger size, ascending to larger sizes the higher the numeral.

There seems to be no set "standard" size or set increase in size for each of the Arabic or Roman numeral size designators used in the collection. The designators are individually specific to each model and bear no relation to the designators on other models.

ADDITIONAL DESIGNATORS

There are a number of pieces in the collection: table lamps, candy boxes, book ends, ash trays, fonts, plaques, music boxes, candle holders, plates and sets of figures, some of which have additional or different designators. The following is a list of them and explanations of how each is marked:

TABLE LAMPS - are numbered in the traditional manner. Some later price lists show the number preceded by an M. Example: M/285.

CANDY BOXES (CANDY BOWLS) - are covered cylindrical deep bowls, the cover being topped with one of the Hummel figures. They are numbered with the appropriate model number for the figure and preceded with the Roman numeral III. **Example:** III/57 is a candy box topped with Hum 57, "Chick Girl".

BOOKS ENDS - are both large figures with provisions for weighting with sand, and smaller figures placed on wooden bookend bases. The only sand-weighted book ends are the "Book Worms". The designation for a book end is accomplished by placing A and B after the assigned Hum model number for the book ends. **Example:** Hum 61/A and Hum 61/B is a set of book ends utilizing Hum 58 and Hum 47, "Playmates" and "Chick Girl". These are the current designations. In some cases, if the figurines are removed from the bookend bases, they are indistinguishable from a regular figurine.

ASH TRAYS - are numbered in the traditional manner.

FONTS - are numbered in the traditional manner. Exception: There is a font, Hum #91, "Angel At Prayer", in two versions. One faces left, the other right. They are numbered 91/A and 91/B respectively.

*This mold number does not exist. Used here as an illustrative example only.

PLAQUES - are numbered in the traditional manner.

MUSIC BOXES - are round wooden boxes in which there is a music box movement, topped with a traditional Hummel model which rotates as the music plays. The number for the music box is the Hummel number for the piece on the box followed by the letter 'M'. If the figure is removed from the top, it will not have the 'M' but will be marked in the traditional manner.

CANDLE HOLDERS - are numbered in the traditional manner. They sometimes have Roman numerals to the left of the model designator. These indicate candle size. I: .6cm. II: 1.0 cm.

PLATES - are numbered in the traditional manner. To date, none has been produced with the size designator, only model number.

SETS OF FIGURES - are numbered with one model number sequence and followed by the designation /A, /B, /C ... /Z, to indicate each figure is part of one set. **Example:** The Nativity Set 214 contains 15 Hummel figures, numbers 214/A, 214/B, 214/C, and so on. In the case of Nativity Sets there are some letters which are not used. The letters I and Q are not utilized because of the possibility of confusing them with the Roman numeral I or Arabic 1 and 0.

SOME ADDITIONAL NOTES ON
SPECIAL MARKINGS

Sets

Any time there have been two or more pieces in the collection which were meant to be matched as a pair or set, the alphabetical listings A through Z appropriately are applied to the Hummel model numbers in some way. Exception: Sometimes called "The Little Band" are the three figures Hum 389, Hum 390, and Hum 391. They do not bear the A, B, C designating them as a set. The piece actually entitled "The Little Band" is Hum 392, an incorporation of these three figures on one base together. References to the "Little Band" and the "Eight Piece Orchestra" are occasionally found in price lists which include Hummel Numbers 2/0, 1/I, 89/I, 89/II, 129, 389, 390, 391. A charming group, but not officially a set.

Mold Induction Dates

The year date incised on the base of many *M.I. Hummel* pieces is the source of much confusion to some collectors. The year date is the Mold Induction Date (MID). The MID is the date the original mold for that particular piece was made and not the date the piece was made. It bears no relationship whatsoever with the date of making the item, only the mold. As a matter of fact there are many molds that are years old and still being used to make figures today. The MID doesn't always appear on the older pieces, but all those currently being made will have it.

THE MAKING OF M.I. HUMMEL FIGURINES AND PLATES BY GOEBEL

The question most asked by those uninitiated to the *Hummel* world is "Why do they cost so much?" It is not an unreasonable question and the answer can be simply that they are hand-made. That, however, really doesn't do justice to the true story. The making of *Hummel* pieces is immensely complex; truly a hand operation from start to finish. The process requires no less than *seven hundred* steps! Those few of you who have been lucky enough to visit Goebel's northern Bavaria facility know how complicated the operation is. Others of you who have seen the Goebel film and/or visited the facsimile factory on its 1985 U.S. tour have a pretty good idea.

To call the facility a factory is misleading, for the word factory causes the majority of us to conjure up an image of machinery and automated assembly lines. It is not that at all. It is an enormous artists' and artisans' studio and workshop complete with friendly relaxed surroundings including good music, hanging baskets and potted plants. In short, a pleasant place to create and work. It is packed with highly trained and skilled artists and craftsmen. Each of them must undergo a full three year apprenticeship before actually taking part in the fashioning of the figurines and other items that are made available to the collector. This apprenticeship is required no matter whether the worker is a mold-maker or painter. Each specialist in the process must understand the duties of the others.

There is insufficient space to elaborate on all seven hundred steps in making the pieces so I have grouped them into six basic areas: Sculpting the Master Model, Mother or Master Mold Making, Molding the Pieces, Bisque Firing, Glaze Firing, Painting and Decor Firing.

1. SCULPTING THE MASTER MODEL

It is estimated that there are 1200-1500 *M.I. Hummel* artworks from which Goebel may pick to render into a three-dimensional piece. Once a piece of art is chosen a master sculptor fashions a model in a water base Bavarian black clay. This is a long process during which the artist must not just reproduce the art but interpret it. He must visualize for instance, what the back of the piece must look like and sculpt it as he thinks *M.I. Hummel* would have rendered it. Once the wax model is deemed acceptable it is taken to the Siessen Convent where it is presented for approval or disapproval. If the preliminary model is approved it is then taken back to Goebel for the next step.

2. MASTER OR MOTHER MOLD MAKING

A figurine cannot be made from a single mold because of its complexity. Therefore after a very careful study of the wax model it is strategically cut into several pieces. Some figurines require being cut up into as many as thirty pieces for molding. For example, Ride Into Christmas had to be cut into twelve separate pieces and Goose Girl into seven. Using the Goose Girl seven pieces we continue. Each of the seven are placed on a round or oval base and secured with more clay. The base is then surrounded by a piece of flexible plastic that extends above the piece to be molded. Liquid plaster of Paris is then poured into it. The dry plaster of Paris is removed resulting in an impression of the part. This process must be repeated for the other side. After each of the seven parts are molded the result is fourteen separate mold halves. From these are made the Mother (sometimes called Master) molds. These are made from an acrylic resin. The mother molds are cream colored and very durable. It is from the mother molds that the working molds are made. The plaster of Paris working molds can be used only about twenty times at which time a new set must be made from the mother molds.

Before full production of a new figure is commenced, a few samples are made. The figure must again be carried to the Siessen Convent for approval or, as the case may be, rejection or recommendations for changes. Once final approval is given the piece is ready for production. That could be immediate or years later.

3. MOLDING AND ASSEMBLY OF THE PIECES

All the pieces in the collection are made of fine earthenware consisting of a mixture of feldspar, kaolin and quartz. It is the finest earthenware available. Both porcelain and earthenware come under the definition of ceramic. Add just a bit more kaolin and the earthenware would become porcelain. Goebel chooses to use earthenware because of its inherent softness. That softness is considered best for Hummel items.

The liquid mixture of the three ingredients plus water is called slip. The slip is poured into the working molds and left for a period of time. The porous character of the plaster of Paris acts like a sponge and draws moisture out of the slip. After a carefully monitored time the remaining slip is poured out of the mold leaving a hollow shell of the desired thickness. The parts are removed from the molds and while still damp, they are assembled using slip as a sort of glue. The assembled piece is then refined, removing all seams and imperfections and detailing the more subtle areas. The piece is then set aside to dry for about a week.

4. THE BISQUE FIRING

Bisque is fired, unglazed ceramic. The dry assembled pieces are gathered together and fired in a kiln for eighteen hours at 2100 degrees Fahrenheit. This results in a white, unglazed bisque figurine.

5. THE GLAZE FIRING

The bisque fired pieces are then dipped into a tainted glaze mixture. The glaze is tinted to assure that the whole piece is covered with the mixture. The tint is usually green and any uncovered area will show up white. The dipped pieces are then fired at 1872 degrees Fahrenheit. When removed from the kiln after cooling, they are a shiny white.

The colors are mixed in small amounts and given to the painters only as needed. Some of the colors react to each other upon firing, so oftentimes the item must be painted with one or a few colors and fired before others can be applied. This results in multiple decor firings before the pieces are finished. In some cases up to ten separate firings are required before they are finished and ready for distribution.

As you can see now, the making of the pieces is a long, involved and painstaking operation. As noted earlier there are 700 separate operations, the workers are highly trained and experienced, and there are 25 different quality control inspection points. In spite of this each is unique because it is a hand operation. No matter how a piece is assembled or painted, no matter how experienced a worker is, he or she is still a human being, inherently incapable of creating identical copies. That is part of the magic. Each piece is a joy, each unique, each a hand-made work of art.

Goebel's Master Sculptor Gerhard Skrobek sculpting the figurine Ring Around the Rosie, Hum 348.

Photo courtesy *M.I. Hummel* Club

The Making (cont'd)

Body of Goose Girl embedded in wax on oval base. Preparatory to surrounding with flexible plastic for containing the plaster of Paris after pouring.

Result of the pouring of plaster of paris. The wax body has not yet been removed. Note the key slots. The one on the right is still in process of being carved out.

The Master or Mother Mold.

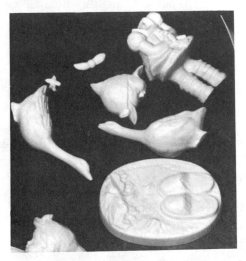

The seven pieces of Goose Girl after removal from the molds and prior to assembly.

The assembled, refined piece prior to bisque firing.

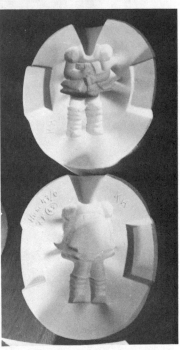

The two halves of a plaster of paris working mold. Note the keys left and right. These insure accuracy of fitting the two halves together for pouring the piece.

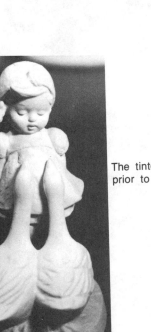

The tinted piece prior to glaze firing

Appearance of the Goose Girl after bisque firing.

(continued)

The Making (cont'd)

Assembling

Assembling the cast parts prior to drying and bisque firing. Umbrella Girl, Hum 152/B
Photo courtesy *M.I. Hummel* Club

Casting

Pouring the slip into the mold.
Photo courtesy *M.I. Hummel* Club

Several hundred assembled figurines just prior to the bisque firing. The various racks and shelves upon which they rest are called "furniture".

Refining the assembled pieces prior to the first firing.

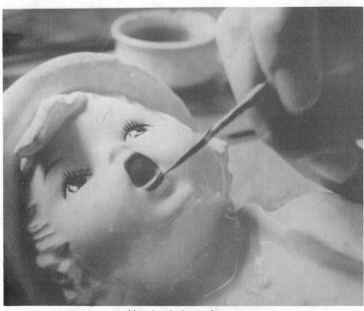

Hand-painting a face.
Photo courtesy *M.I. Hummel* Club

(continued)

The Making (cont'd)

One of the final steps of decorating prior to Decor Firing.

A row of Kilns at the factory

One of the light and cheerful studios where artists are hand-painting the figurines.

CARING FOR, PROTECTING AND DISPLAYING YOUR COLLECTION

Caring For Your Collection

The first consideration is the potential damage from direct sunlight. It can wreak havoc on just about any type of collectible including kiln-fired colors on the pieces and the decals under the glaze. Once this occurs, the damage is irreversible. Another permanent damage is that which some of the older figurines are subject to. A few have discolored somewhat, due to environmental and atmospheric pollution. In the early years the pigments used in the paints, while the finest available, were not as durable and lasting as those used in the present day and are more subject to the caustic elements of air polution.

A simple periodic dusting of earthenware or ceramic pieces as you would any decorative item is always a good idea, but occasionally they may a little freshening up.

Goebel sells, through the *M.I. Hummel* Club, an *M.I. Hummel* Care Kit that consists of two specially formulated cleaning solutions and some brushed all designed specifically with earthenware, ceramic and porcelain collectibles in mind. It also includes an instruction booklet. Should you not wish to obtain this kit you can still clean your items. Use your kitchen sink or a similar large vessel. Line it with a towel or other soft material to minimize the possibility of breakage when handling your figure. Make up a solution of barely warm water and a mild soap such as baby shampoo. Cover the air hole with tape if possible, dip the piece in the solution and scrub gently with a very soft toothbrush or similar soft bristle brush all the while holding it over the towel lined sink. Rinse it off here also. It may take more than one washing if the piece is heavily soiled. Dab it with a soft, absorbent cloth and place on the same type of surface to air dry. Should you be unable to avoid getting water inside the figure, it may take quite some time to dry out.

Many knowledgeable dealers and collectors use strong detergents without harm, but I would be reluctant to use them as they may contain chemicals that could be incompatible with the finish.

If, while handling your figures, you notice a tinkling or rattling sound don't worry. When being made sometimes a small piece comes loose inside the figure and rattles around. Sometimes, depending on the shape and design of the figure, you can stop this by injecting a little household glue into the interior of the figure through the air hole(s) and shaking it until the rattle stops. Place it on its side until it drys. Presto! No more rattle.

Cleaning paper collectibles beyond dusting is not recommended and if you are fortunate enough to own an original drawing or painting, proper archival framing and care of the frame is recommended. Best advice? Don't touch it. Leave the cleaning of such things to the professionals.

Displaying Your Collection

The display of your collection is limited only by your imagination. This section is primarily to help you with display ideas, but to give you some practical information and guidance for displaying your collection safely and securely.

One of the first considerations is the strength of the display case if you choose to go that route. I will never forget photographing a large collection many years ago, that was displayed in several antique china cabinets and etageres. It was indeed elegant, but every time I opened a door or moved a figurine all the others rattled or shook. It was nerve-racking to say the least. I was sure relieved to get it over with. The point is, be sure that your display unit is strong enough to hold your collection safely.

Remember also the severe damage direct sunlight can inflict on just about any type of collectible and try to avoid display on a mantle if there is ever a fire set in the fireplace. You can cause severe damage to any framed artwork placed there.

Safeguarding Your Collection

We have discussed the strength factor with regard to the display fixture, but another consideration should be security. First, if there are any innocent, but mischievous little hands about, keep the displays out of their reach and cabinets latched or locked. More importantly, especially if you have a valuable collection, is security.

After you have given the usual attention to normal home security there are some things you need to consider with respect to your collection. No matter how tempting or flattering, turn down any media attention to your collection. This is a red alert to thieves and yes, there are *Hummel* thieves. Most thefts take place from display tables set at shows and vehicles used to transport them to and from such events, but there have been enough instances of home burglary and armed robbery in the home to keep knowledge of your collection among family and friends. If you don't have a home security system consider installing one. Fairly inexpensive do-it-yourself systems have been developed. Some are even wireless, eliminating the need to run wires all over the house.

What To Do When It's Broken

There are different options depending upon the nature of the item and the value, intrinsic or sentimental. If you attach great meaning to the piece, but it is a relatively inexpensive item, you could simply glue it back together. If it has great sentimental value and you have the wherewithal, by all means have it professionally restored. If you have damaged a very rare or valuable piece, it might be worth having it professionally restored. Restoration can be expensive and take quite some time so you must first decide whether it is worth the trouble and more importantly whether the piece will be worth as much or more than the cost.

There are three types of restoration: "Cold repairing", "Firing" and "Bracing". The method used in the greatest majority of cases where Hummel figures are concerned is Cold Repairing. It is the least expensive of the three and the results are very good. You will not likely be able to detect the repairs with the naked eye. Examination by X-ray and/or Long-wave ultraviolet light is the only way to detect a professionally restored piece of earthenware or porcelain.

In selecting a restorer a personal visit to the shop is advisable. There you can look over work that is in process and maybe even see a few finished restorations. Many keep a photo album of their work as well. Ask for some references, get an estimate for the job and find out how long a wait. In most cases, a long wait (we can be talking months here, folks) means many people on the list and that is usually an indication of a good reputation. The best way to be sure is to get a recommendation from a friend or trusted dealer.

The following list of restorers is a combination of the list provided by the *M.I. Hummel* Club and a list I have developed over the last seventeen years. It is by no means complete, for there are dozens more around the country doing competent, professional restorations. Over the years I have heard from or spoken to dealers and collectors who have not been satisfied with the work or service of some of them, while on the other hand I have heard praise from others regarding the same restorers. In fairness to all of them, I cannot be responsible for recommendations and therefore offer only the list. They are listed alphabetically by each state in which they are located.

ARIZONA

China & Crystal Clinic
243 N. Fraser Drive
Mesa, AZ 85203
(602) 898-8877
(800) 658-9197

CALIFORNIA

Attic Unlimited
22435 E La Palma
Linda, CA 92686
(714) 692-2940

Ceramic Restoration
Gene Gomas
Manteca, CA
(209) 823-3922

Mr. Mark R. Durban
P.O. Box 4084
Big Bear Lake, Ca 92315
(714) 585-9989

Foster Art Restoration
711 West 17th Street
Suite C-12
Costa Mesa, Ca 92627
(800) 824-6967

House of Renew
27601 Forbes Rd., Unit 55
Laguna Niguel, CA 92677
(714) 582-3117

Just Enterprises
2790 Sherwin Avenue #10
Ventura, CA 93003
(805) 644-5837

Barry J. Korngiebel
Geppetto's Restoration
31143 Via Colinas, Suite 506
Westlake Village, CA 91362
(818) 889-0901

Martha A. MacCleary
14851 Jeffrey Road #75
Irvine, CA 92720
(714) 262-9110

Porcelain Repair by Joan
San Diego, CA
(619) 291-6539

Restorations by Linda (Linda M. Peet)
1759 Hemlock Street
Fairfield, CA 94533
Restoration by appointment only
(707) 422-6497

Venerable Classics
645 Fourth St. Suite 208
Santa Rosa, CA 95404
(707) 575-3626

COLORADO

Herbert Klug
2270 South Zang Ct.
Lakewood, CO 80228
(303) 985-9261

Nylander Studios
1650 S. Forest St.
Denver, CO 80222
(303) 758-4313

CONNECTICUT

Walter C. Kahn
76 N. Sylvan Rd.
Westport, CT 06880
(203) 227-2195

(continued)

FLORIDA

Eric Beckus
4511 32nd Avenue North
St. Petersburg, FL 33713
(813) 522-4288

Robert E. Di Carlo, Restoration
P.O. Box 16222
Orlando, FL 32861
(407) 886-7423

Loughlin Restoration Studio
Indian Beach Circle
Sarasota, FL 34234
(813) 355-7318

The Old Coburg, Inc.
Markus A. Paetzold
1300 Tyrone Blvd.
St. Petersburg, FL 33710
(813) 343-1419
By Appointment Only

Eric W. Idstrom Co.
Restorations Objects D'Art
12500 S.E. Highway 301
Belleview, FL 32620
(904) 245-8862

Ginette or Irving Sultan
Maison Gino, Inc.
845 Lincoln Road
Miami Beach, FL 33139
(305) 532-2015

ILLINOIS

John & Betty Bazar
J.B. Services
2302 Sudbury Lane
Geneva, IL 60134

Doe Lasky
Repair and Restoration
Oak Park, IL
(708) 386-1772

Sierra Studios
37 W 222
Rt. 64, St. 103
St. Charles, IL 60175

Wayne Warner
RR 16 Box 557
Bloomington, IL 61704
(309) 828-0994

IOWA

Maxine's Ltd.
7144 University Ave.
Des Moines, IA 50311
(515) 255-3197

MASSACHUSETTS

Rosine Green Associates
45 Bartlett Crescent
Brookline, MA 02146
(617) 277-8368

J. Kevin Samara
The Shropshire
274 South Street
Shrewsbury, MA 01545
(508) 845-4381

NEW JERSEY

Baer Specialty Shop
259 E. Browning Road
Bellmawr, NJ 08031
(609) 931-0696

Ely House
118 Patterson Ave.
Shrewsbury, NJ 07701

Restoration by Dudley, Inc.
47 Stanford Avenue
P.O. Box 345
West Orange, NJ 07033
(201) 731-4449

Restoration by Louis
R.D. 6 Box 340
Hyatt Road
Branchville, NJ 07826
(201) 875-2274

NEW YORK

China & Glass Repair Studios
282 Main Street
Eastchester, NY 10709
(914) 337-1977
also
P.O. Box 598
Somers, NY 10589
(914) 628-5531

Richard Gerhardt
66 Jayson Ave.
Great Neck, NY 11021

Imperial China
22 North Park Avenue
Center, NY 11570
(516) 764-7311

Restoration Unlimited
Donna Curtin, Proprietor
3009 W. Genesee St.
Syracuse, NY 13219
(315) 488-7823 or 1-800-622-8679

Hans-Jurgen Schindhelm
Ceramic Restoration of
Westchester, Inc.
81 Water Street
Ossining, NY 10562
(914) 762-1719

OHIO

Colonial House Antiques & Gifts
22 Front Street Terrace Park
Berea, OH 44017
(216) 826-4169

Old World Restorations
347 Stanley Avenue
Cincinnati, OH 45226
(513) 321-1911 or 1-800-878-1911

Wiebold Studio, Inc.
413 Terrace Place
Cincinnati, OH 45174
(513) 831-2541

PENNSYLVANIA

H.A. Eberhardt & Sons, Inc.
2010 Walnut Street
Philadelphia, PA 19103
(215) 568-4144

A. Ludwig Klein & Son, Inc.
P.O. Box 145 - 683 Sumneytown Pike
Harleysville, PA 19438
(215) 256-9004

The Krauses
97 W. Wheeling St.
Washington, PA 15301
(412) 228-5034

(continued)

SOUTH DAKOTA

D & J Glass Clinic, Inc.
RR 3, Box 330
Sioux Falls, SD 57106
(605) 361-7524

TEXAS

Sharon Lewis
1010 West Monroe Street
Austin, TX 78704
(512) 441-9985

VIRGINIA

Bell Haven Clay Works
P.O. Box 178 Belle Haven Road
Belle Haven, VA 23306
(804) 442-5964

CANADA

British Columbia

J & H China Repairs
8296 St. George St.
Vancouver, BC
CANADA V5X 3C5
(604) 321-1093

Manitoba

Artwork Restoration
30 Hillhouse Rd.
Winnipeg, Manitoba
CANADA R2V 2V9
(204) 334-7090

Toronto

Classic Art Restoration
875 Eglinton Ave. West
Toronto, Ontario
CANADA M6C 3Z9
(416) 787-4794

Cataloging and Insuring Your Collection

With increasing value of your collection through acquisition and appreciations come increasing risk of loss if some or all are lost or damaged. Just about everyone carries some amount of homeowners or household goods insurance against loss due to fire or natural disaster, but so few actually have enough. Many people don't realize that if there is any coverage at all, for collectibles, it is severely limited. Most companies require a separate schedule for collectibles, listing each item individually and others will offer a special policy. Discuss this with your local agent. As for establishing a value for each piece, you can pay for an appraisal by a knowledgeable dealer in your area or, that not being possible, ask your agent if he will accept the values listed in this book. I know many do, for I have been contacted by them on various occasions, for up-to-the-minute valuations on collections. The market has become fairly stable so a one year old value is usually close to the current market and this book rarely goes over a year and a half without being updated.

You will need to catalog your collection for the insurance company and for your own peace of mind in the case of a theft. A record of your collection, especially if it includes photographs, will go a long way toward helping the law enforcement authorities in their investigation of a theft. It will also assure you of identification of your property in the happy case of recovery by the authorities.

You can also place a unique mark beneath the base to aid in identifying the items as yours. The thieves may or may not discover your mark and remove it. There is, however, an even better way to mark them. There is a black ray crayon on the security market that is invisible to the naked eye when used. The marking from it becomes visible under a black light (long-wave ultraviolet light).

Refer to Appendix A of this book for instructions on photographing your collection. Take the pictures and attach them to a written description of each piece including trademarks and any other marks found on the base. These will not usually be in the photos. Record the exact size and any other characteristic unique to your piece. Some put this information on the back of the photo itself. Whatever method you use, be sure to make a duplicate set to be kept in a safe deposit box or some other secure location away from your home or where you keep your collection. You don't want your catalog stolen or burned up with your collection. Your insurance company will very likely require a written list itemized with description and value. Your safely stored photo catalog will be a big help to you and them in the case of a disaster. Don't forget to update the catalog with any new acquisitions and significant changes in value.

RECOMMENDED BOOKS FOR COLLECTORS

AUTHENTIC HUMMEL FIGURINES

Copyright by W. Goebel, Rodental, Germany. This is an illustrated catalog that was, for many years, published by the company. Out or print.

FORMATION OF AN ARTIST, THE EARLY WORKS OF BERTA HUMMEL

James S. Plaut. Copyright 1980, Schmid Brothers, Inc., Randolph, Massachusetts.

This softbound book is actually a catalog of the 1980-82 tour of an exhibition of paintings, drawings, photographs and a tapestry from the collection of the *Hummel* family.

GOEBEL MINIATURES OF ROBERT OLZEWSKI by Dick Hunt. 595 Jackson Ave., Satellite Beach, FL. Hunt's Collectibles.

GUIDE FOR COLLECTORS

Copyright by W. Goebel, Rodental, Germany. Available through the *M.I. Hummel Club,* P.O. Box 11, Pennington, NJ 08534-0011.

This is a beautiful, large format full color catalog of the current Goebel *M.I. Hummel* collection including closed editions. It is updated periodically.

HUMMEL

By Robert L. Miller. Coypright 1979, Portfolio Press Corporation, Huntington, New York 11743.

This is a supplement to the original *Hummel, the Complete Collector's Guide and Illustrated Reference* by Ehrmann and Miller.

THE M.I. HUMMEL ALBUM

First Edition/First Printing. Copyright 1992, Portfolio Press Corporation. Available through the *M.I. Hummel Club* P.O. Box 11, Pennington, NJ 08534-0011.

This is a beautiful, hard cover, large format that any collector and lover of *M.I. Hummel* needs in their library.

HUMMEL ART

By John Hotchkiss. Copyright 1982. Wallace-Homestead Book Co., 1912 Grand Avenue, Des Moines, Iowa 50305.

This is a full color handbook that essentially updates the first and second editions.

THE HUMMEL

by ArsEdition, © 1984 by Verlag Ars Sacra Josef Mueller, Munich, Germany. This is a 78 page, full color hard cover book, full of illustrations by Sister M.I. Hummel with light verse.

THE HUMMEL BOOK

17th Edition; by Berta Hummel and Margarete Seeman. Copyright 1992 by W. Goebel, Roedental, Germany. This copyright is today with ARS AG, Zug, Switzerland.

HUMMEL COPYCATS

By Lawrence L. Wonsch. Copyright 1987. Published by Wallace-Homestead, 580 Waters Edge, Lombard, IL 60148.

This superb treatment of the hundreds of copies of *M.I. Hummel* figurines over the years and around the world.

HUMMEL FACTS

By Pat Arbenz, Misty's Gift Gallery, 228 Fry Blvd., Sierra Vista, Arizona 85635.

This is a reprint collection of all Mr. Arbenz' columns for *Plate Collector Magazine.* It is inexpensive and indispensable to the collector, but probably out of print. You might try. It's possible he has a few copies.

HUMMEL, THE COMPLETE COLLECTOR'S GUIDE AND ILLUSTRATED REFERENCE

By Erich Ehrmann and special contributor, Robert L. Miller, 1976. Portfolio Press Corporation, Huntington, NY 11743.

Mr. Ehrmann, publisher of Collectors Editions Magazine, and Mr. Miller Acknowledged expert and owner of one of the world's largest Hummel collections, have collaborated to present this large work. As a reference it is invaluable to collectors.

M.I. HUMMEL ALBUM

A Goebel publication. See your dealer.

M.I. HUMMEL: THE GOLDEN ANNIVERSARY ALBUM
By Eric W. Ehrmann, Robert L. Miller and Walter Pfeiffer. Copyright 1984, Portfolio Press Corporation, Huntington, NY 11743
  A beautiful book full of color photos and much good information for collectors.

M.I. HUMMEL FIGURINES, PLATES, MORE ... 5th Edition
By Robert L. Miller. Copyright 1992, Portfolio Press Corporation, Huntington, NY 11743
  A well organized and handy reference by this noted collector.

SKETCH ME BERTA HUMMEL
By Sister M. Gonsalva Wiegand, O.S.F. Published in reprint by Robert L. Miller and available at most dealers or from Mr. Miller at P.O. Box 210, Eaton, Ohio 45320.

VIDEO TAPES

THE LIFE OF SISTER M.I. HUMMEL
Produced by W. Goebel. This is a striking 25 minute treatment of Berta Hummel life. Available from the *M.I. Hummel Club*. Goebel Plaza, P.O. Box 11, Pennington, NJ 08534-0011.

M.I. HUMMEL® MARKS OF DISTINCTION
A historical look at the progression of *M.I. Hummel* backstamps from the beginning to the current mark. Available from the *M.I. Hummel Club*. Goebel Plaza, P.O. Box 11, Pennington, NJ 08534-0011.

SOME USEFUL PERIODICALS

The following is a list of periodicals you may find useful in collecting Hummel figurines.

ANTIQUES JOURNAL   (monthly)
P.O. Box 1046
Dubuque, Iowa 52001
  Has occasional articles about Hummel collecting and ads for buying and selling Hummels.

THE ANTIQUE TRADER WEEKLY   (weekly)
P.O. Box 1050
Dubuque, Iowa 52001
  Occasional Hummel articles and extensive ads for buying and selling Hummels.

COLLECTOR EDITIONS (incorporating ACQUIRE)   (quarterly)
170 Fifth Avenue
New York, NY 10010
  Has occasional Hummel column.

COLLECTORS JOURNAL   (weekly)
Box 601
Vinton, Iowa 52349
  Has ads for Hummel buying and selling.

COLLECTORS MART   (bi-monthly)
15100 W. Kellogg
Wichita, Kansas 67235

COLLECTORS NEWS   (monthly)
606 8th Street
Grundy Center, Iowa 50638
  Has ads for Hummel buying and selling occasional Hummel articles.

COLLECTORS' SHOWCASE   (bi-monthly)
P.O. Box 6929
San Diego, California 92106

THE TRI-STATE TRADER   (weekly)
P.O. Box 90
Knightstown, Indiana 46148
    Has ads for Hummel buying and selling.

CLUBS AND ORGANIZATIONS

There are a few dealers and manufacturers who sponsor "collector's clubs". They are designed to market their products to a target audience. This is a good marketing technique that doubles as a means of educating collectors as to what artists and manufacturers are presently doing. The collector of *M.I. Hummel* items is lucky to have a couple of these. They are unique in that they are very large organizations and are very serious about keeping collectors informed. Membership in both is highly recommended.

THE HUMMEL COLLECTOR'S CLUB
1261 University Drive
P.O. Box 157
Yardley, PA 19067
(215) 493-6705, (215) 493-6204

Established in 1975 By Dorothy Dous, she and her husband have developed the club into a very valuable and worthwhile organization for collectors of Hummel collectibles. Mrs. Dous (Dottie) writes an interesting quarterly newsletter which is lengthy, easy to read and crammed with information. The newsletter also includes a long list of members' for sale, trade or wanted lists. The club acts as a gratis go-between for its members. The collector would benefit by becoming a member of this organization.

The M.I. HUMMEL CLUB
Goebel Plaza
P.O. Box 11
Pennington, NJ 08534-0011
(609) 737-8777, 1 (800) 666-2582

This club was founded by the W. Goebel firm in 1976 as the Goebel Collectors' Club and became the *M.I. Hummel* Club in the spring of 1989. The club publishes a beautiful and very informative quarterly newsletter, *Insights*, which no collector should be without. Another advantage of membership is the renewal gifts each year, usually a figurine, and the chance to buy figures that are offered exclusively to members and are specially marked with the club backstamp. They also maintain a referral list of member's items for sale or wanted.

LOCAL CHAPTERS OF THE M.I. HUMMEL® CLUB

In 1993, 117 Local Chapters of the *M.I. Hummel Club* were active in 37 states and 4 provinces in Canada. If you are interested in joining a Local Chapter or starting one of your own if there isn't one in nearby call or write the club in Pennington at the phone or address already given.

The old local chapter patch. The new ones read ''*M.I. Hummel* Club''. Many have their own custom patches made to more personally identify their chapter.

Local Chapters (cont'd)

ARIZONA
Northwest Valley (Sun City)

ARKANSAS
Arkansas Traveler (Harrison)

CALIFORNIA
Bumble Bee (Burbank)
Camarillo
Central Coast (Santa Maria)
Fresno
Hollywood
San Bernardino (Yucaipa)
San Diego
San Gabriel (Camarillo)
San Jose
Whittier (Orange)

COLORADO
Loveland
Mile Hi (Denver)
Pikes Peak (Colorado Springs)
Gateway to the Rockies

CONNECTICUT
Rose City (Norwich)

FLORIDA
Broward County (Hollywood)
Daytona Beach
Fivay (Hudson)
Gulfview Coquettes
Greater Zephyrhills
Jacksonville
Ocala
Orlando Area
Palm Beach (Lake Park)
St. Petersburg
Seven Rivers (Beverly Hills)
Suncoast (Palm Harbor)
Tampa Area

ILLINOIS
Chicago/Niles
Greater Peoria Area
Gateway East
LaGrange Park (Bridgeview)
N.W. Suburban (Palatine)
Springfield
Southern Illinois (Irvington)

INDIANA
Illiana (Crown Point)
Danville

IOWA
Quint Cities (Rock Island)
Siouxland Bees (Sioux City)

KANSAS
Mo-Kan (Kansas City)
Flint Hills (Americus)

LOUISIANA
Cajun Collectors (Baton Rouge)

MAINE
Nor'Easter (Lewiston)

MARYLAND
Silver Spring
Frederick

MASSACHUSETTS
Cape Cod (Sandwich)
Pioneer Valley (Springfield)
Neponset Valley (Dedham)
Quabbin (Belchertown)

MICHIGAN
Dearborn
Great Lakes (Dearborn)
Mid-Michigan (Flushing)
Niles
Saginaw Valley (Bay City)
Tri-County (Shelby Township)

MINNESOTA
Minneapolis/St. Paul (Eagan)
St. Cloud

MISSOURI
Gateway City (St. Peters)
St. Louis Area

MONTANA
Big Sky (Great Falls)

NEBRASKA
Lincoln
Omaha

NEVADA
High Sierra (Reno)

NEW HAMPSHIRE
The Graniteer (Manchester)

NEW JERSEY
Garden State (Maplewood)
Ocean Pines (Whiting)
Raritan Valley (Piscataway)

NEW YORK
Brookhaven (Babylon)
Great South Bay (Amityville)
Nassau-Suffolk (Centereach)
Paumanok (Babylon)
Rochester (Hilton)
Western NY (Buffalo)

NORTH CAROLINA
Carolina Mountain Region
(Hendersonville)

OHIO
Greater Cleveland (Parma)
Firelands Area (Sandusky)
Miami Valley (Dayton)
Toledo
Western Reserve (Cleveland)
Youngstown/Hubbard
Queen City (Cincinnati)
Stark County Hall of Fame

OKLAHOMA
OK Chapter (Oklahoma City)

OREGON
Cascade (Eugene)
Portland (West Linn)

Local Chapters (cont'd)

PENNSYLVANIA

Antietam Valley (Waynesboro)
Berks County (West Lawn)
Central (Muncy)
Pocono (Stroudsburg)
Perkasie (Doylestown)
Philadelphia
Pittsburgh
Schuykill County (Pottsville)
York County (Spring Grove)

PUERTO RICO

El Coqui (Guaynoba)

RHODE ISLAND

Bristol County

SOUTH CAROLINA

Piedmont Carolinas (Fort Mill)

TEXAS

Alamo (San Antonio)
Brazosport (Lake Jackson)
Fort Worth
Heart of Texas (Waco)
Gulf Coast (Houston)
Metroplex (McKinney)
Museum Chapter of New Braunfels

UTAH

Beehive (West Jordan)

VERMONT

Burlington

VIRGINIA

Northern Virginia (Fairfax)
Tidewater Area (Virginia Beach)

WASHINGTON

Bellevue
Puget Sound (Kirkland)
Seattle-Tacoma (Brier)

WISCONSIN

Fox Valley (Fond du Lac)

CANADA

Alberta

Calgary
Edmonton (Sherwood Park)

British Columbia
Greater Vancouver (Langley)

Manchester
Manitoba (Winnipeg)

The M.I. HUMMEL® Club Exclusives

When the club was founded under Goebel sponsorship and management, as part of the benefits of membership the company began producing pieces that would be available only through the club. There are two types of these. One is in the form of a membership renewal premium. For the past several years these have been figurines. The other is each year, subsequent to renewal, the member receives a redemption card(s) allowing the purchase of the exclusive offerings for that year. They are available only through officially sanctioned dealers representing the club. Where practical, until early in 1989, each of these exclusive pieces bore the following inscription:

EXCLUSIVE SPECIAL EDITION
No. (1,2,3, etc) FOR MEMBERS OF THE
GOEBEL COLLECTOR'S CLUB

Concurrent with the transition from the old Goebel Collectors Club the *M.I. Hummel Club* came a change in the club exclusive backstamp. The backstamp now incorporates a black and yellow bumble bee within lined half-circle with *M.I. Hummel* beneath the half-circle.

Base of Hum 479/I Brought You A Gift showing the new special club backstamp described above.

With only one exception, each of the redemption pieces has been based on an original *M.I. Hummel* drawing or painting. This was the third year offering, a bust of Sister M.I. Hummel (Hu-3) designed by Goebel master sculptor Gerhard Skrobek and illustrated here.

M.I. HUMMEL BUST, Hu 3. Last Bee mark (TMK-5), incised 1978 MID, 5¾".

Pins given to members of the *M.I. Hummel* Club (formally Goebel Collectors' Club) upon the fifth, tenth and fifteenth anniversaries of their membership.

4" plaque that was given to members of the Goebel Collectors' Club upon joining until May 31, 1989.

Valentine Gift

What Now?

A most unusual club piece was offered in addition to the figurine for 1983-84 club exclusive. This was a miniature of the first exclusive club piece, "Valentine Gift". It was made in the form of a tiny ¾ inch figurine mounted in a 14K gold plated cage hanging from a chain and worn as a necklace. It is easily removed from the cage for display as a free-standing figurine.

1986 saw the introduction of a second *M.I. Hummel* miniature, "What Now?" as an exclusive piece available to members.

(continued)

For the club year 1991-92 Goebel Miniatures created another miniature figurine exclusive for the club. This one is a freestanding figurine, Morning Concert at ⅞". It is supplied with an earthenware Bavarian Bandstand setting and a protective glass display dome and base. The release price was $175.00.

MORNING CONCERT, Miniature, GMS 269-P. This is shown in the optional display dome and bandstand setting and also with the Goebel English language Miniature Studio display plaque to the left. Note the dime on the right for scale. *M.I. Hummel* club exclusive.

The membership gift for 1990-91. Sterling silver pendant.

Goebel announced in 1984 that from that point on there would be a cut-off date for use of the redemption certificates after which the pieces would no longer be available and the molds destroyed. Following here is a list of each of the exclusive club pieces and their respective cut-off dates. Those that do not bear regular Goebel *Hummel* mold numbers are illustrated and discussed at their appropriate location within the collection listing. The others are illustrated in this section.

Release Date	Name	Mold No.	Cut-off Date
1977-78	Valentine Gift	387	5/31/84
1978-79	Smiling Through (Plaque)	690	5/31/84
1979-80	M.I. Hummel Bust	HU-3	5/31/84
1980-81	Valentine Joy	399	5/31/84
1981-82	Daisies Don't Tell	380	5/31/85
1982-83	It's Cold	421	5/31/85
1983-84	What Now?	422	5/31/85
1984-85	Valentine Gift (Miniature)	--	12/31/84
1984-85	Coffee Break	409	5/31/86
1985-86	Smiling Through	408	5/31/87
1986-87	What Now? (Miniature)	--	5/31/88
1986-87	Birthday Candle	440	5/31/88
**1986-87	Valentine Gift (6" plate)	738	5/31/88
1987-88	Morning Concert	447	5/31/89
**1987-88	Valentine Joy (6" plate)	399	5/31/89

(continued)

Release Date	Name	Mold Number	Cut-off Date
1988-89	The Surprise	431	5/31/89
**1988-89	Daisies Don't Tell (6" plate)	736	5/31/90
1988-89	Daisies Don't Tell	380	5/31/89
*1989-90	I Brought You a Gift	479	5/31/90
**1989-90	It's Cold 6" plate	735	5/31/90
1989-90	Hello World	429	5/31/90
1990-91	I Wonder	486	5/31/91
*1990-91	Merry Wanderer (sterling silver pendant)	--	5/31/91
1991-92	Morning Concert (miniature)	--	5/31/92
*1991-92	Two Hands, One Treat	493	5/31/92
1992-93	My Wish is Small	463/0	5/31/93
*1992-93	Lucky Fellow	560	5/31/93
1993-94	I Didn't Do It	626	5/31/94
*1993-94	A Sweet Offering	549/3/0	5/31/94
***1993-95	Sweet As Can Be	541	

*These are special edition pieces given to all old members who renewed. New members will get the figure for the year they first join.

**A four plate series called the Celebration Plate Series.

***A Preview Edition. This figure will be offered to members exclusively, with the club backstamp for two years. Thereafter it will be a regular production figure with regular markings.

OTHER GOEBEL M.I. HUMMEL® COLLECTIBLES

M.I. HUMMEL® DOLLS

Three current production **HUMMEL DOLLS**. Left to right: CARNIVAL, SIGNS OF SPRING, LOST SHEEP. All have Goebel earthenware heads and hands.

The first Hummel dolls were made in 1950. They were made at the time outside of the Goebel factory by arrangement with another company. The first dolls had rubber heads and soft stuffed bodies, stood 16½ inches tall, and were delivered to the Goebel factory to be dressed in hand-made clothing. Very shortly thereafter the com-

44

(continued)

position of the body was changed (1951) to rubber also. There were only six dolls produced at first in 1952 Goebel took over the entire production of the dolls in-house and added a smaller 10 inch tall size.

Over the years it became apparent that the rubber type used in the dolls was unstable and the compound would sometimes break down. This breakdown is exhibited by overall deterioration of the head and body, areas sinking in or collapsing, cracking or a combination of any or all. By 1963 or 1964 the company changed the composition to rubber and vinyl according to their advertising at the time. The bodies are now all made of soft, durable material which is a type of polyvinylchloride (PVC).

There were nine different dolls of this type produced up until 1983 in a 10 inch size. At that point Goebel introduced a completely new line. These will be discussed on following pages.

NAME	SIMILAR TO	NAME	SIMILAR TO
Bertl	Unknown	Liesl	Unknown
Gretl	Sister	Max	Unknown
Hansel	Unknown	Seppl	Boy with Toothache

Variously over the years the company has called the dolls by different names and have also made an 8 inch high version of some. A 1976 catalog advertised the 8 inch dolls as:

NAME	SIMILAR TO
Vroni	Meditation
Rudi	Home From Market
Seppl	Boy with Toothache
Mariandl	None
Jackl	Happy Traveler (somewhat)
Rosi	Little Sweeper (somewhat)

The 1976 catalog also lists and illustrates a 10 inch tall baby doll in two different costumes (boy and girl) although it is not made completely clear whether or not they are Hummel dolls.

The nine 10 inch dolls that were in production up until the introduction of the new line in 1983 were as follows:

NAME	SIMILAR TO
Felix	Chimney Sweep
Ganseliesl	Goose Girl
Gretl	Sister
Hansl	Brother
Peterle	School Boy
Radibub	For Father
Rosi	School Girl
Striekliesl	A Stitch In Time (somewhat)
Wanderbub	Merry Wanderer

All the bodies of the girls and of the boys were the same (two styles only). It is the costumes and accessories that made them different.

Identification of the above Hummel dolls is made relatively easy by the presence of an incised *M.I. Hummel* signature and Goebel trademark found on the back of the neck of each.

Current Production Dolls

In 1983 the Goebel company announced a completely new line of *M.I. Hummel* dolls. The heads, hands and feet of the new dolls are made of the same or similar ceramic-type material as are the figurines. The bodies are still of a soft, stuffed material.

The new dolls are readily identifiable from the material of the heads, hands and feet but there are additional, unmistakable identifying characteristics. They are 15 inches in height, each having the *M.I. Hummel* signature and the date of production year. The bodies will also carry a label containing the production date along with identifying remarks.

The first four to be released were as follows:

Postman
On Holiday
Boy from Birthday Serenade
Girl from Birthday Serenade

They were released at a suggested retail price of $175.00 each and production was limited to the year 1984. The dolls for the year 1985 and limited in production to that year were as follows:

Lost Sheep
Easter Greetings
Signs of Spring
Carnival

Please turn to the Danbury Mint section on page 117 for more dolls.

EXPRESSIONS OF YOUTH SERIES

During factory tours or the promotional tour where a Goebel artist demonstrates the painting of a figure, Goebel officials noticed that people had a tendency to be drawn toward the figurines in the pure white, glazed stage in their production. Something about the striking shiny pure white figurine was intriguing to them. Over the years collectors have also been drawn to the white overglaze pieces in the collection also. Goebel decided to create a small collection of the white pieces with only the eyes, eyebrows and the lips rendered in color. So far only seven have been put into the collection:

HUM 2/I	Little Fiddler	7½"
HUM 7/I	Merry Wanderer	7"
HUM 13/V	Meditation	13½"
HUM 15/II	Hear Ye, Hear Ye	7½"
HUM 21/II	Heavenly Angel	8¾"
HUM 47/II	Goose Girl	7½"
HUM 89/II	Little Cellist	8"

These figurines are produced as an open edition, but methods of production and the extraordinary quality control required in their production will limit the number available. Each is identified beneath the base with the inscription "Expressions of Youth" in a red color in addition to the trademark and other normal marks.

M.I. HUMMEL® FIGURINES — THE CRYSTAL COLLECTION

In 1991 Goebel began producing twelve of the Hummel figurines in 24% lead crystal. Although not visible in any of the three photographs accompanying, they each bear the incised *M.I. Hummel* signature. They also bear the Missing Bee (TMK-6) and the year date 1991. If they continue to produce them it would be reasonable to assume that as they run out of the present stock they will be produced with the new Hummel Mark (TMK-7). The twelve are:

Apple Tree Girl 3¾"
Botanist 3⅛"
For Mother 2⅞
Little Sweeper 2⅞
March Winds 2⅞
Meditation 3½"
Merry Wanderer 3½"
Postman 3⅞"
Sister 3⅞"
Soloist 3"
Village Boy 3"
Visiting an Invalid 3¾"

Crystal Collection. Left to right: Little Sweeper, Soloist, For Mother, Sister, Village Boy, March Winds.

Crystal Collection. Left to right: Postman, Meditation, Visiting an Invalid.

Crystal Collection. Left to right: The Botanist, Merry Wanderer, Apple Tree Girl.

BUSTS OF M.I. HUMMEL®

There have been only three of these produced over the years. The first was a large size, 15" high, fashioned in a white bisque finish. These were made primarily as display pieces for authorized dealers and were given to them. The number made is not known, but is likely to be fairly limited. First made in 1965 they have the incised mold number "HU 1" and the Three Line Mark (TNK-4).

The second one to be made was a smaller version. The one in my photograph here measured 6⅝" high. It has an incised mold number of "HU 2". As you can see it bears the incised signature on the base at front. Not visible is "1967 Skrobek" on the back of the base. It can be found in both the Three Line Mark (TMK-4) and the Last Bee (TMK-5) mark.

This is the Hu 2, bisque finish bust of *M.I. Hummel* made for sale through dealers. This particular one was taken to a commercial mold ceramic operation, sprayed and fired, giving it this white overglaze finish. They were never produced by Goebel in white overglaze.

The third version appears to be the same as the HU 2, but has the incised mold number "HU 3" and is painted in colors. It was produced in an edition limited to the year of production that it was an exclusive offering to the Goebel Collector's Club (now *M.I Hummel Club*) in the club year 1979-80. It is found bearing the Last Bee (TMK-5) mark.

THE WOODEN MUSIC BOXES

This four music box series was announced in late 1986. This was the first officially authorized hand-carved *M.I. Hummel* design in wood. Designed by Goebel and made in cooperation with the Anri Workshop carvers in Italy, the four designs were rendered in relief on the covers of the boxes. Each music box is accompanied by a sequentially numbered ceramic medallion made by Goebel. Each of the four is limited in production to 10,000. The four motifs are:

1987 **Ride Into Christmas** Release Price - $389.95
1988 **Chick Girl** Release Price - $400.00
1989 **In Tune** Release Price - $425.00
1990 **Umbrella Girl** Release Price - $450.00

WOODEN MUSIC BOXES. 1987, Ride into Christmas and 1988, Chick Girl.

WOODEN MUSIC BOXES. 1989, In Tune and 1990, Umbrella Girl.

PLAQUES, PATCHES AND PINS

Many collectors like to add related articles to their collections. There have been various items made by Goebel as well as some by other companies with Goebel's knowledge and permission, to commemorate events in the world of *M.I. Hummel* collecting. There are probably more than are listed here as this goes on constantly. There are probably a few unauthorized items that are too localized and small in number to precipitate a reaction from the company and probably others that are unknown to them for the same reasons. Whatever the case the following lists and illustrations can give you a good idea of the type of thing that the collector may find.

Plaques

Year	Design	Event
--	Merry Wanderer	Free to each visitor to the Goebel factory 1977 to May 31, 1989
	Merry Wanderer	Free to each new member of the Goebel Collectors' Club. States Membership
1979	Merry Wanderer	Hummel Festival, Eaton, Ohio
1980	Meditation	Hummel Festival, Eaton, Ohio
1981	Little Fiddler	Hummel Festival, Eaton, Ohio
1982	Goose Girl	Hummel Festival, Eaton, Ohio
1983	Little Fiddler Head	Dealer Fest. Jan. 6, 1983

Many small plaques such as these are prepared by the factory for Goebel sanctioned events.

The reverse of the two small plaques showing typical inscriptions.

Year	Design	Event
1983	Merry Wanderer	South Bend Plate Collectors Convention, Goebel Facsimile Factory Display, South Bend, Indiana
1983	Confidentially	*M.I. Hummel* Fiesta Misty's Gift Gallery Sierra Vista, Arizona

Three of the plaques specially made for the U.S. tour of the Goebel Facsimile Factory and the Goebel Archive Tour. There are many others than just these three.

Year	Design	Event
1983	Merry Wanderer	Archive Tour Spenser-Zaring, Ltd., Carefree, Arizona
1983	Merry Wanderer	Archive Tour Carol's Gift Shop Artesia, California
1983	Merry Wanderer	Archive Tour, Henri's, Belmont, California
1985	Jubilee	Free to each visitor to the factory during 1985 Golden Anniversary.
1985	Jubilee	Free to factory visitors

4⅛" plaques given to visitors to Goebel in Rodental. What is not generally known is the existence of the Golden Anniversary version shown on the right here. Normally printed in blue the special version was printed in gold and given to visitors during 1985. The background shows the front of the plaque with Jubilee. Hum 416.

50

Year	Design	Event
1985	Little Fiddler Head	Golden Anniversary Gala Jan. 6, 1985
1989	Rose	World's Fair of Hummels, Rosemont, Illinois, 1989
1991	text only	Commemorates the new Hummel backstamp (TMK-7)

A special plaque commemorating the creation of the new Goebel trademark for exclusive use on Goebel trademark for exclusive use on Goebel *M.I. Hummel* collectibles. It came in a blue velvet presentation pouch.

Patches

Year	Design	Event
1977	Merry Wanderer	Hummel Festival, Eaton, Ohio
1978	Merry Wanderer	Hummel Festival, Eaton, Ohio
1978	Silent Night with Black Child, Hum 31	Hummel Festival Eaton, Ohio
1979	Mountaineer	Hummel Festival, Eaton, Ohio
1979	Singing Lesson (plate)	Collector's Exposition Rosemont, Illinois
1980	Meditation	Hummel Festival, Eaton, Ohio
1981	Little Fiddler	Hummel Festival, Eaton, Ohio
1982	Goose Girl	Hummel Festival, Eaton, Ohio
--	text only	"Goebel Collectors" Club LOCAL CHAPTER MEMBER
1983	Confidentially	*M.I. Hummel* Fiesta Sierra Vista, Arizona
1988	Puppy Love	Bavarian Summer Festival, Eaton, Ohio
1988	text only	World's Fair of Hummels, Rosemont, IL

Pins

Year	Design	Event
--	Merry Wanderer	5 year membership pin for members the Whitier, CA chapter
1983	Confidentially	*M.I. Hummel* Fiesta Misty's Gift Gallery Sierra Vista, Arizona
1982	text only	5 year membership pin for members of the Goebel Collector's Club.
1987	text only	10 year membership pin for members of the Goebel Collector's Club
1988	Home From Market	Hummel Festival Volksmarsch. Eaton, Ohio
1988	Friends	Hummel Festival Volksmarsch. Eaton, Ohio
1989	Latest News	Hummel World's Fair Volksmarsch above without the Volksmarsch banner
1989	Bumblebee on Rose	Created for the 1989 Chicago Show
1991	Crossroads	Hummel Expo '91, Dayton, Ohio
1992	Land in Sight	Miller's Hummel Expo '92, Dayton, Ohio (large badge).

Examples of cloisonne pins made to commemorate event in the Hummel collecting world. These have become increasing expensive to make and are therefore becoming scarce.

1993 button given out at the *M.I. Hummel* Club convention.

Miscellaneous

Year	Design	Event
1986	Commemorative plaque (DeGrazia figure)	Goebel Fest Las Vegas, Nevada
1986	Mug (Chapel Time)	Goebel Fest, Las Vegas, Nevada
1992	On Our Way (metal figure)	Miller's Expo '92 in Dayton, Ohio
1993	Museum Building on Silver Plate Medallion	Opening of the new Hummel Museum, New Braunfels, Texas

Metal Hum 472, On Our Way, cast for the Miller's Expo '92 in Dayton, Ohio.

Base of the metal Hum 472, On Our Way.

54

Jewelry

In past years from time to time an individual or a company has produced jewelry utilizing *M.I. Hummel* design motifs. Goebel keeps tight control of licensing these days, but in the earlier years there were some who took advantage. One such effort turned into the Goebel Miniatures division of the company (see page 60). Refer also to the section on the *M.I. Hummel* Club exclusives for pictures of the pendants offered to the membership.

Most of the items are in the form of pins or brooches. There have probably been in excess of fifty of these to be produced. Quality has ranged from pot metal to silver and gold. Please refer also to page 99.

Calendars

Goebel published the first calendar in 1951. It was in the German language. The following year the first English language version was published and until 1975 when the German language version illustrated the 1975 plate on the cover, the English calendar used the design from the previous years German edition. In 1975 the cover of the

German calendar was the 1975 Annual Plate, so the next years English edition illustrated the 1976 plate. The practice reverted to the German language design preceding the English language edition after that with one other exception in 1964 and 1965. In 1989 the format of the calendars changed completely.

Goebel published a special calendar in 1985 to celebrate the fifty year anniversary of *M.I. Hummel* figurines. This is apart from the annual series of calendars.

There was another special edition calendar published for 1987. This one in commemoration of the tenth anniversary of the founding of the Goebel Collectors' Club (now the *M.I. Hummel* Club). This calendar is apart from the annual series of *Hummel* calendars.

The M.I. Hummel® Annual Calendar Listing

1951	German	Goose Girl
1952	English	Vacation Time plaque
1953	German	Heavenly Protection
1954	English	
1954	German	Festival Harmony with Flute
1955	English	
1955	German	Candle Light candle holder
1956	English	
1956	German	School Girls
1957	English	
1957	German	School Boys
1958	English	
1958	German	Meditation
1959	English	
1959	German	Stormy Weather
1960	English	
1960	German	Bookworm
1961	English	
1961	German	Flower Madonna
1962	English	
1962	German	Telling Her Secret
1963	English	
1963	German	Little Tooter
1964	English	
1964	German	Saint George
1965	English	Goose Girl
1965	German	Spring Dance
1966	English	
1966	German	School Girls
1967	English	
1967	German	Duet
1968	English	
1968	German	Mail Coach
1969	English	

(continued)

Calendars (cont'd)

Year	Language	Title
1969	German }	Ring Around the Rosie
1970	English }	
1970	German }	To Market
1971	English }	
1971	German }	Stormy Weather (detail)
1972	English }	
1972	German }	Adventure Bound
1973	English }	
1973	German }	Umbrella Boy
1974	English }	
1974	German }	Happy Days
1975	English }	
1975	German	1975 Annual Plate
1976	English	1976 Annual Plate
1976	German }	Little Artist
1977	English }	
1977	German }	Follow the Leader
1978	English }	
1978	German }	Happy Pastime
1979	English }	
1979	German }	Smart Little Sister
1980	English }	
1980	German }	School Girl
1981	English }	
1981	German }	Ring Around the Rosie
1982	English }	
1982	German }	Umbrella Girl
1983	English }	
1983	German }	Happy Days
1984	English }	
1984	German }	Merry Wanderer
1985	English }	
1985	German }	Thoughtful
1986	English }	
1986	German }	Auf Wiedersehen
1987	English }	
1987	German }	In Tune
1988	English }	

MISCELLANEOUS OTHER M.I. HUMMEL® COLLECTIBLES

There are more *M.I. Hummel* related collectibles out there than most realize. Following here is a partial list and a description of a few of them. Today, only products licensed by ARS AG, Zug, Switzerland are authentic *M.I. Hummel* products". Many on the list will be covered in the sections describing authorized collectibles made by other companies in the past and present.

Foreign Postage Stamps	Jigsaw Puzzles
First Day Covers	Decoupage Pictures
Framed Stamps	Music Boxes
Christmas Tree Ornaments	Boxed Tapestry Cards
Christmas Tree Balls	Boxed Printed Satinique
Clocks	Glassware
Kitchen Canisters	Calendars
Cookie Jars	Wall Plaques
Spice Jars	Checks and check covers
Salt & Pepper Shakers	Stationery
Collector Plates	Gift Wrapping
Porcelain Eggs	Metal Containers
Porcelain Music Boxes	Photo Frames with Mats
Candle Holders	Greeting Cards
Gold Plated Thimbles	Postcards of Figurines

Needlework

If you are handy with crosstitch, crewelwork, embroidery, etc., there is a treasure trove of needle craft of *M.I. Hummel* designs available. Some of the designs that are listed have been discontinued, but I have seen them, still in kit form, from time to time in antique shops and the like. I have also seen finished kits in the same places and at garage and estate sales. I am acquainted with someone who has had one in her "To Do Someday" bag for fifteen years so you never know where you might turn one up, partially finished, finished or still in the kit form.

There are at least two companies that have produced the kits, JCA Inc., 35 Scales Lane, USA - Townsend, MA 01469 and Paragon Needlecraft from the National Paragon Corporation of New York.

There are round, oval and square shapes and they are also made up for bell pulls and pillows. If you are really talented you are limited only by your imagination. If you make your own from a Hummel design, it's perfectly all right as long as it is for your own private use.

Current JCA, Inc. Hummel Needlecraft Products as of 10/4/93

Cross Stitch Books

84022	The Hikers	(Off To Town, the Little Hiker)	Org.H303,309
84023	Carefree Days	(Meeting In the Meadow, ...Mountain)	Org.H144,145
84024	Little Friends	(Chick Girl, Playmates)	Org.H371,372
84025	School Mates	(School, Little Scholar)	Org.H191,192
84034	Land In Sight		Fig.Hum 530
84035	Blessed Event		Original H102
84036	The Apple Tree	(Apple Tree Girl, Apple Tree Boy)	Org.H297,298
84037	Playtime	(Knit One Purl Two, The Book Worm)	Org.H195,196
84038	Ready for Rain	(Have The Sun..., Umbrella Girl)	Org.H294,296
84039	Alpine Afternoon	(Bashful, The Globetrotter)	Org.H350,216
84042	The Birthday Gifts		Original H283

Needle Treasures Kits

2607	Sunny Weather	Original Art	H287
2608	Ring Around the Rosie	Original Art	H204
2609	Not For You	Original Art	H292
2610	Telling Her Secret	Original Art	H291

(continued)

2633	Washday	Original Art	H232
2634	The Postman	Original Art	H246
2641	Stormy Weather	Original Art	H288
2642	Hansel and Gretel	Original Art	H217
2649	Sunny Weather Afghan	Original Art	H287
4217	Blessed Event Baby Quilt	Original Art	H102
NEW	The Doctor	Original Art	H256
NEW	Follow The Leader	Original Art	H351

Christmas Kits

864	Christmas Angel	Original Art	H431
2865	Candle Light	Original Art	H412
2874	Letter to Santa Claus	Original Art	H318
2882	Silent Night	Figurine Art	Hum54
2891	Celestial Musician	Figurine Art	Hum188

Weekenders

750	Chicken-Licken	Original Art	H376
755	Cinderella	Original Art	H154
2762	Sleepy Time	Original Art	H114
2775	Looks Like Rain	Original Art	H304
2802	What's New	Figurine Art	Hum418

40 Designs Used

Toy Truck

What will we find next?! Yes, as you can see by the accompanying photograph, this is a *Hummel* truck. It was authorized by ARS AG and marketed through a toy company. It is a high quality, highly detailed model about 6" long. Everybody needs a *Hummel* eighteen-wheeler for their collection. Not everybody will get one, however, because although the number manufactured is not presently known, the number is small. They were selling for about $35.00 for a few years, but when word got around recently, that a dealer had a few in stock, they disappeared from the shelves rapidly.

A toy truck authorized by ARS AG for sales through a licensee.

Umbrella Girl Tapestry

In the Spring 1990 issue of *INSIGHTS,* the newsletter of the *M.I. Hummel* Club, there was a tapestry offered. There were only 50 made worldwide. They were hand-knotted of pure silk with 120 lines of knots per foot. They were made in Beijing, China and measured 25¼"x26½". The initial offering was for $1,800.00. See page 95.

THE UNUSUAL AND THE RARE
M.I. Hummel® and Related Pieces

This section is devoted to the unusual and rare items. The most famous of these is, of course, the International Collection. There are some others that are difficult to classify in the normal divisions of derivations of *M.I. Hummel* art and so they are placed here. Still others that could be placed with their respective normal production piece counterpart deserve more to be placed here because of a perceived special status. In some cases they will appear in both places and in other cases they will be cross-referenced.

The Goebel Flying Full Bee

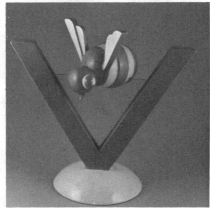

The Flying Bee trademark store display.

Goebel changed their trademark (backstamp) from the Crown Mark (TMK-1) to the Full Bee (TMK-2) in 1950. This large promotional display piece was made depicting the new mark. There are two sizes to be found. The one in the photo here is of the larger size. It is thought to be prototype for there are many more of the smaller size to be found. The secondary market value for any of them should be around $2000-$2500.00

The Miniature Collection

There is another division of Goebel, based in California, Goebel Miniatures. They are sole producers of the painted bronze miniature renditions of *M.I. Hummel* figurines.

There is an interesting story behind the formation of Goebel Miniatures. Back a few years before the division existed, a talented artist named Robert Olszewski produced several miniature replicas of Hummel figurines, innocently unaware of the need to obtain permission to do so. It is unlikely that the company would have allowed it and that's what makes the story interesting. Prior to Goebel finding out about his work and stopping him, he produced miniatures of each of the following five figurines:

Barnyard Hero
Stormy Weather
Kiss Me
Ring Around the Rosie
Ride into Christmas

He had also fashioned a very small number of solid gold bracelets with each one of the above miniatures attached. Those bracelets and the unauthorized have since become highly sought and if sold can command extraordinary high prices.

Out of this incident came Goebel's recognition of Olszewski's talent and the fact that there was a market for the miniature figurines. It resulted in his association with Goebel and the creation of Goebel Miniatures with Olszewski as its head.

Goebel Miniatures produced many other miniatures for Goebel, but our interest is in the series of miniatures of the *M.I. Hummel* figurines that were made.

The series was enhanced by the introduction of six separate little Bavarian buildings and settings that were connected by bridges. They were made to the same scale as the miniatures for their display. The settings are known as KinderWay.

The following is a list of all the miniatures produced:

Valentine Gift (*M.I. Hummel* Club exclusive)
What Now? (*M.I. Hummel* Club exclusive)
Morning Concert (*M.I. Hummel* Club exclusive)
Dealer Display Plaque (German language)
Dealer Display Plaque (English language)
Accordian Boy
Apple Tree Boy
Baker
Busy Student
Doll Bath
Goose Girl
Little Fiddler
Little Sweeper
Little Tooter
Merry Wanderer
Postman
Ride into Christmas
School Boy
Stormy Weather
Visiting an Invalid
Waiter
Wayside Harmony
We Congratulate

Goebel Miniatures. Left to right: We Congratulate, Stormy Weather, Apple Tree Boy, School Boy, Little Sweeper, Merry Wanderer, a U.S. dime for scale.

Goebel Miniatures. Left to right: Little Tooter, Waiter Accordian Boy Little Fiddler, Baker, Goose Girl. A U.S. Dime for scale.

Goebel Miniatures. Left to right: a German language miniature display plaque, Visiting and Invalid, Postman, Ride into Christmas, a U.S. dime for scale.

Goebel Miniatures. Left to right: Doll Bath, Busy Student, a U.S. dime for scale.

MORNING CONCERT, Miniature, GMS 269-P. This is shown in the optional display dome and bandstand setting and also with the Goebel English language Miniature Studio display plaque to the left. Note the dime on the right for scale. *M.I. Hummel* club exclusive.

Goebel announced in early 1992 that the KinderWay Bavarian village settings would be permanently retired, but more importantly, they announced that production of the *M.I. Hummel* figurine miniature would be suspended indefinitely as of the end of 1992. They further stated in the announcement (*INSIGHTS*, Vol. 15, No. 4, page 8): "Though the figurine miniatures have not yet been formally retired, there are currently no plans to resume production".

The International Figures

One of the most interesting and exciting aspects of collecting Hummel figurines and other related pieces is the omnipresent chance to turn up a relatively uncommon to a significantly rare piece. This fortuitous circumstance has happened many times. It has often occurred as a result of painstaking research and detective work, but more often it is pure chance.

One such example is the story of the "Hungarians". A knowledgeable and serious collector of Hummel articles, Mr. Robert L. Miller, regularly advertises that he will buy original Hummel pieces in various collector periodicals around the world. He received a postcard from Europe one day describing some "Hummels" an individual had for sale. After he obtained photographs of a few figurines which appeared to be Hummel designs, some were obviously the familiar figurines but some were apparently in Hungarian costume. In relating his story to the author, Mr. Miller said he felt at first that they were probably not real Hummel pieces but were attractive and he thought they might make a nice Christmas present for his wife. He sent a check and after some thought he called the factory to inquire as to their possible authenticity. He was informed that they knew of no such figures. By the time the pieces arrived he had begun to think that they might be genuine. Upon opening and examining he saw that each bore the familiar "M.I. Hummel" signature! He again called the factory and was told again they knew nothing of them but would investigate. A short time later he received a letter from the W. Goebel firm stating that the eight figurines were indeed produced by the factory as prototypes for a dealer in Hungary before the war and that they believe them to be the only eight ever produced! As most of us are aware now, many more have turned up since Mr. Miller's discovery. In fact there have been something like twenty-six or more different designs to be found. In the beginning, they were so unique that the price they commanded was as much as $20,000.00 at one time! The old law of supply and demand came very much into play as more and more were found. Today the value can go as low as a mid-four figure amount to as high as $15,000 for the very scarce and rare examples.

Unidentified as to country or mold number. 5", no apparent marks.

Mel. 9., BULGARIAN. Stamped Crown Mark, 5¼".

BULGARIAN. The mold number on this example is not evident but is known to be 807. What is there is an incised Bul. 2. and an incised Crown mark (TMK-1). It measures 5".

Hum 810., BULGARIAN. Both have the double Crown Mark (TMK-1) and measure 5⅛".

Hum 8O8, BULGARIAN. Left: 808., double Crown Mark (TMK-1), donut base, 5". Right: No apparent markings, 4¹⁵⁄₁₆".

Hum 811., BULGARIAN. Double Crown Mark, 5¼".

Hum 812, SERBIAN. While similar in costume and pose these two figures are obviously from different molds. Both have donut bases and measure 5¾".

Hum 812, SERBIAN. Base not of one of the two in the previous photo showing the marking.

Hum 813., SERBIAN. Left: Incised Crown Mark (TMK-1), 5¾''. Right: No apparent trademark, 5¾''. There are some color decoration variations between the two.

Hum 813., SERBIAN. Shows markings beneath the base.

Hum 824, SWEDISH. Left: 4⅝'', Right: 4¾'' Obviously inspired by the Merry Wanderer. The one on the right is really stepping out!

Hum 825, SWEDISH. Incised Crown mark (TMK-1) and a stamped Full Bee (TMK-2) trademark, black "Germany", 5".

Two variations on a theme. **Left:** Slovak dress. Mold number is not evident, but is known to be 831. There is an incised number that appears to be an 82 or 89... It measures 5⅝". **Right:** The mold number is 806 and the figure measures 5" tall.

Two international versions of Lost Sheep that curiously have two different mold numbers. **Left:** Czechoslovakian costume with mold number 841. with stamped Crown Mark (TMK-1) and measures 5¾". **Right:** Serbian dress with mold number 968. with a stamped Full Bee (TMK-2) mark, black "Germany", 5½".

Hum 832, Country unknown. There is at least one other 832 design in Slovak costume. Markings are: incised Crown mark colored in blue, measures 5⁷⁄₁₆".

A one-of-a-kind copy of one of the International. Hum 851 in Hungarian dress. It was hand-made for personal enjoyment by a talented artist many years ago.

Hum 842, CZECHOSLOVAKIAN. Left: 842., stamped Crown Mark (TMK-1), 5⅝". Right: 842, Full Bee (TMK-2), black "Germany", 5½. Two obviously different molds.

Hum 852., HUNGARIAN. Incised Crown (TMK-1) and Full Bee (TMK-2) marks, 5".

Hum 851., HUNGARIAN. Left: Double Crown Mark (TMK-1), 5¼". Right: Incised Crown Mark (TMK-1) and stamped Full Bee (TMK-2) mark, black "Germany", 5¼".

Hum 853, HUNGARIAN. Incised Crown Mark
(TMK-1), donut base, 5''.

Two different international versions of Little Fiddler. Although they
obviously reflect the same theme, the molds are very different. **Left:**
No apparent markings. Measures 4⅝'' **Right:** Mold number 904 incised,
Full Bee (TMK-2) mark, 5¼''.

Hum 854., HUNGARIAN.
Double Crown Mark (TMK-1), 5''.

Hum 913, SERBIAN. Left: Measuring 5⅝'' this figure has ''MEL 1940
Unger'' written in pencil beneath the base. No other marks apparent.
Right: 913, registered trademark symbol, 5¼''.

Hum 947/0., SERBIAN. Both have double Crown Marks (TMK-1). The left one measures 4⅞'' and the other, 5''.

For several years these superb figures were erroneously referred to as "The Hungarians", but they are now known as the "Internationals" because as time went by more and more were found wearing costumes from countries other than Hungary. Among them are: Bulgaria, Serbia, Hungary, Czech, Slovakia and Sweden. There may yet be others found. The photos of the International Figures here are also found in the color section.

So far there have been at least 26 unique models found; and counting variations and those figures that are different, but bear the same mold number, there are at least 36. When considering numbers missing in the sequence of those found so far, a conservative estimate of those left unfound would be 25-35, but there is a distinct, however remote, possibility that upwards of 100 may yet be out there.

The following is a list of the different designs that have so far been found.

806	Bulgarian	Similar to SERENADE
807	Bulgarian	Entirely different from other known Hummel designs. Could be a redesign of FEEDING TIME.
808	Bulgarian	Similar to SERENADE
809	Bulgarian	Similar to FEEDING TIME. Has also been found with the Mel 9 designator.
810	Bulgarian	Entirely different from other known Hummel designs. There are four distinct paint variations to be found.
810	Bulgarian	Similar to SERENADE
811	Bulgarian	Entirely different from other known Hummel designs.
812	Serbian	Entirely different from other known Hummel designs.
813	Serbian	Entirely different from other known Hummel designs.

824	Swedish	Similar to MERRY WANDERER. The 824 has also been found with the Mel 24 designtor
825	Swedish	Similar to MEDITATION
831	Slovak	Similar to SERENADE
832	Slovak	Similar to MEDITATION
833	Slovak	Similar to SERENADE, but with different instrument.
841	Czech.	Similar to LOST SHEEP
842	Czech.	Similar to GOOSE GIRL
851	Hungarian	Similar to LITTLE HIKER
852	Hungarian	Entirely different from other known Hummel designs.
853	Hungarian	Similar to NOT FOR YOU
853	Hungarian	Entirely different from other known Hummel designs.
854	Hungarian	Similar to the girl on the right in HAPPY BIRTHDAY
904	Serbian	Similar to LITTLE FIDDLER
913	Serbian	Similar to MEDITATION
947	Serbian	Similar to GOOSE GIRL
968	Serbian	Similar to LOST SHEEP

It was not generally known, but there was a tentative plan in the works to reissue thirty of the International designs in a larger size than the originals. It got to the prototype phase and the plan was reconsidered and finally scrapped. Dealers and collectors lauded this decision as there was much speculation that an issue such as that would have a negative effect on one of the most exciting aspects of collecting *M.I. Hummel* items, i.e. the value of those known Internationals and those yet to be uncovered.

The Internationals were never part of the regular production line. They were never produced and released in large quantities, but rather a very limited number of sample pieces, therefore quite rare.

The MEL Pieces

At least seven of a possible twenty-four or more of these interesting pieces are known to exist today. Some are more common than others, but on a relative basis for they are all scarce. Generally speaking, the rule of identification is that each of the pieces have the three letter prefix "MEL" incised along with the mold number. It is now known that these were produced as prototypes and marked with the last three letters of Hummel to identify them as such. Only two of these so far have been found with the *M.I. Hummel* incised signature and they are unique. The remaining pieces do not have the signature so cannot be considered original Hummel pieces in the strictest sense. Their claim to authenticity otherwise is obvious.

So far those positively identified as MEL pieces are:

Mel 1	Girl with Nosegay	Collector value for these three is about $200-$250
Mel 2	Girl with Fir Tree	
Mel 3	Boy with Horse	
Mel 4	Candy dish or box with a boy on the lid. Collector Value: $6500-7500	
Mel 5	Candy dish or box with a girl on the lid. Collector value: $6500-7500	
Mel 6	Child in Bed candy dish or box. Collector value $2500-3000	
Mel 7	Child (sitting on lid of candy dish). Collector value: $6500-7500	

Mel (cont'd)

Mel 9   International figure (Bulgarian, Hum 809)

Mel 24*   International figure (Swedish, Hum 824)

MEL 6, Child in Bed candy dish.

THREE MEL PIECES, Left to right Mel 1, Mel 2, Mel 3. Each also has a black "Germany" beneath the base.

Of all these the first three are so far the most commonly found. It is a matter of interest that these three (Mel 1 through Mel 3) have subsequently been released as HUM 115, 116 and 117. The other Mel piece with the signature is only assumed to be so through an old Goebel catalog listing for it does not have the Mel prefix in the mold number. It is unique with only one known to exist in a private collection.

There is some information in existence that suggests there may be more of these pieces to be found. There are the obvious missing numbers between nine and twenty-four and factory records of the modeling of Mel 4 and Mel 5, both candy dishes, one with a boy on top and the other with a girl indicate their existence.

*This particular Mel piece bears the incised *M.I. Hummel* signature. Only one known to be in a private collection.

The Wooden Jumbo Display Plaque

There have been at least seven of these plaques found in recent years. They are each magnum sized (34" x 23", 20 lbs.), carved from wood and beautifully painted duplicating the Hum 187 Display Plaque in a jumbo size.

The only identifying mark that could be found on the plaque was a curious "A" within a circle with the crossbar in the "A" appearing to be a bolt of lightening.

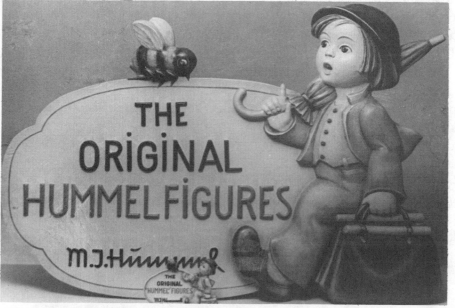

Oversize **Wooden Display Plaque**. Its genuine Hummel, normal size counterpart is placed in the foreground.

Jumbo Plaque (cont'd)

For several years the origin of this plaque remained elusive giving rise to much speculation regarding the circle A mark. The "A" gave rise to the theory that the plaques were produced in the famous ANRI wood carving workshops in Italy for the character of the carving and painting seemed to be the same as their style and quality.

Some of the circle A marks were placed upside down on the back of the plaques and not rendered very clearly. This anomaly made the mark resemble the Goebel Vee and Bee trademark giving rise to yet another theory that it might have been a Goebel product.

Both of these theories have since been discredited as the origin of the plaques has finally been traced. It seems that a furniture company quite close to the Goebel factory in Oeslau, Germany was the manufacturer. In fact Goebel had these made by the company and Goebel artists painted them. When queried about them, the furniture company said they did indeed produce them, but have not done so for 30 or so years. It seems there was some sort of changeover in the type of production facility resulting in the company no longer employing the wood carvers necessary to produce them. No doubt the Goebel company would take a dim view of this endeavor in any case.

There is no record of how many of these were made, but they are in short supply. They have been found both in Europe and the United States. The last one I know of was found in the U.S. Virgin Islands. Secondary market value is around $5000-6000.

The Factory Workers' Plate

The 1971-1980 Factory Workers Plate

This plate was produced for distribution to the Goebel factory workers involved in plate production, in commemoration of the tenth (1980) annual plate. Because it was produced for this purpose it obviously would have been made in an extremely low edition as it was never intended for general distribution and retail sales. The edition is reported to be 60-100. It is not rendered in bas relief as are all the other Goebel plates but was made by utilizing the decal method. The design depicts the ten plates in miniature in a counter clockwise circle with the 1971 plate in the 12 o'clock position.

There are apparently three authorized and one unauthorized versions of this plate. The three legitimate versions are an uncolored plate, a version where each of the illustrated plates is given a single color wash and a third with the single color illustrated plates with the inscription in a black rectangular box. The collector value of these three is $1200-1800.

Of some interest is the unauthorized version of this plate. It seems that someone produced a few of the plates in full color. When Goebel found out about this, they quickly put a stop to it. Some collectors place a value of about $300.00 on these, but most are uninterested because they were not produced by or under the auspices of W. Goebel Porzellanfabrik.

Goebel employee service plaque.

The Goebel Employee Service Plaque

This very unique piece is quite similar to the Hum 187 display plaque but does not have the usual "Original Hummel Figures" inscription. On the occasion of the employee's 25th, 40th and 50th anniversary with the company each is presented with one of these plaques personalized with the employee's name and the date of the event. A very small number of these pieces have surfaced in private collections. They are valued at $1200-1500.

Local Chapter, Goebel Collectors' Club plaque.

The Local Chapter Plaque

Pictured here is an example of a display plaque few collectors are aware of. It is a modified Hum 187 Display Plaque that was made available for a short time, to members of local chapters of the Goebel Collectors' Club (now the *M.I. Hummel* Club). It was personalized with the name of the member and the local chapter name.

The 1948 Christmas Plate

This plate was never put into production, but obvious a few managed to make their way into private hands. Perhaps this happened through samples given to sales representatives or inadvertant loss at trade shows. It measures 7¾" diameter and the reverse side of the plate has three concentric raised circles the center of which has the hand-inked words: "Entw. A. Moller Ausf. H. Sommer nach Hummel". Collector Value Range: Mid five figure range.

Unidentified Holy Water Font

This is a beautiful little font and has an incised *M.I. Hummel* signature, but no other apparent markings whatsoever. I have not been able to find it listed or illustrated in any references. The globe is colored a beautiful deep blue with white stars. Unique, no trading on the secondary market, therefore no valuation is attempted.

Unidentified Goebel Mold Number HS 1

This piece is thought by some to be the forerunner to the Hum 88, Heavenly Protection. The two are quite similar, but the connection has not proved out as yet. It could simply have been inspired by the Heavenly Protection figurine or the painting from which it was derived. The final conclusion must be made by the individual collector until some evidence to support or refute the theory is found.

Another possibility is that it is the Hum 108 prototype. The piece may have been a *M.I. Hummel* design that was not approved for production. Please refer to page 207.

Goose Girl with Bowl

This mysterious piece was uncovered in Germany about 1989. It has an incised Crown mark. It is a 4¾" Goose Girl with an attached bowl. Upon close examination, it appears that they were joined before firing, lending legitimacy to the presumption that it was fashioned at the factory. The bowl is a Double Crown piece with an incised mold number "1".

There have been two more of these unusual pieces found. They are Hum 13, Meditation and Hum 17, Congratulations. The attached pots are different from the one in the picture here. The pots are round, slightly tapered from bottom to a larger diameter at the top and have four ridges around the main body. These are prototypes that were not approved by the convent, therefore never placed into production. The collector value range is $6000-7000.00

74

The limited edition gold gilt base **Little Fiddler**, Hum 2/I.

The underside of the base of the gold base Hum 2/I showing the trademark and the German language Golden Jubilee backstamp. It reads: "50 JAHRE M.I. HUMMEL-FIGUREN 1935-1985".

Limited Edition Fiddler

Little known in the U.S. is the limited production of a 7½", Hum 2/I, Little Fiddler with a gilded gold base. According to company promotional literature only fifty of these were made and they were part of a Goebel contest give-a-way in Germany. This is probably one of the most severely limited production figures that Goebel has ever produced. The collector value is about $1500-$1800.

These two unusual Crown Marks shown here are often found incised on the underside of the base of the Doll Face pieces. The reason for the odd devices over the mark is as yet unexplained.

Faience or "Doll Face" Pieces

In 1986 a U.S. Army officer stationed in Germany discovered a most unusual Little Fiddler with the *M.I. Hummel* incised signature and the Crown trademark in a German flea market. It was painted different, brighter colors than the normal ones and even more unusual was the china white face, hands and base and the very shiny glaze. Subsequent investigation not only authenticated the piece as genuine, but uncovered some new and interesting information with regard to the early history of the development of *M.I. Hummel* figurines. It seems that early on, while experimenting with different mediums for the pieces, glazed porcelain was used. As far as is known, Goebel did not go into mass production of the porcelain pieces for it was found that the fine earthenware with a matte finish was more amenable to the true reproduction of the soft pastel colors used by *M.I. Hummel* in her artwork. What we do know is that they were produced in sufficient numbers for many to end up in private collections. Models and colors vary widely, but the majority reflect the normal colors. The one the officer found had a bright blue coat, red kerchief instead of the normal blue and a brown hat instead of black. Some collectors refer to these as the "Doll Face Pieces". The accompanying photo illustrates the difference between the normal and the Doll Face pieces of the same era, but the difference can be more readily seen if you will turn to the examples shown in the color section. The Faience or "Doll Face" variation can be found on Hum 1 through Hum 15. If found, these are valued about 20% higher than their Crown marked counterparts. It is unusual, but the "doll face" pieces have been found bearing Full Bee and Stylized Bee marks as well. The difference between them is more readily seen in the color section.

(continued)

How They Came to Be

In the early experimenting with the media and paints in which to render the figure in three dimensions, porcelain was among the attempts. In the long run it was found that the inherent "whiteness" of fired porcelain would not lend itself to the rendering of the rosy cheeks so typical of *M.I. Hummel's* children in the paintings and drawings. They did, however cast paint and fire the first fifteen of the designs in porcelain and took them along with the earthenware figures to the Leipzig Fair.

When they displayed the original 46 *M.I. Hummel* at the Leipzig Fair in 1935, they displayed the porcelain ones also. At the end of the fair it was the now-familiar earthenware pieces that proved the most popular. The porcelain pieces apparently languished in some storage area or another, but they obviously somehow made their way into the market. The individual terra cotta pieces will be identified with their respective designs in the Goebel figurine listing.

The Terra Cotta pieces

When Goebel displayed the original 46 figurines they also displayed a number of them rendered in terra cotta, a brownish red, unglazed earthenware. As with the porcelain pieces they did not prove to be popular and subsequently production of the terra cotta pieces was abandoned. There is no way of knowing how many designs and how many of each of the designs were made. What we do know is that they were apparently severely limited in number. For example: an unquestionably genuine terra cotta Puppy Love has been found with an incised "T 1" mold number and the *M.I. Hummel* signature, but it is the only one known to be in a private collection.

Each known terra cotta piece will be individually identified in the collection listing with their respective design.

THE ARS EDITION M.I. HUMMEL® PRODUCTS

Twelve different matted and framed prints. Size: 3¾" x 4½".

The company, Ars Sacra Josef Miller, Munich, Germany (now Ars Edition GmbH) has had a long association with *M.I. Hummel* art.

In March of 1933 the company received a letter from the Siessen Convent that said: "Enclosed please find three proof sheets of the newest sketches of our young artist B. Hummel. We beg to inquire whether and under what conditions an edition of devout pictures in black and white, and later on in color, would be possible."

This modest beginning gave rise to many years of fruitful collaboration, and up to now the publishing house has printed more than 300 *Hummel* motifs in the form of pictures for wall decoration, prayerbooks, postcards and books. Over the years it was possible for the publisher to procure most of these originals from the convent.

In 1983 Ars Edition, Inc., subsequently ARS AG, obtained from the convent exclusive rights for the two-dimensional reproduction of original art works and figures on various products, such as limited editions for commemorative spoons and bells, stained glass, thimbles, note card assortments, candles, books, clocks, boxes and so on.

The reason for listing the various products is to inform the collector interested in these things, what is out there to find. Few of them are assigned a collector value as there is no organized secondary market trading in most of them where possible, the original price and year will be given. As the years go by an organized secondary market will evolve. It is you, the collector, that will dictate values as activity in the market expands.

There may be more than listed here. The catalogs and other material researched did not provide as much date and detail as I would have liked, so keep your eyes open.

The Prints

They range in various sizes from postcards at about 2¾" x 4¼" to approximately 10" x 14". They were not all available in all sizes. Some were sold framed. There are also some limited edition prints, larger in size. The company cataloged all of the pictures by title or subject assigning "H" numbers beginning with H 101 for "Hello There!" and ending with H 626, "A Gift for Jesus" as far as I could determine. There are several groups of consecutive

CAREFREE. Limited to 799 hand-numbered copies, this print is 27" x 24½".

ALLELUJA. Limited to 799 hand-numbered copies, this print is 24⅜''
x 21⅜''.

numbers not used, and a couple of single numbers not used. There is no explanation. Perhaps the numbers are assigned to drawings or paintings not published or were meant to be assigned elsewhere. In many of the catalogs, these numbers are referenced no matter what the product.

In 1982 Ars Edition published a full color booklet/catalog, *The Hummel Collection*, copyright 1981, Ars Edition, Inc. That publication illustrated 292 of *M.I. Hummel's* paintings and drawings alone with illustrations of details of 24 of them. It is with their kind permission that we reproduce them for you here, that you may finally have a reference of much of the artwork that inspired and continues to inspire the many figurines and other collectibles.

H 101 Hello There!

H 102 Blessed Event

H 103 Good Morning

H 104 What's New?

H 105 Loves Laughing

(continued)

H 109 Baby and the Spider

H 110 Baby and the Bee

H 111 Innocence

H 112 The Unexpected Guest

H 113 Friend of the Flowers

H 107 Nature's Child

H 106 My Baby Bumblebee

H 108 Sunflower Shade

H 114 Sleepy Time

H 116 Honey Lovers

H 118 The Song Birds

H 120 Slumber Time

H 121 Wishing Time

H 122 Morning Light

H 123 Daisy Duet

H 124 Sunrise Shepherd

H 125 Springtime Joys

H 128 Daisy

H 132 Dandelion

H 133 My Wish Is Small

H 134 Heidi

H 135 First Portrait

H 136 Portrait of a Little Girl

H 137 Curiosity

H 138 Discovery

H 139 Spring Basket

H 140 The Flower Girl

H 141 Out of Tune

H 142 Child of the Heart/I

H 143 Young Crawler

H 144 Meeting in the Meadow (In Tune)

H 145 Meeting on the Mountain (Whistler's Duet)

H 178 The Opinion/II (Sing Along)

H 147 Tit-for-Tat

H 150 Carefree

H 151 Grandma's Story

H 152 Grandpa's Helper

H 153 On the Other Side

H 154 Cinderella

H 156 Hold Your Head High and Swallow Hard

80

H 157 Feathered Friends

H 158 Retreat to Safety

H 159 On Tiptoes

H 160 Behind the Fence

H 162 Summertime

H 163 Little Thrifty

H 164 Doll Mother

H 165 Prayer Before Battle

H 166 The Golden Rule

H 167 Let's Sing/I

H 191 School Girl

H 192 Little Scholar

H 193 Little Brother's Lesson

H 194 School Chums

H 195 Knit One, Purl Two

H 197 School Girls

H 198 School Boys

H 200 Captive

H 201 Mother's Helper

H 202 Little Bookkeeper

81

H 203 The Mountaineer   H 204 Ring Around the Rosie   H 205 The Goat Girl (Good Friends)   H 206 Vacation Time   H 207 Rosebud

H 208 The Flower Vendor   H 209 Blue Belle   H 210 Bye-Bye!   H 214 Adventure Bound   H 216 The Globetrotter

H 217 Hansel and Gretel   H 218 The Runaway   H 231 Kiss Me   H 232 Washday   H 234 The Little Sweeper

H 235 The Little Goat Herder   H 236 Feeding Time   H 237 The Fisherman (Just Fishing)   H 238 Good Hunting   H 239 The Boss (Hello)

82

H 240 The Professor

H 241 Little Pharmacist

H 242 The Stargazer

H 243 The Baker

H 244 The Waiter

H 245 Latest News

H 246 The Postman

H 247 Too Short to Read

H 248 The Conductor/I

H 249 The End of the Song

H 250 Little Cellist

H 251 The Artist

H 252 The Art Critic

H 253 The Poet

H 254 Confidentially

H 255 Little Boots

H 256 The Doctor

H 257 The Toothache
(Boy with Toothache)

H 258 The Little Tailor

H 260 The Photographer

H 261 Chimney Sweep

H 262 The Draftsman
(The Little Architect)

H 271 Just For You

H 273 Mountain's Peace
(Forest Shrine)

H 276 Prayer Time

H 278 Resting

H 282 Spring's Return

H 283 The Birthday Gifts
(We Wish You the Best)

H 284 Quartet

H 287 Sunny Weather

H 288 Stormy Weather

H 289 Wayside Harmony

H 290 Just Resting

H 291 Telling Her Secret

H 292 Not for You!

H 297 Apple Tree Boy

H 298 Apple Tree Girl

H 299 Girl on Fence/I

H 300 Boy on a Fence

H 301 For Mother

H 302 For Father

H 303 Off to Town

H 304 Looks Like Rain

H 305 His Happy Pastime

H 306 Her Happy Pastime

H 307 Happy John

H 308 Coquettes

H 310 Farewell

H 311 Evening Tide

H 312 Twilight Tune

H 313 The Work Is Done

H 314 Homeward Bound

H 316 Winter Fun
(Ride Into Christmas)

H 317 March Winds

H 333 This Heart Is Mine

H 334 Catch My Heart

H 335 I Like You Boy
(Valentine Gift)

H 336 I Like You Girl
(Valentine Joy)

H 337 Take Me Along

H 338 The Strummers

H 339 To Market, to Market | H 342 Serenade | H 346 Boys Ensemble | H 347 Girls Ensemble | H 348 Special Gift

H 349 Special Delivery | H 350 Bashful | H 352 Max and Moritz | H 354 A Smile Is Your Umbrella | H 355 Begging His Share

H 371 Chick Girl | H 372 Playmates | H 374 A Little Hare | H 375 Favorite Pet | H 376 Chicken-Licken

H 377 Children on the Church Road | H 378 The Shepherd's Tune | H 379 Easter Playmates | H 380 Easter Basket | H 381 And One Makes a Dozen

86

| H 382 Return to the Fold | H 383 In Full Harmony (Eventide) | H 384 Praise to God | H 385 Alleluja | H 386 The Easter Lamb |

| H 401 In Guardian Arms | H 402 Deliver Us from Evil | H 404 The Guardian Angel | H 405 Guardian Angel Preserve Us | H 406 The Renewal |

| H 407 Boy's Communion | H 408 Girl's Communion | H 409 Angel/Trumpet | H 410 Tender Watch | H 411 Angel Duet |

| H 412 Candle Light | H 435 Angel/Horn | H 436 Angelic Care | H 437 Light of the World (Merry Christmas, Plaque) | H 438 Guiding Angel |

H 441 Celestial Musician	H 442 Bearing Christmas Gifts (Christmas Angel)	H 444 The Littlest Candle	H 448 Angel/Harp (Song of Praise)	H 449 Angel/Mandolin

H 451 Watchful Angel	H 452 Star Bethlehem	H 453 Guiding Light	H 454 Angel and Birds	H 471 Trinity

H 475 Alleluja Angel	H 477 Silent Night, Holy Night (Whitsuntide)	H 479 Joyous Christmas	H 480 Flying Angel	H 481 Jubilation

H 482 Prince of Peace	H 483 Merry Christmas and Happy New Year	H 484 Love and Luck	H 485 Glory to God in the Highest	H 486 Bless Your Soul on Christmas

H 487 Joyous Holidays

H 488 Good Luck in the New Year

H 490 For All Men

H 492 God Is Born

H 494 May You Sing

H 496 We Wish the Very Best

H 497 Town Crier (Hear Ye, Hear Ye)

H 500 The Good Shepherd

H 520 Queen of May

H 521 Mary; Queen of May

H 522 Fruit of the Vine

H 523 Mother of God

H 524 Mary Mother, Queen Maid

H 525 Immaculata

H 526 Mother at the Window

H 527 Mother of Christ

H 528 Queen of the Rosary

H 529 Nativity

H 530 At Mary's Knee

H 531 Mary Take Us into Your Care

H 532 Madonna in Green   H 533 Loving Mother and Child   H 537 Born in Bethlehem   H 538 Blessings   H 539 Virgin Mother

H 540 Christ Child Sleeping   H 543 Christ Is Born   H 615 Crossroads   H 616 Teach Me to Fly

H 617 Mail Is Here   H 619 Sunrise   H 620 Sing to the Mountains   H 622 Hard Letters

H 623 Easy Letters (With Loving Greetings)   H 624 Gift Bearers   H 625 Angel's Music   H 626 A Gift for Jesus

Limited Edition Prints - There are at least two prints identified as limited editions by Ars Edition. They are from what is called the "Hummel Gallery" and are limited to 799 hand-numbered prints. See page 77-78 for illustrations of these prints.

Note Cards - There are at least twelve different bi-fold note cards available. There was no size given, only "slightly oversized". Included were colored envelopes whose lining features the *Hummel* signature. They were sold in boxes of twenty.

Calendars - There are four types of calendars, two of which are the traditional month by month and another is the Advent calendar. The fourth is a linen wall hanging type.

The company has produced a couple of types large calendars annually for many years. The older ones are 10½" x 16" at first, then approximately 12 x 16 for a time and spiral bound. They can be found in French, German, of course, and English language. The years the French language version was published is unclear. There have been format changes, lately in 1984 and a significant change in 1989 to a larger 13" x 12" format. It was in 1984 when they began producing the calendar for Goebel.

There is also a small postcard calendar at 4½" x 9½" that features prints that can be detached at ease for framing, etc.

The regular 1987 calendar and the small, Post Card Calendar

This is the old style Advent Calendar.

The Advent Calendars are a tradition. They have windows for each of the 24 days before Christmas. A traditional part of European children's and many American children's Christmas. Each day one window is opened, revealing a piece of Hummel art with a religious theme. Each year the central Hummel picture is different. In 1986 the format was changed. There were four different designs offered then and after. The picture was a depiction of a winter scene utilizing actual *M.I. Hummel* figurines in the scene. The size of these new calendars was given as 15"x11".

There were at least two years that Ars Edition produced a 16" x 21" "Collector's Limited Edition Calendar" printed on linen and fitted with a wooden bar across the top and bottom. The first edition was the 1981 and the theme was "Sunny Day", a drawing much like "Stormy Weather" except the children face right and there is no rain in the picture. The second edition, the 1982 calendar, theme was "Not for You". The next year catalog available for study was 1985 and there was no such calendar listed. The limit of the edition was 15,000.

Wall Plaques - There are several sizes and styles. The prints are mounted on wood and a hard finish is applied making them very durable and attractive. They are square, rectangular and round and there are twenty seven of them to be found. There are many others made by other companies as the prints have been readily available and easy to apply to many types of objects.

Musical Wall Plaques - There are twelve designs of these. Six of them have red ribbon hangers and the others have a hanger on their back. They are 4" round wooden framed prints mounted with a music box movement. The music box is activated by pulling a round wooden knob on a string mounted at the bottom.

Music Boxes - Several different styles and sizes of music boxes have been available from ArsEdition. Today a licensee from ARS AG, Zug, Switzerland, the Art Decor Company in Sorrento, Italy is producing and marketing the music boxes. There are about twenty-five different motifs, five sizes and two basic styles.

The top of the line are furniture grade with a fine finish and turned brass feet on each corner. You can barely see the feet in the accompanying photograph of four. These sold for $55.00 in 1986. There is a slightly larger size in this style that has a lock and key that sold for $79.00 in 1986.

The rest of the music boxes were simple rectangular boxes and ranged in price from about $30.00 to $40.00 in the mid-1980s. A list of the sizes found follows:

10¼" x 8¼"
8¼" x 5¾"
7¼" x 6"
6" x 4½"
5" x 4⅝

(continued)

This **RIDE INTO CHRISTMAS** design is another style of music box by
Ars Edition. It measures 7¼'' x 6''.

This is a double lid music box measuring 5¾'' x 8¼''.

Jigsaw Puzzles - There are at least eight of these to be found. There are four older puzzles that can be identified
by their yellow boxes with red printing. The newer ones have the art printed in full color on the boxes.

Books - Ars Edition has published at least ten small books in English and it is thought, possibly a few more earlier, in German. Most are very small at about 4" x 6". One not illustrated here is *Ride into Christmas*, a book of pictures of figurines and hints for celebrating the Christmas season. It is 8" x 8½". Also there are the 6 assorted little 3" x 4" address books and the book *The Hummel* listed on page 37.

Placemats and Coasters - These are found in sets of six coasters and sets of four placemats. The coasters are 4" squares with rounded corners. The placemats are rectangular and are made in two sizes: 12" x 9" and 15¾" x 11⅞". The illustrations are photographs of actual Goebel *M.I. Hummel* figurines in models of life-like settings.

Wall Clocks - There are nine wall clocks in all. There are two styles. There are three quartz movement, square clocks with a round print in the center. The designs are "Umbrella Boy", "Telling her Secret" and "Meeting in the Meadow". The other style is a small, pendulum movement clock found in at least twelve different designs:

Mother's Helper	Sunny Weather
Follow the Leader	School Girl
Umbrella Girl	School Boys
Coquettes	School Chums
Resting	Globe Trotter
Little Bookkeeper	School Girls

94

Silk Carpets - In a 1988 Ars Edition catalog, a "First Edition" silk carpet, limited to 99 carpets worldwide, was offered. The carpet was described as having been made by hand-knotting 120 knots per square inch. The design was "Celestial Musician" and the size was listed as 31½" x 42". In the Spring 1990 issue of *INSIGHTS*, THE *M.I. Hummel* Club newsletter, another of these was offered in a worldwide limited edition of 50. It was similarly described and offered at $1,800.00. No mention of Ars Edition was made, but it can probably be safely assumed that it was a subsequent edition. The design of this one was "Umbrella Girl" and the size was 35¼" x 26½".

Candles - There is a wide variety of candles in two sizes in the catalogs. They are a high quality candle. One catalog listing describes them as being made of cream colored paraffin as the ideal color for placing the art on.

Gift Wrap and Gift Cards - There are eighteen designs of the gift card. They are 2¼" x 2¾" and come with envelopes. There have also been gift tags offered. There is one gift wrap that illustrates a variety of *M.I. Hummel* artworks, all separated by bright red borders.

Leaded Glass Panels - There have been at least three of these available. The three designs are:

1986 Ring Around the Rosie
1987 The Postman
1988 Sunny Weather (much like Stormy Weather)

The size of these is 6¼" x 8¼". They were limited to 2,500 pieces worldwide and individually numbered. The release price in 1986 was $65.00.

Ring Around the Rosie

Metal Trays - There were two metal trays offered in the early 1980s. The designs were "Apple Tree Boy" and "Apple Tree Girl". They were oval in shape and measure 12" x 16".

This is the fourth edition glass Christmas ornament, "Angel with Light". Similar to "Light up the Night", Hum 622.

Christmas Ornaments - There have been about 35-40 different ornaments offered by Ars Edition over the years. The styles are widely varied. In 1982 they introduced as a "First Edition" a gold satin ball. Apparently they decided to change this to a more traditional glass ball for in 1983 there was another "First Edition", but in glass this time.

Pill Boxes - there are four motifs to be found on the tops of these little 1⅝" x 1½" metal pill boxes:

Wayside Harmony
Chick Girl
Easy Letters (With Loving Greetings, Hum 309)
Playmates

They were no longer in the catalog in 1988. They sold for about $18.00 in the mid-1980s.

Collector Spoons - In 1982, Ars Edition began an annual collector spoon series with a twelve-piece set of silver plate 5" spoons with shield-like enamel finials each bearing a different *M.I. Hummel* design. The backs of the spoons bear the company name, the year of the edition and the *M.I. Hummel* signature. The series ended with the third set. Through many circumstances the sets may have been broken up so they may be found singly. The following is a list of the designs in each set.

First Edition

Sunny Weather	Stormy Weather
School Girl	School Boy
Farewell	Not For You!
Wayside Harmony	Girl on Fence
Chick Girl	Playmates

Second Edition

Hello	Slumber Time
Rosebud	Little Sweeper
On the Other Side	Little Cellist
Blessed Event	Mother's Helper
Little Bookkeeper	Little Goat Herder
Feeding Time	Springtime Joys

Third Edition

The Renewal	Boy's Communion
Innocence	The Postman
Just Resting	Confidentially
Behind the Fence	Serenade
My Dolly	Baker
Star Gazer	Goat Girl (Good Friends)

In 1986 a set of six 4⅜" spoons began a new annual series. The finial shape had changed to round. These were also issued for three years and are listed here by edition in case the sets were broken up, to aid you in identifying them. They each have the company name, the year of issue and the *M.I. Hummel* signature.

First Edition

His Happy Pastime	Her Happy Pastime
Discovery	Tit-for-Tat
Sunny Weather	Stormy Weather

Collector Spoons (cont'd)

Second Edition

Sleepy Time   My Wish is Small
School Girl   Little Scholar
Off to Town   Looks Like Rain

Third Edition

She Loves Me, She Loves Me Not   He Loves Me, He Loves Me Not
We Wish You the Best   Harmony in Four Parts
Special Gift   Special Delivery

There are as many as seven **Mother's Day Spoons** to be found beginning in 1982. They are 25K gold plate and have an enamel finial with the design on it. The length is 4⅜" and each of them has "For Mother" engraved in the bowl. The missing years had no catalog listing for them.

1982 Special Gift
1983 ---
1984 ---
1985 ---
1986 ---
1987 First Outing
1988 For Mother

This is the 1986 Christmas Spoon and Bell, Celestial Musician and the 1986 Annual Bell, Apple Tree Boy.

There was also an **Annual Christmas Spoon, Thimble and Bell Series.** These began in 1982. They are all engraved with the year and "Christmas" in the bowl of the spoon and on the body of the bell. Those missing from the list were not found in the catalogs of the corresponding year.

Christmas Spoon, Bell and Thimble

1982 Guiding Angel
1983 Prayer of Adoration
1984 Heavenly Duo
1985 Guiding Light
1986 Celestial Musician
1987 Candle Light
1988 Angelic Guide

Annual Bells - As far as can be determined, the Annual Bell Series wasn't begun until 1983. They are silver plate and are 3½" high. Where there is a blank in the following listing, there was no catalog entry. Each had the year and design engrave on the body of the bell. When they were first issued they cost about $20.00.

1983	Ring Around the Rosie
1984	Telling Her Secret
1985	Quartet (Harmony in Four Parts)
1986	Apple Tree Boy
1987	Follow the Leader
1988	Max and Moritz

Pendants - At one time the finial portion of the bells was made into pendants. It is not known how many different designs there were, but the one I have seen is of "Sunny Weather" and it is on a 24" chain. They came with a rope chain, but may be found with any other or no chain. They cost $10.00 in the early 1980s.

The third edition of the Annual Thimble Assortment.

Thimbles - The series of six annual editions of six assorted thimbles each began in 1984. These thimbles are silver plate and are 1" high. I was unable to find the designs of the first edition, but the other five are listed below.

Second Edition

Hello there!	Baby and Spider
His Happy Pastime	Her Happy Pastime
Discovery	Tit-For-Tat

The Third Edition

Helping Mother	Little Bookkeeper
Sunny Weather	Stormy Weather
Special Gift	Special Delivery

Thimbles (cont'd)
The Fourth Edition

Apple Tree Girl   Apple Tree Boy
Little Goat Herder   Goat Girl (Friends)
Off to Town   Happy John

The Fifth Edition

Chick Girl   Playmates
Ring Around the Rosie   Harmony in Four Parts
Wayside Harmony   Coquettes

Annual Christmas Plates - This is a four plate series beginning in 1987. They are beautiful porcelain plates in full color and decorated with 24K gold. They were made by Goebel and marketed by Ars Edition. They are 7½" in diameter and limited to 20,000 individually, sequentially numbered plates worldwide.

100

Miniature Annual Plates. Miniature replicas of the 1971-76 plates in an oval wooden frame. Edition limited to 15,000.

Miniature Annual Plates. Miniature replicas of the 1971-82 plates in an oval wooden frame. Edition limited to 15,000.

Miniature Annual Plates

This is a series of six miniature plates (1") that are replicas of the first six plates in the Goebel Annual Plate Series, 1971 through 1976. The total production is 15,000 sets worldwide. The complete set, released in 1986 was offered at $150.00 including a wooden oval display frame designed for the set.

There is a second set depicting the 1977 through the 1982 plates. It was released in 1988.

THE SCHMID BERTA HUMMEL PRODUCTS

The history of the Schmid company's association with the art of *M.I. Hummel* goes all the way back to when the first figurines were put on the market in Germany in 1935. They noticed them, arranged to buy a few and ended up being the Goebel company's U.S. distributor. Their association with the Goebel company ended in 1968. About the same time Schmid began offering a selection of Hummel collectibles of their own manufacture or from other sources and in 1971 they offered a Christmas Plate with using the same original Hummel art as the Goebel first annual Christmas plate. As you might expect the companies ended up in court.

Berta Hummel, as she was known before taking her vows as a Franciscan nun, had created a large amount of work before taking entering the convent. All that work had become the property of the family, her mother Viktoria Hummel in particular, after her death. Schmid made an agreement with Mrs. Hummel allowing them to produce decorative items and other collectibles inspired by or using this early work of the artist.

Prints of Berta Hummel Art

There have been roughly 130 small framed prints offered over the years. Schmid took the existing prints and had them framed in quantities sufficient to wholesale to the trade.

By far the most important of the prints by Schmid are the following described and illustrated limited edition issues:

A Self Portrait. Image size 9⅝'' x 13¼''

This sensitive self portrait, rendered in sepiatone, was released in 1981 in a limited edition of 525. They are each sequentially numbered and signed by the artist's brother, Adolph Hummel. The print was issued at $125.00 and is valued at about $300.00 on the secondary market today.

Poppies. Image size 11½'' x 14½''

The rendering of flowers was issued in 1980-81. Colors are rich earth tones with a cheerful red-orange poppy. The edition was limited to 450 and each was signed by the artist's brother, Adolph Hummel. The release price was $125.00 and it is presently valued at $650.00 on the secondary market.

"A Time to Remember" was issued in 1980-81 in an edition limited to 900. It is a color print depicting a boy with three children on a sled. There is a snow covered fir tree in the background. The edition is 900 numbered prints, each signed by Adolph Hummel, brother of the artist. There is penciled inscription around the border on 180 of the prints in German, that is translated: "Seasons Greetings from the Hummel family home in Massing, Bavaria, West Germany. The Hummel family wishes you and yours a Merry Christmas and a very happy and prosperous New Year". The picture depicts a Hummel family Christmas tradition of going into the woods to pick out a tree. Released originally at $150.00 for the regular prints they are now valued at $300.00. The 180 copies with the Christmas inscription are at about $1200.00.

Moonlight Return. Image size 10¾" x 16½"

"Moonlight Return" is a pastel Berta Hummel did to depict an incident in her brother Adolf's boyhood. The limited edition issue of this print is signed by him. The edition is 900 and the release price was $150.00. It is now valued at $850-$1000.00 on the secondary market.

This print was issued in an edition 400 signed by the artist's brother, Adolph Hummel authenticating the print. 900 of the prints are numbered as usual but the other 200 were given inscriptions in German. The inscriptions began on the left border and went over the top and down the right border. Translated it reads: "May the angel of Christmas abide with you, at Advent, and all year through". This edition is valued at $450.00 and the one with the 75th Anniversary inscription is valued at about $700.00. The regular edition is about $300.00.

Angelic Messenger. Image size 12½" x 16".

Side view of the Schmid Berta Hummel paperweight.

Top view of the Schmid Berta Hummel crystal paperweight.

Paperweight

This was called the "Sister Berta Hummel Visage Paperweight" in promotional literature. It is a beautiful French sulfide paperweight measuring 2¾" in diameter and 1⅞" high. It was limited in production to 400. Each is individually numbered by etching the number on the bottom of the piece.

"Serenity". Limited edition of 15,000.

"Tranquility". Limited edition of 15,000.

"Tranquility" and "Serenity" Plate Series

The first of this two plate issue was "Tranquility" released in 1978. The second, "Serenity", was issued in 1982. Each of these is about 10" in diameter. The editions were limited to 15,000 for each plate. The plate is museum quality porcelain with an application of 24K gold and hand painted. The resulting soft glowing finish was achieved by a unique technique that required six separate kiln firings.

Annual Christmas Plate Series with
Matching Mini-Plates Bells, Cups, Ornaments and Thimbles

YEAR	PLATE DESIGN	PLATE VALUE	BELL	CUP	ORNAMENT
1971	Angel with Candle	$20-25			
1972	Angel with Flute	$15-20	x		
1973	Nativity	$75-95	x		
1974	The Guardian Angel	$10-15	x		x
1975	Christmas Child	$15-20	x	x	x
1976	Sacred Journey	$10-15	x		x
1977	Herald Angel	$10-15	x		x
1978	Heavenly Trio	$10-15	x		x
1979	Starlight Angel	$10-15	x		x
1980	Parade into Toyland	$15-20	x	x	x
1981	A Time to Remember	$25-30	x		x
1982	Angelic Procession	$30-35	x		x
1983	Angelic Message	$25-30	x		x
1984	A Gift From Heaven	$35-40	x		x
1985	Heavenly Light	$30-35	x		x
1986	Tell the Heavens	$40-45	x		x
1987	Angelic Gifts	$35-40	x		x
1988	Cheerful Cherubs	$65-70	x		x
1989	Angelic Musician	$45-50	x		x
1990	Angel's Light	$40-45	x		x

1972 "Angel with Flute" © Schmid Bros. Inc. 1971   1973 "Nativity" © Schmid Bros. Inc. 1972   1974 "The Guardian Angel" © Schmid Bros. Inc. 1973   1975 "Christmas Child" © Schmid Bros. Inc. 1974

1976 "Sacred Journey" © Schmid Bros. Inc. 1975   1977 "Herald Angel" © Schmid Bros. Inc. 1976   1978 "Heavenly Trio" © Schmid Bros. Inc. 1977   1979 "Starlight Angel" © Schmid Bros. Inc. 1978   1980 "Parade Into Toyland" © Schmid 1979

Schmid Christmas Bell Series Depicting the Authentic Art of Berta Hummel

1993 Ornament/Silent Wonder

1994 Ornament/Heavenly Melody

God's Littlest Messenger Series

This is a four year series that began in 1991. The 7½" diameter plates have a $60.00 release price and is limited to 15,000. The matching 4¾" diameter miniature plate is $25.00, the matching 4½" high bell is limited to 5,000 produced at $58.00, the 2½" cup is $40.00, the 1" thimble is $20.00 and the 3¼" ball ornament is $7.50.

1991	A Message from Above
1992	Sweet Blessings
1993	Silent Wonder
1994	Heavenly Melody

1971 "Angel with Candle"
© Schmid Bros., Inc. 1970

1972 "Angel with Flute"
© Schmid Bros., Inc. 1971

1973 "Nativity"
© Schmid Bros., Inc. 1972

1974 "The Guardian Angel"
© Schmid Bros., Inc. 1973

1975 "Christmas Child"
© Schmid Bros., Inc. 1974

1976 "Sacred Journey"
© Schmid Bros., Inc. 1975

1977 "Herald Angel"
© Schmid Bros., Inc. 1976

1978 "Heavenly Trio"
© Schmid Bros., Inc. 1977

1979 "Starlight Angel"
© Schmid Bros., Inc. 1978

1980 "Parade Into Toyland"
© Schmid Bros., Inc. 1979

1981 "A Time To Remember"
© Schmid Bros., Inc. 1980

Schmid Christmas Plate Series Inspired by the Art of Berta Hummel

1982 Christmas Plate, 7½'' Dia., Twelfth Edition

1982 Christmas Ornament, 3¼'' Dia. Ninth Edition

1982 Christmas Bell, 6¼'' High, Eleventh Edition

Christmas Plate, 18th Edition, 7½''Dia., Gift Boxed

Christmas 1988

177-157

Christmas 1992

God's Littlest Messenger Series

Sweet Blessings
Miniature Plate 4¼'' dia.
Plate 7½'' Dia. Ltd. Edition of 15,000
Thimble 1''H.
Ornament 3¼'' Dia.
Cup 2½''H.
Bell 4½''H. Ltd. Edition of 5,000

"A Message From Above"
Plate 7½" Dia. Ltd. Edition of 15,000
Miniature Plate 4¾" Dia.
Thimble 1"H.
Ornament 3¼" Dia.
Bell 4½"H. Ltd. Edition of 5,000
Cup 2½"H.

Silent Wonder
Ornament 3¼"Dia. $7.50   (Not Shown)
Plate 7½"Dia. Ltd. Edition of 15,000
Bell 4½"H Ltd. Edition of 5,000
Miniature Plate 4¾"Dia.
Cup 2½"H
Thimble 1"H   (Not Shown)

God's Littlest Messenger Series

Heavenly Melody

Plate, 7½"Dia., Ltd. Edition of 15,000	$60.00
Bell, 4½"H, Ltd. Edition of 5,000	$58.00
Miniature Plate, 4¾"Dia.	$25.00
Cup, 2½"H	$40.00
Thimble, 1"H (Not Shown)	$20.00
Ornament, 3¼"Dia. (Not Shown)	$7.50

Annual Mother's Day Plates, Bells and Cups

Beginning in 1972 Schmid produced a series of 7½" plates and matching 6½" high bells and 2½" high cups. For some reason the bells and cups in the series did not start until 1976. The Plate series ended with the 1990 plate. In the years 1981 through 1984 there were some other matching pieces made. These were eggs, thimbles and trinket boxes. They will be listed separately later.

YEAR	PLATE DESIGN	PLATE VALUE	BELL	CUP
1972	Playing Hooky	$20		
1973	The Little Fisherman	$40		
1974	The Bumblebee	$30		x
1975	Message of Love	$25		
1976	Devotion for Mothers	$20	x	x
1977	Moonlight Return	$30	x	x
1978	Afternoon Stroll	$20	x	x
1979	Cherub's Gift	$30	x	x
1980	Mother's Helpers	$30	x	
1981	Playtime	$25	x	x
1982	The Flower Basket	$45	x	x

109

Annual Mother's Day Plates/Bells and Cups (cont'd)

YEAR	PLATE DESIGN	PLATE VALUE	BELL	CUP
1983	Spring Bouquet	$35	x	x
1984	A Joy to Share	$30	x	x
1985	A Mother's Journey	$40	x	
1986	Home From School	$40	x	
1987	Mother's Little Learner	$60	x	
1988	Young Reader	$85	x	
1989	Pretty as a Picture	$80	x	
1990	Mother's Little Athlete	$80	x	

1972 "Playing Hookey"
©Schmid Bros., Inc. 1971

1973 "The Little Fisherman"
©Schmid Bros., Inc. 1972

1974 "The Bumblebee"
©Schmid Bros., Inc. 1973

1975 "Message of Love"
©Schmid Bros., Inc. 1974

1976 "Devotion for Mothers"
©Schmid Bros., Inc. 1975

1977 "Moonlight Return"
©Schmid Bros., Inc. 1976

1978 "Afternoon Stroll"
©Schmid Bros., Inc. 1977

1979 "Cherubs Gift"
©Schmid Bros., Inc. 1978

1980 "Mothers Helpers"
©Schmid Bros., Inc. 1979

1981 "Playtime"
©Schmid Bros., Inc. 1980

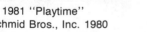

Schmid Mother's Day Plate Series

1976   1977

1978   1979   1980

Schmid Mother's Day Bell Series

Mother's Day (cont'd)

The Little Fisherman. Berta Hummel. 1973 Mother's Day Plate.

1982 Mother's Day Plate, 7½''Dia. Eleventh Edition

1982 Mother's Day Bell, 6¼''High Seventh Edition

"Young Reader", Mother's Day Plate, 17th Edition, 7½''D, Gift Boxed

1982 Annual Cup, 2½''Dia.,
2½''High Tenth Edition

Annual Cups
Twelve in the Series

| ©Schmid Bros. Inc. 1972 | 1974 The Bumblebee © Schmid Bros. Inc. 1973 | 1975 Christmas Child © Schmid Bros. Inc. 1974 | 1976 Devotion for Mothers © Schmid Bros. Inc. 1975 | 1977 Moonlight Return © Schmid Bros. Inc. 1976 | 1978 Afternoon Stroll © Schmid Bros. Inc. 1977 | 1979 Cherub's Gift © Schmid Bros. Inc. 1978 | 1980 Parade Into Toyland © Schmid 1979 |

The Annual Cup Series was introduced in 1973 with an untitled design. The art was of a baby in a basket with a bird and flowers. This cup was not a match to any other piece in the collection. The next year the design matched the 1974 Mother's Day plate and the year following, 1975, the cup design matched that of the same year Christmas Plate. The cup design reverted to match the Mother's Day plate in 1976 for four more years when in 1980 it once again was made matching the Christmas plate. This was the last time for from here on the cups matched the Mother's Day design until the Annual Cup Series ended with the 12th edition in 1984. See chart on pages 109-110.

Stained Glass

For three years Schmid issued a 6" diameter round stained glass decoration. The design was applied to the glass. It is framed in lead in the traditional manner of stained glass and a chain hanger is provided. Six were found cataloged, two each year matching the Christmas and the Mother's Day motifs.

Year	Christmas Design	Mother's Day Design
1976	Sacred Journey	Devotion for Mothers
1977	Herald Angel	Moonlight Return
1978	Heavenly Trio	Afternoon Stroll

Thimbles

The original series of three porcelain thimbles began in 1982. They are 1" high and the designs matched the correspoding designs for the Mother's Day plates. They were issued at a $10,000 retail price.

1982 Thimble - The Flower Basket
1983 Thimble - Spring Bouquet
1984 Thimble - A Joy to Share

Trinket Boxes

At the same time the collector porcelain egg was introduced a three piece series of porcelain trinket boxes with lids was started. These are 2½" in diameter and sold for $20.00 at release.

1982 - The Flower Basket
1988 - Spring Bouquet
1984 - A Joy to Share

Collector Eggs

The original series of four porcelain eggs began in 1981. They are 3" high when placed on the base that came with them. Each design was the same as the corresponding year of the Mother's Day Plate. They were issued at $35.00 retail price.

1981 - Playtime
1982 - The Flower Basket
1983 - Spring Bouquet
1984 - A Joy to Share

The Flower Basket. 1982 egg, 3" high with base. Second edition.

Music Boxes and Other Musical Items

There have been at least 70 different music boxes offered by Schmid over the years. There are also a few other musical items to be found.

Annual Music Boxes

Although seldom cataloged, there were annual, year-dated music boxes made in the same design as the annual releases of the **Christmas** and **Mother's Day** plates beginning in 1974. Although I could only find them referenced in 1976 and 1977 in catalogs and other promotional literature, they were presumably offered every year. The ones found referenced were 4" x 5¾" x 2" high. They sold for $20-$25.00 in the 1970s.

Statuette Ornaments

In 1983 Schmid released the first in a series of what were called "Statuette Ornaments". These were little 4½" figures with bases for standing up and provisions for hanging on the Christmas tree. The second was called "Hark the Herald" and was a boy with a trumpet tucked under his right arm and his left hand stuck in his pocket. The first edition, 1984, was called "Sweetheart" and is similar to the *M.I. Hummel* figurine "Little Shopper", Hum 96. No more were found in the catalogs and literature studied. The retail price at the time was about $18.00. See next page.

"Sweetheart"
Statuette Ornament
Second Edition

"Hark the Herald"
Statuette-Theme Collection

In 1984 Schmid introduced this group of items to commemorate the 75th year since Berta Hummel's birth. Apparently inspired by the 1983 Statuette Ornament "Sweetheart" each of these items had either the three dimensional figure or a bas-relief of it incorporated in its design. The following is a list of the items and their 1984 retail price:

TYPE OF PIECE	SIZE	ISSUE PRICE
Plate	7" diameter	$40.00
Medallion Ornament	2⅞" diameter	$10.00
Bell	5¼" high	$20.00
Mug	3¼" high	$15.00
Thimble	1" high	$10.00
Music Box	5¼" high	$30.00
Trinket Box	3½" diameter	$15.00

Limited Edition Music Box

In 1981 Schmid introduced what their brochure described as a, in part: "...first limited edition inlaid Sorrento wooden music box...". The motif for the box is "Devotion". The edition was limited to 5,000 sequentially numbered music boxes at $150.00. There may be more in this edition, but they are not found in the catalogs and other literature I studied.

Other Music Boxes

There are at least 42 other Berta Hummel design music boxes in varying shapes and sizes. All are made of wood. The shapes and sizes are listed here:

NUMBER OF DIFFERENT DESIGNS	SHAPE	SIZE
42	Rectangular	4¼" x 3" x 2¼" high
12	Rectangular	5¾" x 3⅞" x 2" high
3	Heart shaped	5¾" x 6¼" x 1¾" high
4	Oval shaped	4¼" x 6¼" x 1¾" high

Musical Wall Pictures

There are six of these to be found. They are round, 5¼" in diameter and are activated by a pull cord on the bottom.

Musical Jewelry Boxes

There is a total of 15 of these to be found, in two sizes and shapes. They are footed, metal boxes with a satin top bearing the Berta Hummel art work.

There six different designs found on two sizes of retangular boxes: 3" x 2½" x 2¼" high and 3¾" and 4¾" x 2" high. The other three are heart-shaped and their size is 4½" x 6¼" x 2" high.

Miscellaneous Other Musical and Non-musical Items

6 different Musical Key Chains, 1½" x 1¼"
1 pair of Musical Bookends, 6¼" wide x 7¼" high
1 pair of Bookends, assorted prints, 3⅞" wide x 6" high
1 Musical Cube with 5 different prints, 4" square
1 Wall-mount Key Rack with print
1975 Linen Calendar, 17½" x 30". The design matches the Mother's Day plate of the same year.
Needlepoint kit of the same design as above. 18" x 18".

Candles

There are some dated candles made to match the various limited annual plates, cups, bells etc. There are otherwise, dozens of candles in various sizes bearing Berta Hummel art. The company also offered a wide variety of candle stands made of metal and wood some of which were even musical. None of these had any Berta Hummel designs on them.

Porcelain Coffee Service

This is a German-made 21 piece service for six. It was made for and imported by Schmid in the early 1970's. They were apparently only offered for a short time as few have been found. The assorted designs used on the pieces of the set are those that were accomplished after Berta Hummel became a nun. This may have led to the discontinuing of the service as that work is licensed exclusively to the Goebel Company.

Angelic Procession
1981 Mini-Plate

This little 4" diameter plate is something of an enigma. I found it in a family member's home and assumed that Schmid could fill me in with the necessary details. Alas, they could find no record of it nor could they find anyone in the company that knew anything of it. I contacted the Bradford Exchange and they had no information regarding the plate. I also met with a dead end trying to find any information about the New England Collectors Society. Since the backstamp indicates this is a "First ... Christmas Plate", there *may* be others. It also states that it was copyrighted in 1981 by Schmid and was made in Germany.

If anyone can shed some light on this, please drop me a line.

All the products depicted from page 102 to 116 are by courtesy of Schmid, Inc.

THE DANBURY MINT COLLECTION
Licensed by ARS AG, Zug, Switzerland

This well known division of the Connecticut company MBI has been in the business offering fine collectibles for many, many years. Their products are either made by the Goebel company or licensed by ARS AG, Zug, Switzerland to reproduce items bearing *M.I. Hummel* artwork.

First Day Covers	Christmas Tree Ornaments
Clocks	Cookie Jars
Spice Jars	Kitchen Canisters
Collector Plates	Salt and Pepper Shakers
Porcelain Eggs	Porcelain Music Boxes
Porcelain Dolls	Kitchen Molds
Thimbles	Candle Holders

Porcelain Dolls

Danbury introduced a doll series in 1988 with the first, "Umbrella Girl". The doll's heads, arms and legs were cast and hand-painted in the traditional manner by the artisans at W. Goebel Porzellanfabrik, maker of the *M.I. Hummel* figurines. They bear the signature and the Goebel trademarks on the back of the neck. Although they are cataloged at Goebel by mold number, the dolls do not bear the number. The dolls were released at $250.00. The dolls in the series are listed following:

MOLD NUMBER	DESIGN
512	Umbrella Girl
513	Little Fiddler
514	Friend or Foe
515	——
516	Merry Wanderer
517	Goose Girl
518	Umbrella Boy
519	Ride Into Christmas

The Spice Jars

A collection of 24 porcelain spice jars bearing reproduction of original artwork and 23K decoration was offered beginning in January of 1993 by subscription. They were delivered to the collector at the rate of two every other month for $19.75 plus $1.00 shipping each piece for a total cost of $498.00. A wooden spice rack was also included for displaying the jars.

Kitchen Canisters

A set of four canisters was offered in 1993. They were decorated with pictures of *M.I. Hummel* figurines with an appropriate Bavarian scene for a background. They were offered for $239.40 including shipping in six monthly installments. They came in four different sizes as listed below:

SIZE	DESIGN
5", 12 oz.	Timid Little Sister, Hum 394
6½", 24 oz.	Barnyard Hero, Hum 195
7½", 48 oz.	In Tune, Hum 414
8½", 60 oz.	Little Goat Herder, Hum 200

Danbury Mint (cont'd)

Angels of Christmas Ornament Series

This is a series of full color decorated Christmas ornaments made by Goebel for Danbury for subscription distribution beginning in 1990. They were issued one every other month. They were released at $42.00 each including $2.50 shipping and handling for a total of $420.00. Goebel cataloged them according to mold number, but did not place this number on the figures. Goebel also utilized the same molds to release another series of ornaments. Please refer to page 401. The designs for the Danbury mint ornaments follow:

MOLD NUMBER	SIZE	DESIGN
575	3"	Heavenly Angel, Hum 21
576	3"	Festival Harmony w/ Mandolin, Hum 172
577	3"	Festival Harmony with Flute, Hum 173
578	3"	Celestial Musician, Hum 188
579	2½"	Song of Praise, Hum 454
580	2½"	Angel with Lute, Hum 238/A
581	3"	Prayer of Thanks
582	3"	Gentle Song
585	2½"	Angel in Clouds
586	2½"	Angel with Trumpet, Hum 238/C

Kitchen Molds

There were six of these offered by subscription beginning in 1991. Danbury shipped them to the collector one every three months at $103.50 each including shipping and handling for a total of $621.00. These were made by Goebel and they are cataloged by a Goebel mold number, but the pieces do not bear the number. They do bear the incised signature. The six are listed for you below:

MOLD NUMBER	SIZE	DESIGN
669	7½" diameter	Baking Day, Hum 301
670	7½" diameter	A Fair Measure, Hum 345
671	7½" diameter	As Sweet As Can Be, Hum 541
672	2⅝" x 8"	Girl Holding a Dish
674	2⅝" x 8"	Baker, Hum 128

Candle Holders

The Danbury Mint issued four candle holders made for them by Goebel. The first two were released three months apart in 1989 and the next two were released likewise in 1990. They each cost $145.50 including shipping and handling. Goebel catalogs the molds with mold numbers, but the pieces do not bear those numbers. They are listed below:

MOLD NUMBER	SIZE	MID	DESIGN
676	6½"	1988	Apple Tree Boy, Hum 141
677	6½"	1988	Apple Tree Girl, Hum 142
678	6½"	1989	She Loves Me, She Loves Me Not
679	6½"	1989	Good Friends, Hum 182

Little Companion
Limited Edition Plate Series

In 1992 Danbury issued the first in a series of limited production collector plates. The first edition in the series is APPLE TREE BOY & GIRL. The number of plates in the series is not revealed. This first plate bears the two figurines photographed in a realistic apple orchard setting and applied to an 8½" porcelain plate rimmed in 23K gold. Literature promoting the series states that the edition sized will be ".....forever limited to the production capacity of 14 full firing days". Available by mail order, the release price was $32.45 including shipping and handling costs.

MASTER INDEX
ALPHABETICAL ENGLISH NAME LISTING
OF THE COLLECTION
WITH CORRESPONDING MOLD NUMBER

A few of the names of pieces have been changed by the factory over the years and this has confused collectors from time to time. Some are even known by two names, due to the changes and different translations from the original German name. As many of these as possible have been included in this listing to facilitate location of those figures.

You may look up the name of the figure, ascertain its appropriate mold number and locate it in the Master Listing of the collection. It is arranged in ascending numerical order.

NAME	HUMMEL MOLD NUMBER
The Accompanist	453
Accordian Boy	185
Adoration	23
Adoration with Bird (Bird Lovers)	105
Advent Group - Candle Holders	115, 116 & 117
Advent Group with Candle	31
Adventure Bound, The Seven Swabians	347
An Apple A Day	403
An Emergency	436
Angel At Prayer-Font	facing left 91/A
	facing right 91/B
Angel Cloud-Font	206
Angel Duet	261
Angel Duet-Candle Holder	193
Angel Duet-Font	164
Angel Lights-Candle Holder	241
Angel Serenade with Lamb	83
Angel Trio (Christmas Angels)	
Angel with Lute	238/A
Angel with Trumpet	238/C
The Angel Trio-Candle Holders	
Joyous News-Angel with Love	38
The Angel Trio-Candle Holders	
Joyous News-Angel with Accordian	38
The Angel Trio-Candle Holders	
Joyous News-Angel with Horn	40
Angel in Cloud (ornament)	585
Angel with Lute (ornament)	580
Angel with Trumpet (ornament)	586
Angel with Birds-Font	22
Angelic Care (Watchful Angel)	194
Angelic Sleep-Candle Holder	25
Angelic Song	144
Anniversary Bell	730
Anniversary Plate 1975, Stormy Weather	280
Anniversary Plate 1980, Spring Dance	281
Anniversary Plate 1985, Auf Wiedersehn	282
Annual Bell 1978, Let's Sing	700
Annual Bell 1979, Farewell	701

NAME	HUMMEL MOLD NUMBER
Annual Bell 1980, Thoughtful	702
Annual Bell 1981, In Tune	703
Annual Bell 1982, She Loves Me, She Loves Me Not	704
Annual Bell 1983, Knit One	705
Annual Bell 1984, Mountaineer	706
Annual Bell 1985, Girl With Sheet Music	707
Annual Bell 1986, Sing Along	708
Annual Bell 1987, With Loving Greetings	709
Annual Bell 1988, Busy Student	710
Annual Bell 1989, Latest News	711
Annual Bell 1990, What's New?	712
Annual Bell 1991, Favorite Pet	713
Annual Bell 1992, Whistler's Duet	714
Annual Plate 1971, Heavenly Angel	264
Annual Plate 1972, Hear Ye, Hear Ye	265
Annual Plate 1973, Globe Trotter	266
Annual Plate 1974, Goose Girl	267
Annual Plate 1975, Ride Into Christmas	268
Annual Plate 1976, Apple Tree Girl	269
Annual Plate 1977, Apple Tree Boy	270
Annual Plate 1978, Happy Pastime	271
Annual Plate 1979, Singing Lesson	272
Annual Plate 1980, School Girl	273
Annual Plate 1981, Umbrella Boy	274
Annual Plate 1982, Umbrella Girl	275
Annual Plate 1983, Postman	276
Annual Plate 1984, Little Helper	277
Annual Plate 1985, Chick Girl	278
Annual Plate 1986, Playmates	279
Annual Plate 1987, Feeding Time	283
Annual Plate 1988, Little Goat Herder	284
Annual Plate 1989, Farm Boy	285
Annual Plate 1990, Shepherd's Boy	286
Annual Plate 1991, Just Resting	287
Annual Plate 1992, Wayside Harmony	288
Annual Plate 1993, Doll Bath	289
Apple Tree Boy (Fall)	142
Apple Tree Boy	252/A
and	
Apple Tree Girl-Bookends	252/B
Apple Tree Boy-Lamp	230
Apple Tree Girl (Spring)	141
Apple Tree Girl-Table Lamp	229
Arithmetic Lesson	303
Art Critic	318
The Artist	304
At The Fence	324
Auf Wiedersehen	153
Autumn Harvest	355
Ba-Bee Rings	30 A&B
Baker	128

NAME	HUMMEL MOLD NUMBER
Band Leader	129
Band Leader (plate)	742
Banjo Betty (Joyful)	53
Barnyard Hero	195
Bashful	377
Bath Time	412
Being Punished (plaque)	326
Begging His Share	9
Behave!	339
Be Patient	197
Big Housecleaning	363
Bird Duet	169
Bird Lovers (Adoration with Bird)	105
Bird Watcher	300
Birthday Candle	440
Birthday Present	341
Birthday Serenade	218
Birthday Serenade-Table Lamp	231
Birthday Serenade-Table Lamp	234
Birthday Wish	338
Blessed Event	333
Blessed Mother	372
Blue Cloak Madonna (Madonna)	151
Bookworm	3
Bookworm	8
Bookworms-Bookends	14 A&B
Boots	143
The Botanist	351
Boy With Accordian (Part of Little Band)	390
Boy With Toothache	217
Brother (Our Hero)	95
A Budding Maestro	477
The Builder	305
Busy Student	367
Call to Worship (clock)	441
Candlelight	192
Carnival	328
Celestial Musician	188
Celestial Musician (bell)	779
Celestial Musician (ornament)	578, 646
Chapel Time (clock)	442
Cheeky Fellow	554
Chef Hello (Hello)	124
Chick Girl	57
Chick Girl-Candy Box	111/57
Chicken-Licken	385
Chicken-Licken (mini-plate)	748
Child-In-Bed-Plaque	137
Child Jesus-Font	26
Child with Flowers-Font	36

NAME	HUMMEL MOLD NUMBER
Children Standing	
Girl With Flowers	239/A
Girl With Doll	239/B
Boy With Toy Horse	239/C
Children's Prayer	448
Chimney Sweep (Smokey)	12
Christmas Angels (Angel Trio)	238/A,B&C
Christmas Bells here and ornaments	
Christmas Song	343
Christ Child	18
Cinderella	337
Close Harmony	336
Coffee Break	409
Companions	370
Concentration	302
Confidentially	314
Congratulations	17
Coquettes	179
Country Song (clock)	443
Cradle Song (Lullaby)-Candle Holder	24
Crossroads	331
Culprits	56/A
Culprits-Table Lamp	44/A
Christmas Bell 1988, Ride into Christmas	775
Christmas Bell 1990, Letter to Santa Claus	776
Christmas Bell 1991, Hear Ye, Hear Ye	777
Christmas Bell 1992, Harmony in Four Parts	778
Christmas Ornament 1990, Peace on Earth	484
Christmas Ornament 1991, Angelic Guide	571
Christmas Ornament 1992, Light Up the Night	622
Daddy's Girls	371
Daisies Don't Tell	380
Daisies Don't Tell (6" plate)	736
Delicious	435
Delivery Angel	301
Devotion-Font	147
Display Plaque (Tally)	460
Do I Dare?	411
Doctor	127
Doll Bath	319
Doll Mother	67
Doll Mother	76/A
and	
Prayer Before Battle-Book Ends*	76/B
Don't Be Shy	379
Dove (font)	393
Drummer (Little Drummer)	240
Duet	130
Easter Greetings	378
Easter Playmates	384
Errand Girl (The Little Shopper)	96

*Not known to exist in any collector's hands.

NAME	HUMMEL MOLD NUMBER
Eventide	99
Evening Prayer	495
A Fair Measure	345
Farewell (Goodbye)	65
Farewell-Table Lamp*	103
Farm Boy (Three Pals)	66
Farm Boy	60/A
and	
Goose Girl-Bookends	60/B
Fall (Apple Tree Boy)	142
Father's Joy (For Father)	87
Favorite Pet	361
Feathered Friends	344
Feeding Time	199
Festival Harmony with Flute	173
Festival Harmony with Flute (ornament)	577
Festival Harmony with Madonna	172
Festival Harmony with Madonna (ornament)	576
Flitting Butterfly-Plaque	139
The Florist	349
Flower Girl	548
Flower Madonna	10
Flower Vendor	381
Flowers for Mother (plate)	500
Flute Song	407
Flying Angel	366
Flying High	452
Follow the Leader	369
Forest Shrine	183
For Father (Father's Joy)	87
For Father (7" plate)	293
Forty Winks	401
A Free Flight	569
Friend or Foe	434
Friends	136
Meditation	292
For Father	293
Sweet Greetings	294
Surprise	295
Gay Adventure (Joyful Adventure)	356
A Gentle Glow	439
Gentle Song (ornament)	586
A Gift From a Friend	485
Girl With Frog (Little Velma)	219
Girl With Horn (Part of Little Band)	391
Girl With Sheet Music (Part of Little Band)	389
Globe Trotter	79
Going to Grandma's	52
Goodbye (Farewell)	65
Good Friends	182

*Not known to exist in any collector's hands.

NAME	HUMMEL MOLD NUMBER
Good Friends and	251/A
She Loves Me, She Loves Me Not (Bookends)	251/B
Good Friends-Table Lamp	228
Good Hunting	307
Good Luck	419
Good Night	214C
Good Shepherd	42
Good Shepherd-Font	35
Goose Girl	47
Grandma's Girl	561
Grandpa's Boy	562
Guardian, The	455
Guardian Angel-Font	29
Guardian Angel-Font	248
Guiding Angel	357
Happiness	86
Happiness, Puppy Love & Serenade	
(triple figure on a wooden base)*	122
Happy Birthday	176
Happy Bugler (Tuneful Goodnight) Plaque	180
Happy Days (Happy Little Troubadours)	150
Happy Days-Table Lamp	232
Happy Days-Table Lamp	235
Happy Little Troubadours (Happy Days)	150
Happy New Year (Whitsuntide)	163
Happy Pastime	69
Happy Pastime-Ash Tray	62
Happy Pastime-Candy Box	111/69
Happy Traveler	109
Harmony in Four Parts	471
Hear Ye, Hear Ye	15
Heavenly Angel	21
Heavenly Angel-Font	207
Heavenly Angel (ornament)	575
Heavenly Lullaby	262
Heavenly Protection	88
Heavenly Song**	113
Hello (Chef, Hello)	124
Hello World	429
Helping Mother	325
Herald Angels-Candle Holder	37
Herald on High (ornament)	623
High Tenor (Soloist)	135
The Holy Child	70
Holy Family-Font	246
Home From Market	198
Homeward Bound	334
Honey Lover	312
Horse Trainer	423
Hosanna	480

*Not known to exist in any private collection.
**Removed by Goebel from "Open Edition" status in mid-1981.

NAME	HUMMEL MOLD NUMBER
I Brought You a Gift	479
I Didn't Do It	626
I Forgot	362
I Wonder	486
I Won't Hurt You	428
I'll Protect Him	438
I'm Here	478
In D-Major	430
In The Meadow	459
In Tune	414
Infant of Krumbad	78
Is it Raining?	420
It's Cold	421
It's Cold (6" Plate)	735
Joyful (Betty Banjo)	53
Joyful Adventure (Gay Adventure)	356
Joyful and Let's Sing (double figure on a wooden base)*	120
Joyful-Ash Tray	33
Joyful-Candy Box	111/53
Joyous News	27
Jubilee	416
Just Resting	112
Just Resting-Table Lamp	225
Kindergartner	467
Knit One, Purl One	432
Kiss Me	311
Knitting Lesson	256
Land in Sight	530
Latest News	184
Let's Sing	110
Let's Sing-Ash Tray	114
Let's Sing-Candy Box	111/110
Let's Tell the World	487
Letter to Santa Claus	340
Little Architect	410
Little Band	see Hummel Nos. 389, 390, 391
Little Band	392
Little Band-Candle Holder	388
Little Band-Candle Holder/Music Box	388/M
Little Band-Music Box	392/M
Little Bookkeeper	306
Little Cellist	89
Little Drummer (Drummer)	240
Little Fiddler (Violinist)	2
Little Fiddler (Violinist)	4
Little Fiddler-Plaque	93
Little Fiddler-Plaque	107
Little Gabriel	32
Little Gardener	74
Little Goat Herder	200

*Not known to exist in any collector's hands.

NAME	HUMMEL MOLD NUMBER
Little Goat Herder	250/A
and	
Feeding Time-Bookends	250/B
Little Guardian	145
Little Helper	73
Little Hiker	16
Little Nurse	376
The Little Pair	449
Little Pharmacist	322
Little Scholar	80
Little Shopper (Errand Girl)	96
Little Sweeper	171
Little Tailor	308
Little Thrifty	118
Little Velma (Girl with Frog)	219
Littlest Angel	365
Lost Sheep	68
Love From Above (ornament)	481
Lost Stocking	374
Lucky Boy	335
Lucky Fellow	560
Lullaby (Cradle Song)-Candle Holder	24
Lute Song	368
Madonna-Plaque	48
Madonna ("Blue Cloaked Madonna")	151
Madonna Plaque (with metal frame)	222
Madonna and Child-Font	243
Madonna praying (no halo)	46
Madonna with Halo	45
Mail Coach-Plaque	140
Mail Coach (The Mail Is Here)	226
Make A Wish	475
March Winds	43
Max and Moritz	123
Meditation	13
Meditation (7" plate)	292
Merry Wanderer	7
Merry Wanderer	11
Merry Wanderer-Plaque	92
Merry Wanderer-Plaque	106
Merry Wanderer-Plaque	263
Mischief Maker	342
Morning Concert	447
Morning Stroll	375
Mother's Aid	325
Mother's Day Plate (Flowers for Mother)	500
Mother's Darling	175
Mother's Helper	133
Mountaineer	315
My Wish is Small	463
A Nap	534

NAME	HUMMEL MOLD NUMBER
Nativity Set	214/A,B,C,D,E,F,G,H,J,K,M,N,O
Nativity Set (large)	260/A,B,C,D,E,F,G,H,J,M,N,O,P,R
Naughty Boy (Being Punished)	326
Not For You	317
Off To School	329
One for You, One for Me	482
On Holiday	350
On Our Way	472
On Secret Path	386
One Plus One	556
Our Hero (Brother)	95
Out of Danger	56B
Out of Danger-Table Lamp	44/B
Parade of Lights	616
The Poet	397
The Photographer	178
Playmates	58
Playmates-Candy Box	111/58
Playmates	61/A
and	
Chick Girl-Bookends	61/B
Pay Attention	426
Pleasant Journey	406
Pleasant Moment	425
Postman	119
Prayer Before Battle	20
Prayer of Thanks (ornament)	581
The Professor	320
Puppy Love	1
Quartet-Plaque	134
Relaxation	316
Retreat To Safety	201
Retreat To Safety-Plaque	126
Ride Into Christmas	396
Ring Around The Rosie	348
The Run-Away	327
Sad Song	404
Scamp	553
School Boy (School Days)	82
School Boys	170
School Days (School Boy)	82
School Girl	81
School Girls	177
Seated Angel (with bird)-Font	167
Sensitive Hunter	6
Serenade	85
She Loves Me, She Loves Me Not	174
She Loves Me, She Loves Me Not-Table Lamp	227
Shepherd Boy	395
Shepherd's Boy	64
Shining Light	358
Shrine-Table Lamp	100

NAME	HUMMEL MOLD NUMBER
Signs of Spring	203
Silent Night-Candle Holder	54
Sing Along	433
Sing With Me	405
Singing Lesson-Ash Tray	34
Singing Lesson	63
Singing Lesson-Candy Box	111/63
Sister	98
Skier	59
Sleep Tight	424
Smiling Through	408
Smiling Through-Plaque	690
Smokey (Chimney Sweep)	12
The Smart Little Sister	346
Soldier Boy	332
Soloist (High Tenor)	133
Song of Praise	454
Song of Praise (ornament)	579
Sounds of the Mandolin	438
Sound the Trumpet	457
Spring (Apple Tree Boy)	141
Spring Bouquet	398
Spring Cheer	72
Spring Dance	353
Standing Boy-Plaque	168
Star Gazer	132
St. George	55
A Stitch in Time	255
A Stitch in Time (mini-plate)	747
Store Plaque (English)	187
Store Plaque (English) (Schmid Brothers plaque)	210
Store Plaque (English)	211
Store Plaque (French)	208
Store Plaque (German)	205
Store Plaque (Spanish)	213
Store Plaque (Swedish)	209
Store Plaque (English, new in 1986)	460
Stormy Weather (Under One Roof)	71
Storybook Time	458
Street Singer	131
Strolling Along	5
Sunny Morning	313
Supreme Protection	364
Surprise	94
Surprise (7" plate)	295
The Surprise	431
Swaying Lullaby	165
Sweet as Can Be	541
Sweet Greetings	352
Sweet Greetings (7" plate)	294
Sweet Music	186

NAME	HUMMEL MOLD NUMBER
A Sweet Offering	549
Tally (display plaque)	460
Telling Her Secret	196
Thoughtful (I Forgot)	415
Three Pals (Farm Boy)	66
Timid Little Sister	394
To Market	49
To Market-Table Lamp	101
To Market-Table Lamp	223
Truant	410
True Friendship	402
Trumpet Boy	97
Tuba Player	437
Tuneful Angel	359
Tuneful Goodnight (Happy Bugler)-Plaque	180
Two Hands, One Treat	493
Umbrella Boy	152/A
Umbrella Girl	152/B
Under One Roof (Stormy Weather)	71
Vacation Time-Plaque	125
Valentine Gift	387
Valentine Gift (6" Plate)	738
Valentine Joy	399
Valentine Joy (6" Plate)	737
Village Boy	51
Violinist (Little Fiddler)	2
Visiting An Invalid	382
Volunteers	50
Volunteers-Table Lamp	102
Waiter	154
Wall Vases (3)	
Boy and Girl	360/A
Boy	360/B
Girl	360/C
Wash Day	321
Watchful Angel (Angelic Care)	194
Wayside Devotion	28
Wayside Devotion	90/A
and	
Adoration-Bookends	90/B
Wayside Devotion-Table Lamp	104
Wayside Harmony	111
Wayside Harmony and Just Reading	121
(double figure on a wooden base)*	
Wayside Harmony-Table Lamp	224
Weary Wanderer	204
We Congratulate	214E
We Congratulate (with base)	220
We wish You the Best	600
Welcome Spring	635

*Existence unsubstantiated outside factory archives.

Pieces listed chronologically by Mold Number beginning on page 132.

THE HUMMEL COLLECTION LISTING

The following list of pieces in the Hummel collection is arranged by the appropriate Hummel mold number in ascending order. To fully understand all of the notations you must read and study the first 75 pages of this book very carefully.

You will find the price listings almost complete, but it is impossible to conscientiously assign a value to each and every model that exists today. (Please refer to the introduction and to pages 10-13 for a discussion of value determination). I have tried to count the possible number of pieces according to size and the number in the listing is approximately 1500. This number does not take into consideration all of the size variations due to mold size variation, color variation and model design differences, so as you can see the number would be incredibly large. Where it was impossible to obtain any pricing information on a particular figure size or variation, the appropriate space is left blank or the listing is omitted altogether. In the latter case, it was not possible to ascertain and document all existing models. From time to time it is possible to establish the existence of a piece but without sure information as to size or trademark. In these cases the corresponding space is left blank.

As evidence by this tenth edition, the book is periodically updated and improved as information is gained and these values and other information will be incorporated in subsequent editions.

As stated earlier, the sizes are approximate, but as accurate as was possible to establish. Almost all lists are contradictory, but in most cases within reasonable agreement. The sizes listed are those most frequently encountered in those listings and notated as the Basic Size. (See definition in glossary). Most of the time this is the smallest size for each figure. Frequently, however, there would be one smaller size listed, but the preponderance of other listings would indicate a ¼" or ½" larger size. In these cases the larger size was assumed the more representative.

For purposes of simplification the various trademarks have been abbreviated in the list. Most are obvious but, should you encounter any trouble interpreting them, refer to the list of abbreviations below or to the Glossary.

Crown	CM	TMK-1	1934-1950
Full Bee	FB	TMK-2	1940-1959
Stylized Bee	Sty Bee	TMK-3	1958-1972
Three Line Mark	3-line	TMK-4	1964-1972
Last Bee Mark	LB	TMK-5	1970-1980
Missing Bee Mark	MB	TMK-6	1979-1991
Hummel Mark (Current)	HM	TMK-7	1991-Present

PUPPY LOVE, Hum 1. Left: Decimal designator in the mold number 1, incised Crown Mark (TMK-1), donut base, black "Germany", 5". Center: Full Bee (TMK-2) in an incised circle, black "Germany", 5¼". Right: Last Bee (TMK-5), donut base, 4⅞".

PUPPY LOVE
Hum 1

Part of the original 46 pieces offered in 1935 it was first known as the "Little Violinist". It can be found in Crown Mark (TMK-1) through the Missing Bee (TMK-6). It was retired in 1988 never to be produced again. Many of the original group have been found rendered in terra cotta and Puppy Love is no exception although so far only one is known to exist.

The most significant variation occurs in Crown pieces only. In this variation the head is tilted slightly to the right instead of the normal left tilt, he wears a black hat and he wears no neck tie. This very rare variation can bring $4,500 on the collector market.

There is a mold number variation that you may encounter. It seems that in the initial stages of planning and modeling the figurines there was no formal designation of the mold number. Puppy Love has been found with the mold number "FF 15". It is not likely, however, that you will encounter this variation.

HUM NO.	BASIC SIZE	TRADE MARK		CURRENT VALUE
1	5"	TMK-1	CM	450-700.00
1	5"	TMK-2	FB	300-350.00
1	5"	TMK-3	Sty. Bee	235-275.00
1	5"	TMK-4	3-line mark	200-225.00
1	5"	TMK-5	LB	180-190.00
1	5"	TMK-6	MB	170-180.00

LITTLE FIDDLER
Hum 2

Originally known as the "Violinist" this little fellow is almost always wearing a brown derby with an orange hat band. It has been made in five sizes since its initial introduction as part of the original 46. The two largest sizes were temporarily withdrawn from production in 1989. The smallest, Hum 2/4/0, was introduced into the line in 1984 and will remain as an open edition. It was the first of a new series of very small figurines issued as a matching piece to a series of mini plates introduced at the same time. A few Little Fiddlers with the Crown Mark (TMK-1) have been found in "Doll Face" or Faience finish. These are valued at about 20% more than the regular Crown pieces.

There is a mold number variation where the mold number is "FF 16". In the days before the figurines were given the official "Hum" designation the "FF" was used (on the first three models). It is possible, but not likely that you will encounter this variation.

LITTLE FIDDLER, Hum 2. Left: 2/II. This figure has an incised Crown Mark (TMK-1) that is colored in green. Note the unusually pale face. This black and white photo doesn't show it well, but this is an example of what collectors refer to as a "Doll Face" or "Faience" piece (see color section and page 75). It has a donut base and measures 10¹⁵⁄₁₆". Right: Has mold number 2/II, Last Bee (TMK-5) trademark, incised 1972 MID and measures 11".

LITTLE FIDDLER, Hum 2/0. The left figure has a small Stylized Bee (TMK-3) trademark, a brown color derby hat with an orange hat band and measures 5¾". The figure on the right is of the older vintage Full Bee (TMK-2) trademark era. It has a black hat, a black "Germany" beneath the base and is 5¼" tall. Both figures have a donut base.

HUM NO.	BASIC SIZE	TRADE MARK		CURRENT VALUE
2/4/0	3½"	TMK-6	MB	90.00
2/0	6"	TMK-1	CM	400-500.00
2/0	6"	TMK-2	FB	290-325.00
2/0	6"	TMK-3	Sty. Bee	225-250.00
2/0	6"	TMK-4	3-line mark	205-225.00
2/0	6"	TMK-5	LB	205.00
2/0	6"	TMK-6	MB	205.00
2/I	7½"	TMK-1	CM	520-650.00
2/I	7½"	TMK-2	FB	375-400.00
2/I	7½"	TMK-3	Sty. Bee	300-325.00
2/I	7½"	TMK-4	3-line mark	280-300.00
2/I	7½"	TMK-5	LB	260.00
2/I	7½"	TMK-6	MB	260.00

The underside of the base of the gold base Hum 2/I showing the trademark and the German language Golden Jubilee backstamp. It reads: "50 JAHRE M.I. HUMMEL-FIGUREN 1935-1985".

Doll Face **LITTLE FIDDLER,** Hum 2. This unusual example of the Little Fiddler bears an incised Crown mark (TMK-1) that is colored in green. It has a donut base and measures $10^{15}/_{16}$".

The limited edition gold gilt base **Little Fiddler,** Hum 2/I. See page 75.

HUM NO.	BASIC SIZE	TRADE MARK		CURRENT VALUE
2/II	11"	TMK-1	CM	1700-2150.00
2/II	11"	TMK-2	FB	1200-1400.00
2/II	11"	TMK-3	Sty. Bee	1000-1100.00
2/II	11"	TMK-4	3-line mark	925-950.00
2/II	11"	TMK-5	LB	850-900.00
2/II	11"	TMK-6	MB	850.00
2/III	12¼"	TMK-1	CM	2000-2500.00
2/III	12¼"	TMK-2	FB	1400-1600.00
2/III	12¼"	TMK-3	Sty. Bee	1200-1300.00
2/III	12¼"	TMK-4	3-line	1100.00
2/III	12¼"	TMK-5	LB	1000-1100.00
2/III	12¼"	TMK-6	MB	1000.00

BOOK WORM
Hum 3

BOOKWORM, Hum 3. Left: Crown Mark, 5½". Right: 3/I, Missing Bee mark, 5½".

BOOKWORM, Hum 3. There is no apparent trademark on either of these. There are, however, the regular incised mold numbers, 3/3. The left one is a "Doll Face" or Faience piece (see color section and page 75). It is rather gaudily painted and it appears as if some of the paint ran before drying or during firing this experimental piece. It measures 9½". The white overglaze piece measures 10".

One of the original 46 released in 1935, this figure appears more than once in the collection. A girl reading a book. It is also found in a smaller size as Hum 8 and in the Hum 14A and B, bookends with a companion figure of a boy reading. The larger Hum 3/II and Hum 3/III have been out of current production for some time. The Hum 3/III with older trademarks is avidly sought by collectors. The numbers 3/II and 3/III are occasionally found with the Arabic number size designator (3/2 and 3/3 respectively). The two larger sizes have been temporarily withdrawn from current production.

There is a mold number variation. In the days before the figurines were given official status "Hum" mold numbers this figure was given the incised mold number "FF 17". It is possible, but not likely that you will encounter this variation.

HUM NO.	BASIC SIZE	TRADE MARK		CURRENT VALUE
3/I	5½"	TMK-1	CM	525-550.00
3/I	5½"	TMK-2	FB	400-420.00
3/I	5½"	TMK-3	Sty. Bee	330-355.00
3/I	5½"	TMK-4	3-line mark	290-310.00
3/I	5½"	TMK-5	LB	270-280.00
3/I	5½"	TMK-6	MB	270.00
3/II	8"	TMK-1	CM	1350-1690.00
3/II	8"	TMK-2	FB	1000-1200.00
3/II	8"	TMK-3	Sty. Bee	800-850.00
3/II	8"	TMK-5	LB	675-700.00
3/II	8"	TMK-6	MB	675.00
3/III	9½"	TMK-1	CM	2000-2500.00
3/III	9½"	TMK-2	FB	1400-1600.00
3/III	9½"	TMK-3	Sty. Bee	1200-1400.00
3/III	9½"	TMK-5	LB	1000-1200.00
3/III	9½"	TMK-6	MB	1000.00

LITTLE FIDDLER
Hum 4

This is the same design as the Hum 2, Little Fiddler. The difference is of course, that this is a smaller size than any of the original three sizes of the Hum 2. One wonders why they used two different mold numbers for the same basic piece in the original 46 released in 1935. Another difference is that the hat, Little Fiddler, Hum 4 wears is colored black. There is a significant variation found in some of the Crown Mark (TMK-1) pieces. The head is tilted to his right instead of the normal tilt to his left and he wears no tie. This variation can fetch $4,500 on the collector market. Refer to the color section to see a photo of a Hum 4 with this variation that is also in the Faience or "Doll Face" finish. The mold number is sometimes found with the decimal point (46.) designator. When found with it, it could increase its value by up to 10%.

HUM NO.	BASIC SIZE	TRADE MARK		CURRENT VALUE
4	4¾"	TMK-1	CM	370-460.00
4	4¾"	TMK-2	FB	265-285.00
4	4¾"	TMK-3	Sty. Bee	220-240.00
4	4¾"	TMK-4	3-line mark	200-210.00
4	4¾"	TMK-5	LB	185-195.00
4	4¾"	TMK-6	MB	185.00

STROLLING ALONG
Hum 5

LITTLE FIDDLER, Hum 4. The left piece is the Doll Face. Note the very pale face and hands, the completely different head position and the lack of a neck kerchief. Each has the decimal point mold number designation, 4., Crown mark and measure 5⅛".

STROLLING ALONG, Hum 5. Left: Mold number is 5., has a Double Crown Mark, a black "Germany" and measures 5". Right: Last Bee mark, 4⅞".

One of the first 46 figures released in 1935 appears in only one basic size, 4¾". This figure similar to Hum 7, MERRY WANDERER. The most notable version found in Hum 5 is that the latest figures to be produced have the boy looking straight ahead while the older ones have him looking to the side. Strolling Along was removed from production at the end of 1989.

HUM NO.	BASIC SIZE	TRADE MARK		CURRENT VALUE
5	4¾"	TMK-1	CM	450-700.00
5	4¾"	TMK-2	FB	300-350.00
5	4¾"	TMK-3	Sty. Bee	235-275.00
5	4¾"	TMK-4	3-line mark	200-225.00
5	4¾"	TMK-5	LB	180-190.00
5	4¾"	TMK-6	MB	170-180.00

SENSITIVE HUNTER
Hum 6

SENSITIVE HUNTER, Hum 6. Left: Decimal point designator in the mold number 6., double Crown mark (TMK-1), donut base, black "Germany", red rabbit, 4¾". Center: 6/0, Full Bee (TMK-2) mark, donut base, black "Germany", red rabbit, 4¾". Right: 6/0, Missing Bee (TMK-6), brown rabbit, 4¹¹⁄₁₆".

Rear view of Hum 6 showing the "H" and "X" suspenders configuration discussed in the text.

Called "The Timid Humer" when first released among the original 46 it has remained in production ever since. The most notable variation is the "H" shape of the suspenders used with the lederhosen. This variation is associated with all of the Crown marked figures and most of those with the Full Bee. The "H" variation will generally bring about 30% more than the value for the "X" pieces. The later models have an "X" shape configuration. Crown mark pieces have been found having the "X" shape suspenders. The color of the rabbit was usually orange until 1981 when the company changed it to brown for all newly produced pieces. Sensitive Hunter can also be found with the decimal (6.) designator. This can add up to 10% to its collector value.

The smallest of the sizes listed here, Hum 6/2/0, was added in 1985 as the second in a series of new smaller figurines to go along with a mini plate using the same design.

Effective December 31, 1984 Goebel has announced that the new production piece in the 7½" size (Hum 6/II) was placed on a temporary withdrawn from production status.

HUM NO.	BASIC SIZE	TRADE MARK		CURRENT VALUE
6/2/0	4"	TMK-6	MB	90 135.00
6	4¾"	TMK-1	CM	500.00 +
6/0	4¾"	TMK-1	CM	350-440.00
6/0	4¾"	TMK-2	FB	250-270.00
6/0	4¾"	TMK-3	Sty. Bee	225-250.00
6/0	4¾"	TMK-4	3-line mark	190-200.00
6/0	4¾"	TMK-5	LB	175-185.00
6/0	4¾"	TMK-6	MB	175.00
6/I	5½"	TMK-1	CM	450-575.00
6/I	5½"	TMK-2	FB	335-350.00
6/I	5½"	TMK-3	Sty. Bee	280-300.00
6/I	5½"	TMK-4	3-line	250-260.00
6/I	5½"	TMK-5	LB	230-240.00
6/I	5½"	TMK-6	MB	230.00
6/II	7½"	TMK-1	CM	800-1000.00
6/II	7½"	TMK-2	FB	575-625.00
6/II	7½"	TMK-3	Sty. Bee	480-515.00
6/II	7½"	TMK-4	3-line	425-450.00
6/II	7½"	TMK-4	3-line	425-450.00
6/II	7½"	TMK-5	LB	400-425.00
6/II	7½"	TMK-6	MB	400.00

MERRY WANDERER
Hum 7

MERRY WANDERER, Hum 7/I. This Stylized Bee marked figurine shows the rare Stepped-up base.

One of the original 46 figurines released in 1935 it also appears as Hum 11. The Merry Wanderer is probably found in more sizes and variations than any other single figure in the collection. There are at least twelve different sizes known to exist. There is even a huge six foot concrete replica of the figure on the factory grounds in Germany and another even larger, eight foot high Merry Wanderer. The latter was displayed on the grounds of the former location of the *M.I. Hummel* Club in Tarrytown, New York. It is presently in storage, but will once again be proudly displayed at the new Goebel Gallery and *M.I. Hummel* Museum when it opens in 1994 in Rosemont, Illinois. It is also part of every dealer and collector's display plaque made prior to the introduction of the Tally display plaque, Hum 460, introduced in 1986 and used until 1990 when the Merry Wanderer display plaque was reintroduced.

The most difficult of the sizes to be found is the Hum 7/III size. It was temporarily withdrawn from production in 1991. Any reinstatement date has yet to be revealed.

The rarest of the base variations is illustrated in the accompanying photograph. Collectors refer to it variously as the "double base", "stepped up base" or the "stair step" base. It is found on the Hum 7/I size of all the Crown Mark (TMK-1) and Full Bee (TMK-2) 7/I's, but only on the older Stylized Bee (TMK-3) pieces.

The 7/III size has been found in Faience or "doll face" finish. These can bring up to 20%-50% more than the top value for the Crown Mark pieces.

In 1993, as part of a special Disneyland and Disney World promotion an unknown number of the small Merry Wanderers were given a special, decal transfer mark to commemorate the occasion. The piece was supposed to be sold along with a similar size Mickey Mouse. The problem is that the Merry Wanderers did not make it to the theme parks in time for the promotion. The last I heard about them was that they were being sold by private individuals out of their hotel room, for $650.00 a set at the site of the *M.I. Hummel* Club Member Convention in Milwaukee, Wisconsin in May of 1993 and have been advertised for as high as $1000.00 (continued)

Merry Wanderer (cont'd)

HUM NO.	BASIC SIZE	TRADE MARK		CURRENT VALUE
7/0	6¼"	TMK-1	CM	480-520.00
7/0	6¼"	TMK-2	FB	365-380.00
7/0	6¼"	TMK-3	Sty. Bee	300-335.00
7/0	6¼"	TMK-4	3-line	275-285.00
7/0	6¼"	TMK-5	LB	245-260.00
7/0	6¼"	TMK-6	MB	245.00
7/I (double step base)	7"	TMK-1	CM	1200-1500.00
7/I (double step base)	7"	TMK-2	FB	900-1000.00
7/I (double step base)	7"	TMK-3	Sty. Bee	750-850.00
7/I (plain base)	7"	TMK-3	Sty. Bee	320-360.00
7/I	7"	TMK-4	3-Line	265-280.00
7/I	7"	TMK-5	LB	250-260.00
7/I	7"	TMK-6	MB	250.00
7/II	9½"	TMK-1	CM	1700-2200.00
7/II	9½"	TMK-2	FB	1300-1600.00
7/II	9½"	TMK-3	Sty. Bee	1050-1100.00
7/II	9½"	TMK-4	3-line	935-970.00
7/II	9½"	TMK-5	LB	850-900.00
7/II	9½"	TMK-6	MB	850-900.00
7/III	11¼"	TMK-1	CM	1850-2250.00
7/III	11¼"	TMK-2	FB	1375-1425.00
7/III	11¼"	TMK-3	Sty. Bee	1200-1300.00
7/III	11¼"	TMK-4	3-line	1000-1200
7/III	11¼"	TMK-5	LB	925-950.00
7/III	11¼"	TMK-6	MB	925.00
7/X	*30"	TMK-5	LB	10,000-15,000.00

*1990 suggested retail. There are a few of these "Jumbo" figures in collectors' hands. They are generally used as promotional figures in showrooms and shops. They rarely bring full retail price. The Aug. 1990 price list from Goebel states "Production Suspended".

BOOK WORM
Hum 8

BOOKWORM, Hum 8. A comparison between the normal skin coloration (left) and the pale coloration on the Doll Face pieces. Both measure 4¼". The left bears a Stylized Bee mark. The one on the right is a "doll face" piece with a double Crown mark.

(continued)

Bookworm (cont'd)

This figure is the same as Hum 3 except much smaller. One of the original 46 to be offered at the Leipzig Fair in 1935. It is found in only the one basic size and has been found in terra cotta. There is only one of these terra cotta Book Worms known to be in collectors hands, but if one exists, that suggests that more may be out there to find.

HUM NO.	BASIC SIZE	TRADE MARK	CURRENT VALUE
8	4"	TMK-1 CM	390-480.00
8	4"	TMK-2 FB	230-250.00
8	4"	TMK-3 Sty. Bee	215-225.00
8	4"	TMK-4 3-line	205-215.00
8	4"	TMK-5 LB	195-205.00
8	4"	TMK-6 MB	195.00

BEGGING HIS SHARE
Hum 9

BEGGING HIS SHARE candle holder, Hum 9. Left: Stamped Crown mark (TMK-1), 5¼". A very unusual piece. Note the lack of the traditional base. The oversize shoes utilized as a base. Probably a prototype that never went into regular production. Right: Stylized Bee in the incised circle, black "Western Germany", 5¼".

BEGGING HIS SHARE, Hum 9. The Doll Face piece is on the left. Note the much more pale face. Both have the decimal point designator in the mold number, 9., double Crown marks, donut bases and measure 5⅝".

There are two notable variations to be found on this piece. Although originally designed to be a candle holder it can be found with and without the hole in the cake to hold the candle until 1964 when the hole was eliminated in a remodeling of the figurine. The Stylized Bee (TMK-3) pieces seem to be the one found most often without the hole. The Crown Mark (TMK-1) is the rarest occurrence of the no-hole variation.

Although not a major variation the fact that the earliest of the TMK-1 pieces have brightly colored striped socks is worth mentioning. Also, the earliest of these are also the ones more likely to be found without the hole in the cake.

A very rare variation is illustrated by the left figure in the accompanying photo. This no base, large shoes figure may have been intended to be utilized as a bookend piece or was simply an experiment. Whatever the case, if found it would command a low five figure sum.

HUM NO.	BASIC SIZE	TRADE MARK	CURRENT VALUE
9 (hole)	5½"	TMK-1 CM	600.00
9 (w/o hole)	5½"	TMK-1 CM	900-1000.00
9 (hole)	5½"	TMK-2 FB	500.00
9 (w/o hole)	5½"	TMK-2 FB	395.00
9 (hole)	5½"	TMK-3 Sty. Bee	275-325.00
9 (w/o hole)	5½"	TMK-3 Sty. Bee	225-240.00
9	5½"	TMK-4 3-line mark	220.00
9	5½"	TMK-5 LB	220.00
9	5½"	TMK-6 MB	220.00

FLOWER MADONNA
Hum 10

FLOWER MADONNA, Hum 10. Left to right, A through D as follows:
A. The mold number has decimal designators as follows: 10./1.. Has an incised Crown Mark (TMK-1) and a stamped Crown Mark green in color. The overall color is beige and the robe has no piping. Measures 8⅜".
B. Mold number is the regular 10/1. It has a large Stylized Bee (TMK-3) in an incised circle, is beige with orange piping, measures 8" and has a green "Western Germany" beneath.
C. The mold number is rendered in pencil, 10/1/11 and incised as 10. There is a green Germany stamped beneath. There are no other apparent markings. The color is blue cloak over a green gown.
D. 10/1, white overglaze, large Stylized Bee (TMK-3), measures 9⅜".

There are several color and mold variations known. The figure appears in color and in white overglaze in both sizes. There have been reports of the figure occurring in tan, beige or brown, and in a royal blue. Has also been found in terra cotta in 10/III (13") and in 10/I size (9½") with the Crown mark.

The Crown mark pieces all have the open style or "doughnut" type halo. The figure was remodeled in the mid 1950's eliminating the hole in the halo (closed halo). Because this took place during a trademark transition from the Crown to the Full Bee marks, the Full Bee trademarked figures are the pieces in which both type halos are found. The Full Bee pieces with open halo bring about 20% more than those with closed halos. This variation has no significant influence on the white overglaze pieces.

The values of the significantly early color variations are $1,500 to $2,200 for the 10/I size and $2000 to $2800 for the 10/III size.

HUM NO.	BASIC SIZE	TRADE MARK		CURRENT VALUE
10/I (white)	9½"	TMK-1	CM	330-420.00
10/I (white)	9½"	TMK-2	FB	230-250.00
10/I (white)	9½"	TMK-3	Sty. Bee	195-215.00
10/I (white)	8¼"	TMK-5	LB	165.00
10/I (color)	9½"	TMK-1	CM	775-970.00
10/I (color)	9½"	TMK-2	FB	575-600.00
10/I (color)	8¼"	TMK-3	Sty. Bee	480-500.00
10/I (color)	8¼"	TMK-5	LB	390-400.00
10/I (color)	8¼"	TMK-6	MB	390.00
10/III (white)	13"	TMK-1	CM	600-750.00
10/III (white) - open halo	13"	TMK-2	FB	470-500.00

Flower Madonna (cont'd)

Shows open and closed halo versions.

HUM NO.	BASIC SIZE	TRADE MARK		CURRENT VALUE
10/III (white) closed halo	13"	TMK-2	FB	420-460.00
10/III (white)	13"	TMK-3 Sty. Bee		370-390.00
10/III (white)	11½"	TMK-5	LB	300.00
10/III (white)	11½"	TMK-6	MB	1000-1300.00
10/III (color) open halo	13"	TMK-2	FB	775-825.00
10/III (color) closed halo	13"	TMK-2	FB	725-775.00
10/III (color)	13"	TMK-3 Sty. Bee		600-625.00
10/III (color)	11½"	TMK-5	LB	500.00
10/III (color)	11½"	TMK-6	MB	500.00

MERRY WANDERER
Hum 11

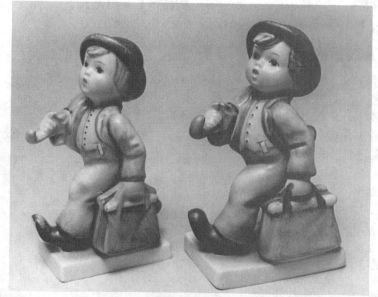

MERRY WANDERER, Hum 11. Left: Double Crown mark, split base (quartered), 4⅞". Right: 11., Crown mark, "Made in U.S. ZONE", black "Germany", split base (quartered), 5¼".

(continued)

Merry Wanderer (cont'd)

MERRY WANDERER, Hum 11. Left: 11 2/0, Full Bee in an incised circle, black "Germany", 7 buttons on vest, 4⅜". Right: 11/0, Stylized Bee mark, 5 buttons, 4⅝".

MERRY WANDERER. Bears the decimal mold number designator 11., a double Crown mark and a split (quartered) base. Valued at about $500.00. It is not likely to be a demonstration piece due to its age. It is placed here because of its similarity to the others known to be such.

This is the same design as the Hum 7, MERRY WANDERER. Although most of the Hum 77's found have five buttons on their vest, there are six and seven button versions to be found on the 11/2/0 size. These bring a bit more than the five button version of the 11/2/0 size, but it is not significant (about 10%).

The Hum 11 model of the Merry Wanderer has been found faience or "doll face" finish.

HUM NO.	BASIC SIZE	TRADE MARK		CURRENT VALUE
11/2/0	4¼"	TMK-1	CM	250-315.00
11/2/0	4¼"	TMK-2	*FB	180-200.00
11/2/0	4¼"	TMK-3	Sty. Bee	150-160.00
11/2/0	4¼"	TMK-4	3-line	135-145.00
11/2/0	4¼'	TMK-5	LB	125-135.00
11/2/0	4¼"	TMK-6	MB	125.00
11/0	4¾"	TMK-1	CM	350-435.00
11/0	4¾"	TMK-2	FB	250-275.00
11/0	4¾"	TMK-3	Sty. Bee	215-225.00
11/0	4¾"	TMK-4	3-line	190-200.00
11/0	4¾"	TMK-5	LB	175-185.00
11/0	4¾"	TMK-6	MB	175.00

*The 6 and 7 button variation of this one will bring $200-225.00

Crown	CM	TMK-1	1934-1950
Full Bee	FB	TMK-2	1940-1959
Stylized Bee	Sty Bee	TMK-3	1958-1972
Three Line Mark	3-line	TMK-4	1964-1972
Last Bee Mark	LB	TMK-5	1970-1980
Missing Bee Mark	MB	TMK-6	1979-1991
Hummel Mark (Current)	HM	TMK-7	1991-Present

CHIMNEY SWEEP
Hum 12

CHIMNEY SWEEP, Hum 12. Left: 12/1, Full Bee mark, donut base, 6⅜".
Right: 12/I, Stylized Bee, donut base 5¾".

When first introduced in 1935 as part of the original group displayed at the Leipzig Fair it was called "Smokey". The small 4" size was not added to the line until well into the 1950's consequently no Crown Mark (TMK-1) pieces are found in that size. There are no significant variations, but there are many variations in sizes. Examples found in sales lists are 4", 5½", 6¼" and 6⅜".

There was a surprise in store for those who bought the 1992 Sampler (A Hummel introductory kit). In it was the usual club membership discount and that years figurine was Chimney Sweep. Along with the figure came a special display base of a roof top and chimney.

HUM NO.	BASIC SIZE	TRADE MARK		CURRENT VALUE
12/2/0	4"	TMK-2	FB	155-175.00
✳12/2/0	4"	TMK-3	Sty. Bee	135-145.00
12/2/0	4"	TMK-4	3-line	120-125.00
12/2/0	4"	TMK-5	LB	110-120.00
12/2/0	4"	TMK-6	MB	110.00
12	5½"	TMK-1	CM	400-460.00
12	5½"	TMK-2	FB	300-365.00
12/I	5½"	TMK-1	CM	380-405.00
12/I	5½"	TMK-2	FB	290-315.00
12/I	5½"	TMK-3	Sty. Bee	240-260.00
12/I	5½"	TMK-4	3-line	210-225.00
12/I	5½"	TMK-5	LB	195-205.00
12/I	5½"	TMK-6	MB	195.00

MEDITATION
Hum 13

The Hum 13/0 and the Hum 13/II sizes were the first to be released in 1935. The most significant variations are with regard to the flowers in the baskets. When first released the 13/II had flowers in the basket, but sometime in the Last Bee mark (TMK-5) era it was restyled to reflect no flowers in the basket and the style remains so today.

Variations in the Hum 13/0 are with regard to the pigtails. The first models of the figure in the Crown Mark (TMK-1) era sported short pigtails with a painted red ribbon. By the time the Full Bee (TMK-2) mark was being utilized the ribbon had disappeared and the pigtails had grown longer.

The larger Hum 13/V was copyrighted in 1957 and has a basket filled with flowers. It is scarce in the older trademarks and hardly ever found for sale. It was temporarily withdrawn from production as of December 31, 1989 with no stated date for reinstatement.

There is a very unusual and probably unique Meditation that has a bowl attached to its side. There have been three different figurines found with bowls attached (see page 74).

MEDITATION, Hum 13. Left: the old style 13/2, 7'' size with flowers in the basket. Double Crown mark and ''Made in Germany'' beneath the base. Right: The newer style 13/II, 7'' size without any flowers in the basket. The latter has the Missing Bee trademark.

HUM NO.	BASIC SIZE	TRADE MARK		CURRENT VALUE
13/2/0	4¼"	TMK-2	FB	260-325.00
13/2/0	4¼"	TMK-3	Sty. Bee	160-175.00
13/2/0	4¼"	TMK-4	3-line	140-155.00
13/2/0	4¼"	TMK-5	LB	130-140.00
13/2/0	4¼"	TMK-6	MB	130.00
13/0	5¼"	TMK-1	CM	410-500.00
13/0	6"	TMK-2	FB	295-325.00
13/0	5¼"	TMK-3	Sty. Bee	245-265.00
13/0	5"	TMK-4	3-line	215-230.00
13/0	5"	TMK-5	LB	205-210.00
13/0	5"	TMK-6	MB	205.00
13/II (13/2) (w/flowers)	7"	TMK-1	CM	3000-4500.00
13/II (13/2) (w/flowers)	7"	TMK-2	FB	2500-4000.00
13/II (13/2) (w/flowers)	7"	TMK-3	Sty. Bee	2250.00
13/II	7"	TMK-5	LB	400-450.00
13/II	7"	TMK-6	MB	400.00
13/V	13¾"	TMK-2	FB	4000-5000.00
13/V	13¾"	TMK-3	Sty. Bee	1800-2500.00
13/V	13¾"	TMK-4	3-line	1200-1500.00
13/V	13¾"	TMK-5	LB	1000-1200.00
13/V	13¾"	TMK-6	MB	1000-1200.00

BOOK WORMS
(Bookends)
Hum 14A and Hum 14B

BOOKWORMS bookends, Hum 14 A and Hum 14 B. Both have the Stylized Bee mark (TMK-3) in an incised circle, black "Western Germany" and measure 5¾".

These are two figures, a boy and a girl (see Hum 3 and Hum 8). As far as is known to date, there is no other occurrence of the Boy Bookworm anywhere else in the collection. It occurs only in conjunction with the book ends (Hum 14 A and B) in only one size. There are no wooden bases as is the case with the other book ends in the collection. There are holes provided where the figures are weighted with sand, etc., and usually sealed with a factory sticker, gold in color. These are listed as "Temporarily Withdrawn" on current Goebel lists.

HUM NO.	BASIC SIZE	TRADE MARK		CURRENT VALUE
14/A&B	5½"	TMK-1	CM	1000-12000.00
14/A&B	5½"	TMK-2	FB	550-650.00
14/A&B	5½"	TMK-3	Sty. Bee	500-550.00
14/A&B	5½"	TMK-4	3-line	450-500.00
14/A&B	5½"	TMK-5	LB	400-450.00
14/A&B	5½"	TMK-6	MB	400-450.00

HEAR YE, HEAR YE
Hum 15

HEAR YE, HEAR YE, Hum 15. Left: 15/0, stamped Crown Mark (TMK-1), donut base, 5⅜". Right: 15/0, Full Bee (TMK-2), donut base, black "Germany", 5⅝".

(continued)

Hear Ye, Hear Ye (cont'd)

Among the first 46 to be released by Goebel at the Leipzig Fair it was first called "Night Watchman" and remained so until around 1950. Serious collectors seek out the larger 7½" size with the Arabic size designator, 15/2 for it represents the oldest of Crown Marked (TMK-1) figures.

HUM NO.	BASIC SIZE	TRADE MARK		CURRENT VALUE
15/2/0	4"	TMK-5	LB	135-145.00
15/2/0	4"	TMK-6	MB	135.00
15/0	5"	TMK-1	CM	375-500.00
15/0	5"	TMK-2	FB	265-285.00
✗15/0	5"	TMK-3	Sty. Bee	225-245.00
15/0	5"	TMK-4	3-line	195-220.00
15/0	5"	TMK-5	LB	180-190.00
15/0	5"	TMK-6	MB	180.00
15/I	6"	TMK-1	CM	450-600.00
15/I	6"	TMK-2	FB	330-350.00
15/I	6"	TMK-3	Sty. Bee	275-290.00
15/I	6"	TMK-4	3-line	245-260.00
15/I	6"	TMK-5	LB	225-240.00
15/I	6"	TMK-6	MB	225.00
15/II	7½"	TMK-1	CM	900-1500.00
15/II	7½"	TMK-1	CM	800-1100.00
15/II	7½"	TMK-2	FB	440-600.00
15/II	7½"	TMK-3	Sty. Bee	410-440.00
15/II	7½"	TMK-4	3-line	410-440.00
15/II	7½"	TMK-5	LB	375-390.00
15/II	7½"	TMK-6	MB	375.00

LITTLE HIKER
Hum 16

One of the original 46 released in 1934 in the 16/I and 16/2/0 sizes. The only significant variation is with the mold number. The mold number is sometimes found with only the "16" and sometimes with the decimal designator "16." in the 5½" to 6" size. These are found with the Crown (TMK-1) and the Full Bee (TMK-2) trademark and will bring about 15% more than comparably trademarked 16/I's.

LITTLE HIKER, Hum 16. Left is a Double Crown Marked (TMK-1) piece measuring 5½" with a black "Made in Germany" beneath the base. The One on the right has an incised Full Bee (TMK-2) and a stamped Full Bee mark as well. It measures 5⅞" and has a black "Germany beneath the base.

(continued)

Little Hiker (cont'd)

HUM NO.	BASIC SIZE	TRADE MARK		CURRENT VALUE
16/2/0	4¼"	TMK-1	CM	220-280.00
16/2/0	4¼"	TMK-2	FB	150-175.00
16/2/0	4¼"	TMK-3	Sty. Bee	125-145.00
16/2/0	4¼"	TMK-4	3-line	120-125
16/2/0	4¼"	TMK-5	LB	110-120.00
16/2/0	4¼"	TMK-6	MB	110.00
16/I	5½"	TMK-1	CM	400-500.00
16/I	5½"	TMK-2	FB	280-320.00
16/I	5½"	TMK-3	Sty. Bee	225-240.00
16/I	5½"	TMK-4	3-line	215-225.00
16/I	5½"	TMK-5	LB	200-210.00
16/I	5½"	TMK-6	MB	200.00

CONGRATULATIONS
Hum 17

CONGRATULATIONS, Hum 17. Left: 17/0, Double Crown Mark (TMK-1), 3¾". Right: 17/0, Small Stylized Bee (TMK-3), 3¾".

One of the original 1935 releases, there is a very unusual, perhaps unique, version of it where a bowl is attached to the figure's right rear. The figure in this version does not have the normal base.

When first modeled the figure had no socks. Later versions (after 1970) have a new hairstyle that also appears to be a little longer, flowers in the pot are larger and she wears socks. This change was made during the Three Line mark (TMK-4) and Stylized Bee (TMK-5) era so you can find either version with these marks. Obviously the no-socks piece would be the more desirable one.

MOLD NUMBER	BASIC SIZE	TRADE MARK	CURRENT VALUE
17/0 (no socks)	6"	TMK-1 CM	360-450.00
17/0 (no socks)	6"	TMK-2 FB	260-285.00
17/0 (no socks)	6"	TMK-3 Sty. Bee	240-260.00
17/0 (socks)	6"	TMK-3 Sty. Bee	215-235.00
17/0 (no socks)	6"	TMK-4 3-line	210-225.00
17/0 (socks)	6"	TMK-4 3-line	190-210.00
17/0 (socks)	6"	TMK-5 LB	180-190.00
17/0 (socks)	6"	TMK-6 MB	180.00
17/2 or 17/II	8¼"	TMK-1 CM	5000-7500.00
17/2 or 17/II	8¼"	TMK-2 FB	4000-5000.00
17/2 or 17/II	8¼"	TMK-3 Sty. Bee	3000-4000.00

CHRIST CHILD
Hum 18

This figure is very similar to the Christ Child figure used in the Nativity Sets, Hum 214 and 260. It is known to have been produced in a solid white overglaze. The white piece is rare. Christ Child has been temporarily withdrawn from production.

CHRIST CHILD, Hum 18.

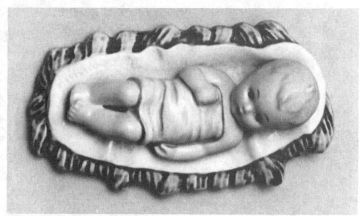

CHRIST CHILD, Hum 18. Stylized Bee mark, 3¼" x 5⅞".

HUM NO.	BASIC SIZE	TRADE MARK		CURRENT VALUE
18	2"x6"	TMK-1	CM	260-325.00
18	2"x6"	TMK-2	FB	185-200.00
18	2"x6"	TMK-3	Sty. Bee	155-170.00
18	2"x6"	TMK-4	3-line	135-145.00
18	2"x6"	TMK-5	LB	130-135.00
18	2"x6"	TMK-6	MB	130.00

PRAYER BEFORE BATTLE
Ashtray
Hum 19
Closed Number

Until 1986, when one of these surfaced in the United States, it was thought this was a Closed Number and the piece never produced. Even though one was found (temporarily) it may well be the only one ever made. The reason I noted "temporarily" found follows: It seems that a lady brought the piece to the Goebel Collectors' Club in Tarrytown, NY for identification. The paint finish was badly damaged as a result of her putting it in a dishwasher to clean it, Goebel Master Sculptor Gerhard Skrobek coincidentally was there. He speculated that the reason the paint was damaged was because it was probably a sample piece, painted but never fired so that the paint had not bonded to the figurine. Subsequent investigation of Goebel records revealed that the design was rejected by the Siessen Convent therefore never placed in production. Furthermore there is no example in the company archives. How it got out of the factory and to the U.S. remains a mystery. It seems the lady left, taking her piece with her, and no one present could remember her name or where she was from. Unique. Cannot place a realistic value on it.

PRAYER BEFORE BATTLE
Hum 20

There has been little change of any significance since its initial release in 1935. Has been listed at 4' and 4½" in the price lists over the years, but is presently 4¼".

There has been one most unusual figure uncovered, that exhibits peculiar color variations (see accompanying photograph). The horse is gray, black and white instead of the normal tan, the wagon is a dark green with red wheels, the socks are the same green color and his clothes are dark green and brown. The horn is a shiny gold gilt. This may be a one-of-a-kind experimental piece that somehow made it out of the factory, but who knows? It is from the late Ed Wunner's collection and the photo is courtesy of Rue Dee Marker.

PRAYER BEFORE BATTLE, Hum 20. Left: Full Bee (TMK-2) mark, black "Germany", 4½". Right: Last Bee (TMK-5) mark, 4⅛".

PRAYER BEFORE BATTLE, Hum 20, with odd paint decoration (see text).

Another view of the PRAYER BEFORE BATTLE with the unusual paint colors.

HUM NO.	BASIC SIZE	TRADE MARK		CURRENT VALUE
20	4¼"	TMK-1	CM	310-390.00
20	4¼"	TMK-2	FB	220-240.00
20	4¼"	TMK-3	Sty. Bee	190-210.00
20	4¼"	TMK-5	LB	155-165.00
20	4¼"	TMK-6	MB	155.00

HEAVENLY ANGEL
Hum 21

First known as the "Little Guardian" and later "Advent Angel", it was among the 46 original releases in 1935. This is the same motif as that used on the famous 1971 Annual plate of both Goebel and Schmid. The 21/0 size was the first to be introduced. It was followed by the larger sizes soon after.

The only variation of any significance in terms of value is the white overglaze model. It has not been found, but factory records indicate that it was produced at some time.

HEAVENLY ANGEL, Hum 21. Left: Small Stylized Bee (TMK-3) mark, 5¾''. Right: Last Bee (TMK-5) mark, 5¾''. Both have the mold number rendered thus: 21/0.

HUM NO.	BASIC SIZE	TRADE MARK		CURRENT VALUE
21/0	4¼"	TMK-1	CM	220-275.00
21/I	4¼"	TMK-2	FB	150-170.00
✗21/0	4¼"	TMK-3	Sty. Bee	135-145.00
21/0	4¼"	TMK-4	3-line	115-125.00
21/0	4¼"	TMK-5	LB	110-120.00
21/0	4¼"	TMK-6	MB	110.00
*21/0/½	6"	TMK-1	CM	400-500.00
*21/0/½	6"	TMK-2	FB	265-285.00
*21/0/½	6"	TMK-3	Sty. Bee	230-250.00
*21/0/½	6"	TMK-4	3-line	205-220.00
*21/0/½	6"	TMK-5	LB	190-200.00
*21/0/½	6"	TMK-6	MB	190.00
21/I	6¾"	TMK-1	CM	450-585.00
21/I	6¾"	TMK-2	FB	330-355.00
21/I	6¾"	TMK-3	Sty. Bee	280-300.00
21/I	6¾"	TMK-4	3-line	245-260.00
21/I	6¾"	TMK-5	LB	230-240.00
21/I	6¾"	TMK-6	MB	230.00
21/II	8¾"	TMK-1	CM	825-1025.00
21/II	8¾"	TMK-2	FB	600-625.00
21/II	8¾"	TMK-3	Sty. Bee	500-525.00
21/II	8¾"	TMK-4	3-line	450-465.00
21/II	8¾"	TMK-5	LB	415-425.00
21/II	8¾"	TMK-6	MB	415.00

*One of the only two pieces in the Goebel collection where this "½" designator is used. The other is "Blessed Child", Hum 78.

ANGEL WITH BIRD or ANGEL SITTING
Holy Water Font
Hum 22

ANGEL WITH BIRD Font, Hum 22/0. Stylized Bee, 3⅞".

Sometimes known as Seated or Sitting Angel with birds. This font has variations in bowl design and appears in two basic sizes. The mold number 22 has been known to appear with the decimal point size designator. The latter will bring about 15% more than the 22/0 counterpart in the Crown mark. The 22/I size is a closed edition.

HUM NO.	BASIC SIZE	TRADE MARK		CURRENT VALUE
22/0	2¾"x3½"	TMK-1	CM	85-100.00
22/0	2¾"x3½"	TMK-2	FB	55-65.00
22/0	2¾"x3½"	TMK-3	Sty. Bee	45-55.00
22/0	2¾"x3½"	TMK-4	3-line	40-45.00
22/0	2¾"x3½"	TMK-5	LB	40.00
22/0	2¾"x3½"	TMK-6	MB	40.00
22/I	3¼"x4"	TMK-1	CM	400-500.00
22/I	3¼"x4"	TMK-2	FB	350-400.00
22/I	3¼"x4"	TMK-3	Sty. Bee	300-350.00

ADORATION
Hum 23

Known in the early years as "Ave Maria" and "At the Shrine" this member of the original group released in 1935 in the smaller size. Soon after came the 23/III.

Both sizes have been produced in white overglaze, but they are quite scarce. When found for sale they usually go for about $3500-3800.00

HUM NO.	BASIC SIZE	TRADE MARK		CURRENT VALUE
23/I	6¼"	TMK-1	CM	650-810.00
23/I	6¼"	TMK-2	FB	470-500.00
23/I	6¼"	TMK-3	Sty. Bee	395-415.00
23/I	6¼"	TMK-4	3-line	350-370.00
23/I	6¼"	TMK-5	LB	325-340.00
23/I	6¼"	TMK-6	MB	325.00
23/III	9"	TMK-1	CM	1000-1300.00

(continued)

Adoration (cont'd)

HUM NO.	BASIC SIZE	TRADE MARK	CURRENT VALUE
23/III	9"	TMK-2 FB	720-760.00
23/III	9"	TMK-3 Sty. Bee	625-650.00
23/III	9"	TMK-4 3-line	545-570.00
23/III	9"	TMK-5 LB	510-530.00
23/III	9"	TMK-6 MB	510.00

ADORATION, Hum 23. Left: 23/1, Stylized Bee mark (TMK-3) in an incised circle, black "Western Germany", 6½". Right: 23/III, Last Bee mark (TMK-5), split base diagonally), 9".

LULLABY
Candleholder
Hum 24

This piece is quite similar to Hum 262, except that this one is a candleholder.

The larger 24/III was withdrawn from production for some time and reinstated in the early 1980s. It has, however, disappeared from the Goebel price lists for the past several years. The other, 24/I size has been listed as temporarily withdrawn since the end of 1989.

The larger (Hum 24/III) was out of production for some time, but has recently been reissued. The 24/III bearing older marks commands premium prices. The 24/III is sometimes found as 24/3.

HUM NO.	BASIC SIZE	TRADE MARK	CURRENT VALUE
24/I	3¼"x5"	TMK-1 CM	385-460.00
24/I	3¼"x5"	TMK-2 FB	250-275.00
24/I	3¼"x5"	TMK-3 Sty. Bee	215-235.00
24/I	3¼"x5"	TMK-4 3-line	180-195.00

153

Lullaby (cont'd)

HUM NO.	BASIC SIZE	TRADE MARK		CURRENT VALUE
24/I	3¼"x5"	TMK-5	LB	175.00
24/I	3¼"x5"	TMK-6	MB	175.00
24/III	6"x8"	TMK-1	CM	1400-1700.00
24/III	6"x8"	TMK-2	FB	500-700.00
24/III	6"x8"	TMK-3	Sty. Bee	310-400.00
24/III	6"x8"	TMK-5	LB	250-300.00
24/III	6"x8"	TMK-6	MB	250-300.00

LULLABY (candle holder), Hum 24. Left: Bears the mold number 24/1 and a small Stylized Bee (TMK-3) mark. Right: Bears the mold number 24/1 and the Last Bee (TMK-5). Both measure 3⅜". Note the candle hole variation. The older one is molded in so that the hole is not obvious without the candle in it.

ANGELIC SLEEP
Candleholder
Hum 25

One of the original 46 displayed at the Leipzig Fair in 1935. It was made in white overglaze for a short period, but these were not for export to the U.S. They are considered rare and can bring up to $2500 when sold.

ANGELIC SLEEP, Hum 25. Left: Full Bee (TMK-2) trademark, 3⅞", black "Germany". Right: Small Stylized Bee (TMK-3), 3½".

(continued)

ANGELIC SLEEP, Hum 25. Rear view of the above showing the hole variations between the two.

HUM NO.	BASIC SIZE	TRADE MARK		CURRENT VALUE
25	3½"x5"	TMK-1	CM	325-410.00
25	3½"x5"	TMK-2	FB	225-250.00
25	3½"x5"	TMK-3	Sty. Bee	190-215.00
25	3½"x5"	TMK-4	3-line	170-185.00
25	3½"x5"	TMK-5	LB	160-170.00
25	3½"x5"	TMK-6	MB	160.00

CHILD JESUS
Holy Water Font
Hum 26

One of the original 1935 releases. There is a very significant variation. The color of the robe is normally a deep orange-red. The rare variation has appeared only in the Stylized Bee (TMK-3) mark, 26/0 size to date.

The font has been produced in two sizes all along although the larger size has not appeared in the Goebel price list for some years.

HUM NO.	BASIC SIZE	TRADE MARK		CURRENT VALUE
26/O	1½"x5"	TMK-1	CM	85-100.00
26/0	1½"x5"	TMK-2	FB	55-65.00
26/0	1½"x5"	TMK-3	Sty. Bee	45-55.00
26/0	1½"x5"	TMK-4	3-line	25-45.00
26/0	1½"x5"	TMK-5	LB	40.00
26/0	1½"x5"	TMK-6	MB	40.00
26/I	2½"x6"	TMK-1	CM	350-500.00
26/I	2½"x6"	TMK-2	FB	300-350.00
24/I	2½"x6"	TMK-3	Sty. Bee	250-300.00

CHILD JESUS Font, Hum 26/0. Stylized Bee mark, 5⅛".

JOYOUS NEWS
Hum 27

JOYOUS NEWS, Hum 27/3. Large Stylized Bee (TMK-3) in an incised circle, black "Western Germany", 4½".

This piece is considered to be fairly scarce in the first three trademarks. As far as is presently known, there are probably less than 100 in collector's hands. The 27/III is sometimes found as 27/3. It was out of production for several years, but has been back in production for some time now. Older marked figures commands a premium price. There is smaller size (27/I) but it is rare. This 2¾" version is a candleholder. There are only four presently known to exist. The Crown mark 27/I's are valued at $350-500.00. The Full Bee 27/I's are valued at $250-350.00

HUM NO.	BASIC SIZE	TRADE MARK		CURRENT VALUE
27/III	4¼"x4¾"	TMK-1	CM	1200-1800.00
27/III	4¼"x4¾"	TMK-2	FB	750-1000.00
27/III	4¼"x4¾"	TMK-3	Sty. Bee	500-750.00
27/III (27/3)	4¼"x4¾"	TMK-5	LB	160-185.00
27/III	4¼"x4¾"	TMK-6	MB	195.00

WAYSIDE DEVOTION
Hum 28

This figurine is one of the initial 1935 designs displayed at the Leipzig Fair.

Both sizes have been found with the Arabic size designator 28/2 and 28/3. The larger, 8½" size also appears without the designator at all on the Crown mark (TMK-1) figurines. These are valued at roughly 20% above the regularly marked counterpart.

It was produced for a short time in white overglaze. These are considered rare and are valued at about $2,500.00

HUM NO.	BASIC SIZE	TRADE MARK		CURRENT VALUE
28/II	7½"	TMK-1	CM	790-990.00
28/II	7½"	TMK-2	FB	585-615.00
28/II	7½"	TMK-3	Sty. Bee	480-505.00
28/II	7½"	TMK-4	3-line	425-450.00
28/II	7½"	TMK-5	LB	395-410.00
28/II	7½"	TMK-6	MB	395.00

(continued)

WAYSIDE DEVOTION, Hum 28/II. Left: Stylized Bee, 6⅞". Right: Last Bee (TMK-5) 7½".

HUM NO.	BASIC SIZE	TRADE MARK		CURRENT VALUE
28	8¾"	TMK-1	CM	1300-1600.00
28/III	8½"	TMK-1	CM	1000-1300.00
✶28/III	8½"	TMK-2	FB	750-780.00
28/III	8½"	TMK-3	Sty. Bee	625-670.00
28/III	8½"	TMK-4	3-line	550-585.00
28/III	8½"	TMK-5	LB	520-535.00
28/III	8½"	TMK-6	MB	520.00

GUARDIAN ANGEL
Holy Water Font
Hum 29

GUARDIAN ANGEL Font, Hum 29. Incised Crown Mark, 5¾".

Crown	CM	TMK-1	1934-1950
Full Bee	FB	TMK-2	1940-1959
Stylized Bee	Sty Bee	TMK-3	1958-1972
Three Line Mark	3-line	TMK-4	1964-1972
Last Bee Mark	LB	TMK-5	1970-1980
Missing Bee Mark	MB	TMK-6	1979-1991
Hummel Mark (Current)	HM	TMK-7	1991-Present

Guardian Angel (cont'd)

This figure is not in current production and highly sought by collectors. A similar piece (Hum 248) exists and is considered to be a redesign of Hum 29. It is, therefore, unlikely to ever be reissued. It has been known to have been found with the decimal point designator.

HUM NO.	BASIC SIZE	TRADE MARK		CURRENT VALUE
29.	2¾"x6"	TMK-1	CM	1100-1350.00
29/0	2½"x5⅝"	TMK-1	CM	1100-1350.00
29/0	2½"x5⅝"	TMK-2	FB	1000-1200.00
29/0	2½"x5⅝"	TMK-3	Sty. Bee	900-1000.00
29/I	3"x6⅜"	TMK-1	CM	1500-1800.00
29/I	3"x6⅜"	TMK-2	FB	1300-1500.00

BA-BEE RINGS
Wall Plaques
Hum 30A and Hum 30B

BA—BEE RINGS. Left: 30/0 B., Crown Mark, red in color, 4⅝". Right: 30/1., double Crown Mark, red in color, 5⅜".

BA—BEE RINGS. Left: 30/1., double Crown Mark, light tan color, 5⅜". Right 30./1 B, incised Crown Mark, light tan color, 5⅜".

(continued)

Ba-Bee Rings (cont'd)

Part of the original collection released in 1935, they are found in two basic sizes.

There are some with the rings painted red in the Crown (TMK-1) era in both sizes and there has been at least one reported in bisque finish. Both of these are considered rare. They are also possibly found in the white overglaze finish. Value in red rings: $5000-8000.00.

They remain in production in a buff color (rings) in the 5" size only.

HUM NO.	BASIC SIZE	TRADE MARK		CURRENT VALUE
30/A&B	5"diam.	TMK-1	CM	325-425.00
30/A&B	5"diam.	TMK-2	FB	250-300.00
30/OA&B	5" diam.	TMK-3	Sty. Bee	200-220.00
30/OA&B	5"diam.	TMK-4	3-line	180-200.00
30/OA&B	5"diam.	TMK-5	LB	170-180.00
30/OA&B	5"diam.	TMK-6	MB	170.00
30/IA&B	6"diam.	TMK-1	CM	2500-3000.00

ADVENT GROUP
Candleholder
Hum 31

ADVENT GROUP, Hum 31. Both measure 3½" and bear the incised Crown Mark (TMK-1).

It was often called Advent Group or Silent Night "with Black Child" until several of the same mold numbers began showing up with a white child where the black child was ordinarily. It is thought by some that, in fact, the white child version may be the more rare of the two. Whatever the case, that both are quite rare is without question. Very similar to Hum 54, Silent Night, this was produced first in 1935 with the other original 45. Both versions have been found in the Crown Mark (TMK-1) only.

Collector value for the Hum 31 with black child: $15,000-20,000

Collector value for the Hum 31 with white child: $15,000-20,000

Crown	CM	TMK-1	1934-1950
Full Bee	FB	TMK-2	1940-1959
Stylized Bee	Sty Bee	TMK-3	1958-1972
Three Line Mark	3-line	TMK-4	1964-1972
Last Bee Mark	LB	TMK-5	1970-1980
Missing Bee Mark	MB	TMK-6	1979-1991
Hummel Mark (Current)	HM	TMK-7	1991-Present

LITTLE GABRIEL
Hum 32

When first released in 1935 it was called "Joyous News". It continues to be produced today, but only in the 5" size (Hum 32 without the "/I" designator).

Little Gabriel has been redesigned. The older pieces have the arms that are attached to each other up to the hands. The new design has the arms separated.

LITTLE GABRIEL, Hum 32. Left: figure is a Hum 32/0 with a Full Bee (TMK-2) mark. It measures 5⅛''. On the right is a Missing Bee (TMK-6) mold number 32 measuring 5'' tall.

HUM NO.	BASIC SIZE	TRADE MARK		CURRENT VALUE
32/O	5"	TMK-1	CM	250-315.00
32/O	5"	TMK-2	FB	180-195.00
32/O	5"	TMK-3	Sty. Bee	150-160.00
32/O	5"	TMK-4	3-line	130-140.00
32/O	5"	TMK-5	LB	125-130.00
32/O	5"	TMK-6	MB	125.00
32	5"	TMK-6	MB	125.00
32	6"	TMK-1	CM	2200-3000.00
32	6"	TMK-2	FB	1800-2000.00
32/I	6"	TMK-1	CM	2200-3000.00
32/I	6"	TMK-2	FB	1800-200.00
32/I	6"	TMK-3	Sty. Bee	1500-1700.00

JOYFUL
Ashtray
Hum 33

An ashtray utilizing a figure very similar to Hum 53 and with the addition of a small bird on the edge of the tray next to the figure. This piece has been temporarily removed from current production effective December 31, 1984 with no date for reinstatement given.

Has been found in the faience finish. This will bring a mid to high five figure amount when found.

HUM NO.	BASIC SIZE	TRADE MARK		CURRENT VALUE
33	3½"x6"	TMK-1	CM	300-400.00
33	3½"x6"	TMK-2	FB	200-250.00
33	3½"x6"	TMK-3	Sty. Bee	160-180.00

(continued)

Joyful Ashtray (cont'd)

HUM NO.	BASIC SIZE	TRADE MARK	CURRENT VALUE
33	3½"x6"	TMK-4 3-line	130-150.00
33	3½"x6"	TMK-5 LB	100-125.00
33	3½"x6"	TMK-6 MB	100-125.00

JOYFUL ashtray, Hum 33. Both bear the Crown Mark (TMK-1) and measure 3¾''. The one on the left is an example of the faience pieces. This one is rather poorly and gaudily painted. See color section and page 75.

SINGING LESSON
Ashtray
Hum 34

An ashtray utilizing a figure very similar to Hum 64, with a small bird perched on the edge of the tray instead of the boy's shoes.

This ashtray was listed as temporarily withdrawn from production at the end of 1989 with no date of reinstatement given.

SINGING LESSON ashtray, Hum 34. Left: Full Bee mark (TMK-2). This is an oversize ashtray measuring 4'' x 6½''. Right: Stylized Bee mark (TMK-3), 3⅞'' x 6³⁄₁₆''.

HUM NO.	BASIC SIZE	TRADE MARK	CURRENT VALUE
33	3½"x6"	TMK-1 CM	285-350.00
33	3½"x6"	TMK-2 FB	195-220.00
33	3½"x6"	TMK-3 Sty. Bee	165-185.00
33	3½"x6"	TMK-4 3-line	130-150.00
33	3½"x6"	TMK-5 LB	100-140.00
33	3½"x6"	TMK-6 MB	100-125.00

THE GOOD SHEPHERD
Holy Water Font
Hum 35

Part of the original collection released in 1935, this figurine has had only minor modifications over the years. With no significant variations it remains in production today.

THE GOOD SHEPHERD Font, Hum 35.
Left: Double Crown mark, 5½". Right: No apparent mark other than the mold number, 4⅝".

GOOD SHEPHERD Font, 35/0.
Stylized Bee mark, 4¹³⁄₁₆".

HUM NO.	BASIC SIZE	TRADE MARK		CURRENT VALUE
35/0	2¼"x4¾"	TMK-1	CM	80-100.00
35/0	2¼"x4¾"	TMK-2	FB	55-60.00
35/0	2¼"x4¾"	TMK-3	Sty. Bee	45-55.00
35/0	2¼"x4¾"	TMK-4	3-line	45.00
35/0	2¼"x4¾"	TMK-5	LB	40.00
35/0	2¼"x4¾"	TMK-6	MB	40.00
35	2¼"x4¾"	TMK-1	CM	275.00-325.00
35/I	2¾"x5¾"	TMK-1	CM	250-300.00
35/I	2¾"x5¾"	TMK-2	FB	200-250.00
35/I	2¾"x5¾"	TMK-3	Sty. Bee	150-200.00

CHILD WITH FLOWERS
Holy Water Font
Hum 36

Part of the original 46 released in 1935 there have been only minor modifications over the years. It remains in production today.

Has been found with the decimal point designator, "36." in the Crown mark, 36/I size.

HUM NO.	BASIC SIZE	TRADE MARK		CURRENT VALUE
36/0	2¾"x4"	TMK-1	CM	80-100.00
36/0	2¾"x4"	TMK-2	FB	55-65.00
36/0	2¾"x4"	TMK-3	Sty. Bee	45-55.00
36/0	2¾"x4"	TMK-4	3-line	45.00
36/0	2¾"x4"	TMK-5	LB	40.00
36/0	2¾"x4"	TMK-6	MB	40.00
36.	3½"x4½"	TMK-1	CM	350-400.00
36/I	3½"x4½"	TMK-1	CM	300-350.00
36/I	3½"x4½"	TMK-2	FB	150-250.00
36/I	3½"x4½"	TMK-3	Sty. Bee	100-150.00

CHILD WITH FLOWERS Font, Hum 36/0. Last Bee mark, 4¼".

HERALD ANGELS
Candleholder
Hum 37

HERALD ANGELS candle holder, Hum 37. Small Stylized Bee (TMK-3), 2⅞" x 4⅝".

This is a group of figures very similar to Hum 38, 39 and 40, placed together on a common round base and provided with a candle receptacle in the center. There are two versions, one with a low and one with a higher candle holder. The higher holder is found on the older pieces. This candleholder has been temporarily withdrawn from current production.

HUM NO.	BASIC SIZE	TRADE MARK	CURRENT VALUE
37	2¼"x4"	TMK-1 CM	320-400.00
37	2¼"x4"	TMK-2 FB	230-250.00
37	2¼"x4"	TMK-3 Sty. Bee	180-210.00
37	2¼"x4"	TMK-4 3-line	170-180.00
37	2¼"x4"	TMK-5 LB	160.00
37	2¼"x4"	TMK-6 MB	160.00

THE ANGEL TRIO
Candleholders
Hum 38, Hum 39, Hum 40

ANGEL TRIO candle holders.
Left: **Angel with Lute**, Hum 38, Full Bee mark, black "Germany", 2¾".
Center: **Angel with Accordian**, Hum 39, Full Bee mark black "Germany", 2⅝".
Right: **Angel with Horn**, Hum 40, Full Bee mark, black "Germany", 2⅝".

(continued)

The Angel Trio (cont'd)

These three figures are presented as a set of three and are usually sold as a set. They each come in three versions according to size and candle size. For some unknown reason only the Hum 38, Angel with Lute is in the current price list.

Hum 38 **Joyous News** — Angel with Lute — *2 full bees* / *full bee*
Hum 39 **Joyous News** — Angel with Accordian
Hum 40 **Joyous News** — Angel with Horn
I/38/0, I/39/0, I/40/0, 2", 0.6 cm candle diameter
III/38/0, III/39/0, III/40/0, 2", 1.0 cm candle diameter
III/38/I, III/39/I, III/40/I, 2¾", 1.0 cm candle diameter

TMK-1	Crown Mark (as a set)	$250-300.00
TMK-2	Full Bee (as a set)	175-185.00
TMK-3	Stylized Bee (as a set)	145-155.00
TMK-4	3-line mark (as a set)	130-135.00
TMK-5	Last Bee (as a set)	120.00
TMK-6	Missing Bee (as a set)	120.00

SINGING LESSON
Hum 41
Closed Number

Has been listed as a closed number but the existence of this piece has now been substantiated. Details are not known but the piece is said to be similar to Hum 63 "Singing Lesson" without the base. There are no known examples, but prototypes in this category have turned up from time to time.

THE GOOD SHEPHERD
Hum 42

The 42 Mold number has been found with the decimal point designator. There are two very rare variations; a blue gown rather than the normal brownish color and a white gown with blue stars. This is found on the 42/0 size in the Crown (TMK-1) and Full Bee (TMK-2) figures.

No longer produced in the 7½" size.

GOOD SHEPHERD, Hum 42. Left: Incised Crown Mark (TMK-1) colored blue, 7⅝". Right: 42/0, Full Bee (TMK-2) trademark, black "Germany", 6½".

(continued)

Good Shepherd (cont'd)

HUM NO.	BASIC SIZE	TRADE MARK		CURRENT VALUE
42.	6¼"	TMK-1	CM	500-600.00
42/0	6¼"	TMK-1	CM	440-550.00
42/0	6¼"	TMK-2	FB	310-340.00
42/0	6¼"	TMK-3	Sty. Bee	265-285.00
42/0	6¼"	TMK-4	3-line	235-250.00
42/0	6¼"	TMK-5	LB	220.00
42/0	6¼"	TMK-6	MB	220.00
42/I	7½"	TMK-1	CM	6500-7500.00
42/I	7½"	TMK-2	FB	5500-6500.00

MARCH WINDS
Hum 43

MARCH WINDS, Hum 43. The Left figure bears the Full Bee (TMK-2) trademark, is 5½" and bears a black "Germany" beneath the base. The one on the right has a small Stylized Bee (TMK-3) trademark and is 4⅞" tall.

This is one of the original 46 released in 1935.

There appear to be two slightly different designs. In the earlier pieces the boy looks more toward the rear than in the newer ones, but there are no significant variations to be found. It is still in production today.

HUM NO.	BASIC SIZE	TRADE MARK		CURRENT VALUE
43	5"	TMK-1	CM	290-360.00
43	5"	TMK-2	FB	200-225.00
43	5"	TMK-3	Sty. Bee	170-190.00
43	5"	TMK-4	3-line	150-160.00
43	5"	TMK-5	LB	145-150.00
43	5"	TMK-6	MB	145.00

CULPRITS	OUT OF DANGER
Table Lamp	Table Lamp
Hum 44/A	Hum 44/B

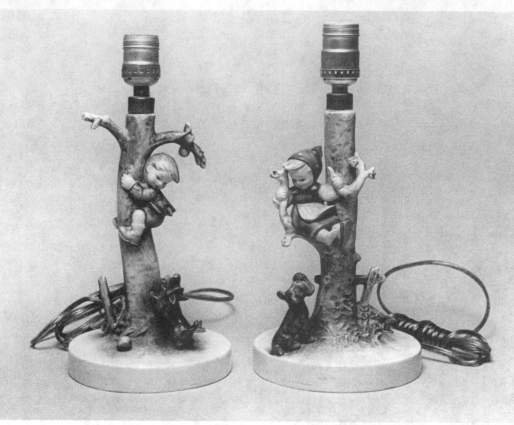

Left: **CULPRIT** table lamp, Hum 44/A. Double Full Bee mark (TMK-2)
incised and stamped, black "Germany", © W. Goebel, 9¼".
Right: **OUT OF DANGER** table lamp, Hum 44/B. Full Bee mark (TMK-2),
black "Germany", Copr. W. Goebel, 8⅜".

Both of these lamps were part of the original 46 designs that were released in 1935. Both are about 9" tall and were temporarily withdrawn from production at the end of 1989. No date for reinstatement was given.

There are no significant variations that would affect the collector value of either one. Only minor changes such as the location of the switch.

HUM NO.	BASIC SIZE	TRADE MARK		CURRENT VALUE
44/A	9½"	TMK-1	CM	450-600.00
44/A	9½"	TMK-2	FB	350-400.00
44/A	9½"	TMK-3	Sty. Bee	275-320.00
44/A	9½"	TMK-4	3-line	225-260.00
44/A	9½"	TMK-5	LB	225-260.00
44/A	9½"	TMK-6	MB	225-260.00
44/B	9½"	TMK-1	CM	450-600.00
44/B	9½"	TMK-2	FB	350-400.00
44/B	9½"	TMK-3	Sty. Bee	275-320.00
44/B	9½"	TMK-4	3-line	225-260.00
44/B	9½"	TMK-5	LB	225-260.00
44/B	9½"	TMK-6	MB	225-260.00

MADONNA WITH HALO
Hum 45

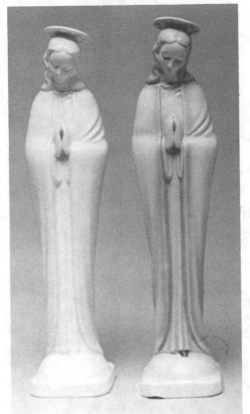

MADONNA WITH HALO, Hum 45/0. Left: White overglaze, small Stylized Bee (TMK-3), 10¾''. Right: Full Bee (TMK-2) trademark in an incised circle, red stars in the halo, 10½''. The halo has blue stars in the Last Bee (TMK-5) era.

MADONNA WITHOUT HALO
Hum 46

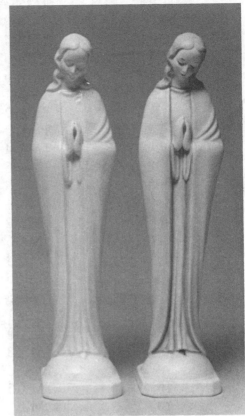

MADONNA WITHOUT HALO, Hum 46/0. Left is white overglaze and right is painted. Both are small Stylized Bee (TMK-3) pieces measuring 10½''.

These Madonnas were part of the original 46 figures that were released in 1935 at the Leipzig Fair. They are often confusing to collectors because of their similarity. Apparently they are also occasionally confused with each other at the factory. Sometimes the mold number appears on the wrong piece, possibly explained in some cases by the fact that the halo is an add-on piece during assembly and without it they are identical. The fact that they are sometimes found with both mold numbers incised on one piece lends evidence to the theory that the body is from the same mold and the mold number is impressed after assembly, but before firing.

At least nine legitimate variations have been found. The chief differences are in size and in color and glaze treatment. They are found in color and white overglaze. The known color variations are beige, rose, light blue, royal blue and ivory. They have also been found in terra cotta.

In 1982 both the 45/III and the 46/III were temporarily withdrawn from production and in 1984 the 45/0 and 46/0 were also withdrawn temporarily. Also the 46/I was temporarily withdrawn in 1989 leaving only the 45/I, Madonna with Halo available to collectors. It is listed as available in either the regular color or the white overglaze.

While variations are rampant only the appearance in terra cotta and one other has any significant effect on value. There is a variation where there are red-painted stars on the underside of the halo. This variation can as much as triple the value for its counterpart without the stars. The terra cotta Madonnas are valued at about $1500-2500.00

(continued)

HUM NO.	BASIC SIZE	TRADE MARK		CURRENT VALUE (White)	CURRENT VALUE (Color)
45/0	10½"	TMK-2	FB	80-120.00	100-170.00
✗45/0 *Blue stars*	10½"	TMK-3	Sty. Bee	50-70.00	85-100.00
45/0	10½"	TMK-4	3-line	40-50.00	70-85.00
45/0	10½"	TMK-5	LB	40.00	60-70.00
45/0	10½"	TMK-6	MB	40.00	60.00
45/I	12"	TMK-1	CM	140-175.00	225-300.00
45/I	12"	TMK-2	FB	100-115.00	165-185.00
45/I	12"	TMK-3	Sty. Bee	80-90.00	140-150.00
45/I	12"	TMK-4	3-line	75-80.00	125-130.00
45/I	12"	TMK-5	LB	70.00	115.00
45/I	12"	TMK-6	MB	70.00	115.00
45/III	16¼"	TMK-1	CM	190-220.00	300-400.00
45/III	16¼"	TMK-2	FB	140-165.00	200-225.00
45/III	16¼"	TMK-3	Sty. Bee	120-130.00	170-185.00
45/III	16¼"	TMK-4	3-line	100-120.00	150-165.00
45/III	16¼"	TMK-5	LB	100.00	140.00
45/III	16¼"	TMK-6	MB	100.00	140.00
46/0	10¼"	TMK-1	CM	125-195.00	200-250.00
46/0	10¼"	TMK-2	FB	80-120.00	100-170.00
46/0	10¼"	TMK-3	Sty. Bee	50-70.00	85-100.00
46/0	10¼"	TMK-4	3-line	40-50.00	70-85.00
46/0	10¼"	TMK-5	LB	40.00	60-70.00
46/0	10¼"	TMK-6	MB	40.00	60.00
46/I	11¼"	TMK-1	CM	140-175.00	225-300.00
46/I	11¼"	TMK-2	FB	100-115.00	165-185.00
46/I	11¼"	TMK-3	Sty. Bee	80-90.00	140-150.00
46/I	11¼"	TMK-4	3-line	75-80.00	125-130.00
46/I	11¼"	TMK-5	LB	70.00	115.00
46/I	11¼"	TMK-6	MB	70.00	115.00
46/III	16"	TMK-1	CM	190-220.00	300-400.00
46/III	16"	TMK-2	FB	140-165.00	200-225.00
46/III	16"	TMK-3	Sty. Bee	120-130.00	170-185.00
46/III	16"	TMK-4	3-line	100-120.00	150-165.00
46/III	16"	TMK-5	LB	100.00	140.00
46/III	16"	TMK-6	MB	100.00	140.00

Crown	CM	TMK-1	1934-1950
Full Bee	FB	TMK-2	1940-1959
Stylized Bee	Sty Bee	TMK-3	1958-1972
Three Line Mark	3-line	TMK-4	1964-1972
Last Bee Mark	LB	TMK-5	1970-1980
Missing Bee Mark	MB	TMK-6	1979-1991
Hummel Mark (Current)	HM	TMK-7	1991-Present

GOOSE GIRL
Hum 47

A very popular piece, probably the most famous among collectors and non-collectors alike. Interestingly, for a model that dates back practically to day one and in three sizes there are no variations significant enough to have an effect on collector value. The occurrence of the decimal designator might have a slight influence with *some* collectors, but not to any significant degree even with them.

There is, of course, the Goose Girl with a bowl attached (see photo on next page). This piece is thought to be unique; a prototype that somehow found its way into the collector market. I photographed this one in a home in Germany. No others have turned up. There are two similar pieces, one in Congratulations, Hum 17 and the other is Meditation, Hum 13.

GOOSE GIRL, Hum 47. Left: 47/0, Full Bee mark, black "Germany", 5¼". Center: 47/0, Stylized Bee mark, 4¾". Right: 47 3/0, Full Bee mark, black "Germany", 4¼".

HUM NO.	BASIC SIZE	TRADE MARK		CURRENT VALUE
47/3/0	4"	TMK-1	CM	310-390.00
47/3/0	4"	TMK-2	FB	220-245.00
47/3/0	4"	TMK-3	Sty. Bee	190-215.00
47/3/0	4"	TMK-4	3-line	165-180.00
47/3/0	4"	TMK-5	LB	155-160.00
47/3/0	4"	TMK-6	MB	155.00
47	5"	TMK-1	CM	410-515.00
47/0	4¾"	TMK-1	CM	410-515.00
47/0	4¾"	TMK-2	FB	290-320.00
47/0	4¾"	TMK-3	Sty. Bee	245-265.00
47/0	4¾"	TMK-4	3-line	215-235.00
47/0	4¾"	TMK-5	LB	205-210.00
47/0	4¾"	TMK-6	MB	205.00
47/II	7½"	TMK-1	CM	800-1000.00
47/II	7½"	TMK-2	FB	575-625.00
47/II	7½"	TMK-3	Sty. Bee	485-520.00
47/II	7½"	TMK-4	3-line	425-450.00
47/II	7½"	TMK-5	LB	400-420.00
47/II	7½"	TMK-6	MB	400.00

(continued)

GOOSE GIRL Bowl. This exceedingly rare piece was found in Germany in 1989. It measures 4⅞" and has an incised Crown mark. Upon examining it closely, it appears that the bowl was attached to the figurine before firing, lending legitimacy to the presumption that it was fashioned by Goebel. The bowl is a double Crown mark piece and has an incised mold number "1". There have been two other bowl pieces show up with a different style bowl, **Meditation,** Hum 13 and **Congratulations,** Hum 17.

MADONNA
Wall Plaque
Hum 48

This plaque has been known to appear in a white overglaze in the 48/0 and the 48/II sizes in a bisque finish. The 48/II can sometimes be found as 48/2. There are two variations of the 48/II in the Crown Mark. The 48/II size in current-use trademark has been temporarily withdrawn from production. The effective date was December 31, 1984 with no reinstatement date given.

The white overglaze pieces appear in the Crown Mark (TMK-1) and are very rare.

MADONNA Plaque, Hum 48/2. Left: Stylized Bee mark, 4⅝" x 5¾", white overglaze. Right: Full Bee mark, 4⅝" x 5⅝".

HUM NO.	BASIC SIZE	TRADE MARK		CURRENT VALUE
48/0	3"x4"	TMK-1	CM	250-300.00
48/0	3"x4"	TMK-2	FB	115-130.00
48/0	3"x4"	TMK-3	Sty. Bee	95-115.00
48/0	3"x4"	TMK-4	3-line	90-95.00
48/0	3"x4"	TMK-5	LB	80-85.00 (continued)

Madonna Wall Plaque (Cont'd)

HUM NO.	BASIC SIZE	TRADE MARK		CURRENT VALUE
48/0	3"x4"	TMK-6	MB	80.00
48	4¾"x6"	TMK-1	CM	450-570.00
48/II	4¾"x6"	TMK-1	CM	400-520.00
48/II	4¾"x6"	TMK-2	FB	200-220.00
48/II	4¾"x6"	TMK-3 Sty. Bee		145-160.00
48/II	4¾"x6"	TMK-5	LB	135-145.00
48/II	4¾"x6"	TMK-6	MB	135.00
48/V	8¼"x10½"	TMK-1	CM	1500-1800.00
48/V	8¼"x10½"	TMK-2	FB	1300-1400.00
48/V	8¼"x10½"	TMK-3 Sty. Bee		1000-1200.00

TO MARKET
Hum 49

TO MARKET, Hum 49. Left: 49./0., double Crown Mark, donut base, 5⁷⁄₁₆". Right: 49/0, Last Bee mark, 5⅜".

The 49/I size was out of current production for at least 20 years and then reinstated in the early 1980's. Once again it is out of current production. Goebel placed it on a temporarily withdrawn from production status on December 31, 1984. The 49 mold number has occasionally been found with the decimal point size designator. There have been 49/0's surface having no bottle in the basket. The 49/3/0 size is routinely produced with no bottle in the basket.

HUM NO.	BASIC SIZE	TRADE MARK		CURRENT VALUE
49/3/0	4"	TMK-1	CM	300-375.00
49/3/0	4"	TMK-2	FB	215-240.00
49/3/0	4"	TMK-3 Sty. Bee		180-200.00
49/3/0	4"	TMK-4	3-line	160-175.00
49/3/0	4"	TMK-5	LB	150-160.00
49/3/0	4"	TMK-6	MB	150.00
49/0	5½"	TMK-1	CM	500-650.00
49/0	5½"	TMK-2	FB	330-400.00
49/0	5¼"	TMK-3 Sty. Bee		300-320.00
49/0	5½"	TMK-4	3-line	265-295.00
49/0	5½"	TMK-5	LB	250-265.00
49/0	5½"	TMK-6	MB	250.00
49.	6¼"	TMK-1	CM	1100-1300.00
49.	6¼"	TMK-2	FB	750-900.00
49/I	6¼"	TMK-1	CM	800-1100.00
49/I	6¼"	TMK-2	FB	600-700.00
49/I	6¼"	TMK-3 Sty. Bee		500-600.00
49/I	6¼"	TMK-4	3-line	440-450.00
49/I	6¼"	TMK-5	LB	400-440.00
49	6¼"	TMK-6	MB	400.00

VOLUNTEERS
Hum 50

The 50/0 and 50/I sizes were out of production for some years and difficult to find with the older trademarks. Both were reinstated in 1979 with the new pieces having the Last Bee (TMK-5). The 50/I has once again been withdrawn from current production with no published reinstatement date.

VOLUNTEERS, Hum 50. Left: 50/0, incised Crown Mark, black "Germany", 5⅞". Center: 50/0, Full Bee in an incised circle, black "Western Germany", 6¹⁄₁₆". Right: 50 2/0, Missing Bee mark, 4⅞", white overglaze.

"Volunteers" an M.I.Hummel Figurine by W.Goebel Porzellanfabrik is being produced with special commemorative Desert Shield - Desert Storm backstamp in limited quantity. This special commemorative piece will only be available through US. Military Exchanges.

M.I.Hummel
Goebel

VOLUNTEERS, Hum 50. 50 2/0, Hummel Mark current use mark or (TMK-7), 4¾". This is the Volunteers with the special Desert Shield/Desert Storm backstamp.

(continued)

Volunteers (cont'd)

Photo showing the Desert Shield/Desert Storm backstamp on the base of the Volunteers figurine.

The small, Hum 50/2/0 Volunteers was released with a special backstamp commemorating the allied victory in Operation Desert Storm. Reportedly limited to 10,000 pieces worldwide, it was to be sold only through military post and base exchanges. This particular variation has already risen to a range of $275-350.00 on the collector market.

HUM NO.	BASIC SIZE	TRADE MARK		CURRENT VALUE
50/2/0	5"	TMK-1	CM	400-500.00
50/2/0	5"	TMK-2	FB	305-415.00
50/2/0	5"	TMK-3	Sty. Bee	245-270.00
50/2/0	5"	TMK-4	3-line	220-235.00
50/2/0	5"	TMK-5	LB	205-215.00
50/2/0	5"	TMK-6	MB	205.00
50/0	5½"	TMK-1	CM	540-600.00
50/0	5½"	TMK-2	FB	375-425.00
50/0	5½"	TMK-3	Sty. Bee	325-375.00
50/0	5½"	TMK-5	LB	270.00
50/0	5½"	TMK-6	MB	270.00
50.	6½"	TMK-1	CM	1000-1500.00
50/I	6½"	TMK-1	CM	900-1400.00
50/I	6½"	TMK-2	FB	600-700.00
50/I	6½"	TMK-3	Sty. Bee	470-485.00
50/I	6½"	TMK-5	LB	430-450.00
50/I	6½"	TMK-6	MB	430.00

VILLAGE BOY
Hum 51

Placed in production around 1934-35, this figure is still being produced. The 51/I was taken out of production sometime in the 1960's and the early figures are considered rare. Out of production for some twenty years, the 51/I was placed back in production for a short time and has once again been temporarily withdrawn effective December 31, 1984 with no known date for reinstatement.

There were many minor variations over the years, but the one most important to collectors occurs in the Crown Mark (TMK-1) 51/3/0 size. The boy wears a blue jacket and a yellow kerchief instead of the normal green jacket and red kerchief. When found, this variation is valued at about $2500.00

(continued)

Village Boy (cont'd)

VILLAGE BOY, Hum 51. Left: 51./0., double Crown mark, donut base, 6½" Right: 51/0, Last Bee mark, 6⅜".

HUM NO.	BASIC SIZE	TRADE MARK		CURRENT VALUE
51/3/0	4"	TMK-1	CM	225-265.00
51/3/0	4"	TMK-2	FB	150-175.00
51/3/0	4"	TMK-3	Sty. Bee	135-150.00
51/3/0	4"	TMK-4	3-line	120.00
51/3/0	4"	TMK-5	LB	110.00
51/3/0	4"	TMK-6	MB	110.00
51/2/0	5"	TMK-1	CM	250-315.00
51/2/0	5"	TMK-2	FB	185-200.00
51/2/0	5"	TMK-3	Sty. Bee	155-170.00
51/2/0	5"	TMK-4	3-line	135-150.00
51/2/0	5"	TMK-5	LB	125-135.00
51/2/0	5"	TMK-6	MB	125.00
51/0	6"	TMK-1	CM	440-550.00
51/0	6"	TMK-2	FB	320-350.00
51/0	6"	TMK-3	Sty. Bee	260-290.00
51/0	6"	TMK-4	3-line	235-250.00
51/0	6"	TMK-5	LB	220-235.00
51/0	6"	TMK-6	MB	220.00
51	7¼"	TMK-1	CM	500-650.00
51/I	7¼"	TMK-1	CM	450-600.00
51/I	7¼"	TMK-2	FB	300-375.00
51/I	7¼"	TMK-3	Sty. Bee	250-300.00
51/I	7¼"	TMK-5	LB	225-240.00
51/I	7¼"	TMK-6	MB	225.00

GOING TO GRANDMA'S
Hum 52

A very early figurine in the line. All of the older pieces in both sizes are found in the square base. A redesign and a new, oval base was accomplished with the transition taking place in the Last Bee (TMK-5) era. You can, therefore find TMK-5 pieces with either base with the older, square base being the most desirable.

Has been found with the decimal designator in the Crown Mark (TMK-1).

HUM NO.	BASIC SIZE	TRADE MARK		CURRENT VALUE
52/0	4¾"	TMK-1	CM	500-600.00
52/0	4¾"	TMK-2	FB	350-400.00
✗52/0	4¾"	TMK-3	Sty. Bee	325-350.00
52/0	4¾"	TMK-4	3-line	275-325.00
52/0 (square base)	4¾"	TMK-5	LB	275-300.00
52/0 (oval base)	4¾"	TMK-5	LB	250-270.00
52/0	4¾"	TMK-6	MB	250.00
52.	6"	TMK-1	CM	900-1200.00
52/I	6"	TMK-1	CM	700-1000.00
52/I	6"	TMK-2	FB	520-550.00
52/I	6"	TMK-3	Sty. Bee	425-470.00
52/I	6"	TMK-5	LB	350-400.00
52/I	6"	TMK-6	MB	350.00

GOING TO GRANDMA'S, Hum 52. Left: Decimal designator in the mold number 52., incised Crown Mark (TMK-1), black "Made in Germany" stamped on and lacquered over, 6". Right: 52/I, Stylized Bee (TMK-3) mark in an incised circle, black "Western Germany", 6¼".

GOING TO GRANDMA'S, Hum 52. Shows the appearance of the cone when it holds candies and the later model oval base.

JOYFUL
Hum 53

JOYFUL, Hum 53. Left: Full Bee (TMK-2) mark in an incised circle, black "Germany", 3¾". Right: Missing Bee (TMK-5), 3¾".

This figure was once known as "Banjo Betty". There are major size variations. As the figure emerged from the Crown Mark (TMK-1) era and transitioned into the Full Bee (TMK-2) period, it began to grow larger. Both the normal sizes and the larger variations appeared during the Full Bee (TMK-2) period and by the time the transition to the Stylized Bee (TMK-3) was finished, it was back to the normal 4" basic size. The oversize pieces consistently bring a higher price than the normal size pieces. They are valued at about 20%-25% more than the normal size.

There is a much more rare variation. There are some very early Crown mark (TMK-1) "Joyfuls" that have an orange dress instead of the normal blue. Collector value $3000-3500.00

HUM NO.	BASIC SIZE	TRADE MARK		CURRENT VALUE
53	4"	TMK-1	CM	225-300.00
53	4"	TMK-2	FB	150-175.00
53	4"	TMK-3	Sty. Bee	130-150.00
53	4"	TMK-4	3-line	115-130.00
53	4"	TMK-5	LB	110-115.00
53	4"	TMK-6	MB	110.00

JOYFUL
Candy Box
Hum III/53

JOYFUL candy dish, Hum III/53. Old style bowl left, and new style on the right.

Joyful Candy Box (cont'd)

There are two styles of candy boxes. The transition from the old to the new took place in the Stylized Bee (TMK-3) period. There are, therefore, the old and the new styles to be found with the Stylized Bee trademark. The older style would, of course, be the more desirable to collectors.

HUM NO.	BASIC SIZE	TRADE MARK		CURRENT VALUE
III/53	6¼"	TMK-1	CM	450-530.00
III/53	6¼"	TMK-2	FB	350-400.00
III/53 (old style)	6¼"	TMK-3	Sty. Bee	275-325.00
III/53 (new style)	6¼"	TMK-3	Sty. Bee	150-200.00
III/53	6¼"	TMK-4	3-line	120-150.00
III/53	6¼"	TMK-5	LB	120-150.00
III/53	6¼"	TMK-6	MB	120-150.00

SILENT NIGHT
Candle Holder
Hum 54

SILENT NIGHT, Hum 54. Left: Full Bee (TMK-2), black "Germany", 3¾". Center: Double Full Bee (TMK-2), incised and stamped; black "Germany", 3¾". Right: Last Bee (TMK-6), 3½".

This piece is almost identical to the Hum 31, "Advent Group" candle holder. Where most of the 31's have a black child on the left, most of the left children on the 54's are white.

There have been at least three distinctly different molds including the current production model.

The significant variation to be found, and the most valuable, is that of the black child. These can be found in the Crown mark (TMK-1) and the Full Bee (TMK-2) trademarks only. They are valued at $8000-10,000.00

HUM NO.	BASIC SIZE	TRADE MARK		CURRENT VALUE
54	4¾"x5½"	TMK-1	CM	540-675.00
54	4¾"x5½"	TMK-2	FB	380-420.00
54	4¾"x5½"	TMK-3	Sty. Bee	340-365.00
54	4¾"x5½"	TMK-4	3-line	295-335.00
54	4¾"x5½"	TMK-5	LB	270-290.00
54	4¾"x5½"	TMK-6	MB	270.00

ST. GEORGE
Hum 55

SAINT GEORGE, Hum 55. The mold number is incised with the decimal designator on this particular example thus: "55.". It has an incised Crown Mark *and* stamped Full Bee mark and measures 7".

This figure is substantially different in style from most others in the collection and is difficult to locate most of the time, even though it is listed as in current production. Sizes encountered in various lists: 6¼", 6⅝", 6¾". Some of the early (Crown mark) pieces will have a bright red painted saddle. This is the rarest variation and brings $1500-2000.00 when sold. Has been reported to appear in white overglaze.

It is reportedly being restyled to make the sword blade less vulnerable to breakage.

HUM NO.	BASIC SIZE	TRADE MARK	CURRENT VALUE
55	6¾"	TMK-1 CM	600-750.00
55	6¾"	TMK-2 FB	425-475.00
55	6¾"	TMK-3 Sty. Bee	360-395.00
55	6¾"	TMK-4 3-line	325-350.00
55	6¾"	TMK-5 LB	300-325.00
55	6¾"	TMK-6 MB	300.00

CULPRITS
Hum 56/A

OUT OF DANGER
Hum 56/B

"Culprits" was released in the mid-1930's while "Out of Danger was not introduced until the early 1950's. There have been minor changes over the years, but none having any influence on normal collector values.

HUM NO.	BASIC SIZE	TRADE MARK	CURRENT VALUE
56	6¼"	TMK-1 CM	425-525.00
56	6¼"	TMK-2 FB	375-400.00
56/A	6¼"	TMK-2 FB	375-400.00

(continued)

Culprits/Out of Order (cont'd)

HUM NO.	BASIC SIZE	TRADE MARK		CURRENT VALUE
✗56/A	6¼"	TMK-3	Sty. Bee	310-350.00
56/A	6¼"	TMK-4	3-line	275-300.00
56/A	6¼"	TMK-5	LB	250-275.00
56/A	6¼"	TMK-6	MB	250.00
56/B	6¼"	TMK-2	FB	375-400.00
56/B	6¼"	TMK-3	Sty. Bee	310-350.00
56/B	6¼"	TMK-4	3-line	275-300.00
56/B	6¼"	TMK-5	LB	250-275.00
56/B	6¼"	TMK-6	MB	250.00

CULPRITS, Hum 56/A. Left: Stylized Bee mark, 6⅜". Right: Last Bee mark, 6¾".

OUT OF DANGER, Hum 56/B. Left: Small Stylized Bee (TMK-3) piece measuring 6¼". Right has the Missing Bee (TMK-6) mark and is 6⅛" tall.

CHICK GIRL
Hum 57

There are many mold types and sizes. The chief mold variation show different numbers of chicks on the base. For instance, the 57/0 has two chicks and the larger, 57/I, has three. Has been found with mold number and no size designator in the 4¼" size, "57".

CHICK GIRL, Hum 57. Left: Double Crown Mark (TMK-1), 4⅛". Right: 57/I, Stylized Bee mark (TMK-3), 4⁵⁄₁₆".

Chick Girl (cont'd)

HUM NO.	BASIC SIZE	TRADE MARK	CURRENT VALUE
57/2/0	3"	TMK-5 LB	135-140.00
57/2/0	3"	TMK-6 MB	135.00
57/0	3½"	TMK-1 CM	310-400.00
57/0	3½"	TMK-2 FB	225-250.00
57/0	3½"	TMK-3 Sty. Bee	190-215.00
57/0	3½"	TMK-4 3-line	165-180.00
57/0	3½"	TMK-5 LB	155-165.00
57/0	3½"	TMK-6 MB	155.00
57	4¼"	TMK-1 CM	550-650.00
57/I	4¼"	TMK-1 CM	500-600.00
57	4¼"	TMK-2 FB	400-440.00
57/I	4¼"	TMK-2 FB	360-395.00
57/I	4¼"	TMK-3 Sty. Bee	300-325.00
57/I	4¼"	TMK-4 3-line	260-285.00
57/I	4¼"	TMK-5 LB	250-260.00
57/I	4¼"	TMK-6 MB	250.00

CHICK GIRL
Candy Box
Hum III/57

There are two styles of candy boxes. The transition from the old to the new took place in the Stylized Bee period. There are, therefore, the old and the new to be found with the Stylized Bee (TMK-3) mark with the old style naturally being the more desirable.

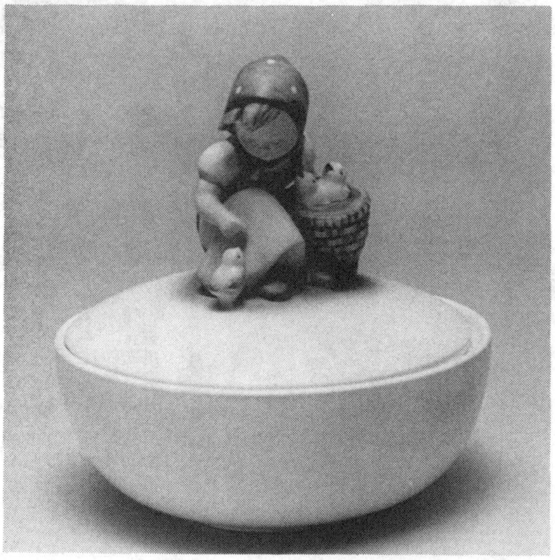

CHICK GIRL candy dish, Hum III 57. Stylized Bee mark (TMK-3). Old style bowl.

HUM NO.	BASIC SIZE	TRADE MARK	CURRENT VALUE
III/57	5¼"	TMK-1 CM	450-530.00
III/57	5¼"	TMK-2 FB	350-400.00
III/57(old)	5¼"	TMK-3 Sty. Bee	275-325.00
III/57(new)	5¼"	TMK-3 Sty. Bee	150-200.00
III/57	5¼"	TMK-4 3-line	120-150.00
III/57	5¼"	TMK-5 LB	120-150.00
III/57	5¼"	TMK-6 MB	120-150.00

PLAYMATES
Hum 58

PLAYMATES, Hum 58/0. Left: Full Bee (TMK-2), black "Germany", 3⅞". Right: Small Stylized Bee (TMK-3), mark, 3⅞".

There are no variations within each trademark era that have any significant effect on value. Similar figure used on bookend Hum 61/A and candy box following.

HUM NO.	BASIC SIZE	TRADE MARK		CURRENT VALUE
58/2/0	3½"	TMK-5	LB	135-140.00
58/2/0	3½"	TMK-6	MB	135.00
58/0	4"	TMK-1	CM	310-400.00
58/0	4"	TMK-2	FB	225-250.00
✶ 58/0	4"	TMK-3	Sty. Bee	190-215.00
58/0	4"	TMK-4	3-line	165-180.00
58/0	4"	TMK-5	LB	155-165.00
58/0	4"	TMK-6	MB	155.00
58	4½"	TMK-1	CM	550-650.00
58/I	4½"	TMK-1	CM	500-600.00
58	4½"	TMK-2	FB	385-420.00
58/I	4½"	TMK-2	FB	360-395.00
58/I	4½"	TMK-3	Sty. Bee	300-325.00
58/I	4½"	TMK-4	3-line	260-285.00
58/I	4½"	TMK-5	LB	250-260.00
58/I	4½"	TMK-6	MB	250.00

Crown	CM	TMK-1	1934-1950
Full Bee	FB	TMK-2	1940-1959
Stylized Bee	Sty Bee	TMK-3	1958-1972
Three Line Mark	3-line	TMK-4	1964-1972
Last Bee Mark	LB	TMK-5	1970-1980
Missing Bee Mark	MB	TMK-6	1979-1991
Hummel Mark (Current)	HM	TMK-7	1991-Present

PLAYMATES
Candy Box
Hum III/58

PLAYMATES candy dish, Hum III/58. Old style bowl.

There are two styles of candy boxes. The transition from the old to the new took place during the Stylized Bee (TMK-3) period therefore each may be found with that trademark. The older style would, of course, be the more desirable to collectors.

Temporarily withdrawn from production at the end of 1989 with no reinstatement date given.

HUM NO.	BASIC SIZE	TRADE MARK		CURRENT VALUE
III/58	5¼"	TMK-1	CM	450-530.00
III/58	5¼"	TMK-2	FB	350-400.00
III/58(old)	5¼"	TMK-3	Sty. Bee	275-325.00
III/58(new)	5¼"	TMK-3	Sty. Bee	150-200.00
III/58	5¼"	TMK-4	3-line	120-150.00
III/58	5¼"	TMK-5	LB	120-150.00
III/58	5¼"	TMK-6	MB	120-150.00

SKIER
Hum 59

SKIER, Hum 59. Left: Stylized Bee mark (TMK-3), wooden Poles. Center: Last Bee mark (TMK-5), metal poles. Right: Last Bee mark, plastic poles. All measure 5¼".

(continued)

Skier (cont'd)

Newer models have metal ski poles and older have wooden poles. For a short time this figure was made with plastic poles. The poles are replaceable and are not considered significant in the valuation of the piece in the case of wooden and metal poles. There is, however, some difficulty with the plastic ski poles found on most of the Stylized Bee (TMK-3) pieces. The small round discs at the bottom of the poles are molded integral with the pole. Some collectors and dealers feel that the intact plastic ski poles on the Stylized Bee pieces are a bit more valuable than those with wooden or metal replacements.

HUM NO.	BASIC SIZE	TRADE MARK		CURRENT VALUE
59.	5¼"	TMK-1	CM	425-500.00
59	5¼"	TMK-1	CM	425-500.00
59	5¼"	TMK-2	FB	375-400.00
✗59	5¼"	TMK-3	Sty. Bee	245-270.00
59	5¼"	TMK-4	3-line	210-235.00
59	5¼"	TMK-5	LB	195-210.00
59	5¼"	TMK-6	MB	195.00

FARM BOY and GOOSE GIRL
Bookends
Hum 60/A and Hum 60/B

FARM BOY, Hum 60 A and **GOOSE GIRL,** Hum 60 B bookends. Left figure measures 3⅜" and the other 4⅞". Both bear the Stylized Bee mark (TMK-3).

The overall height of the bookends is 6". The figurines themselves measure 4¾". Notice the lack of bases on the figurines. Most often the trademark is found stamped on the base and not on the figurines. Noted collector Robert Miller has confirmed, by removing the boy from a 60/A bookend, that some of the earliest production pieces are occasionally found with the mold number incised on the bottom of feet. The mold number has also been observed on the back of the slippers on other early pieces.

There are no significant variations affecting value.

These bookends have been temporarily withdrawn from current production status effective December 31, 1984 with no date for reinstatement given.

HUM NO.	BASIC SIZE	TRADE MARK		CURRENT VALUE
60/A&B	6"	TMK-1	CM	500-575.00
60/A&B	6"	TMK-2	FB	400-450.00
60/A&B	6"	TMK-3	Sty. Bee	300-325.00
60/A&B	6"	TMK-5	LB	225-300.00
60/A&B	6"	TMK-6	MB	225-300.00

PLAYMATES and CHICK GIRL
Bookends
Hum 61/A and Hum 61/B

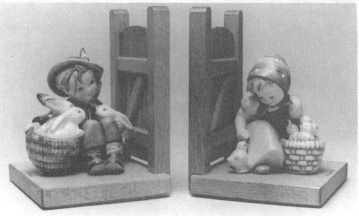

PLAYMATES, Hum 61A and CHICK GIRL, Hum 61 B bookends. Both have Stylized Bee marks (TMK-3). Left measures 4¼'' and right, 4''.

Overall height of each is 6". The figures are 4". Note that the figures used do not have the usual base. The trademark is usually marked on the wood portion. The trademark and mold number may or may not appear on the bottom of the figures if removed from the base. Some bookend pieces are marked so, especially the earliest.

The bookends have been temporarily withdrawn from current production status effective December 31, 1984 with no date for reinstatement given.

HUM NO.	BASIC SIZE	TRADE MARK		CURRENT VALUE
60/A&B	6"	TMK-1	CM	500-575.00
60/A&B	6"	TMK-2	FB	400-450.00
60/A&B	6"	TMK-3	Sty. Bee	300-325.00
60/A&B	6"	TMK-5	LB	225-300.00
60/A&B	6"	TMK-6	MB	225-300.00

HAPPY PASTIME
Ashtray
Hum 62

HAPPY PASTIME ashtray, Hum 62. Last Bee mark (TMK-5), 3½''.

There are no significant variations affecting the value. This, as all ashtrays, has been temporarily withdrawn from production with no published reinstatement date.

Figure used is similar to Hum 69 except that the bird is positioned on the edge of the tray rather than on the girl's leg.

HUM NO.	BASIC SIZE	TRADE MARK		CURRENT VALUE
62	3½"x6¼"	TMK-1	CM	300-400.00
62	3½"x6¼"	TMK-2	FB	200-250.00
62	3½"x6¼"	TMK-3	Sty. Bee	160-180.00
62	3½"x6¼"	TMK-4	3-line	130-150.00
62	3½"x6¼"	TMK-5	LB	100-125.00
62	3½"x6¼"	TMK-6	MB	100-125.00

184

SINGING LESSON
Hum 63

SINGING LESSON, Hum 63. Left: 63., incised Crown Mark (TMK-1), U.S. Zone Germany, 3". Center: 63., double Crown Mark, Made in Germany, 2¾". Right: Last Bee mark (TMK-5), 3".

First offered in the late 1930's "Singing Lesson" has changed a little over the years, but has no significant variations. It has been found with the decimal designator occasionally, on the Crown mark (TMK-1). That is an indication that it is an early Crown piece, but does not have a significant impact on value.

HUM NO.	BASIC SIZE	TRADE MARK	CURRENT VALUE
63	2¾"	TMK-1 CM	225-280.00
63	2¾"	TMK-2 FB	150-175.00
63	2¾"	TMK-3 Sty. Bee	130-145.00
63	2¾"	TMK-4 3-line	115-135.00
63	2¾"	TMK-5 LB	110-115.00
63	2¾"	TMK-6 MB	110.00

SINGING LESSON
Candy Box
Hum III/63

There are two styles of bowls. The transition from the old to the new took place in the Stylized Bee (TMK-3) period, therefore both are found with the Stylized Bee trademark. The old style with this mark is, of course, the more desirable to collectors.

SINGING LESSON candy dish, Hum III/63. Left: Last Bee mark (TMK-5). Right: Stylized Bee mark (TMK-5), old style bowl.

Singing Lesson Candy Dish (cont'd)

HUM NO.	BASIC SIZE	TRADE MARK		CURRENT VALUE
III-63	5¼"	TMK-1	CM	450-530.00
III-63	5¼"	TMK-2	FB	350-400.00
III-63(old)	5¼"	TMK-3	Sty. Bee	275-325.00
III-63(new)	5¼"	TMK-3	Sty. Bee	150-200.00
III-63	5¼"	TMK-4	3-line	120-150.00
III-63	5¼"	TMK-5	LB	120-150.00
III-63	5¼"	TMK-6	MB	120-150.00

SHEPHERD'S BOY
Hum 64

SHEPHERD'S BOY, Hum 64. Left: Full Bee mark (TMK-2) with a registered trademark symbol associated, black "Germany", 5¾". Right: Last Bee (TMK-5), 5½".

SHEPHERD'S BOY, Hum 64. Full Bee mark, black "Germany", 6⅛".

There are no significant variations that could affect the normal pricing of the various trademarked figurines. There seem to be a number of size variations to be found.

HUM NO.	BASIC SIZE	TRADE MARK		CURRENT VALUE
64	5½"	TMK-1	CM	400-500.00
64	5½"	TMK-2	FB	290-315.00
64	5½"	TMK-3	Sty. Bee	250-275.00
64	5½"	TMK-4	3-line	210-240.00
64	5½"	TMK-5	LB	200-210.00
64	5½"	TMK-6	MB	200.00

FAREWELL
Hum 65

The first models of this figurine, the 65/0 size, in a small 4" basic size is very rare and highly sought by serious collectors. They apparently made a very limited number of them. They are found in the Crown Mark (TMK-1) and the Full Bee (TMK-2) only.

The 4¾" basic size carried the 65/I mold number for a while, but in the late 1970's it became 65 only. This size is also sometimes found with the decimal designator on the early Crown Mark and Full Bee mark pieces.

There is an interesting variation that occured in the Missing Bee mark (TMK-6) era. It seems that a few of the baskets were attached wrong resulting in a gap between the arm and the basket on the inside. The pieces with this variation are valued at a bit above the normal by some collectors. Mistakes such as this are not common, but do happen once in a while. For instance, sometimes a bottle is inadvertently left out of a basket during assembly. Most of the time it is only an interesting oddity, but there were a sufficient number of the "Farewell" basket errors to make it attractive to some.

"Farewell" is a retired figurine. The mold was scheduled to be broken up on December 31, 1993. All produced during 1993 will bear a special "Final Issue" backstamp and will be accompanied by a small medallion proclaiming it as a "Final Issue" in 1993.

HUM NO.	BASIC SIZE	TRADE MARK		CURRENT VALUE
65/0	4"	TMK-2	FB	6000-7500.00
65/0	4"	TMK-3	Sty. Bee	5000-6000.00
65.	4¾"	TMK-1	CM	450-500.00
65/I	4¾"	TMK-1	CM	450-500.00
65.	4¾"	TMK-2	FB	360-400.00
65/I	4¾"	TMK-2	FB	360-400.00
65/I	4¾"	TMK-3	Sty. Bee	300-350.00
65/I	4¾"	TMK-4	3-line	265-300.00
65	4¾"	TMK-5	LB	240-265.00
65	4¾"	TMK-6	MB	240.00

FAREWELL, Hum 65. Left: Incised Crown Mark *and* a stamped Full Bee mark, black "Germany", 4⅞". Right: Full Bee mark in an incised circle, black "Germany", 4⅞".

FARM BOY
Hum 66

FARM BOY, Hum 66. Left: Decimal designator in mold number 66., double Crown Mark (TMK-1), donut base. "Made in Germany" stamped on base and lacquered over, 5⅛". Right: Full Bee (TMK-2) in an incised circle, black "Germany", donut base, 6".

Similar figure used in Bookends Hum 60/A. Older versions have larger shoes than the newer ones. In fact, the whole piece appears fatter over all. Has been known as "THREE PALS" in the past and is occasionally found with the decimal point size designator.

HUM NO.	BASIC SIZE	TRADE MARK		CURRENT VALUE
66.	5¼"	TMK-1	CM	500-575.00
66	5¼"	TMK-1	CM	500-575.00
66	5¼"	TMK-2	FB	400-450.00
66	5¼"	TMK-3	Sty. Bee	300-325.00
66	5¼"	TMK-4	3-line	275-300.00
66	5¼"	TMK-5	LB	225-275.00
66	5¼"	TMK-6	MB	225-275.00

DOLL MOTHER
Hum 67

Released in the late 1930's, "Doll Mother" was first known as "Little Doll Mother".
There are no significant mold or paint variations within each trademark period that have any effect on value.

DOLL MOTHER, Hum 67. Left: 67., double Crown Mark, "Made in Germany", 4⅜". Right: Full Bee mark, black "Germany, 4¾".

(continued)

Doll Mother (cont'd)

HUM NO.	BASIC SIZE	TRADE MARK		CURRENT VALUE
67.	4¾"	TMK-1	CM	380-470.00
67	4¾"	TMK-1	CM	380-470.00
67	4¾"	TMK-2	FB	275-300.00
✗ 67	4¾"	TMK-3	Sty. Bee	230-250.00
67	4¾"	TMK-4	3-line	200-225.00
67	4¾"	TMK-5	LB	190-200.00
67	4¾"	TMK-6	MB	190.00

LOST SHEEP
Hum 68

LOST SHEEP, Hum 68. Left: Incised Full Bee (TMK-2) trademark and a donut base with a black "Germany" beneath, 6". Right: 68/0 mold number with the Last Bee (TMK-5) trademark. Measures 5½".

Sizes found referenced in lists are as follows: 4¼", 4½", 5½" and 6½". This figure is found most commonly with green pants. A reference to a figure with orange pants (6½") was found, but the color variation considered rare is the one with brown pants. The collector value for the brown pants variation is about 25% above the value for the normal green pants piece.

There are four or five different color variations involving the coat, pants and shirt of the figure. Oversize pieces bring premium prices.

The decimal point designator has been found on some early Crown mark (TMK-1) figures.

The 68/0 and 68/2/0 sizes were retired at the end of 1992. Each of them made in 1992 bear the special "Final Issue" backstamp indicating this. See the introductory pages for an explanation and illustration of this mark. In addition there will be a medallion accompanying these particular figures.

HUM NO.	BASIC SIZE	TRADE MARK		CURRENT VALUE
68/2/0	4½"	TMK-2	FB	185-200.00
68/2/0	4½"	TMK-3	Sty. Bee	155-180.00
68/2/0	4½"	TMK-4	3-line	135-155.00
✗ 68/2/0	4½"	TMK-5	LB	125-135.00
68/2/0	4½"	TMK-6	MB	125.00
68.	5½"	TMK-1	CM	405-495.00
68	5½"	TMK-1	CM	405-495.00
68	5½"	TMK-2	FB	325-350.00
68/0	5½"	TMK-2	FB	300-325.00
68	5½"	TMK-3	Sty. Bee	285-310.00
68/0	5½"	TMK-3	Sty. Bee	260-280.00
68/0	5½"	TMK-4	3-line	190-215.00
68/0	5½"	TMK-5	LB	180-190.00
68/0	5½"	TMK-6	MB	180.00

HAPPY PASTIME
Hum 69

HAPPY PASTIME, Hum 69. Left: Small Stylized Bee (TMK-3), 3⅜''. Right: Missing Bee (TMK-6), 3⅜''.

This piece was in a group that was issued a short time after the initial 46 were released in 1935. There have been changes over the years, but nothing significant enough to influence the normal pricing within each trademark era.

HUM NO.	BASIC SIZE	TRADE MARK		CURRENT VALUE
69	3¼"	TMK-1	CM	300-360.00
69	3¼"	TMK-2	FB	215-235.00
69	3¼"	TMK-3	Sty. Bee	175-200.00
69	3¼"	TMK-4	3-line	150-170.00
69	3¼"	TMK-5	LB	145-150.00
69	3¼"	TMK-6	MB	145.00

HAPPY PASTIME
Candy Box
Hum III/69

HAPPY PASTIME candy dish, Hum III/69. Last Bee mark (TMK-5).

There are two styles of candy boxes. The transition from the old to the new took place during the Sytlized Bee (TMK-3) period. There are, therefore, both the old and new to be found bearing the Stylized Bee (TMK-3) trademark.

There have been no other significant changes.

HUM NO.	BASIC SIZE	TRADE MARK		CURRENT VALUE
III/69	6"	TMK-1	CM	450-530.00
III/69	6"	TMK-2	FB	350-400.00
III/69(old)	6"	TMK-3	Sty. Bee	275-325.00
III/69(new)	6"	TMK-3	Sty. Bee	150-200.00
III/69	6"	TMK-4	3-line	120-150.00
III/69	6"	TMK-5	LB	120-150.00
III/69	6"	TMK-6	MB	120-150.00

THE HOLY CHILD
Hum 70

There have been no paint and finish variations significant enough to affect the value of each trademark era piece. There was a general restyling of the whole collection over the years, to the more textured finish of the clothing of the figures in the collection today.

There are some oversize pieces that are sought after. They are generally valued at about 20% above the normal value listed.

THE HOLY CHILD, Hum 70. Left: Full Bee (TMK-2), black "Germany", 7⅜". Right: Last Bee (TMK-5), 6⅞".

HUM NO.	BASIC SIZE	TRADE MARK		CURRENT VALUE
70	6¾"	TMK-1	CM	320-400.00
70	6¾"	TMK-2	FB	225-250.00
70	6¾"	TMK-3	Sty. Bee	190-215.00
70	6¾"	TMK-4	3-line	170-180.00
70	6¾"	TMK-5	LB	160-170.00
70	6¾"	TMK-6	MB	160.00

STORMY WEATHER
Hum 71

This figure has been known as "Under One Roof". Some earlier models were produced with a split base under. The split base model with the Full Bee mark, upon examination, shows that the split is laterally oriented. The new models also have the split base, but it is oriented longitudinally.

There has been a Crown mark Stormy Weather found that is different from the norm. Among other things the boy figure in the piece has no kerchief. It is most likely a prototype inasmuch as it is not signed. Other than the oddity described above there were no significant variations over the years until the new smaller, 5", 71/2/0 was introduced. After a period of time it became obvious that the method of painting the underside of the umbrella had changed. The first models released exhibit the brush strokes of hand-painting while the later ones had been air

Stormy Weather (cont'd)

brushed. Serious collectors seek this variation out. It is valued at about $600.

The 71 mold number was changed to 71/I during the Missing Bee Mark (TMK-6) period. The mold number can be found rendered either way on those pieces.

HUM NO.	BASIC SIZE	TRADE MARK		CURRENT VALUE
71/2/0	5"	TMK-6	MB	270.00
71	6¼"	TMK-1	CM	825-930.00
71	6¼"	TMK-2	FB	600-640.00
71	6¼"	TMK-3	Sty. Bee	500-525.00
71	6¼"	TMK-4	3-line	445-470.00
71	6¼"	TMK-5	LB	415-440.00
71	6¼"	TMK-6	MB	415.00
71/I	6¼"	TMK-6	MB	415.00

STORMY WEATHER, Hum 71. Left: Crown Mark, split base, 6''. Right: Stylized Bee mark in an incised circle, black "Western Germany", split base, 6''.

Crown	CM	TMK-1	1934-1950
Full Bee	FB	TMK-2	1940-1959
Stylized Bee	Sty Bee	TMK-3	1958-1972
Three Line Mark	3-line	TMK-4	1964-1972
Last Bee Mark	LB	TMK-5	1970-1980
Missing Bee Mark	MB	TMK-6	1979-1991
Hummel Mark (Current)	HM	TMK-7	1991-Present

SPRING CHEER
Hum 72

Released soon after the initial issue of 46, this figurine was originally called "It's Spring".

There have been some significant variations in this figurine. It was initially released in a yellow dress and with no flowers in her right hand. These can be found in the Crown Mark (TMK-1), the Full Bee mark (TMK-2) and the Stylized Bee (TMK-3). During the Stylized Bee (TMK-3) it was redesigned in a green dress and with flowers in the right hand. This latter is the way the current productions pieces are configured. There were, however, some of the old no flowers in right hand models left, so they painted them with the green dress to match the new model. This is the rarest of the two green dress models.

The company lists the figurine a temporarily withdrawn from production as of December 31, 1984 with no reinstatement date.

Value of the green dress, no flowers in right hand $1500-1800.00

HUM NO.	BASIC SIZE	TRADE MARK		CURRENT VALUE
72	5"	TMK-1	CM	400-500.00
72	5"	TMK-2	FB	275-300.00
✳72	5"	TMK-3	Sty. Bee	225-250.00
72	5"	TMK-4	3-line	200-225.00
72	5"	TMK-5	LB	165-185.00
72	5"	TMK-6	MB	165-185.00

SPRING CHEER, Hum 72. Left: Full Bee (TMK-2), black "Germany", 5½". Note there are no flowers in the right hand. The dress is yellow. Center: Stylized Bee (TMK-1) mark, no flowers in right hand, green dress, 5¼". All newer versions have flowers in the right hand as in the right figurine in the photo.

LITTLE HELPER
Hum 73

There are no significant variations affecting the normal values for this figurine in the various trademark evolutions.

LITTLE HELPER, Hum 73. The older is on the right. It has an incised Full Bee trademark (TMK-2) and measures 4⅜". The one on the left is a 4" Stylized Bee (TMK-3) piece.

HUM NO.	BASIC SIZE	TRADE MARK		CURRENT VALUE
73	4¼"	TMK-1	CM	220-280.00
73	4¼"	TMK-2	FB	150-175.00
✶73	4¼"	TMK-3	Sty. Bee	125-145.00
73	4¼"	TMK-4	3-line	120-125.00
73	4¼"	TMK-5	LB	110-120.00
73	4¼"	TMK-6	MB	110.00

LITTLE GARDENER
Hum 74

This figure was found in several lists with the following sizes: 4", 4¼", 4½". Earlier versions are found on an oval base; newer to current pieces are on the round base. The major variation encountered is a dark green dress rather than the present lighter colored dress. Some of the earliest models have a very light green or yellowish dress.

Some other variations make it easy to spot the older pieces. On the Crown mark (TMK-1) and Full Bee (TMK-2) figures, the flower at the base is tall and almost egg-shaped. On the Stylized Bee (TMK-3) marked figures, the flower is about one-half the height of the earlier flowers and from the Last Bee (TMK-5) on them are rather flattened in comparison.

These variations, however, have no effect on the normal value of the piece for their respective trademarks. They represent normal changes through the years.

There is one variation that bears watching. In the spring of 1992, Goebel took this figurine out of normal production and will not resume until 1994. From the Spring of 1992 until the end of the year, Little Gardener was used as a District Managers special promotion piece and each bears a special promotion back-stamp.

The only place they were available was at promotions at authorized *M.I. Hummel* dealers conducting District Manager Special Promotions and in Canada at Artist's Promotions. Not all promotions were so sponsored. The figurines were available on a first-come, first-served basis to all comers.

(continued)

Little Gardener (cont'd.)

LITTLE GARDENER, Hum 74. Last Bee (TMK-5), 4¼".

LITTLE GARDENER, Hum 74. Left: 74., incised Crown Mark, split base, 4⅜". Note the height of the flower. Right: Missing Bee trademark, 4½".

HUM NO.	BASIC SIZE	TRADE MARK		CURRENT VALUE
74	4¼"	TMK-1	CM	220-280.00
74	4¼"	TMK-2	FB	150-175.00
74	4¼"	TMK-3	Sty. Bee	125-145.00
74	4¼"	TMK-4	3-line	120-125.00
74	4¼"	TMK-5	LB	110-120.00
74	4¼"	TMK-6	MB	110.00

WHITE ANGEL
Holy Water Font
Hum 75

Although this piece is known as the Angelic Prayer or White Angel Font it is painted in color. It has been produced in two sizes, 1¾" x 3½" and 3" x 4¼", but only the larger is still produced. It is the older and smaller one which is usually called the White Angel Font.

HUM NO.	BASIC SIZE	TRADE MARK		CURRENT VALUE
75	1¾"x3½"	TMK-1	CM	75-100.00
75	1¾"x3½"	TMK-2	FB	55-70.00
75	1¾"x3½"	TMK-3	Sty. Bee	45-55.00
75	1¾"x3½"	TMK-4	3-line	45.00
75	1¾"x3½"	TMK-5	LB	40-45.00
75	1¾"x3½"	TMK-6	MB	40.00

WHITE ANGEL Font, Hum 75. Stylized Bee mark, 4⅜".

DOLL MOTHER and PRAYER BEFORE BATTLE
Bookends
Hum 76/A and Hum 76/B

These book ends are unique. It is possible, but not likely that they might be found. There are no known examples in private hands. Factory archives only.

CROSS WITH DOVES
Holy Water Font
Hum 77

In the last edition of this book it was reported that there was only one example of this piece and it was in the factory archives. Eight now reside in private collections. The one in the photo accompanying is an incised Crown mark piece with the *M.I. Hummel* signature on the back. It has been reported found in white. If sold, this font would likely bring $7000-10,000, in color or white.

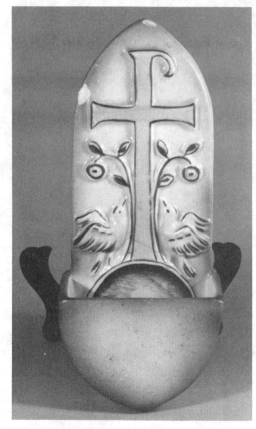

Back side of the Hum 77. Font showing the Crown mark and the *M.I. Hummel* incised signature.

CROSS WITH DOVES Font, Hum 77.

CROSS WITH DOVES Font, Hum 77. The same piece after professional restoration.

BLESSED CHILD
Hum 78

This piece can be found in seven different sizes and three finishes. All sizes except one, have either been retired or have been temporarily withdrawn from production with no stated reintroduction date.

The normal finish is a brown-tone bisque. They were available painted in full color for a time, withdrawn, reissued and finally discontinued. There was also a white overglaze finish reportedly produced for a European market only. The color pieces are valued at two times the normal value listed for the size and the white overglaze figure are valued at about two to three times the normal value, also depending on the size.

There are two pieces still available. One is the small 78/0, 2¼" size, but it is difficult to get. This size was discontinued in the Stylized Bee (TMK-3) period. It has been redesigned and issued in the brown-tone finish without the "78/0" incised mold number. It bears only the Missing Bee (TMK-6) or the Hummel Mark (TMK-7) and is sold in the Siessen Convent only. It is unavailable elsewhere. The other one is also available only at the convent. It is the 4½", Hum 78/11½" mold.

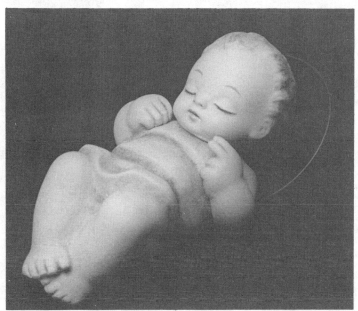

BLESSED CHILD or **INFANT OR KRUMBAD,** Hum 78. This one bears the Full Bee trademark, measures 4¾" in length and has the original wire halo.

HUM NO.	BASIC SIZE	TRADE MARK		CURRENT VALUE
78/0	1¾"	TMK-2	FB	200-250.00
78/0	1¾"	TMK-3	Sty. Bee	150-200.00
78/0	1¾"	TMK-6	MB	100.00
78/I	2½"	TMK-3	Sty. Bee	35-55.00
78/I	2½"	TMK-4	3-line	30-40.00
78/I	2½"	TMK-5	LB	30-40.00
78/I	2½"	TMK-6	MB	30-40.00
78/II	3½"	TMK-3	Sty. Bee	45-65.00
78/II	3½"	TMK-4	3-line	35-45.00
78/II	3½"	TMK-5	LB	35-45.00
78/II	3½"	TMK-6	MB	35-45.00
78/III	5¼"	TMK-1	CM	250-300.00
78/III	5¼"	TMK-2	FB	150-250.00
78/III	5¼"	TMK-3	Sty. Bee	50-60.00
78/III	5¼"	TMK-4	3-line	40-55.00
78/III	5¼"	TMK-5	LB	40-55.00
78/III	5¼"	TMK-6	MB	40-55.00
78/V	7¾"	TMK-3	Sty. Bee	75-125.00
78/V	7¾"	TMK-4	3-line	75-100.00

Blessed Child (cont'd)

78/V	7¾"	TMK-5	LB	50-100.00
78/V	7¾"	TMK-6	MB	50-75.00
78/VI	10"	TMK-1	CM	300-500.00
78/VI	10"	TMK-2	FB	200-300.00
78/VI	10"	TMK-3	Sty. Bee	150-200.00
78/VI	10"	TMK-4	3-line	150-200.00
78/VI	10"	TMK-5	LB	100-150.00
78/VI	10"	TMK-6	MB	100-150.00
78/VIII	13½"	TMK-1	CM	450-650.00
78/VIII	13½"	TMK-2	FB	400-500.00
78/VIII	13½"	TMK-3	Sty. Bee	250-400.00
78/VIII	13½"	TMK-4	3-line	250-350.00
78/VIII	13½"	TMK-5	LB	250-300.00
78/VIII	13½"	TMK-6	MB	200-300.00
*78/11½"	4"	TMK-6	MB	100-150.00

*One of the two only pieces in the collection to use this "½" designator. The other is Hum 21. Heavenly Angel.

GLOBE TROTTER
Hum 79

One of the earlier, pre-WW II releases. There are no significant variations that directly affect the value of the pieces with the various trademarks, but there are some interesting ones that can help you spot the earlier ones without examining the marks. The Crown Mark (TMK-1), Full Bee (TMK-2) and exhibit a double weave in the baskets (see accompanying photos). The weaving changed from the double weave to the single weave during the Stylized Bee (TMK-3) era so you may find them in either configuration in that trademark. A few of the older marked figures will also sport a dark green hat instead of the normal reddish brown color. This piece was permanently retired in 1991.

GLOBE TROTTER, Hum 79. Left: Stamped Crown Mark (TMK-1), donut base, 4⅞". Right: Incised Full Bee (TMK-2), black "Germany", donut base, 5¼".

GLOBE TROTTER, Hum 79. Rear shot showing the old style double weave basket.

(continued)

Globe Trotter (cont'd)

GLOBE TROTTER, Hum 79. Rear view showing the different basket weave patterns discussed in text. Older is on the left.

GLOBE TROTTER, Hum 79. This photo shows the Final Issue Medallion and the new style single weave basket.

HUM NO.	BASIC SIZE	TRADE MARK	CURRENT VALUE
79	5"	TMK-1 CM	500-650.00
79	5"	TMK-2 FB	350-450.00
79(old style)	5"	TMK-3 Sty. Bee	250-300.00
79(new style)	5"	TMK-3 Sty. Bee	220-240.00
79	5"	TMK-4 3-line	200-210.00
79	5"	TMK-5 LB	180-190.00
79	5"	TMK-6 MB	180-190.00

LITTLE SCHOLAR
Hum 80

LITTLE SCHOLAR, Hum 80. Has the Full Bee (TMK-2) trademark, donut base, black "Germany" and measures 5⅝".

Little Scholar (cont'd)

There are no variations that have an effect on the normal value of each of the figures with the various trademarks. There is one variation, however, that may help you pick out the older pieces without picking them up and examining the bases. The Crown mark (TMK-1) and the Full Bee mark (TMK-2) pieces will have dark brown shoes instead of the lighter color of those afterward.

HUM NO.	BASIC SIZE	TRADE MARK		CURRENT VALUE
80	5½"	TMK-1	CM	390-480.00
80	5½"	TMK-2	FB	280-315.00
✗80	5½"	TMK-3	Sty. Bee	235-260.00
80	5½"	TMK-4	3-line	205-225.00
80	5½"	TMK-5	LB	195-205.00
80	5½"	TMK-6	MB	195.00

SCHOOL GIRL
Hum 81

There are no variations affecting the value of any of the models of this piece. There are, however, some worth noting. The smallest of the figures, the 81/2/0, 4" basic size, has flowers evident in the basket. All other sizes are devoid of flowers. The older figures have a black book bag and a pink blouse.

Has been found with the decimal point designator on the Crown mark (TMK-1), larger 5¼" basic size.

HUM NO.	BASIC SIZE	TRADE MARK		CURRENT VALUE
81/2/0	4¼"	TMK-1	CM	270-335.00
81/2/0	4¼"	TMK-2	FB	195-225.00
81/2/0	4¼"	TMK-3	Sty. Bee	165-175.00
81/2/0	4¼"	TMK-4	3-line	145-155.00
✗81/2/0	4¼"	TMK-5	LB	135-145.00
82/2/0	4¼"	TMK-6	MB	135.00
81.	5¼"	TMK-1	CM	400-485.00
81/0	5¼"	TMK-1	CM	350-435.00
81	5¼"	TMK-2	FB	300-325.00
81/0	5¼"	TMK-2	FB	250-270.00
81/0	5¼"	TMK-3	Sty. Bee	220-245.00
81/0	5¼"	TMK-4	3-line	185-210.00
81/0	5¼"	TMK-5	LB	175-185.00
81/0	5¼"	TMK-6	MB	175.00

SCHOOL GIRL, Hum 81. Left: 81/0 Full Bee mark, black "Germany", donut base, 5¼". Right: 81/0, Last Bee mark, 4⅞".

SCHOOL GIRL, Hum 81. Note the flowers in the basket. Stylized Bee trademark, 4½".

SCHOOL BOY
Hum 82

Sizes found in various lists are 4", 4¾", 5½" and 7½". Has been known as School Days in the past. Is occasionally found having the decimal point size designator in the Crown mark (TMK-1) pieces.
There are no other significant variations.

SCHOOL BOY, Hum 82/0. Left: Double Crown Mark, donut base, 4⅞". Center: Full Bee mark in an incised circle, black "Germany", 5". Right: Full Bee mark, black "Germany", donut base, 5¾".

HUM NO.	BASIC SIZE	TRADE MARK		CURRENT VALUE
82/2/0	4"	TMK-1	CM	270-335.00
82/2/0	4"	TMK-2	FB	195-225.00
82/2/0	4"	TMK-3	Sty. Bee	165-175.00
82/2/0	4"	TMK-4	3-line	145-155.00
82/2/0	4"	TMK-5	LB	135-145.00
82/2/0	4"	TMK-6	MB	135.00
82.	5½"	TMK-1	CM	400-485.00
82	5½"	TMK-1	CM	350-435.00
82	5½"	TMK-2	FB	300-325.00
82/0	5½"	TMK-2	FB	250-270.00
82/0	5½"	TMK-3	Sty. Bee	220-245.00
82/0	5½"	TMK-4	3-line	185-210.00
82/0	5½"	TMK-5	LB	175-185.00
82/0	5½"	TMK-6	MB	175.00
82/II	7½"	TMK-1	CM	800-1000.00
82/II	7½"	TMK-2	FB	575-650.00
82/II	7½"	TMK-3	Sty. Bee	475-550.00
82/II	7½"	TMK-5	LB	400-450.00
82/II	7½"	TMK-6	MB	400.00

ANGEL SERENADE WITH LAMB
Hum 83

There is another piece in the collection with a similar name. The other is in the nativity set. They are dissimilar, but the name may confuse you.

There are no significant variations, only minor changes over the years, but until recently there were apparently made in limited quantities in the trademarks from the Stylized Bee (TMK-3) until the Missing Bee mark (TMK-6) period to now where they seem to be available in quantities again.

ANGEL SERENADE WITH LAMB, Hum 83. Full Bee mark in an incised circle, black "Germany", 5¾".

HUM NO.	BASIC SIZE	TRADE MARK		CURRENT VALUE
83	5"	TMK-1	CM	395-500.00
83	5"	TMK-2	FB	275-315.00
83	5"	TMK-3	Sty. Bee	240-260.00
83	5"	TMK-4	3-line	210-230.00
83	5"	TMK-5	LB	195-210.00
83	5"	TMK-6	MB	195.00

Crown	CM	TMK-1	1934-1950
Full Bee	FB	TMK-2	1940-1959
Stylized Bee	Sty Bee	TMK-3	1958-1972
Three Line Mark	3-line	TMK-4	1964-1972
Last Bee Mark	LB	TMK-5	1970-1980
Missing Bee Mark	MB	TMK-6	1979-1991
Hummel Mark (Current)	HM	TMK-7	1991-Present

WORSHIP
Hum 84

Sizes reported in various lists are 5", 6¾", and 14½". Has been found with the decimal point size designator. The 84/V was temporarily withdrawn from production at the end of 1989 with no reinstatement date revealed. The small piece, 84/0 has been found in white overglaze. These are valued at $800-1000.00

WORSHIP, Hum 84. Mold number is rendered as 84./5. and the figurine bears the large Stylized Bee mark (TMK-3). It measures 13⅛" tall.

HUM NO.	BASIC SIZE	TRADE MARK		CURRENT VALUE
84.	5"	TMK-1	CM	340-400.00
84/0	5"	TMK-1	CM	290-360.00
84/0	5"	TMK-2	FB	210-240.00
84/0	5"	TMK-3	Sty. Bee	175-195.00
84/0	5"	TMK-4	3-line	155-175.00
84/0	5"	TMK-5	LB	145-155.00
84/0	5"	TMK-6	MB	145.00
84/V	13"	TMK-1	CM	1800-2800.00
84/V, 84/5	13"	TMK-2	FB	1350-1800.00
84/V, 84/5	13"	TMK-3	Sty. Bee	1100-1350.00
84/V, 84/5	13"	TMK-4	3-line	800-1100.00
84/V, 84/5	13"	TMK-5	LB	800-1100.00
84/V, 84/5	13"	TMK-6	MB	800-1100.00

SERENADE
Hum 85

Introduced in the late 1930's. It has undergone normal changes of style, colors and finishes over the years since, but none have had a significant impact on the collector value.

An interesting variation is with the boy's fingers on the flute. You can find them with some fingers extended (see color section for an example) while other versions have all fingers down. It seems, however, that there is no association with any particular mark or marks one way or the other.

The decimal designator can be found with the mold number on the older Crown mark (TMK-1) pieces in both sizes.

There is a beautiful blue colored Hum 85 in the 7½" size illustrated in the color section. It has no apparent markings. There has also been a Serenade found with the incised mold number 85/0. This one is painted with an air brush rather than the usual brush. Both of these are most likely prototypes that did not obtain the approval of the convent.

SERENADE, Hum 85/2. Full Bee mark, black "Germany", donut base, 7⅝".

HUM NO.	BASIC SIZE	TRADE MARK		CURRENT VALUE
85/4/0	3½"	TMK-5	LB	70-85.00
85/4/0	3½"	TMK-6	MB	90.00
85/0	4¾"	TMK-1	CM	240-305.00
✗85/0	4¾"	TMK-2	FB	175-190.00
85/0	4¾"	TMK-3	Sty. Bee	145-165.00
85/0	4¾"	TMK-4	3-line	130-145.00
85/0	4¾"	TMK-5	LB	120-130.00
85/0	4¾"	TMK-6	MB	120.00
85.	7½"	TMK-1	CM	875-1100.00
85/II	7½"	TMK-1	CM	825-1025.00
85/II	7½"	TMK-2	FB	585-635.00
85.	7½"	TMK-2	FB	635-685.00
85/II	7½"	TMK-3	Sty. Bee	490-525.00
85/II	7½"	TMK-4	3-line	440-465.00
85/II	7½"	TMK-5	LB	410-430.00
25/II	7½"	TMK-6	MB	410.00

HAPPINESS
Hum 86

Another late 1930's entry into the collection. There have been no changes or variations significant enough to affect value.

Sizes reported in various lists are 4½",4¼", 5", and 5½".

HAPPINESS, Hum 86. Left: Full Bee (TMK-2), black "Germany", 5⅛". Right: Last Bee (TMK-5) mark, 5½".

HUM NO.	BASIC SIZE	TRADE MARK		CURRENT VALUE
86	4¾"	TMK-1	CM	240-305.00
86	4¾"	TMK-2	FB	175-190.00
✗86	4¾"	TMK-3	Sty. Bee	145-165.00
86	4¾"	TMK-4	3-line	130-145.00
86	4¾"	TMK-5	LB	120-130.00
86	4¾"	TMK-6	MB	120.00

FOR FATHER
Hum 87

FOR FATHER, Hum 87. Left: Full Bee mark (TMK-2), donut base, black "Germany", red radishes, 5¹¹/₁₆". Right: Stamped Full Bee mark (TMK-2) in an incised circle, black "Western Germany", donut base, brown radishes, 5¾".

(continued)

For Father (cont'd)

For Father is yet another late 1930's release, formerly called "Father's Joy". The significant variations have to do with the beer stein and the color of the radishes.

A few early production, Crown mark (TMK-1) pieces have been found with the initials "HB" painted on the stein (see accompanying photograph). The radishes on these have a definite greenish cast and are rare.

The other important variation is found on Full Bee (TMK-2) and Stylized Bee (TMK-3) trademark figures only where the radishes are colored orange. The collector value for this variation is $3000-4200.00.

FOR FATHER, Hum 87. Mold number is rendered with the decimal designator 87., double Crown Mark, donut base. Note the "HB" on the stein standing for Hofbrau House in Munich. This is a very scarce item. Also there is a very distinct green highlighting on the radishes not appearing on any other variations.

HUM NO.	BASIC SIZE	TRADE MARK		CURRENT VALUE
87.	5½"	TMK-1	CM	395-500.00
87	5½"	TMK-1	CM	395-500.00
87	5½'	TMK-2	FB	275-315.00
87	5½"	TMK-3	Sty. Bee	240-260.00
87	5½"	TMK-4	3-line	210-230.00
✗ 87	5½"	TMK-5	LB	195-210.00
87	5½"	TMK-6	MB	195.00

HEAVENLY PROTECTION
Hum 88

HEAVENLY PROTECTION, Hum 88. Left: Full Bee (TMK-2) mark, base split in quarters beneath, black "Germany", 9⅜". Right: 88/II, small Stylized Bee (TMK-3), donut base, 8⅝".

(continued)

206

Heavenly Protection (cont'd)

It was first introduced in the late 1930's in the 9¼" size with a decimal designator 88. or 88 without the decimal in the Crown mark (TMK-1), the Full Bee (TMK-2) and the Stylized Bee (TMK-3) trademarks. The transition from the 88 to the 88/II mold number took quite some time. It began in the Full Bee era and was completed in the Stylized Bee era, so you can find the mold number rendered either way with those trademarks.

The large size has been found in white overglaze in the Crown and Full Bee marks.

There is a similar piece in the Goebel line that some theorize may have either inspired Heavenly Protection or was inspired by it. It is mold number HS 1 and is illustrated on page 74. Also see Hum 108.

HUM NO.	BASIC SIZE	TRADE MARK	CURRENT VALUE
88/I	6¾"	TMK-3 Sty. Bee	495-525.00
88/I	6¾"	TMK-4 3-line	425-450.00
88/I	6¾"	TMK-5 LB	400-425.00
88/I	6¾"	TMK-6 MB	395.00
88. or 88	9¼"	TMK-1 CM	1200-1500.00
88. or 88	9¼"	TMK-2 FB	950-1050.00
88. or 88	9¼"	TMK-3 Sty. Bee	750-850.00
88/II	9¼"	TMK-2 FB	850-1000.00
88/II	9¼"	TMK-3 Sty. Bee	725-800.00
88/II	9¼"	TMK-4 3-line	650-700.00
88/II	9¼"	TMK-5 LB	600-650.00
88/II	9¼"	TMK-6 MB	600.00

LITTLE CELLIST
Hum 89

There have been no major variations over the years, that would have an impact on the collector value of the figurine.

There are some differences worth noting. The newer models have a base that has flattened corners (see accompanying photograph). The older models have squared off corners. Also, in the older models, the boy's head is up and his eyes are wide open whereas on the new models the head is down and the eyes cast down as if concentrating on where he is stepping. The transition from old to new style was during the Stylized Bee (TMK-3) era so either the old or new can be found with this mark, the older obviously being the more desirable to collectors.

LITTLE CELLIST, Hum 89. Left: 89/I, double Crown Mark (TMK-1), 4⁹⁄₁₆". Right: 89/I, small Stylized Bee (TMK-3) mark, 5⁵⁄₁₆". Note the difference in the eyes and the bases of the old verses the newer piece.

LITTLE CELLIST, Hum 89. Left: 89/II, Stylized Bee (TMK-3) stamped in an incised circle, 7⅞", black "Western Germany". Right: 89/II, Last Bee (TMK-5) trademark, 7½". Note the textured hat and clothing on the newer of the two pieces and the different bases. (continued)

Little Cellist (cont'd)

HUM NO.	BASIC SIZE	TRADE MARK		CURRENT VALUE
89/I	6"	TMK-1	CM	395-500.00
89/I	6"	TMK-2	FB	275-315.00
89/I	6"	TMK-3	Sty. Bee	240-260.00
89/I	6"	TMK-4	3-line	210-230.00
89/I	6"	TMK-5	LB	195.00-210.00
89/I	6"	TMK-6	MB	195.00
89.	8"	TMK-1	CM	1400-1750.00
89	8"	TMK-1	CM	1200-1500.00
89/II	8"	TMK-2	FB	875-940.00
89/II	8"	TMK-3	Sty. Bee	700-800.00
89/II	8"	TMK-4	3-line	650-675.00
89/II	8"	TMK-5	LB	600-650.00
89/II	8"	TMK-6	MB	600.00

EVENTIDE and ADORATION
Bookends
Hum 90/A and Hum 90/B

Up until late 1984 it was thought that these pieces were never produced except in prototype and never released on the market. The Adoration half of the set has been found. It is not likely that these bookends were ever put into production, but more than one was obviously made as at least two of the Adoration halves have made it into private collections.

ADORATION bookend , Hum 90/B. No apparent markings. Measures 3¾" (figure only).

ANGEL AT PRAYER
Holy Water Font
Hum 91

The only notable variation is that the older ones have no halo and the newer models do. The transition from no halo to halo took place in the Stylized Bee (TMK-3) era there they may be found either way in that trademark.

(continued)

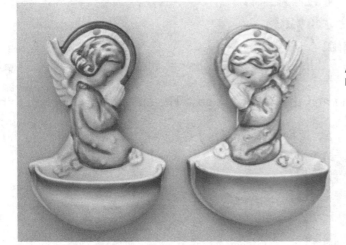

ANGELS AT PRAYER Font, Hum 91 A and Hum 91 B. Left: 91 B, Last Bee mark, 5''. Right: 91 A, Stylized Bee mark, 4⅞''.

HUM NO.	BASIC SIZE	TRADE MARK		CURRENT VALUE
91/A&B	2"x4¾"	TMK-1	CM	250-350.00
91/A&B	2"x4¾"	TMK-2	FB	150-200.00
91/A&B	2"x4¾"	TMK-3	Sty. Bee	130-140.00
91/A&B	2"x4¾"	TMK-3	Sty. Bee	120-130.00
91/A&B	2"x4¾"	TMK-4	3-line	100-110.00
91/A&B	2"x4¾"	TMK-5	LB	90-100.00
91/A&B	2"x4¾"	TMK-6	MB	90-100.00

MERRY WANDERER
Wall Plaque
Hum 92

There are two distinct sizes to be found in the Crown (TMK-1) and Full Bee (TMK-2) trademark pieces. The newer ones are all the smaller size. There are also some differences with regard to the placement of the incised *M.I. Hummel* signature, but there are no variations having a significant impact on the collector value. They have been found with the decimal designator in some older Crown mark examples.

MERRY WANDERER Plaque, Hum 92. Last Bee mark, 4¾'' x 5''.

HUM NO.	BASIC SIZE	TRADE MARK		CURRENT VALUE
92.	4¾"x15⅛"	TMK-1	CM	350-425.00
92	4¾"x5⅛"	TMK-1	CM	300-375.00
92	4¾"x5⅛"	TMK-2	FB	200-250.00
92	4¾"x5⅛"	TMK-3	Sty. Bee	185-200.00
92	4¾"x5⅛"	TMK-4	3-line	160-175.00
92	4¾"x5⅛"	TMK-5	LB	150-160.00
92	4¾"x5⅛"	TMK-6	MB	150.00

LITTLE FIDDLER
Wall Plaque
Hum 93

In current production, this plaque bears the Little Fiddler motif which appears many times in the collection. Less background detail in older models.

The accompanying photograph shows both the old and the newer designs. The older one is valued at about $2000-2500.00

Has been temporarily withdrawn from production as of December 31, 1991.

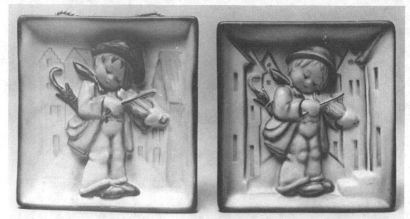

LITTLE FIDDLER Plaque, Hum 93. Left: 93., double Crown Mark, 4¾" x 5⅛". Right: Last Bee mark, 4¾" x 5⅛".

HUM NO.	BASIC SIZE	TRADE MARK		CURRENT VALUE
93	4¾x5⅛"	TMK-1	CM	300-375.00
93	4¾x5⅛"	TMK-2	FB	200-250.00
93	4¾x5⅛"	TMK-3	Sty. Bee	185-200.00
93	4¾x5⅛"	TMK-4	3-line	160-175.00
93	4¾x5⅛"	TMK-5	LB	150-160.00
93	4¾x5⅛"	TMK-6	MB	150.00

SURPRISE
Hum 94

First placed in the line in the late 1930's in two basic sizes, this figurine continues in production in those sizes today.

The 94/I size has been found erroneously marked 94/II. The error was apparently caught early for only a very few have shown up.

Older examples of the 94/I size have been found without the "/I".

SURPRISE, Hum 94. Left: Crown Mark, "U.S.-ZONE Germany", 5¾". Right: 94/1, Stylized Bee mark, 5½".

Surprise (cont'd)

HUM NO.	BASIC SIZE	TRADE MARK		CURRENT VALUE
94/3/0	4¼"	TMK-1	CM	280-350.00
94/3/0	4¼"	TMK-2	FB	200-240.00
94/3/0	4¼"	TMK-3	Sty. Bee	170-190.00
94/3/0	4¼"	TMK-4	3-line	150-170.00
94/3/0	4¼"	TMK-5	LB	140-150.00
94/3/0	4¼"	TMK-6	MB	149.00
94	5½"	TMK-1	CM	575-700.00
94	5½"	TMK-2	FB	400-440.00
94/I	5½"	TMK-1	CM	520-650.00
94/I	5½"	TMK-2	FB	375-415.00
94/I	5½"	TMK-3	Sty. Bee	315-350.00
94/I	5½"	TMK-4	3-line	275-300.00
94/I	5½"	TMK-5	LB	260-275.00
94/I	5½"	TMK-6	MB	260.00

BROTHER
Hum 95

The earliest Crown Mark (TMK-1) pieces can be found with the decimal point designator. There are no other variations of any great significance.

The figure has been known as "Our Hero". Older mold style comes with a blue coat.

BROTHER, Hum 95. Left: 95., no apparent trademark, but probably a Crown era piece, donut base, 5½". Center: Stylized Bee mark (TMK-3), 5⅝". Right: Missing Bee mark (TMK-6), 5⅝".

HUM NO.	BASIC SIZE	TRADE MARK		CURRENT VALUE
95.	5½"	TMK-1	CM	385-475.00
95	5½"	TMK-1	CM	360-450.00
95	5½"	TMK-2	FB	260-290.00
95	5½"	TMK-3	Sty. Bee	225-250.00
95	5½"	TMK-4	3-line	190-225.00
95	5½"	TMK-5	LB	180-190.00
95	5½"	TMK-6	MB	180.00

LITTLE SHOPPER
Hum 96

Introduced in the late 1930's, this figurine has changed little over the years. There are no changes or variations that have any influence on the collector value.

LITTLE SHOPPER, Hum 96. Small Stylized Bee (TMK-3), 4½''.

HUM NO.	BASIC SIZE	TRADE MARK		CURRENT VALUE
96	4¾''	TMK-1	CM	360-450.00
96	4¾''	TMK-2	FB	260-290.00
96	4¾''	TMK-3	Sty. Bee	225-250.00
96	4¾''	TMK-4	3-line	190-225.00
96	4¾''	TMK-5	LB	180-190.00
96	4¾''	TMK-6	MB	180.00

TRUMPET BOY
Hum 97

TRUMPET BOY, Hum 97. Stylized Bee mark (TMK-3), 4½''.

TRUMPET BOY, Hum 97. Shows the unique mold number rendering discussed in the accompanying text.

(continued)

Trumpet Boy (cont'd)

The boy's coat is normally green. Some of the older models, particularly the post-war U.S. Occupation era, have a blue painted coat. Trumpet Boy in the Crown mark (TMK-1) is fairly rare, but is found. The crown mark era piece will have "Design Patent No. 116, 464" inscribed beneath instead (see accompanying photo).

A query with a photograph to Goebel regarding this anomaly brought the following response: "The Trumpet Boy shown in the photo seems to be a very old figurine dating back to pre-war years. The bottom of the piece allows the assumption that production date may go back as far as the late 1930's (possibly cast from the first model). The stamp *Design Patent No. 116.464* indicates that the piece was originally shipped to England. All merchandise shipped at that time to that country was liable to be marked with the respective design patent number...".

The collector value for a Trumpet Boy so marked is $800-1200.00.

HUM NO.	BASIC SIZE	TRADE MARK		CURRENT VALUE
97	4¾"	TMK-1	CM era	240-305.00
97	4¾"	TMK-2	FB	175-190.00
97	4¾"	TMK-3	Sty. Bee	145-165.00
97	4¾"	TMK-4	3-line	130-145.00
97	4¾"	TMK-5	LB	120-130.00
97	4¾"	TMK-6	MB	120.00

SISTER
Hum 98

Introduced in the late 1930's in the 5¾" basic size, a smaller size was introduced during the Stylized Bee (TMK-3) trademark period.

Some of the large size from the Crown mark (TMK-1) era through the Stylized Bee (TMK-3) are found with the 98 mold number with and without the decimal designator.

SISTER, Hum 98. Left: Full Bee mark (TMK-2), black "Germany", donut base, 5¾". Right: 98/2/0, Last Bee mark (TMK-5), 1962 MID, 4¾".

(continued)

Sisters (cont'd)

HUM NO.	BASIC SIZE	TRADE MARK		CURRENT VALUE
98/2/0	4¾"	TMK-3	Sty. Bee	160-180.00
98/2/0	4¾"	TMK-4	3-line	140-155.00
98/2/0	4¾"	TMK-5	LB	130-140.00
98/2/0	4¾"	TMK-6	MB	130.00
✗98.	5¼"	TMK-1	CM	385-500.00
98.	5¾"	TMK-2	FB	285-340.00
98.	5¾"	TMK-3	Sty. Bee	250-300.00
98/0	5¾"	TMK-3	Sty. Bee	225-250.00
98/0	5¾"	TMK-4	3-line	190-225.00
98/0	5¾"	TMK-5	LB	180-190.00
98/0	5¾"	TMK-6	MB	180.00

EVENTIDE
Hum 99

There are three versions of this figurine to be found. Apparently when first released in the late 1930's the lambs were placed toward the left side of the base. For whatever reason they were moved to the right side soon after and there they remain to this day on current production models. This piece has also been found without the sheep appearing at all. The collector value range for both the left sheep and the no sheep variation is $2300-2800. There is also a rare white overglazed version valued at about the same.

EVENTIDE, Hum 99. Stylized Bee mark (TMK-3), 4½''.

HUM NO.	BASIC SIZE	TRADE MARK		CURRENT VALUE
99	4¾"	TMK-1	CM	630-825.00
99	4¾"	TMK-2	FB	450-500.00
99	4¾"	TMK-3	Sty. Bee	380-410.00
99	4¾"	TMK-4	3-line	335-360.00
99	4¾"	TMK-5	LB	315-335.00
99	4¾"	TMK-6	MB	315.00

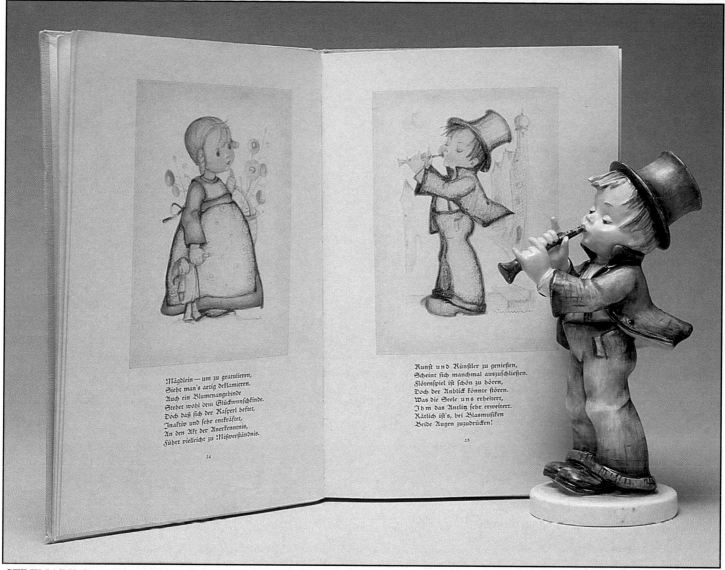

SERENADE, Hum 85 in all blue clothing. It measures 7½" high and has a donut base. No apparent markings. Displayed here with a like illustration from a German book illustrating Hummel drawings. It is likely a prototype that never made it into routine production.

RIDE INTO CHRISTMAS. An interesting five piece set from the Goebel factory illustrating an abbreviated version of painting process.

Left to Right: **MOTHER'S DARLING**, Hum 175. *Far Left:* Crown Mark, the bag in the right hand is pinkish and the upper part of her dress very light; Hum 175, Stylized Bee trademark, bag in right hand is blue and the upper part of the dress very dark.
SOLDIER BOY, Hum 332. Both of these bear the Three Line Mark. The one on the far right has the red medallion found on the earlier, more desirable pieces for collectors.

Left to Right: **WEARY WANDERER**, Hum 204. Both of these bear the Full Bee. The one on the left is probably the older of the two (the Full Bee is incised) and is referred to as the Blue eye variation. **LOST SHEEP**, Hum 68. Bears an incised Full Bee mark. It is the brown pants variation found on the older pieces. *Far Right:* Last Bee trademark figurine illustrating the normal clothing colors.

Left to Right: **KISS ME**, Hum 311. Bears the Three Line Mark, this is the older "socks on the doll variation"; Missing Bee mark with the regular no socks version. **HAPPY BIRTHDAY**, Hum 176. Both are Crown Marked pieces with the decimal designator 176., but the one on the far right also has a Full Bee mark. You can see that they are from different molds.

Left to Right: **HELLO**, Hum 124. The Figure on the far left is the green pants, pink vest variation found on the older pieces. The Last Bee marked figure to the right of the first one right is the norm for later releases. Next is **WAITER**, Hum 154, the older of the two Waiters, has an incised Crown Mark. It has gray pants. The far right figurine has the brown pants found on the newer releases.

SPRING CHEER, Hum 72. *Left to Right* there is a Full Bee piece, a small Stylized and a large Stylized Bee piece, a small Stylized and a large Stylized Bee piece. These three represent the major variations found in the older releases. The dress colors and the lack of flowers in the right hand are significant.

SENSITIVE HUNTER, Hum 6. The left, mold number 6, is a Crown Mark piece with the orange rabbit and "H" shaped suspenders on the back. The newer one on the right, 6/0 and missing Bee trademark, has the now common brown rabbit and "X" configuration of the suspenders.

WITH LOVING GREETINGS, Hum 309. The figurine on the left is an early (Full Bee) release. Note the presence of a stopper for the blue ink well. The Next two are both later (Missing Bee or TMK-6) and have the blue and purple inkwells respectively.

MAMAS AND PAPAS, Hum 189 and Hum 181. There are no apparent marks on these two examples.

BOOKWORM, Hum 3. *Left* is a Crown Mark piece. Note the black and white duck on the book. On the *right* is the later, Missing Bee piece with the duck in color. Each of these is the mold number 3/3, 9½" size. The left hand figure is a "Doll Face" or Faience piece. The other is a white overglaze. For further information please refer to the listing for Bookworm, Hum 3.

FRIENDS, Hum 136. A white overglaze and a terra cotta version. Both are Crown Mark pieces.

Holy Water Fonts. The *left* font bears the *M.I. Hummel* incised signature, but has no other apparent markings whatever.
The *center* one is the **Cross With Doves** font, Hum 77. It has the Crown (TMK-1) Mark and the incised signature on the back.
The font on the *right* is Hum 241, **Angel With Lute** that was never placed into regular production.

Left to Right: **BOOKWORM,** Hum 3. *Far left* is a Crown Mark mold number 3. Next is a mold number 3/I with the Missing Bee trademark. The next pair is **MEDITATION**, Hum 13. The first has a double Crown Mark. Note the flowers in the basket. *Far right,* the newer, Missing Bee marked piece has no flowers in the basket. The latter is todays normal production.

Left to Right: **BEGGING HIS SHARE**, Hum 9. A very unusual Crown Mark Hum 9 utilizing oversize shoes as a base instead of the regular base. The next is a Full Bee mark Hum 9. The next pair is **AUF WIEDERSEHN**, Hum 153. These are examples of the handkerchief / no handkerchief in the boy's left hand variation. The first of this pair is a Full Bee and the second, far right is a Stylized Bee piece.

Left Pair: **HEAVENLY SONG CANDLE HOLDER**, Hum 113. The left one in this pair bears a double Crown Mark and the right one, a Stylized Bee. *Right pair:* **ADVENT GROUP CANDLE HOLDER**, Hum 31. Both are Crown Mark pieces and bear the incised 31. mold number (note the decimal point).

SILENT NIGHT CANDLE HOLDER, Hum 54. *Left to Right:* Double Full Bee mark, incised and stamped; Full Bee mark; Last Bee mark.

Reading *Left to Right* the first pair is **SIGNS OF SPRING**, Hum 203 2/0. Both are Full Bee pieces. The left figure has both feet down and wearing shoes. The other is the variation with a raised bare foot. The third figure is **BIRD LOVERS** or **ADORATION WITH BIRD**, Hum 105. Full Bee, incised 1948 Mold Induction Date. *Far right* is **LITTLE VELMA**, Hum 219/2/0, Full Bee.

LET'S SING ASHTRAY, Hum 114. Both are Full Bee Marked. Shows the reverse mold variation on the left.

JOYFUL ASHTRAY, Hum 33. The one on the left ia a "Doll Face" or faience piece. Typically porcelain-like with unusual coloration. Both bear the Crown Mark.

Internationals. *Left to Right:* **HUNGARIAN**, Hum 851, double Crown Mark; **HUNGARIAN**, Hum 851, Crown and Full Bee marks; **SWEDISH**, Hum 825, Crown and Full Bee marks; No apparent marks, but known to be **SERBIAN**, Hum 812; No apparent marks, but known to be **SERBIAN**, Hum 812.

Internationals. *Left to Right:* **BULGARIAN**, no incised mold number, Hum 808, no trademark; **BULGARIAN**, Hum 808, Crown Mark, no country identification, no apparent marks; **HUNGARIAN**, Hum854, double Crown Mark.

Internationals. *Left to Right:* **SERBIAN** with no apparent mold number or trademark; **SERBIAN**, Hum 813, Crown Mark; **CZECHO-SLOVAKIAN**, Hum 968, Full Bee mark; **CZECHOSLOVAKIAN**, Hum 841, Crown Mark.

Internationals. *Left to Right:* **HUNGARIAN**, Hum 853, Crown Mark; **HUNGARIAN**, Hum 852, Crown Mark; **SWEDISH**, Hum 824; **SWEDISH**, Hum 824; **SWEDISH**, Hum 824. Note the blue eyes.

Internationals. *Left to Right:* **CZECHOSLOVAKIAN**, Hum 842, Full Bee mark; **CZECHOSLOVAKIAN**, Hum 842, Crown Mark; Country unknown, Crown Mark; **SERBIAN**, Hum 913; **SERBIAN**, Hum 913, "(R)".

Internationals. *Left to Right:* **SERBIAN**, Hum 947/0, Crown Mark; **SERBIAN**, Hum 947/0, double Crown Mark; **BULGARIAN**, Hum 810, double Crown Mark; **BULGARIAN**, Hum 810, Crown Mark.

Internationals. *Left to Right:* **BULGARIAN**, Mel. 9, double Crown Mark; **BULGARIAN**, Bul.2, Crown Mark; **SERBIAN**, Hum 904, Full Bee mark; **BULGARIAN**, Hum 811, double Crown Mark.

Internationals. *Left to Right:* Country unknown, no apparent markings; **SLOVAK** dress, there is an incised 82 or 89, but known to be Hum 831; Probably **SERBIAN**, Hum 806.

Left to Right: **FOR FATHER**, Hum 87, Full Bee mark with orange turnips (carrots?); Full Bee mark with the normal color turnips. **CONGRATULATIONS**, Hum 17/0. Last Bee trademark. *Far right:* Older, Stylized Bee mark. Note the absence of socks and other differences.

Left to Right: A pair of **CINDERELLAS,** Hum 337. *Far left:* A Full Bee piece with a fourth bird (on left shoulder). From the collection of Katherine Stephens. *Center:* A Last Bee marked, normal version. *Far Right:* A yet to be released **LITTLEST ANGEL,** Hum 365 with the Three Line Mark and an incised 1964 MID.

MADONNA HOLDING CHILD. *Left to Right:* Blue clock, Hum 151, Full Bee; Brown clock, Hum 151, Crown and Full Bee marks; White overglaze, Hum 151, double Full Bee mark.

FLOWER MADONNA. *Left to Right:* Normal color, Hum 10/III, Stylized Bee mark; Beige robe with orange piping, Hum 10/3, Stylized Bee mark; White overglaze, Hum 10/III, Stylized Bee mark.

MADONNA WITH HALO.
Detail of the halos showing the stars on the underside of the Hum 45's and the color variations.

FLOWER MADONNA.
Left to Right: Beige robe with orange piping, Hum 10/1, Stylized Bee mark; Beige robe with no piping, Hum 10./1, double Crown Mark; Blue robe, blue bird, Hum 10/1, Stylized Bee mark; White overglaze, Hum 10/1, Stylized Bee mark.

MADONNAS WITH HALO, Hum 45/0 and **WITHOUT HALOS,** Hum 46/0.
Left to Right: With halo, normal color, blue stars in halo, Last Bee mark; With halo, white overglaze, Stylized Bee mark; With halo, normal color, red stars in halo, Full Bee mark; Without halo, normal color, Stylized Bee mark; Without halo, white overglaze, Stylized Bee mark.

SHRINE
Table Lamp
Hum 100

Extremely rare 7½" table lamp. As far as can be determined only three or four exist in collector's hands presently. The lamps found so far bear the Crown or the Full Bee trademarks. There are two versions of lamp post. The most common is the tree trunk post. The rarest is the fluted post and valued at about $4000-5000.00

TO MARKET
Table Lamp
Hum 101

There are two versions of this 7½" lamp with regard to the lamp stem or post. Of the few that have been found most exhibit the "tree trunk" base (see accompanying photograph). The more rare is the less elaborate, fluted stem.

HUM NO.	BASIC SIZE	TRADE MARK	CURRENT VALUE
101(plain)	7½"	TMK-1 CM	4000-5000.00
101(tree trunk)	7½"	TMK-1 CM	1200-1500.00
101	7½"	TMK-2 FB	700-1000.00
101	7½"	TMK-3 Sty. Bee	500-600.00

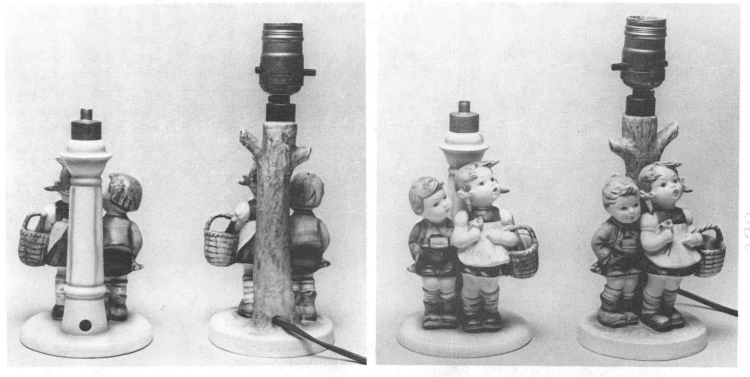

TO MARKET table lamp, Hum 101. Rear view showing the regular and the tree trunk style lamp stem.

TO MARKET table lamp, Hum 101. Left: Full Bee mark (TMK-2), 6½''. Right: Stylized Bee in an incised circle, 7⅛''.

215

VOLUNTEERS
Table Lamp
Hum 102

There are only a few examples of this piece known to exist in private collections at present. The few found so far all bear the Crown trademark and have a plain white post. They are valued at $4000-5000.00

FAREWELL
Table Lamp
Hum 103

This is an extremely rare piece of which there are very few known to exist presently. If sold it could bring up to $5000.00

EVENTIDE
Table Lamp
Hum 104

Very few examples of this table lamp known to be in any collector's hands at present. If sold it could bring up to $5000.00

ADORATION WITH BIRD or BIRD LOVERS
Hum 105

First discovered about 1977 this piece was not previously thought to exist. It bears the mold number 105. This number was a "Closed Number", a number supposedly never having been used and never to be used on an original Hummel piece. There have been at least 10 to 15 more found since the initial discovery. As is custom the original finder named the piece "Bird Lovers". It is sometimes known as "Adoration with Bird" because of its similarity to Hum 23, "Adoration". The major variation in them is in the girl's pigtail. A Hum 105 in fine condition is valued at $5000-7000.00

BIRD LOVERS or **ADORATION WITH BIRD,** Hum 105. Double Crown Mark (TMK-1), split base, 4¹³⁄₁₆''.

MERRY WANDERER
Wall Plaque in a Wooden Frame
Hum 106

Limited examples of this extremely rare plaque have been found. It was apparently only made a short time. Perhaps this is because the plaque is basically the same as Hum 92 except for the wooden frame. Those that have been found all have the Crown Mark (TMK-1). They are valued at about $4000.00

LITTLE FIDDLER
Wall Plaque in a Wooden Frame
Hum 107

Limited examples of this extremely rare plaque have been found. It was apparently only made for a short time. Perhaps this is because the plaque is basically the same as Hum 93 except for the wooden frame. Those that have been found all have the Crown mark (TMK-1). They are valued at about $4000.00

ANGEL WITH BOY AND GIRL AT FEET
Wall Plaque in Relief
Hum 108 (Closed Number)

It is unlikely that any of these will ever find their way into collectors' hands. It cannot be certain that it is even an angel with children as described in the name above. There is a 1950's Goebel catalog listing for a plaque as described, but it is not listed as a Hummel design. The deduction is made because of the description similar to the name and the mold number designation of 108 listed in factory records. Please refer to pages 74 & 207.

HAPPY TRAVELER
Hum 109

This figurine was placed in production in the late 1930's in a 5" basic size. An 8" basic size was added in the Full Bee (TMK-2) era. The large size was retired in 1982.

There has been a curious variation to surface in the 109/0 size. The normal colors for the figurine is a brown hat and green jacket. The variation has a green hat and a blue jacket. It has no trademark and is the only one known. It may be unique.

HUM NO.	BASIC SIZE	TRADE MARK		CURRENT VALUE
109/0	5"	TMK-1	CM	260-325.00
109/0	5"	TMK-2	FB	190-210.00
109/0 or 109	5"	TMK-3	Sty. Bee	100-180.00
109/0 or 109	5"	TMK-4	3-line	140-155.00
109/0 or 109	5"	TMK-5	LB	130-140.00
109/0	5"	TMK-6	MB	130.00
109.	8"	TMK-1	CM	1000-1200.00
109/II	8"	TMK-2	FB	700-800.00
109/II	8"	TMK-3	Sty. Bee	400-500.00
109/II	8"	TMK-4	3-line	350-400.00
109/II	8"	TMK-5	LB	325-350.00
109/II	8"	TMK-6	MB	325-350.00

(continued)

HAPPY TRAVELER, Hum 109. Left is mold number 109/0 with Full Bee (TMK-2) mark, a donut base, 5⅛", black "Germany". Right has mold number 109, Last Bee (TMK-5) trademark and measures 4¾".

HAPPY TRAVELER, Hum 109/0. Left: a Full Bee piece with black "Germany", donut base and the normal green color coat. Right: This is a doll face Hum 109/0 with a blue plaid coat. It has no apparent base markings. Both measure 5".

LET'S SING
Hum 110

One of the group of new designs to be introduced in the late 1930's there have been no variations significant enough to have any impact on the normal pricing structure for the various pieces.

LET'S SING, Hum 110. Left: Bears no mold number, Full Bee (TMK-2) trademark, 3½", black "Germany", "© W. Goebel". Center: Mold number 110/0, Three Line Mark (TMK-4), 1938 MID, 3". Right: Mold number 110/0, Last Bee (TMK-5), 3¼".

HUM NO.	BASIC SIZE	TRADE MARK		CURRENT VALUE
110	3½"	TMK-1	CM	350-480.00
110	3½"	TMK-2	FB	250-325.00
110/0	3¼"	TMK-1	CM	230-400.00
110/0	3¼"	TMK-2	FB	160-190.00
110/0	3¼"	TMK-3	Sty. Bee	140-160.00

(continued)

Let's Sing (cont'd)

110/0	3¼"	TMK-4	3-line	125-140.00
✗110/0	3¼"	TMK-5	LB	115-125.00
110/0	3¼"	TMK-6	MB	115.00
110/I	3⅞"	TMK-1	CM	310-400.00
110/I	3⅞"	TMK-2	FB	220-250.00
110/I	3⅞"	TMK-3	Sty. Bee	190-220.00
110/I	3⅞"	TMK-4	3-line	165-180.00
110/I	3⅞"	TMK-5	LB	155-165.00
110/I	3⅞"	TMK-6	MB	155.00

LET'S SING
Hum III/110
Candy Box

There are two styles of candy boxes. The transition from the old to the new took place during the Stylized Bee (TMK-3) period. There are, therefore, the old and the new to be found in the Stylized Bee mark. Temporarily removed from production in 1989 with no reinstatement date.

LET'S SING candy dish, Hum III/110. Last Bee mark (TMK-5).

HUM NO.	BASIC SIZE	TRADE MARK		CURRENT VALUE
III/110	6"	TMK-1	CM	450-530.00
III/110	6"	TMK-2	FB	350-400.00
III/110(old)	6"	TMK-3	Sty. Bee	275-325.00
III/110(new)	6"	TMK-3	Sty. Bee	150-200.00
III/110	6"	TMK-4	3-line	120-150.00
III/110	6"	TMK-5	LB	120-150.00
III/110	6"	TMK-6	MB	120-150.00

Crown	CM	TMK-1	1934-1950
Full Bee	FB	TMK-2	1940-1959
Stylized Bee	Sty Bee	TMK-3	1958-1972
Three Line Mark	3-line	TMK-4	1964-1972
Last Bee Mark	LB	TMK-5	1970-1980
Missing Bee Mark	MB	TMK-6	1979-1991
Hummel Mark (Current)	HM	TMK-7	1991-Present

WAYSIDE HARMONY
Hum 111

Introduced in the late 1930's. It has changed a bit over the years, but there are no variations that have any significant impact on the value.

There does exist a curious variation where the bird is missing. This is an aberation wherein the bird was probably inadvertently left off during assembly. This sometimes happens to small parts and is not considered a rare variation.

This piece has been known to appear with Roman Numeral size designators instead of the Arabic number indictated.

HUM NO.	BASIC SIZE	TRADE MARK		CURRENT VALUE
111/3/0	3¾"	TMK-1	CM	270-335.00
111/3/0	3¾"	TMK-2	FB	195-220.00
111/3/0	3¾"	TMK-3	Sty. Bee	165-190.00
111/3/0	3¾"	TMK-4	3-line	145-165.00
111/3/0	3¾"	TMK-5	LB	135-145.00
111/3/0	3¾"	TMK-6	MB	135.00
111.	5"	TMK-1	CM	535-650.00
111/1	5"	TMK-1	CM	490-610.00
111/1	5"	TMK-2	FB	350-390.00
111/1	5"	TMK-3	Sty. Bee	300-330.00
111/1	5"	TMK-4	3-line	265-285.00
111/1	5"	TMK-5	LB	245-265.00
111/1	5"	TMK-6	MB	245.00

WAYSIDE HARMONY, Hum 111. Left: 111/1, incised Full Bee mark, black "Germany", © W. Goebel", 5½". Right: 111/I, Three Line Mark, incised 1938 MID, 5⅛".

WAYSIDE HARMONY
Table Lamp
Hum II/111 or Hum II/112

This lamp was made for a short period of time in the 1950's. Perhaps to avoid confusion and/or to conform with the mold numbering system, the lamp was slightly redesigned and assigned a new number, 224 (see page 286). Whatever the reason, there are a few of these II/111 Wayside Harmony lamps around. They occur in the Crown, Full Bee and Stylized Bee trademarks. Quite scarce, but for some reason are valued at only $300-450.00

JUST RESTING
Table Lamp
Hum II/112

This lamp was made for a short period of time in the 1950's. Perhaps to avoid confusion and/or conform the mold numbering system the number was changed to 225 with a concurrent slight redesign. Whatever the reason, there are a few of these II/112 Just Resting lamps around. They occur in the Crown, Full Bee and Stylized Bee trademarks. Quite scarce, for some reason they are valued at only $300-450.00

JUST RESTING
Hum 112

There have been no variations significant enough to influence the normal pricing structure of this piece. There has been one example of a curious variation found on the 112/1 size where there is no basket present on the base. This is probably an inadvertant omission while then it was being assembled, that somehow slipped by the quality control inspectors. It happens occasionally with small pieces such as bottles in baskets and birds. It is not usually considered important, just a curiosity.

JUST RESTING, Hum 112/1. Left: Stamped and incised Full Bee (TMK-2) mark, black "Germany", W. Goebel, 5⅛". Right: Three Line Mark (TMK-4), 1938 MID, 4⅞".

Just Resting (cont'd)

HUM NO.	BASIC SIZE	TRADE MARK		CURRENT VALUE
112/3/0	3¾"	TMK-1	CM	265-330.00
✗112/3/0	3¾"	TMK-2	FB	195-215.00
112/3/0	3¾"	TMK-3	Sty. Bee	165-185.00
112/3/0	3¾"	TMK-4	3-line	145-160.00
112/3/0	3¾"	TMK-5	LB	135-145.00
112/3/0	3¾"	TMK-6	MB	135.00
112	5"	TMK-1	CM	545-665.00
112/I	5"	TMK-1	CM	500-625.00
112/I	5"	TMK-2	FB	360-400.00
112/I	5"	TMK-3	Sty. Bee	300-340.00
112/I	5"	TMK-4	3-line	260-290.00
112/I	5"	TMK-5	LB	250-260.00
112/I	5"	TMK-6	MB	250.00

HEAVENLY SONG
Candleholder
Hum 113

HEAVENLY SONG candle holder, Hum 113. Left. Double Crown Mark (TMK-1), 3½". Note the shiny, porcelain-like finish and atypical paint. Right: Large Stylized Bee (TMK-3) in an incised circle, black "Western Germany", 2⅝".

This four figure piece is a candleholder. It is quite similar to Hum 54 and was produced in extremely small numbers. There are in fact, only a few known to reside in private collections. The actual number is not known, but less than 50 would be a reasonable estimation. They do pop up from time to time and have been found in the Crown, Full Bee, Stylized Bee and Last Bee trademarks. The Goebel company announced in 1981 that they were removing Heavenly Song from production permanently. It is considered extremely rare in any of the trademarks.

HUM NO.	BASIC SIZE	TRADE MARK		CURRENT VALUE
113	3½x4¾"	TMK-1	CM	5000-6000.00
113	3½x4¾"	TMK-2	FB	4000-5000.00
113	3½x4¾"	TMK-3	Sty. Bee	3000-4000.00
113	3½x4¾"	TMK-5	LB	1000-2000.00

LET'S SING
Ashtray
Hum 114

This piece is an ashtray with a figure very like Hum 110 at the edge of the dish. It is found with the figure on either the right or left side of the tray. The older ones have the figure on the right side. There are very few of this variation known. It was changed during the Full Bee (TMK-2) so it can be found with either the Crown or Full Bee trademark.

    This, as all the ashtrays in the line is listed as temporarily withdrawn from production with no reinstatement given.

LET'S SING ashtray, Hum 114. Left: Last Bee Mark (TMK-5), 3⅝". Right: Full Bee mark (TMK-2), 3½".

HUM NO.	BASIC SIZE	TRADE MARK		CURRENT VALUE
114 (rev. mold)	3½"x6¾"	TMK-1	CM	400-500.00
114 (rev. mold)	3½"x6¾"	TMK-2	FB	300-350.00
114	3½"x6¾"	TMK-2	FB	200-225.00
114	3½"x6¾"	TMK-3	Sty. Bee	150-175.00
114	3½"x6¾"	TMK-4	3-line	125-140.00
114	3½"x6¾"	TMK-5	LB	100-110.00
114	3½"x6¾"	TMK-6	MB	100-110.00

ADVENT GROUP
Candleholders
Hum 115, Girl with Nosegay
Hum 116, Girl with Fir Tree
Hum 117, Boy with Horse

    This is a group of three figures with a Christmas theme, each of the figures provided with a candle receptacle. Hum 115 is a girl holding flowers, Hum 116 is a girl with a Christmas tree, and Hum 117 is a boy with a toy horse. The original models were made with the "Mel" prefix followed by 1, 2 and 3 for 115, 116 and 117 respectively. These were prototypes, but many apparently got into the market (see page 70).

HUM NO.	BASIC SIZE	TRADE MARK		CURRENT VALUE
115,116,117	3½"	TMK-1	CM	400-480.00(set)
115,116,117	3½"	TMK-2	FB	185-200.00(set)
115,116,117	3½"	TMK-3	Sty. bee	175-185.00(set)
115,116,117	3½"	TMK-4	3-line	160-175(set)
115,116,117	3½"	TMK-5	LB	150-160.00(set)
115,116,117	3½"	TMK-6	MB	150(set)

(continued)

ADVENT GROUP candle holders. Left: Hum 115, small Stylized Bee (TMK-3) mark, 3½''. Center: Hum 116, small Stylized Bee mark, 3⅝''. Right: Hum 117, small Stylized Bee, 3½''.

LITTLE THRIFTY
Hum 118

This figurine, introduced in the late 1930's, is also a coin bank. It is usually found with a key and lockable metal plug beneath the base, but these are sometimes lost over the years.

Although not terribly significant in terms of value there is a difference in designs between the older and the newer pieces. The most obvious is a less thick base on the new design. This design change took place during the Stylized Bee (TMK-3) trademark period, so the old and the new designs can be found with that mark.

HUM NO.	BASIC SIZE	TRADE MARK		CURRENT VALUE
118	5''	TMK-1	CM	260-350.00
118	5''	TMK-2	FB	200-225.00
118	5''	TMK-3	Sty. Bee	160-180.00
118	5''	TMK-4	3-line	140-155.00
118	5''	TMK-5	LB	130-140.00
118	5''	TMK-6	MB	130.00

LITTLE THRIFTY, Hum 118. The one on the left represents the older design. It measures 5½'', has the large Stylized Bee (TMK-3) trademark and bears a black "Germany" beneath the base. The one on the right has the Last Bee (TMK-5) trademark and is 5⅛'' in height. Note the variation in the bases.

POSTMAN
Hum 119

Introduced about 1940 there have been several different sizes and distinct mold variations despite the one size always listed until the new smaller version 119/2/0 was released in 1989. With the release of the 119/2/0, the larger 119 became 119/0 beginning with the Missing Bee (TMK-6) trademark pieces.

There are no variations significant enough to influence normal values for the Postman.

HUM NO.	BASIC SIZE	TRADE MARK		CURRENT VALUE
119/2/0	4½"	TMK-6	MB	115-120.00
119	5¼"	TMK-1	CM	250-315.00
119	5¼"	TMK-2	FB	180-200.00
119	5¼"	TMK-3	Sty. Bee	150-170.00
119	5¼"	TMK-4	3-line	135-150.00
119	5¼"	TMK-5	LB	125-135.00
119	5¼"	TMK-6	MB	125.00
119/0	5¼"	TMK-6	MB	125.00

POSTMAN, Hum 119. Left: Stylized Bee (TMK-3) mark, 4⅞".
Right: 119 2/0, Missing Bee (TMK-6) mark, 1985 MID, 4½".

JOYFUL and LET'S SING
Double Figure on a Wooden Base
Hum 120

No examples known to be in a private collection. Factory records only.

WAYSIDE HARMONY and JUST RESTING
Bookends
Hum 121/A and Hum 121/B

No examples known to be in a private collection. Factory archives only. The figures on the wooden bases of the bookends are very similar to the Hum 111 and Hum 112, but have different incised mold numbers.

PUPPY LOVE and SERENADE WITH DOG
Bookends
Hum 122

No examples known to be in a private collection. Factory archives only. These are the figurines without bases mounted on wooden bases of bookends.

MAX AND MORITZ
Hum 123

Released about 1940 this figurine was once known as "Good Friends".

There is an important variation to be noted. There have been a few Crown Mark (TMK-1) examples found that have black hair rather than the lighter, blonde hair. In fact, they appear to be painted in darker colors overall. When found, these pieces are valued at about $3000.00

MAX AND MORITZ, Hum 123. The one on the right is the older, bearing the Full Bee Mark (TMK-2) it has a donut base and an incised 1939 MID, is 5⅜" tall and has W. Goebel inscribed in script. The left figure has the 3-line mark (TMK-4), measures 5" and has a donut base.

HUM NO.	BASIC SIZE	TRADE MARK		CURRENT VALUE
123	5¼"	TMK-1	CM	420-525.00
123	5¼"	TMK-2	FB	305-325.00
123	5¼"	TMK-3	Sty. Bee	245-275.00
123	5¼"	TMK-4	3-line	215-245.00
123	5¼"	TMK-5	LB	205-215.00
123	5¼"	TMK-6	MB	205.00

HELLO
Hum 124

Introduced around 1940, this figurine was once known as "Chef, Hello". When first released it had grey pants and coat and a pink vest. This changed to green pants, brown coat and pink vest and then finally to the brown coat and pants with white vest used on the pieces from sometime in the Stylized Bee (TMK-3) trademark period to the present. The variation in shortest supply is the green pants version.

It has been found with the decimal designator in the Crown and Full Bee trademarked figures. The 124/I size has been temporarily removed from production with no reinstatement date given.

HUM NO.	BASIC SIZE	TRADE MARK		CURRENT VALUE
124.	6½"	TMK-1	CM	650-750.00
124.	6½"	TMK-2	FB	400-500.00
124/0	6¼"	TMK-2	FB	275-315.00
124/0	6¼"	TMK-3	Sty. Bee	240-260.00
124/0	6¼"	TMK-4	3-line	210-230.00
124/0	6¼"	TMK-5	LB	195-210.00
124/0	6¼"	TMK-6	MB	195.00
124/I	7"	TMK-1	CM	550-650.00
124/I	7"	TMK-2	FB	350-450.00

(continued)

Hello (cont'd)

HUM NO.	BASIC SIZE	TRADE MARK		CURRENT VALUE
124/I	7"	TMK-3	Sty. Bee	275-325.00
124/I	7"	TMK-4	3-line	240-250.00
124/I	7"	TMK-5	LB	220-230.00
124/I	7"	TMK-6	MB	220-230.00

HELLO, Hum 124. Right: 124/0, Full Bee (TMK-2) in an incised circle, donut base, black "Germany" beneath the base, five buttons on vest only four of which are painted, green pants, brown jacket, red hair, 6¼". Right: 124/I, Missing Bee (TMK-5) mark, donut base, five painted buttons, brown pants, purple jacket, brown hair, 6⅜".

VACATION TIME
Wall Plaque
Hum 125

There are two distinctly different designs. The transition from the old to the new took place in the Stylized Bee (TMK-3) period, so you can find the old and the new styles in that trademark. The newest style has now lost one fence picket for a count of five. The old has six.

VACATION TIME Plaque, Hum 125. Left: Full Bee mark, 6 pickets in the fence, 4⅜" x 5⅜". Right: Last Bee mark, 5 pickets in the fence, 4 x 4⅞".

Vacation Time (cont'd)

HUM NO.	BASIC SIZE	TRADE MARK		CURRENT VALUE
125	4⅜"x5¼"	TMK-1	CM	500-600.00
125	4⅜"x5¼"	TMK-2	FB	250-325.00
125	4"x4¾"	TMK-3	Sty. Bee	185-195.00
125	4"x4¾"	TMK-4	3-line	180.00
125	4"x4¼"	TMK-5	LB	175.00
125	4"x4¼"	TMK-6	MB	175.00

RETREAT TO SAFETY
Wall Plaque
Hum 126

This plaque was released around 1940 and has been in continuous production until 1989 when it was temporarily withdrawn from production. No reinstatement date has been given.

RETREAT TO SAFETY Plaque, Hum 126.

HUM NO.	BASIC SIZE	TRADE MARK		CURRENT VALUE
126	4¾"x4¾"	TMK-1	CM	500-600.00
126	4¾"x4¾"	TMK-2	FB	250-325.00
126	4¾"x4¾"	TMK-3	Sty. Bee	185-195.00
126	4¾"x4¾"	TMK-4	3-line	180-185.00
126	4¾"x4¾"	TMK-5	LB	175-185.00
126	4¾"x4¾"	TMK-6	MB	175.00

DOCTOR
Hum 127

Introduced in the line about 1940. On the Crown Mark (TMK-1) and Full Bee (TMK-2) figures the doll's feet extend slightly beyond the edge of the base. They must have proved vulnerable because the feet were restyled so they no longer exend over the base. The sizes in various lists range from 4¾" to 5¼". The larger sizes are generally the older pieces.

HUM NO.	BASIC SIZE	TRADE MARK		CURRENT VALUE
127	4¾"	TMK-1	CM	290-360.00
127	4¾"	TMK-2	FB	200-250.00
127	4¾"	TMK-3	Sty. Bee	175-200.00
127	4¾"	TMK-4	3-line	150-175.00
127	4¾"	TMK-5	LB	145-150.00
127	4¾"	TMK-6	MB	145.00

(continued)

Doctor (cont'd)

DOCTOR, Hum 127. Full Bee mark, black "Germany", donut base, 5¼".

BAKER
Hum 128

Although this figure, like most, underwent changes over the years none are important enough to influence the normal values of the pieces in each trademark.

HUM NO.	BASIC SIZE	TRADE MARK		CURRENT VALUE
128	4¾"	TMK-1	CM	350-445.00
128	4¾"	TMK-2	FB	250-285.00
128	4¾"	TMK-3	Sty. Bee	220-245.00
128	4¾"	TMK-4	3-line	185-220.00
128	4¾"	TMK-5	LB	175-185.00
128	4¾"	TMK-6	MB	175.00

BAKER, Hum 128. Left: Full Bee mark, black "Germany", donut base, 51/8". Center: Stylized Bee mark, 4¾". Right: Missing Bee mark, 4⅞".

BAND LEADER
Hum 129

Another circa 1940 release. This figure has not been found with any significant mold variations.

There was a new, smaller size without the music stand introduced in 1987 as the fourth in a four part series of small figurines matching four mini-plates in the same motif.

BAND LEADER, Hum 129. Left: Full Bee mark in an incised circle, black Germany, split base in quarters, 6". Right: Last Bee mark 5⅛".

HUM NO.	BASIC SIZE	TRADE MARK		CURRENT VALUE
129/4/0	3½"	TMK-5	LB	90-100.00
129/4/0	3½"	TMK-6	MB	90.00
129	5¼"	TMK-1	CM	360-450.00
129	5¼"	TMK-2	FB	260-290.00
129	5¼"	TMK-3	Sty. Bee	230-260.00
129	5¼"	TMK-4	3-line	190-215.00
129	5¼"	TMK-5	LB	180-190.00
129	5¼"	TMK-6	MB	180.00

DUET
Hum 130

Some older Crown trademark pieces have a very small lip on the front of the base; sort of a mini version of the stepped or double base variation on the Merry Wanderer. These lip base Duets also have incised musical notes on the sheet music and are valued at about $1000-1200.00.

Another variation is the absence of the kerchief on the figure sporting the top hat. This is found on some Full Bee (TMK-2) and Stylized Bee (TMK-3) pieces. If found, these are valued at about $2000-3500.00

HUM NO.	BASIC SIZE	TRADE MARK		CURRENT VALUE
130	5¼"	TMK-1	CM	500-625.00
130	5¼"	TMK-2	FB	350-400.00
130	5¼"	TMK-3	Sty. Bee	300-330.00
130	5¼"	TMK-4	3-line	260-290.00
130	5¼"	TMK-5	LB	250-260.00
130	5¼"	TMK-6	MB	250.00

(continued)

Duet (cont'd)

DUET, Hum 130. Left: 130., double incised Crown Marks one of which is colored blue, 5¼". Right: Full Bee mark, black "Germany", 5⅝".

STREET SINGER
Hum 131

This figure was introduced about 1940 in one size and has remained in one size to current production. There are no significant mold variations to be found.

STREET SINGER, Hum 131. Left: The mold number is 131., but there is no trademark apparent. The underlined word "Originalmuster" on the side of the base is partially visible in the photo here. This indicates that this was at one time a master model. Right: Stylized Bee mark, 5".

HUM NO.	BASIC SIZE	TRADE MARK		CURRENT VALUE
131	5"	TMK-1	CM	340-410.00
131	5"	TMK-2	FB	240-275.00
131	5"	TMK-3	Sty. Bee	200-240.00
131	5"	TMK-4	3-line	180-200.00
131	5"	TMK-5	LB	170-180.00
131	5"	TMK-6	MB	170.00

STAR GAZER
Hum 132

A few of the older Crown mark (TMK-1) have a darker blue or purple shirt while the normal color after that is a lighter blue or purple.

The straps on the boy's lederhosen are normally crossed in the back. If there are no straps, the value is increased; perhaps valued at 20% above the normal value.

STARGAZER, Hum 132. Left: Full Bee mark in an incised circle, black "Germany", 4⅞". Right: Stylized Bee mark, split base, 4⅞".

HUM NO.	BASIC SIZE	TRADE MARK		CURRENT VALUE
132	4¾"	TMK-1	CM	395-500.00
132	4¾"	TMK-2	FB	275-315.00
✗132	4¾"	TMK-3	Sty. Bee	240-260.00
132	4¾"	TMK-4	3-line	210-230.00
132	4¾"	TMK-5	LB	195-210.00
132	4¾"	TMK-6	MB	195.00

MOTHER'S HELPER
Hum 133

Released about 1939-1940 in a 5" basic size, this figurine has remained essentially unchanged since. The basic size of 5" has also remained the same although older versions of it are generally larger than the newer models.

MOTHER'S HELPER, Hum 133. The original 1939 design is represented by the figure on the left. It bears the small Stylized Bee (TMK-3) trademark in an incised circle and measures 5". The right figure in the photo is a Last Bee (TMK-5) piece. It has a donut base and is 4¾" tall.

(continued)

Mother's Helper (cont'd)

HUM NO.	BASIC SIZE	TRADE MARK		CURRENT VALUE
133	5"	TMK-1	CM	350-420.00
133	5"	TMK-2	FB	250-290.00
133	5"	TMK-3	Sty. Bee	205-250.00
133	5"	TMK-4	3-line	185-205.00
133	5"	TMK-5	LB	175-185.00
133	5"	TMK-6	MB	175.00

QUARTET
Wall Plaque
Hum 134

Another of the circa 1940 releases, the plaque has remained in the line since in the same basic size. There are no significant mold variations influencing the normal pricing structure. It has been temporarily removed from production without a reinstatement date.

QUARTET, Plaque, Hum 134. Stylized Bee mark, 5½" x 6¼".

HUM NO.	BASIC SIZE	TRADE MARK		CURRENT VALUE
134	6"x6"	TMK-1	CM	600-725.00
134	6"x6"	TMK-2	FB	360-400.00
134	6"x6"	TMK-3	Sty. Bee	300-350.00
134	6"x6"	TMK-4	3-line	265-285.00
134	6"x6"	TMK-5	LB	250-265.00
134	6"x6"	TMK-6	MB	250.00

SOLOIST
Hum 135

Released in the early 1940's and called High Tenor at the time, it has remained in continuous production since. It has no significant mold variations influencing values.

There was a new smaller version, 135/4/0 released in 1986, as the third in a series of small figurines and matching mini plates for a total of four in the series. Because of the new size designator in the smaller model the larger model is now incised with the mold number 135/0. This change was instigated in the Missing Bee mark (TMK-6) era.

HUM NO.	BASIC SIZE	TRADE MARK		CURRENT VALUE
135/4/0	3½"	TMK-5	MB	90-100.00
135/4/0	3½"	TMK-6	LB	90.00
135	4¾"	TMK-1	CM	240-310.00
135	4¾"	TMK-2	FB	175-200.00

(continued)

Soloist (cont'd)

SOLOIST, Hum 135. 4⅞", Stylized Bee (TMK-3) trademark, black "Western Germany".

HUM NO.	BASIC SIZE	TRADE MARK		CURRENT VALUE
⚹135	4¾"	TMK-3	Sty. Bee	150-175.00
135	4¾"	TMK-4	3-line	130-150.00
135	4¾"	TMK-5	LB	120-150.00
135	4¾"	TMK-6	MB	120.00
135/0	4¾"	TMK-6	MB	120.00

FRIENDS
Hum 136

Sizes found in various lists were 5", 10¾", and 11½". There have been at least two examples of this piece found that are made of a terra cotta. These are in the 136/V size. The terra cotta pieces are valued at about $9000-12,000.

Released circa 1940 in two sizes, it was originally known as "Good Friends".

Also found in white overglaze in the Crown mark (TMK-1), this very rare variation is valued at $3,500-4,000.

FRIENDS, Hum 136. Left: 136., Crown Mark, white overglaze, 11¼". Center: 136., Crown Mark, terra cotta finish, 10¼". Right: 136., Crown Mark, "U.S. ZONE Germany", 10¾".

234

(continued)

Friends (cont'd)

HUM NO.	BASIC SIZE	TRADE MARK		CURRENT VALUE
136/I	5"	TMK-1	CM	400-500.00
136/I	5"	TMK-2	FB	275-325.00
136/I	5"	TMK-3	Sty. Bee	250-275.00
136/I	5"	TMK-4	3-line	210-250.00
136/I	5"	TMK-5	LB	195-210.00
136/I	5"	TMK-6	MB	195.00
136	10¾"	TMK-1	CM	3000-3300.00
136	10¾"	TMK-2	FB	2000-2200.00
136/V	10¾"	TMK-1	CM	2000-2300.00
136/V	10¾"	TMK-2	FB	1500-1700.00
136/V	10¾"	TMK-3	Sty. Bee	1300-1400.00
136/V	10¾"	TMK-4	3-line	1100-1300.00
136/V	10¾"	TMK-5	LB	1080-1100.00
136/V	10¾"	TMK-6	MB	1080.00

CHILD IN BED
Wall Plaques
Hum 137/A and Hum 137/B

The mold number is found as "137/B" until the Last Bee (TMK-5) when the "B" was dropped. Until recently it was speculated that there might have been a matching piece with the mold number 137/A. A few of these have now surfaced. Apparently they were never produced in any quantity and are valued at $5,000-7500.00.

Hum 137 (no B) is in current production.

HUM NO.	BASIC SIZE	TRADE MARK		CURRENT VALUE
137/B	2¾"x2¾" (round)	TMK-1	CM	300-400.00
137/B	2¾"x2¾" (round)	TMK-2	FB	150-175.00
137/B	2¾"x2¾" (round)	TMK-3	Sty. Bee	100-125.00
137/B	2¾"x2¾" (round)	TMK-4	3-line	65-70.00
137	2¾"x2¾" (round)	TMK-5	LB	60-65.00
137	2¾"x2¾" (round)	TMK-6	MB	60.00

CHILD IN BED Plaque, Hum 137/B. Stylized Bee mark, 3".

BABY IN CRIB
Wall Plaque
Hum 138

    Although all records of the factory indicate that this piece was never released for sale to the consumer and only prototypes were produced, at least six are known to reside in private collections. It dates from around 1940.

    They have only been found with the Full Bee (TMK-2) trademark to date. They are valued at $4000-5500.00 presently.

FLITTING BUTTERFLY
Wall Plaque
Hum 139

    This piece was out of current production for some time. It has been reissued in a new mold design with the same number.

    Released circa 1940, it has not undergone any significant mold variation that would affect the normal value for the various trademarked pieces.

HUM NO.	BASIC SIZE	TRADE MARK		CURRENT VALUE
139	2½"x2½"	TMK-1	CM	120-175.00
139	2½"x2½"	TMK-2	FB	85-100.00
139	2½"x2½"	TMK-3	Sty. Bee	70-85.00
139	2½"x2½"	TMK-4	3-line	65-70.00
139	2½"x2½"	TMK-5	LB	60-65.00
139	2½"x2½"	TMK-6	MB	60.00

FLITTING BUTTERFLY Plaque, Hum 139. Full Bee mark in an incised circle, 2⅜" square.

THE MAIL IS HERE
or
MAIL COACH
Wall Plaque
Hum 140

MAIL COACH Plaque, Hum 140. Last Bee trademark, 6¾" x 4½".

236

(continued)

Mail Coach Plaque (cont'd)

This plaque predates the figurine by the same name and design. It was introduced into the line around 1940.

While there are no significant mold variations there is a finish variation of importance. There were some of these plaques produced in white overglaze for the European market in the early days. They are found bearing the Crown mark (TMK-1) and are valued at $1000-1500.00

HUM NO.	BASIC SIZE	TRADE MARK		CURRENT VALUE
140	4½"x6¼"	TMK-1	CM	500-600.00
140	4½"x6¼"	TMK-2	FB	250-350.00
140	4½"x6¼"	TMK-3	Sty. Bee	185-200.00
140	4½"x6¼"	TMK-4	3-line	180-185.00
140	4½"x6¼"	TMK-5	LB	175-180.00
140	4½"x6¼"	TMK-6	MB	175.00

APPLE TREE GIRL
Hum 141

This figure has also been known as "Spring". Sizes found in various lists are as follows: 4", 4¼", 6", 6¾", 10", 10½", 29". Two references were made in the list to a "rare old base" and a "brown base". This is apparently a reference to the "tree trunk base" variation. When found this variation will bring about 30% more than the value in the chart below. The 4" size has no bird perched on the branch as do all the larger sizes, although there has been at least one, a 141/I, reported having no bird. Perhaps it was inadvertently omitted by a factory worker.

APPLE TREE GIRL, Hum 141. Left 141 3/0, Full Bee mark, black "Germany", painted brown base, 4⁵⁄₁₆". Right: 141 3/0, Full Bee mark, black "Germany", 4¼".

HUM NO.	BASIC SIZE	TRADE MARK		CURRENT VALUE
141/3/0	4"	TMK-1	CM	260-325.00
141/3/0	4"	TMK-2	FB	200-220.00
141/3/0	4"	TMK-3	Sty. Bee	160-190.00
141/3/0	4"	TMK-4	3-line	140-160.00

(continued)

Apple Tree Girl (cont'd)

HUM NO.	BASIC SIZE	TRADE MARK		CURRENT VALUE
✱ 141/3/0	4"	TMK-5	LB	130-140.00
141/3/0	4"	TMK-6	MB	130.00
141	6"	TMK-1	CM	600-750.00
141	6"	TMK-2	FB	400-450.00
141/I	6"	TMK-1	CM	500-650.00
141/I	6"	TMK-2	FB	350-400.00
141/I	4"	TMK-3	Sty. Bee	300-350.00
141/I	6"	TMK-4	3-line	260-300.00
141/I	6"	TMK-5	LB	245-260.00
141/I	6"	TMK-6	MB	245.00
141/V	10½"	TMK-3	Sty. Bee	1350-1400.00
141/V	10½"	TMK-5	LB	1080-1200.00
141/V	10½"	TMK-6	MB	1080.00
141/V	10½"	TMK-5	LB	*16,900.00

*There are a few of these "Jumbo" figures in collectors' hands. They are generally used as promotional figures in showrooms and shops. Rarely do they bring full retail price. They have been temporarily withdrawn from production.

APPLE TREE BOY
Hum 142

This figure has also been known as "Fall". Sizes found in various lists are as follows: 3¾", 4", 4½", 6", 6½", 10", 10½" and 29". Two references were made in the list to a "rare old base" and a "brown base". This is apparently a reference to the "tree trunk base" variation. When found this variation will bring about 30% more than the figure in the value chart on the next page. The 4" size has no bird perched on the branch as do all the larger sizes.

APPLE TREE BOY, Hum 142. Left: 142 3/0, double Full Bee mark (incised and stamped), black "Germany", old style rounded, brown color base, 4". Right: 142 3/0, Stylized Bee mark in an incised circle, newer style base, 3¹⁵⁄₁₆".

(continued)

Apple Tree Boy (cont'd)

HUM NO.	BASIC SIZE	TRADE MARK		CURRENT VALUE
142/3/0	4"	TMK-1	CM	260-325.00
142/3/0	4"	TMK-2	FB	200-220.00
✗ 142/3/0	4"	TMK-3	Sty. Bee	160-190.00
142/3/0	4"	TMK-4	3-line	140-160.00
142/3/0	4"	TMK-5	LB	130-140.00
142/3/0	4"	TMK-6	MB	130.00
142	6"	TMK-1	CM	600-750.00
142	6"	TMK-2	FB	400-450.00
142/I	6"	TMK-1	CM	500-650.00
142/I	6"	TMK-2	FB	350-400.00
142/I	6"	TMK-3	Sty. Bee	300-350.00
142/I	6"	TMK-4	3-line	260-300.00
142/I	6"	TMK-5	LB	245-260.00
142/I	6"	TMK-6	MB	245.00
142/V	10¼"	TMK-3	Sty. Bee	1350-1400.00
142/V	10¼"	TMK-5	LB	1080-1200.00
142/V	10¼"	TMK-6	MB	1080.00
142/X	29"	TMK-5	LB	*16,900.00

*There are a few of these "Jumbo" figures in collectors' hands. They are generally used as promotional figures in showrooms and shops. Rarely do they bring full retail price. They have been temporarily withdrawn from production.

BOOTS
Hum 143

First released around 1940 in two basic sizes. Although there are many size variations to be encountered, none of the variations is significant in terms of affecting value.

BOOTS, Hum 143. Left: Full Bee mark, black "Germany", donut base 6¹³⁄₁₆". Right: 143/1, Stylized Bee mark, donut base, 6¾".

(continued)

Boots (cont'd)

HUM NO.	BASIC SIZE	TRADE MARK		CURRENT VALUE
143/0	5¼"	TMK-1	CM	360-450.00
143/0	5¼"	TMK-2	FB	260-290.00
143/0	5¼"	TMK-3	Sty. Bee	225-250.00
143/0	5¼"	TMK-4	3-line	190-225.00
143/0	5¼"	TMK-5	LB	180-190.00
143/0	5¼"	TMK-6	MB	180.00
143/I	6¾"	TMK-1	CM	600-750.00
143/I	6¾"	TMK-2	FB	400-500.00
143/I	6¾"	TMK-3	Sty. Bee	350-400.00
143/I	6¾"	TMK-4	LB	300-350.00
143/I	6¾"	TMK-5	MB	300.00

ANGELIC SONG
Hum 144

There are no significant variations of Angelic Song affecting the normal values of the pieces bearing the various trademarks. First released about 1940.

HUM NO.	BASIC SIZE	TRADE MARK		CURRENT VALUE
144	4¼"	TMK-1	CM	270-335.00
144	4¼"	TMK-2	FB	200-225.00
144	4¼"	TMK-3	Sty. Bee	165-185.00
144	4¼"	TMK-4	3-line	145-160.00
144	4¼"	TMK-5	LB	135-145.00
144	4¼"	TMK-6	MB	135.00

ANGELIC SONG, Hum 144. Last Bee mark, 4⅛".

Crown	CM	TMK-1	1934-1950
Full Bee	FB	TMK-2	1940-1959
Stylized Bee	Sty Bee	TMK-3	1958-1972
Three Line Mark	3-line	TMK-4	1964-1972
Last Bee Mark	LB	TMK-5	1970-1980
Missing Bee Mark	MB	TMK-6	1979-1991
Hummel Mark (Current)	HM	TMK-7	1991-Present

LITTLE GUARDIAN
Hum 145

Released in the early 1940's. This figurine has no variation significant enough to affect values. It is still in production today.

HUM NO.	BASIC SIZE	TRADE MARK		CURRENT VALUE
145	3¾"	TMK-1	CM	270-335.00
145	3¾"	TMK-2	FB	200-225.00
145	3¾"	TMK-3	Sty. Bee	165-185.00
145	3¾"	TMK-4	3-line	145-165.00
145	3¾"	TMK-5	LB	135-145.00
145	3¾"	TMK-6	MB	135.00

LITTLE GUARDIAN, Hum 145. Measures 3⅝" tall and has the Last Bee (TMK-5) trademark.

ANGEL DUET
Holy Water Font
Hum 146

There have been many variations with regard to the shapes and positions of the heads and wings, but none significant. This font has been in continuous production since their introduction in the early 1940's.

HUM NO.	BASIC SIZE	TRADE MARK		CURRENT VALUE
146	2"x4¾"	TMK-1	CM	395-500.00
146	2"x4¾"	TMK-2	FB	275-315.00
146	2"x4¾"	TMK-3	Sty. Bee	240-260.00
146	2"x4¾"	TMK-4	3-line	210-230.00
146	2"x4¾"	TMK-5	LB	195-210.00
146	2"x4¾"	TMK-6	MB	195.00

ANGEL DUET Font, Hum 146. Stylized Bee mark, 4⅝".

ANGEL SHRINE
Holy Water Font
Hum 147

In continuous production since its release in the early 1940's, there are no important mold or finish variations affecting their value.

HUM NO.	BASIC SIZE	TRADE MARK		CURRENT VALUE
147	3"x5"	TMK-1	CM	100-150.00
147	3"x5"	TMK-2	FB	75-90.00
147	3"x5"	TMK-3	Sty. Bee	60-75.00
147	3"x5"	TMK-4	3-line	55-60.00
147	3"x5"	TMK-5	LB	50-55.00
147	3"x5"	TMK-6	MB	50.00

DEVOTION Font, Hum 147. Stylized Bee mark, 5¼".

UNKNOWN
Hum 148
Closed Number Designation

Records indicate that this piece could be a Farm Boy (Hum 66) with no base. No examples have even been found. You can remove the figure from the bookend Hum 60/A and have the same figure, but the mold number would not be present.

UNKNOWN
Hum 149
Closed Number Designation

Records indicate that this could be a Goose Girl (Hum 47) with no base. No known examples in collectors' hands. You can remove the figure from the bookend Hum 60/B and have the same piece, but the mold number would not be present.

HAPPY DAYS
Hum 150

Sizes reference in price lists were: 4¼", 5¼", 6" and 6¼". Has been known as "Happy Little Troubadours" in the past. Known to appear with the decimal point size designator.

There are no mold or finish variations significant enough to influence values.

HUM NO.	BASIC SIZE	TRADE MARK		CURRENT VALUE
150/2/0	4¼"	TMK-2	FB	225-260.00
150/2/0	4¼"	TMK-3	Sty. Bee	200-225.00
150/2/0	4¼"	TMK-4	3-line	170-200.00
150/2/0	4¼"	TMK-5	LB	160-170.00
150/2/0	4¼"	TMK-6	MB	160.00
150/0	5¼"	TMK-2	FB	375-425.00

(continued)

Happy Days (cont'd)

HUM NO.	BASIC SIZE	TRADE MARK		CURRENT VALUE
150/0	5¼"	TMK-3	Sty. Bee	325-375.00
150/0	5¼"	TMK-4	LB	270.00
150/0	5¼"	TMK-5	MB	270.00
150	6"	TMK-1	CM	1000-1500.00
150	6"	TMK-2	FB	700-800.00
150/I	6"	TMK-1	CM	900-1400.00
150/I	6"	TMK-2	FB	600-700.00
150/I	6"	TMK-3	Sty. Bee	470-485.00
150/I	6"	TMK-5	LB	430-450.00
150/I	6"	TMK-6	MB	430.00

HAPPY DAYS, Hum 150. Left: 150/0. Full Bee (TMK-2) mark, black "Germany", split base, 5¼". Right: 150/0, Last Bee (TMK-5) mark, 5⅛".

MADONNA HOLDING CHILD
Hum 151

Sometimes called the "Blue Cloaked Madonna" because of its most common painted finish, this figure was temporarily withdrawn from production in 1989, but is back in production in the blue and white overglaze as per the 1993 Goebel price listing.

It has also appeared in other finishes. The three finishes that are the most rare and sought after are those with the rich dark brown cloak, a dark blue and an ivory colored cloak. Always occurring in the Crown mark (TMK-1) these are valued at $8000-12,000.00 depending on condition.

Sizes found referenced range from 12" to 14" and it has appeared with the Crown, Full Bee and Stylized Bee marks. It has appeared in blue cloak, white overglaze, and in a brown cloak. The brown cloak is the most rare. (See color section.) The white overglaze and blue cloak are both listed as reinstated.

MADONNA HOLDING CHILD, Hum 151. Left: The Brown Cloak Madonna with decimal designator mold number "151.". It has an incised Crown Mark (TMK-1) and a stamped Full Bee (TMK-2) mark, a black Germany and measures 12½". Center: Double Full Bee (TMK-2), one incised and one stamped. White overglaze measuring 12⅞". Right: Blue cloak, Full Bee mark, 12¾".

HUM NO.	BASIC SIZE	TRADE MARK		CURRENT VALUE	
				(color)	(white)
151	12"	TMK-1	CM	1350-1750.00	600-700.00
151	12"	TMK-2	FB	800-1100.00	460-500.00
151	12"	TMK-4	LB	675-725.00	320-375.00
151	12"	TMK-5	MB	675.00	320.00

Crown	CM	TMK-1	1934-1950
Full Bee	FB	TMK-2	1940-1959
Stylized Bee	Sty Bee	TMK-3	1958-1972
Three Line Mark	3-line	TMK-4	1964-1972
Last Bee Mark	LB	TMK-5	1970-1980
Missing Bee Mark	MB	TMK-6	1979-1991
Hummel Mark (Current)	HM	TMK-7	1991-Present

UMBRELLA BOY
Hum 152/A

Introduced in one size in the early 1940's. A second, smaller size was introduced in the Full Bee mark (TMK-2) period.

There are no mold or finish variation that have any affect on value.

The earliest Crown mark (TMK-1) examples were produced with the incised mold number "152".

Left: **UMBRELLA BOY**, Hum 152/A. 152 O A, Three Line Mark (TMK-4), incised 1957 MID, 4⅝" Right: **UMBRELLA GIRL**, Hum 152/B. 152/O B, Three Line Mark, incised 1957 MID, 4¾".

HUM NO.	BASIC SIZE	TRADE MARK		CURRENT VALUE
152/0A	5"	TMK-2	FB	775-825.00
152/0A	5"	TMK-3	Sty. Bee	650-680.00
152/0A	5"	TMK-4	3-line	550-600.00
152/0A	5"	TMK-5	LB	530-550.00
152/0A	5"	TMK-6	MB	530.00
152	8"	TMK-1	CM	3000-5000.00
152/A	8"	TMK-2	FB	2000-2500.00
152/A	8"	TMK-3	Sty. Bee	1500-1700.00
152/A	8"	TMK-4	3-line	1400-1450.00
152/A	8"	TMK-5	LB	1300-1400.00
152/A	8"	TMK-6	MB	1300.00

UMBRELLA GIRL
Hum 152/B

Obviously created to match the Umbrella Boy, one wonders why it was introduced several years after it at the end of the 1940's. In any case, it also may be found in two sizes, the smaller appearing in the Full Bee trademark period. There are not significant variations affecting values.

HUM NO.	BASIC SIZE	TRADE MARK		CURRENT VALUE
152/0B	4¾"	TMK-2	FB	775-825.00
152/0B	4¾"	TMK-3	Sty. Bee	650-680.00
152/0B	4¾"	TMK-4	3-line	550-600.00

(continued)

Umbrella Girl (cont'd)

HUM NO.	BASIC SIZE	TRADE MARK		CURRENT VALUE
152/0B	4¾"	TMK-5	LB	530-550.00
152/0B	4¾"	TMK-6	MB	530.00
152/B	8"	TMK-1	CM	3000-5000.00
152/B	8"	TMK-2	FB	2000-2500.00
152/B	8"	TMK-3	Sty. Bee	1500-1700.00
152/B	8"	TMK-4	3-line	1400-1450.00
152/B	8"	TMK-5	LB	1300-1400.00
152/B	8"	TMK-6	MB	1300.00

AUF WIEDERSEHEN
Hum 153

First released in the mid-1940's in the 7" basic size, the English translation is "Good Bye". A smaller size was introduced during the Full Bee (TMK-2) era.

There is an extremely rare version of this double figure piece where the little boy wears a Tyrolean cap. This variation is found only in the 153/0 size. In most examples of these pieces he wears no hat but is waving a handkerchief as is the girl. The rare version is valued at about $2500-3000.00. Sizes referred in various lists follow: 5½", 5⅞". (See color section) The 153/I size is listed as reinstated.

HUM NO.	BASIC SIZE	TRADE MARK		CURRENT VALUE
153/0	5¼"	TMK-1	CM	440-550.00
153/0	5¼"	TMK-2	FB	315-350.00
153/0	5¼"	TMK-3	Sty. Bee	260-290.00
153/0	5¼"	TMK-4	3-line	230-260.00
153/0	5¼"	TMK-5	LB	220-230.00
153/0	5¼"	TMK-6	MB	220.00
153/0	5¼"	TMK-1	CM	540-725.00
153/0	5¼"	TMK-2	FB	375-425.00
153/0	5¼"	TMK-3	Sty. Bee	285-320.00
153/0	5¼"	TMK-5	LB	270-285.00
153/0	5¼"	TMK-6	MB	270.00

AUF WIEDERSEHN, Hum 153. Left: 153/O, Full Bee mark, black "Germany", 5¼". Right: 153/O Stylized Bee, 5⅜".

WAITER
Hum 154

First released in the 1940's in two sizes.

This figure has appeared with several different labels on the wine bottle. All are now produced with a "Rhine Wine" label. Earlier versions have much darker pants than those in current production. The variation where the label on the bottle reads "Whiskey" is in the Full Bee (TMK-2) era and is valued at $2000.00

WAITER, Hum 154. Left to right, A through D.
A. 154., Crown mark, donut base, "U.S. ZONE Germany", 6½".
B. 154., Crown mark, donut base, black "Germany", 6½".
C. 154/O, Full Bee mark, Donut base, Black "Germany", 6⅛".
D. 154/1 Stylized Bee mark, donut base, 6¹³⁄₁₆".

HUM NO.	BASIC SIZE	TRADE MARK		CURRENT VALUE
154/0	6"	TMK-1	CM	395-500.00
154/0	6"	TMK-2	FB	275-325.00
154/0	6"	TMK-3	Sty. Bee	240-260.00
154/0	6"	TMK-4	3-line	210-230.00
✳154/0	6"	TMK-5	LB	195-210.00
154/0	6"	TMK-6	MB	195.00
154	7"	TMK-1	CM	750-850.00
154	7"	TMK-2	FB	400-450.00
154	7"	TMK-1	CM	520-650.00
154	7"	TMK-2	FB	375-425.00
154	7"	TMK-3	Sty. Bee	300-350.00
154	7"	TMK-5	LB	260-300.00
154	7"	TMK-6	MB	260.00

UNKNOWN
Hum 155
Closed Number Designation

Records indicate this to possibly be a Madonna holding child. No known examples.

UNKNOWN
Hum 156
Closed Number Designation

Records indicate this to possibly be a wall plaque of a mother and child. No known examples.

UN-NAMED
Hum 157
Closed Number

This is a 1940's prototype of a figurine where the boy is dressed much more formally than that of the typical figurine. This figurine was apparently not approved by the convent and was never put into regular production. No examples are known to be outside factory archives.

UN-NAMED
Hum 158
Closed Number

This is a 1940's prototype of a figurine where the girl is dressed much more formally than that of the typical figurine. This figure was apparently not approved by the convent and was never put into regular production. No examples are known to be outside factory archives.

Hum 157 & 158.
Referred to as "Town Children", this boy and girl were never named or produced. As you'll recognize immediately, the subjects are slimmer and more citified than the rural look that is typical of *M.I. Hummel* children. These samples were sculpted in 1943.
Photo courtesy *M.I. Hummel* Club.

CLOSED NUMBERS
Hum 156 through Hum 162
Closed Number Designations

Until recently these numbers have been listed as unknown. Records indicate these six were modeled and considered for production but never released. There are sample models of some of them in the Goebel archives and they are atypical of *M.I. Hummel* figurines. They do not wear the traditional costumes, but rather appear to be dressed in more modern clothes. Sister Maria Innocentia is known to have asked on at least one occasion, "How shall I draw for the Americans?" It is pure conjecture, but one can only wonder if these pieces were possibly an attempt to produce a few for the American market and not approved. None known outside the archives. See photo on page 248.

WHITSUNTIDE
Hum 163

This figure is sometimes known as "Happy New Year". It is one of the early, (mid 1940) releases and was removed from production about 1960 and reinstated in 1977. The older pieces are very scarce and highly sought by collectors. The angel below appears holding a red or a yellow candle in older versions, without the candle in newer ones.

HUM NO.	BASIC SIZE	TRADE MARK		CURRENT VALUE
163.	7¼"	TMK-1	CM	1000-1200.00
163	7¼"	TMK-1	CM	800-1000.00
163	7¼"	TMK-2	FB	600-750.00
163	7¼"	TMK-3	Sty. Bee	350-335.00
163	7¼"	TMK-4	3-line	305-335.00
163	7¼"	TMK-5	LB	290-305.00
163	7¼"	TMK-6	MB	290.00

WHITSUNTIDE, Hum 163. Left: Incised Crown Mark, red candle in angels hand. Right: Last Bee trademark (TMK-5), no candle. Both measure 6¾".

WHITSUNTIDE, Hum 163. Full Bee mark in an incised circle, black "Western Germany", split base (in quarters), 7".

WORSHIP
Holy Water Font
Hum 164

From its introduction to the line in the mid-1940's to current production models there have been no significant variations that have any impact on value.

WORSHIP Font, Hum 164. Left: 164., Crown Mark, black "Germany", 4¹³⁄₁₆''. Right: Stylized Bee mark, 4⅞''.

HUM NO.	BASIC SIZE	TRADE MARK		CURRENT VALUE
164	2¾''x4¾''	TMK-1	CM	100-150.00
164	2¾''x4¾''	TMK-2	FB	70-80.00
164	2¾''x4¾''	TMK-3	Sty. Bee	60-70.00
164	2¾''x4¾''	TMK-4	3-line	55-60.00
164	2¾''x4¾''	TMK-5	LB	50-55.00
164	2¾''x4¾''	TMK-6	MB	50.00

SWAYING LULLABY
Wall Plaque
Hum 165

Introduced in the 1940's, this plaque was apparently made in limited quantities and then removed from production at some point in time. It does occur in all trademarks, however, and was reinstated in 1978, only to be withdrawn from production again in 1989 with no specific date given for reinstatement.

HUM NO.	BASIC SIZE	TRADE MARK		CURRENT VALUE
165	4½''x5¼''	TMK-1	CM	600-750.00
165	4½''x5¼''	TMK-2	FB	400-500.00
165	4½''x5¼''	TMK-3	Sty. Bee	300.00
165	4½''x5¼''	TMK-5	LB	200.00
165	4½''x5¼''	TMK-6	MB	200.00

SWAYING LULLABY Plaque, Hum 165. Full Bee mark, 4½'' x 5¼''.

BOY WITH BIRD
Ashtray
Hum 166

Introduced into the collection in the mid-1940's it has been in continuous production until 1989 when it was listed as temporarily withdrawn with no reinstatement date. There are no significant mold or finish variations.

BOY WITH BIRD Ashtray, Hum 166. Last Bee mark (TMK-5), 3¼'' x 6''.

HUM NO.	BASIC SIZE	TRADE MARK		CURRENT VALUE
166	3¼"x6¼"	TMK-1	CM	300-400.00
166	3¼"x6¼"	TMK-2	FB	200-250.00
166	3¼"x6¼"	TMK-3	Sty. Bee	160-180.00
166	3¼"x6¼"	TMK-4	3-line	130-150.00
166	3¼"x6¼"	TMK-5	LB	100-125.00
166	3¼"x6¼"	TMK-6	MB	100-125.00

ANGEL WITH BIRD
Holy Water Font
Hum 167

Sometimes called "Angel Sitting" this font was placed in the line in the 1940's. There have been changes over the years, but none that have any effect on the normal values for pieces with the various trademarks. Still in production today.

HUM NO.	BASIC SIZE	TRADE MARK		CURRENT VALUE
167	3¼"x4¼"	TMK-1	CM	100-125.00
167	3¼"x4¼"	TMK-2	FB	75-85.00
167	3¼"x4¼"	TMK-3	Sty. Bee	60-70.00
167	3¼"x4¼"	TMK-4	3-line	55-60.00
167	3¼"x4¼"	TMK-5	LB	50-55.00
167	3¼"x4¼"	TMK-6	MB	50.00

ANGEL WITH BIRD Font, Hum 167. Stylized Bee mark, 4¼''.

STANDING BOY
Wall Plaque
Hum 168

Originally placed in the line in the Mid-1940's. It must have been produced in limited numbers in the first twenty years because examples in the first three trademarks have never been available in any but small numbers. It was taken out of production in the Stylized Bee (TMK-3) period, reinstated in 1978 and taken out of production yet again in 1989 with no reinstatement date published.

HUM NO.	BASIC SIZE	TRADE MARK		CURRENT VALUE
168	4⅛"x5½"	TMK-1	CM	500-600.00
168	4⅛"x5½"	TMK-2	FB	300-400.00
168	4⅛"x5½"	TMK-3	Sty. Bee	200-250.00
168	4⅛"x5½"	TMK-5	LB	125-150.00
168	4⅛"x5½"	TMK-6	MB	125-150.00

STANDING BOY Plaque, Hum 168. Full Bee mark in an incised circle, 4" x 5½".

BIRD DUET, Hum 169. Left: Crown Mark, 4". Right: Last Bee mark, 4".

BIRD DUET
Hum 169

There are many variations in the figure, but none that have any impact on the normal values of the pieces bearing the various trademarks. Introduced in th 1940's, it has been in continuous production since.

HUM NO.	BASIC SIZE	TRADE MARK		CURRENT VALUE
169	4"	TMK-1	CM	260-325.00
169	4"	TMK-2	FB	185-220.00
169	4"	TMK-3	Sty. Bee	160-185.00
169	4"	TMK-4	3-line	140-160.00
169	4"	TMK-5	LB	130-140.00
169	4"	TMK-6	MB	130.00

SCHOOL BOYS
Hum 170

Released in only one size originally in the 1940's, a new smaller size was introduced in the Stylized Bee (TMK-3) period.

There are no variations important enough to affect values.

The larger size, 180/III was permanently retired by Goebel in 1982. It is now considered a Closed Edition.

HUM NO.	BASIC SIZE	TRADE MARK		CURRENT VALUE
170/I	7½"	TMK-3	Sty. Bee	1350-1450.00
170/I	7½"	TMK-4	3-line	1150-1250.00
170/I	7½"	TMK-5	LB	1100-1150.00
170/I	7½"	TMK-6	MB	1100.00
170	10"	TMK-1	CM	4000-4500.00
170	10"	TMK-2	FB	3000-3500.00
170	10"	TMK-3	Sty. Bee	1800-2200.00
170/III	10"	TMK-3	Sty. Bee	1600-1800.00
170/III	10"	TMK-4	3-line	1500.00
170/III	10"	TMK-5	LB	1500.00
170/III	10"	TMK-6	MB	1500.00

SCHOOL BOYS, Hum 170/I. Last Bee trademark, 1961 MID, 7¾".

LITTLE SWEEPER
Hum 171

There are no variations significant enough to have an impact of values.

First released in the mid-1940's in one size, 171, a smaller size, 171/4/0, was introduced in 1988 as part of a four piece series with matching mini-plates. As a result of this new mold number, the old 171 was changed to 171/0.

HUM NO.	BASIC SIZE	TRADE MARK		CURRENT VALUE
171/4/0	3"	TMK-5	LB	90-100.00
171/4/0	3"	TMK-6	MB	90.00

Little Sweeper (cont'd)

HUM NO.	BASIC SIZE	TRADE MARK		CURRENT VALUE
171	4½"	TMK-1	CM	240-305.00
171	4½"	TMK-2	FB	175-200.00
✗ 171	4½"	TMK-3	Sty. Bee	150-175.00
171	4½"	TMK-4	3-line	130-150.00
171	4½"	TMK-5	LB	120-130.00
171	4½"	TMK-6	MB	120.00
171/0	4½"	TMK-6	MB	120.00

LITTLE SWEEPER, Hum 171. Left: Full Bee (TMK-2), 4¾", black "Germany". Right: Last Bee (TMK-5), 4¼".

FESTIVAL HARMONY
Angel with Mandolin
Hum 172

The major variations to be found are the Crown and Full Bee trademarked figures. The earliest (CM) and some FB (very rare) have flowers extending from the base well up onto the gown and the bird is perched on top of the flowers rather than on the mandolin as on later models. This variation piece is valued at $3000-3500.00

The majority of the Full Bee pieces show the flowers just barely extending up over the bottom edge of the gown and the bird is situated on the mandolin as in later designs.

The 172/II size was temporarily withdrawn from current production effective December 31, 1984 with no reinstatement date given.

The above variations invariably are found on the pieces marked with the plain incised mold number 172.

There is one example in existence where the bird is perched on the arm rather than on the mandolin. This was probably an error in assembly that somehow made it past the quality control inspection. There are several instances of this with other figures with small pieces such as bottles in baskets and usually does not influence value.

HUM NO.	BASIC SIZE	TRADE MARK		CURRENT VALUE
172/0	8"	TMK-4	3-line	300-350.00
172/0	8"	TMK-5	LB	280-300.00
172/0	8"	TMK-6	MB	280.00
172(bird on flowers)	10¾"	TMK-1	CM	2700-3200.00
172(bird on flowers)	10¾"	TMK-2	FB	2200-2500.00
172(bird on mandolin)	10¾"	TMK-2	FB	1000-1300.00
172(bird on mandolin)	10¾"	TMK-3	Sty. Bee	700-1000.00
172/II	10¾"	TMK-3	Sty. Bee	600-700.00
172/II	10¾"	TMK-4	3-line	500-550.00
172/II	10¾"	TMK-5	LB	400-425.00
172/II	10¾"	TMK-6	MB	400-425.00

(continued)

FESTIVAL HARMONY, Hum 172. Reading from left to right A through D:
A. Incised Crown MArk (TMK-1) *and* a stamped Full Bee (TMK-2) trademark. It has a donut base, measures 10¾''
and ''© W. Goebel'' beneath the base.
B. Same as the previous except for a different bird and a black ''Germany''.
C. A Full Bee piece exhibiting the same characteristics listed for the previous figure except for the now very small
flowers and the bird moved to the mandolin. The bird is colored brown.
D. This one has a small Stylized Bee trademark. Note the textured gown and the altered flowers. The bird is now
colored blue. It measures 10⅛''.

FESTIVAL HARMONY
Angel with Flute
Hum 173

The major variations to be found are on the Crown and Full Bee trademarked pieces. The Crown and some Full Bee (very rare) pieces have the flowers extending from the base well up onto the gown front. This variation piece is valued at $3000-3500.00

The Hum 173 Crown and Full Bee trademarked figures seem to be in shorter supply than those same pieces in the 172 mold number. It is probable they were not sold in the same quantities because of the vulnerability to breakage of the flutes.

The Full Bee pieces have the flowers barely extending from the base up over the bottom edge of the gown.

These variations invariable are found on the pieces marked with the plain incised 173 with no size designator.

The 173/II size was temporarily withdrawn from current production effective December 31, 1984 with no reinstatement date given.

HUM NO.	BASIC SIZE	TRADE MARK		CURRENT VALUE
173/0	8''	TMK-3	Sty. Bee	350-375.00
173/0	8''	TMK-4	3-line	300-350.00
173/0	8''	TMK-5	LB	280-300.00
173/0	8''	TMK-6	MB	280.00
173(high flowers)	11''	TMK-1	CM	2900-3400.00
173(high flowers)	11''	TMK-2	FB	2400-2700.00
173(medium flowers)	11''	TMK-2	FB	1200-1500.00

HUM NO.	BASIC SIZE	TRADE MARK		CURRENT VALUE
173(low flowers)	11"	TMK-3	Sty. Bee	700-1000.00
173/II	11"	TMK-3	Sty. Bee	600-700.00
173/II	11"	TMK-4	3-line	500-550.00
173/II	11"	TMK-5	LB	400-425.00
173/II	11"	TMK-6	MB	400-425.00

FESTIVAL HARMONY, Hum 173.
Reading from left the right, A through D:
A. Bears the mold number with decimal size designator, 172., an incised Crown Mark (TMK-1) *and* stamped Full Bee (TMK-2). It measures 1¼", has a donut base and a black "Germany".
B. Exhibits the same characterists as the previous one except it measures 11".
C. The mold number on this one is a plain 173. It has a Full Bee trademark, donut base, measures 11" and has a black "Germany". Note the bird is much smaller and the very small flowers.
D. This mold number is 173/II bears the Missing Bee (TMK-6) trademark and measures 10⅞". Note the absence of flowers and the textured gown.

SHE LOVES ME, SHE LOVES ME NOT
Hum 174

SHE LOVES ME, SHE LOVES ME NOT, Hum 174. Left: Full Bee mark in an incised circle, black "Western Germany", 4⅜". Center: Three Line Mark, incised 1955 MID, 4⅜". Right: Stylized Bee mark, 4¼".

256

(continued)

She Loves Me, She Loves Me Not (cont'd)

Released originally in the 1940's in one size only, it has remained so to today.

The earliest were produced with eyes open and a very small feather in the hat compared to later models. A flower was added to the left fence post and the feather grew larger on the Full Bee (TMK-2) pieces although some are found in the older style. The third change was manifest by the time the Three Line mark (TMK-4) was in use, where the fence post flower is missing and the boy's eyes are cast down. There are transition pieces for each of these changes, so you may encounter the changes associated with more than one trademark. The current production pieces have the eyes down.

HUM NO.	BASIC SIZE	TRADE MARK		CURRENT VALUE
174	4¼"	TMK-1	CM	450-550.00
174	4¼"	TMK-2	FB	350-400.00
174 (eyes up)	4¼"	TMK-3	Sty. Bee	250-300.00
174 (eyes down)	4¼"		Sty. Bee	200-225.00
174	4¼"	TMK-4	3-line	180-190.00
174	4¼"	TMK-5	LB	170.00
174	4¼"	TMK-6	MB	170.00

MOTHER'S DARLING
Hum 175

The most significant variation found is in the color of the bags. The older versions find the bags colored light pink and yellow-green. The newer ones are blue and red. These variations are not significant except in the case of spotting the older pieces without examining the bases. The value is reflected in the earlier trademark rather than the color in this case.

HUM NO.	BASIC SIZE	TRADE MARK		CURRENT VALUE
175	5½"	TMK-1	CM	395-500.00
175	5½"	TMK-2	FB	275-315.00
175	5½"	TMK-3	Sty. Bee	240-260.00
175	5½"	TMK-4	3-line	210-330.00
175	5½"	TMK-5	LB	195-210.00
175	5½"	TMK-6	MB	195.00

MOTHER'S DARLING, Hum 175. The left figure is the older with an incised Crown Mark (TMK-1) *and* a black Full Bee (TMK-2) trademark. The one on the right has the Stylized Bee (TMK-3) trademark. They both measure 5½".

HAPPY BIRTHDAY
Hum 176

The 176/0 has been known to be written "176" without using the "slash 0" designator in the Crown and Full Bee marks and in the 5⅓" size it utilizes the decimal point designator, "176." in the same trademarks.

Released in the 1940's, there are no mold or finish variations that have any influence on value. Still in production today.

HUM NO.	BASIC SIZE	TRADE MARK		CURRENT VALUE
176.	5⅓"	TMK-1	CM	390-500.00
176.	5⅓"	TMK-2	FB	300-340.00
176/0	5½"	TMK-2	FB	275-315.00
176/0	5½"	TMK-3	Sty. Bee	240-260.00
176/0	5½"	TMK-4	3-line	210-230.00
✗ 176/0	5½"	TMK-5	LB	195-210.00
176/0	5½"	TMK-6	MB	195.00
176	6½"-7"	TMK-1	CM	565-700.00
176	6½"-7"	TMK-2	FB	400-450.00
176/I	6"	TMK-1	CM	540-675.00
176/I	6"	TMK-2	FB	385-430.00
176/I	6"	TMK-3	Sty. Bee	320-360.00
176/I	6"	TMK-5	LB	270-300.00
176/I	6"	TMK-6	MB	270.00

HAPPY BIRTHDAY, Hum 176. Left: Decimal designator in the mold number 176., incised Crown Mark (TMK-1), black "Germany", 5⅝". Right: Decimal designator in the mold number 176., incised Crown Mark (TMK-1) *and* Full Bee (TMK-2), donut base, black "Germany", 5½".

SCHOOL GIRLS
Hum 177

First produced in the 1940's, it remains in the line in one smaller size today. There are no mold or finish variations that have an influence on value outside the normal evolutionary changes on the various trademarked figures. The 177/III was permanently retired in 1989. It is now a Closed Edition.

HUM NO.	BASIC SIZE	TRADE MARK		CURRENT VALUE
177/I	7½"	TMK-3	Sty. Bee	1350-1450.00
177/I	7½"	TMK-4	3-line	1150-1250.00
177/I	7½"	TMK-5	LB	1100-1150.00
177/I	7½"	TMK-6	MB	1100.00
177	9½"	TMK-1	CM	4000-4500.00
177	9½"	TMK-2	FB	3000-3500.00
177	9½"	TMK-3	Sty. Bee	1800-2200.00
177/III	9½"	TMK-3	Sty. Bee	1600-1800.00
177/III	9½"	TMK-4	3-line	1500.00
177/III	9½"	TMK-5	LB	1500.00
177/III	9½"	TMK-6	MB	1500.00

SCHOOL GIRLS, Hum 177/I. Last Bee trademark, 1961 MID, 7½".

THE PHOTOGRAPHER
Hum 178

Released about 1950 in one size only, it remains so in current production.

There are color and mold variations, but these are due to the ordinary evolution of the figure and, outside of the value changes due to the trademark changes, they have no influence on the value of the pieces.

HUM NO.	BASIC SIZE	TRADE MARK		CURRENT VALUE
178	4¾"	TMK-1	CM	520-650.00
178	4¾"	TMK-2	FB	375-425.00

(continued)

The Photographer (cont'd)

HUM NO.	BASIC SIZE	TRADE MARK		CURRENT VALUE
178	4¾"	TMK-3	Sty. Bee	300-350.00
178	4¾"	TMK-4	3-line	275-300.00
178	4¾"	TMK-5	LB	260-275.00
178	4¾"	TMK-6	MB	260.00

THE PHOTOGRAPHER, Hum 178. Left: Three Line Mark (TMk-4), incised copyright symbol ©, 1948 MID, 4¾". Right: Missing Bee (TMK-6), 1948 MID, 4⅝".

COQUETTES
Hum 179

Older versions of this figure have a blue dress and yellow flowers on the back of the fence posts, the girls are a bit chubbier and the hairstyle of the girl with the red kerchief is swept back.

First released around 1950, there are no significant mold or finish variations that affect value.

COQUETTES, Hum 179. Stylized Bee mark (TMK-3), 5".

(continued)

Coquettes (cont'd)

HUM NO.	BASIC SIZE	TRADE MARK		CURRENT VALUE
179	5¼"	TMK-1	CM	520-650.00
179	5¼"	TMK-2	FB	375-425.00
179	5¼"	TMK-3	Sty. Bee	300-350.00
179	5¼"	TMK-4	3-line	275-300.00
179	5¼"	TMK-5	LB	260-275.00
179	5¼"	TMK-6	MB	260.00

TUNEFUL GOODNIGHT
Wall Plaque
Hum 180

This plaque is quite rare in the older marks. Sometimes called "Happy Bugler" it is 5" x 4¾" in size and was redesigned toward the end of the Last Bee trademark era. The newer design has the bugle in a more forward position making it very vulnerable to breakage.

It was originally released about 1950. There are no important variations affecting value.

HUM NO.	BASIC SIZE	TRADE MARK		CURRENT VALUE
180	4"x4¾"	TMK-1	CM	500-600.00
180	4"x4¾"	TMK-2	FB	350-450.00
180	4"x4¾"	TMK-3	Sty. Bee	250-300.00
180	4"x4¾"	TMK-4	3-line	200-225.00
180	4"x4¾"	TMK-5	LB	200.00
180 (new style)	4"x4¾"	TMK-6	LB	200.00

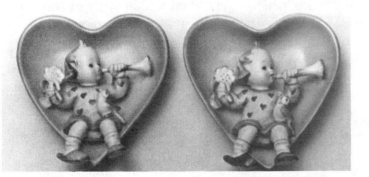

TUNEFUL GOOD NIGHT Plaque, Hum 180. Left: Incised Crown Mark, 4¾" x 5". Right: Stylized Bee in an incised circle, black "West Germany", 4¾" x 5".

OLD PEOPLE
"THE MAMAS AND THE PAPAS"
Hum 181, 189, 190, 191 and 202
Closed Numbers

These are the only known examples of the *M.I. Hummel* figurines to feature old people as their subject. They are more like characatures than realistic renderings. The first four were discovered in Europe by an American collector. The fifth piece, a table lamp (Hum 202), has subsequently turned up. These discoveries filled in the gaps in the mold number sequence previously unknown and designated as Closed Numbers, the term Goebel applies to pieces never placed in production. At least three complete sets of the five pieces are positively known to exist, a set in the company archives and two others in private collections. There have been other single pieces found and there are reports of three or more sets in the U.S. There is little doubt that some others do exist, either singly or in sets, but the number is likely to be extremely small. They were made in samples only and apparently rejected by the Siessen Convent as atypical of Hummel art. Collector value is about $20,000 for each.

THE MAMAS AND PAPAS. Left: Hum 181, **OLD MAN READING NEWSPAPER**, 6⅜''. Right: Hum 189 **OLD WOMAN KNITTING**, 6¹³⁄₁₆''.

Hum 181   OLD MAN READING NEWSPAPER
Hum 189   OLD WOMAN KNITTING
Hum 190   OLD WOMAN WALKING TO MARKET
Hum 191   OLD MAN WALKING TO MARKET
Hum 202   Hum 181 above as TABLE LAMP

GOOD FRIENDS
Hum 182

Released around the late 1940's, Good Friends remains in production today. Produced in one size only there are no significant variations influencing the regular collector value for the various trademarked pieces.

HUM NO.	BASIC SIZE	TRADE MARK		CURRENT VALUE
182	4"	TMK-1	CM	350-425.00
182	4"	TMK-2	FB	250-280.00
✳182	4"	TMK-3	Sty. Bee	215-240.00
182	4"	TMK-4	3-line	185-210.00
182	4"	TMK-5	LB	175-185.00
182	4"	TMK-6	MB	175-185.00

GOOD FRIENDS, Hum 182. Left: Stylized Bee (TMK-3), donut base, 4''. Right: Missing Bee (TMK-6), 4¼''.

FOREST SHRINE
Hum 183

The figure was released sometime around the late 1940's. Apparently they were produced in limited quantities because those with the early trademarks are in short supply. They were removed from production sometime around the end of the Stylized Bee (TMK-3) period, but put back in 1977. This is probably the reason they are not found bearing the Three Line mark (TMK-4).

HUM NO.	BASIC SIZE	TRADE MARK		CURRENT VALUE
183	7"x9"	TMK-1	CM	1000-1200.00
183	7"x9"	TMK-2	FB	800-900.00
183	7"x9"	TMK-3	Sty. Bee	600-700.00
183	7"x9"	TMK-5	LB	500.00
183	7"x9"	TMK-6	MB	500.00

FOREST SHRINE, Hum 183. Left: Decimal designator with mold number, 183., incised Crown mark (TMK-1) *and* stamped Full Bee (TMK-2) mark, black "Germany", split base, 9". Right: Missing Bee (TMK-6), 9".

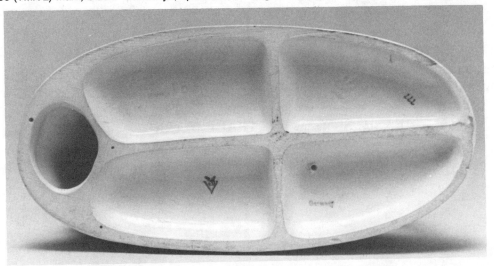

FOREST SHRINE, Hum 183. showing the base split in quarters.

LATEST NEWS
Hum 184

First produced about 1946, the older pieces have square bases and wide open eyes. They are found with a variety of newspaper names. In fact there was a period of time when some were produced with any name requested by merchants, i.e. their hometown newspapers. The piece was remodeled in the 1960's and given a round base and lowered eyes so the boy appears more like he is reading his paper. Later models bear the newspaper names: "Das Allerneuste", "Latest News" and "Muchner Press". As of 1985 the only newspaper name used is "Latest News". These three titles are the most common. Some of the more rare titles can range in value from $750 to $2500 for the most rare titles. Be careful in cleaning these. If you rub too hard or use harsh cleaners there is a danger of rubbing them off overtime. They were produced for a time with no titles, so you may find anything printed on them.

HUM NO.	BASIC SIZE	TRADE MARK		CURRENT VALUE
184	5¼"	TMK-1	CM	520-650.00
184	5¼"	TMK-2	FB	375-425.00
✱184	5¼"	TMK-3	Sty. Bee	300-350.00
184	5¼"	TMK-4	3-line	275-300.00
184	5¼"	TMK-5	LB	260-275.00
184	5¼"	TMK-6	MB	260.00

LATEST NEWS, Hum 184. Reading from left to right, A through D:
A. "Daily Mail". Has the decimal designator in the mold number 184., Crown Mark (TMK-1), U.S. ZONE Germany in a rectangular box beneath.
B. "Bermuda News, 1909-1959".
C. "Latest News". Stylized Bee (TMK-3) mark in an incised circle, black "Western Germany".
D. "LB Goebel - NACH". Last Bee (TMK-5) trademark. Note the round base. All four measure 5⅛".

ACCORDIAN BOY
Hum 185

First released sometime around the late 1940's, this model remains in the line today. Produced in only one size through the years, there have been no significant variations in the mold or the finish that would affect value.

HUM NO.	BASIC SIZE	TRADE MARK		CURRENT VALUE
185	5¼"	TMK-1	CM	360-450.00
185	5¼"	TMK-2	FB	260-290.00
185	5¼"	TMK-3	Sty. Bee	225-250.00
185	5¼"	TMK-4	3-line	190-225.00
185	5¼"	TMK-5	LB	180-190.00
185	5¼"	TMK-6	MB	180.00

(continued)

ACCORDIAN BOY, Hum 185. Left: 185., incised Full Bee mark, black "Germany", donut base, 5½". Right: Stylized Bee mark, 5⅜".

SWEET MUSIC
Hum 186

This piece appeared in the collection around the late 1940's.

The most significant variation of Sweet Music is the striped slippers shown on the figure in the accompanying photo. It is found on the Crown mark (TMK-1) figures and will bring $1500-1800 depending upon condition. The plain painted slippers are also found on Crown mark era figures.

SWEET MUSIC, Hum 186. Left: Full Bee mark, black "Germany", 5¼". Right: Stylized Bee mark, black "Western Germany", 5".

SWEET MUSIC, Hum 186. This is the scarce striped slipper variation found on some Crown mark (TMK-1) era examples of the piece. This one bears an incised Crown Mark, has a donut base and measures 5³⁄₁₆".

HUM NO.	BASIC SIZE	TRADE MARK		CURRENT VALUE
186	5¼"	TMK-1	CM	360-450.00
186	5¼"	TMK-2	FB	260-290.00
186	5¼"	TMK-3	Sty. Bee	225-250.00
186	5¼"	TMK-4	3-line	190-225.00
186	5¼"	TMK-5	LB	180-190.00
186	5¼"	TMK-6	MB	180.00

DEALER PLAQUES and DISPLAY PLAQUES
Hum 187

The 187 mold number is the one used on all dealer plaques produced until 1986 when it was taken out of production (see page 384). The older pieces have the traditional bumblebee perched on top but was redesigned in 1972. The newer design has a raised round area known as the "moon top" in its place and is imprinted with the Stylized Bee trademark. The plaques in current production do not have this round medallion like area.

Some of the plaques have been found with the mold numbers 187/A and 187/C.

The picture above is of a special edition of the display plaque make available to local chapter members of the Goebel Collectors' Club for a short time. As you can see they were personalized with chapter and member name.

There are a number of the 187 plaques in existence in Europe that were made specifically for individual stores and bearing the store name in addition to the traditional wordings.

Please see Service Plaque on page 73.

HUM NO.	BASIC SIZE	TRADE MARK		CURRENT VALUE
187	4"x5½"	TMK-1	CM	650.00
187	4"x5½"	TMK-2	FB	550.00
187	4"x5½"	TMK-3	Sty. Bee	450.00
187(with bumblebee)	4"x5½"	TMK-4	3-line	600.00
187(with Moon Top)	4"x5½"	TMK-4	3-line	325-375.00
187*	4"x5½"	TMK-5	LB	125-150.00
187*	4"x5½"	TMK-6	MB	125-150.00

STORE or **DISPLAY PLAQUE**, Hum 187, Full Bee mark, "© W. Goebel".

*A current suggested retail price list from a few years ago indicates the availability of a "Display Plaque Retailer" and a "Display Plaque Retailer" and a "Display Plaque Collector". The list suggested that each bears the 187 mold number. Neither are offered anymore.

266

(continued)

A specially customized Hum 187 Dealer Plaque. Goebel has been known to do this for dealers from time to time.

STORE or **DISPLAY PLAQUE,** Hum 187. Full Bee mark in an incised circle.

STORE or **DISPLAY PLAQUES,** Hum 187. Left to right A through D:
A. Stylized Bee In the "moon top", plaque bears the Three Line Mark and an incised 1947 MID on the base, 3¾".
B. 187/A, Last Bee mark, incised 1976 MID, 3⅝".
C. 187/A, Missing Bee mark, incised 1976 MID, 3⅝".
D. Last Bee mark, incised 1947 MID, 3⅝".

STORE or **DISPLAY PLAQUES.** Left to right, A through D:
A. Hum 187, but there is no apparent mold number or trademark. Measures 3¾".
B. Hum 187, Full Bee mark, 3¾". "SCHMID BROS. Inc. BOSTON" painted on the satchel.
C. Hum 211, Full Bee, white overglaze, 3⅞".
D. Hum 213, Spanish language, Full Bee mark, "(R)", 4".

267

CELESTIAL MUSICIAN
Hum 188

Up until 1983 this piece was made in only one size, 7". The mold number was simply 188. Production of a smaller size was begun. The smaller size is 5½" and bears the mold number 188/0. At the same time the mold number of the 188 was changed to 188/I on the TMK-7, current production pieces, to reflect the difference.

It has reportedly surfaced in white overglaze. Other than that faint possibility, there have been no significant variations that would influence the normal values for the various trademarked pieces.

HUM NO.	BASIC SIZE	TRADE MARK		CURRENT VALUE
188/4/0	3⅛"	TMK-6	MB	90.00
188/0	5"	TMK-5	LB	195.00
188/0	5"	TMK-6	MB	195.00
188	7"	TMK-1	CM	500-650.00
188	7"	TMK-2	FB	355-405.00
188	7"	TMK-3	Sty. Bee	300-355.00
188	7"	TMK-4	3-line	260-290.00
188	7"	TMK-5	LB	250-260.00
188	7"	TMK-6	MB	250.00

CELESTIAL MUSICIAN, Hum 188. Left: Three Line Mark, incised 1948 MID, 6¾". Right: Missing Bee mark, incised 1948 MID, 7".

OLD PEOPLE
"THE MAMAS AND THE PAPAS"
Hum 189, Hum 190, Hum 191
(See pages 261-262)

CANDLELIGHT
Hum 192

There are two distinct versions of this piece. The chief difference is found in the candle receptacle. This variation is found on the Crown mark (TMK-1) and Full Bee (TMK-2) figurines. The transition from this older style to the newer one where the candle socket is held in the hand (no extension) took place in the Stylized Bee (TMK-3) era so you may also find the old design so marked.

HUM NO.	BASIC SIZE	TRADE MARK		CURRENT VALUE
192(long candle)	6¼"	TMK-1	CM	700-800.00
192(long candle)	6¾"	TMK-2	FB	500-600.00
192(long candle)	6¾"	TMK-3	Sty. Bee	350.00
192(regular)	6¾"	TMK-3	Sty. Bee	250-275.00
192(regular)	6¾"	TMK-4	3-line	220-250.00
192(regular)	6¾"	TMK-5	LB	210-220.00
192(regular)	6¾"	TMK-6	MB	210.00

CANDLELIGHT, Hum 192. Left: Incised Full Bee mark (TMK-2), "© W. Goebel", black "Germany", donut base, 6¾". Right: Last Bee mark (TMk-5), jncised 1948 MID, 6¾".

ANGEL DUET candle holder, Hum 193. Missing Bee mark (TMK-6), 5".

ANGEL DUET
Candle Holder
Hum 193

Essentially the same design as Hum 261 except that the 261 is not a candleholder. Has been produced in two variations. The variations are seen in the rear of the figure. One shows the angel not holding the song book and has an arm around the waist of the other, the other has the hand on the shoulder of the angel. Both versions are found on the Crown mark (TMK-1) and the Full Bee (TMK-2) marked figures. The transition to the new, arm around waist, took place during the Full Bee trademark period.

Has been found in white overglaze. The value of this variation is $1200-1500.00

HUM NO.	BASIC SIZE	TRADE MARK		CURRENT VALUE
193	5"	TMK-1	CM	400-500.00
193	5"	TMK-2	FB	275-325.00
193	5"	TMK-3	Sty. Bee	235-275.00
193	5"	TMK-4	3-line	210-235.00
193	5"	TMK-5	LB	200-210.00
193	5"	TMK-6	MB	200.00

WATCHFUL ANGEL
Hum 194

Once called "Angelic Care", this figurine entered the line around the late 1940's. There are no significant mold or finish variations reported.

HUM NO.	BASIC SIZE	TRADE MARK		CURRENT VALUE
194	6½"	TMK-1	CM	580-725.00
194	6½"	TMK-2	FB	410-460.00
194	6½"	TMK-3	Sty. Bee	350-385.00
194	6½"	TMK-4	3-line	305-345.00
194	6½"	TMK-5	LB	290-305.00
194	6½"	TMK-6	MB	290.00

WATCHFUL ANGEL, Hum 194. Three Line mark, incised 1948 MID, 6½".

BARNYARD HERO
Hum 195

Introduced into the line in the late 1940's. It has undergone some major mold changes over the years as it evolved, but most were associated with a trademark change or a change in finish of the entire collection. There may be some slight variation from the standard valuations for the figures with the various trademarks, but not substantial.

HUM NO.	BASIC SIZE	TRADE MARK		CURRENT VALUE
195/2/0	4"	TMK-2	FB	300-375.00
195/2/0	4"	TMK-3	Sty. Bee	180-220.00
195/2/0	4"	TMK-4	3-line	160-180.00
195/2/0	4"	TMK-5	LB	150-160.00
195/2/0	4"	TMK-6	MB	150.00
195	5¾"-6"	TMK-1	CM	700-800.00
195	5¾-6"	TMK-2	FB	500-550.00
195/I	5¾"-6"	TMK-2	FB	450-500.00
195/I	5¾"	TMK-3	Sty. Bee	375-400.00
195/I	5¾"	TMK-4	3-line	310-350.00
195/I	5¾"	TMK-5	LB	290-310.00
195/I	5¾"	TMK-6	MB	290.00

(continued)

BARNYARD HERO, Hum 195. Left: Incised Crown mark *and* a stamped
Full Bee mark, split base, black "Germany", blue "© W. Goebel", 5¾"
Right: 195/1, Three Line mark, incised 1948 MID, 5¾".

TELLING HER SECRET
Hum 196

This figure was introduced sometime in the late 1940's in a 6¾" basic size. During the Full Bee (TMK-2) trademark period a second, smaller size, 196/0, was introduced. With this came a change of the mold number for the larger one from "196" to "196/I". The Full Bee (TMK-2) can be found with either style of mold number.

TELLING HER SECRET, Hum 196. Left: 196/I, Full Bee mark in an incised circle, incised 1948 MID, black "Western Germany", 6½". Right:
196/O, Missing Bee mark, incised 1948 MID, 5½". White overglaze.

(continued)

Telling Her Secret (cont'd)

HUM NO.	BASIC SIZE	TRADE MARK		CURRENT VALUE
196/0	5¼"	TMK-2	FB	375-425.00
196/0	5¼"	TMK-3	Sty. Bee	325-375.00
196/0	5¼"	TMK-4	3-line	280-325.00
196/0	5¼"	TMK-5	LB	270-280.00
196/0	5¼"	TMK-6	MB	270.00
196	6¾"	TMK-1	CM	900-1400.00
196/I	6¾"	TMK-2	FB	700-800.00
196/I	6¾"	TMK-2	FB	600-700.00
196/I	6¾"	TMK-3	Sty. Bee	470-485.00
196/I	6¾"	TMK-4	3-line	450-470.00
196/I	6¾"	TMK-5	LB	430-450.00
196/I	6¾"	TMK-6	MB	430.00

BE PATIENT
Hum 197

There are no important mold or finish variations to be found on this late 1940's release. There is, however, a mold number variation that is significant. The figure was first produced in only one size and the incised mold number was "197" accordingly. When a smaller size, 197/2/0, was produced in the Stylized Bee (TMK-3) period, the mold number on the larger one was changed to 197/I.

HUM NO.	BASIC SIZE	TRADE MARK		CURRENT VALUE
197/2/0	4¼"	TMK-2	FB	300-375.00
197/2/0	4¼"	TMK-3	Sty. Bee	180-220.00
197/2/0	4¼"	TMK-4	3-line	160-180.00
✳197/2/0	4¼"	TMK-5	LB	150-160.00
197/2/0	4¼"	TMK-6	MB	150.00
197	6¼"	TMK-1	CM	700-800.00
197	6¼"	TMK-2	FB	500-550.00
197/I	6¼"	TMK-2	FB	450-500.00
197/I	6¼"	TMK-3	Sty. Bee	375-400.00
197/I	6¼"	TMK-4	3-line	310-350.00
197/I	6¼"	TMK-5	LB	290-310.00
197/I	6¼"	TMK-6	MB	290.00

BE PATIENT, Hum 197. Left: Full Bee mark "© W. Goebel", black "Germany", 6½". Right: 197/I, Last Bee mark, incised 1948 MID, 6".

HOME FROM MARKET
Hum 198

There are no important mold or finish variations to be found on this late 1940's release. There is, however, a mold number variation that is significant. The figure was first produced in only one size and the incised mold number was "198" accordingly. When a smaller size, 198/2/0, was issued in the Stylized Bee (TMK-3) period, the mold number was changed to 198/I on the larger one.

HOME FROM MARKET, Hum 198. Left: Full Bee mark in an incised circle, 1948 MID, black "Germany",© by W. Goebel, 5⅞". Right: 198/1, Three Line mark (TMK-4), 1948 MID, donut base, 5½".

A **HOME FROM THE MARKET**, Hum 198 with a red line on the base. This indicates that this particular piece was a master model at one time. Note the archive medallion wired and sealed around the legs.

HUM NO.	BASIC SIZE	TRADE MARK		CURRENT VALUE
198/2/0	4¾"	TMK-2	FB	180-225.00
198/2/0	4¾"	TMK-3	Sty. Bee	155-180.00
198/2/0	4¾"	TMK-4	3-line	140-150.00
198/2/0	4¾"	TMK-5	LB	130-140.00
198/2/0	4¾"	TMK-6	MB	130.00
198	5¾"	TMK-1	CM	290-500.00
198	5¾"	TMK-2	FB	300-350.00
198/I	5¾"	TMK-2	FB	275-315.00
198/I	5¾"	TMK-3	Sty. Bee	240-260.00
198/I	5¾"	TMK-4	3-line	210-230.00
✶198/I	5¾"	TMK-5	LB	195-210.00
198/I	5¾"	TMK-6	MB	195.00

FEEDING TIME
Hum 199

There are no major mold or finish variations outside the normal evolution of the figurine. There is, however, a mold number variation that is important. It was first produced in the late 1940's in only one size and its incised mold number was "199" accordingly. It was sometimes found as "199." with the decimal designator also. When a new smaller, 199/0, size was introduced during the Stylized Bee (TMK-3) era, the trademark on the larger one was changed to 199/I.

The older pieces have blonde hair and the newer ones dark hair.

(continued)

Feeding Time (cont'd)

FEEDING TIME, Hum 199. Left: Full Bee mark, black "Germany", "© W. Goebel", donut base, 5½". Right: 199/1. Full Bee in an incised circle, black "Germany", "© W. Goebel", incised 1948 MID, donut base, 5½".

HUM NO.	BASIC SIZE	TRADE MARK		CURRENT VALUE
199/0	4¼"	TMK-2	FB	250-275.00
199/0	4¼"	TMK-3	Sty. Bee	210-250.00
199/0	4¼"	TMK-4	3-line	185-215.00
199/0	4¼"	TMK-5	LB	175-185.00
199/0	4¼"	TMK-6	MB	175.00
199 or 199.	5¾"	TMK-1	CM	480-600.00
199 or 199.	5¾"	TMK-2	FB	350-450.00
199/I	5¾"	TMK-2	FB	325-400.00
199/I	5¾"	TMK-3	Sty. Bee	275-325.00
199/I	5¾"	TMK-4	3-line	250-275.00
199/I	5¾"	TMK-5	LB	240-250.00
199/I	5¾"	TMK-6	MB	240.00

LITTLE GOAT HERDER
Hum 200

LITTLE GOAT HERDER, Hum 200. Both of these are the same basic size according to their mold numbers though they differ in actual measurement. The larger one on the left is the 200/1 measuring 5¾", has a Full Bee (TMK-2) trademark in an incised circle, a "© by W. Goebel", a black "Germany" and a 1948 MID. The one on the right is the 200/I measuring 5¼" is a Three Line Mark (TMK-4) piece and also has an incised 1948 MID.

(continued)

274

Little Goat Herder (cont'd)

There are no important mold or color variations outside those occurring during the normal evolution of the figure. There is, however, a mold number variation that is significant. The figure was first produced in only one size and given the incised mold number "200" accordingly. It sometimes appeared with the decimal designator, "200." also. When a new smaller, 4¾" basic size was introduced in the Stylized Bee (TMK-3) era, the mold number on the larger one was changed to 200/I.

HUM NO.	BASIC SIZE	TRADE MARK	CURRENT VALUE
200/0	4¾"	TMK-2 FB	250-275.00
200/0	4¾"	TMK-3 Sty. Bee	210-250.00
200/0	4¾"	TMK-4 3-line	185-215.00
200/0	4¾"	TMK-5 LB	175-185.00
200/0	4¾"	TMK-6 MB	175.00
200 or 200.	5½"	TMK-1 CM	440-550.00
200 or 200.	5½"	TMK-2 FB	325-400.00
200/I	5½"	TMK-2 FB	300-350.00
200/I	5½"	TMK-3 Sty. Bee	250-300.00
200/I	5¼"	TMK-4 3-line	230-250.00
200/I	5¼"	TMK-5 LB	220-230.00
200/I	5¼"	TMK-6 MB	220.00

RETREAT TO SAFETY
Hum 201

There are not important mold or finish variations outside those occurring during the normal evolution of the figure. There is, however, a mold number variation that is significant. The figure was first produced in one size only and given the incised mold number "201" accordingly. It sometimes also appeared with the decimal point designator as well. When a new, smaller 4" size was introduced during the Stylized Bee (TMK-3) era, the mold number on the 5½" size was changed to 201/I.

RETREAT TO SAFETY, Hum 201. Left: Full Bee mark with a "(R)" associated, "© W. Goebel", black "Germany", split base, 6". Right: 201/I, 3-line mark, incised 1948 MID, 5⅜".

HUM NO.	BASIC SIZE	TRADE MARK	CURRENT VALUE
201/2/0	4"	TMK-2 FB	300-375.00
201/2/0	4"	TMK-3 Sty. Bee	180-220.00
201/2/0	4"	TMK-4 3-line	160-180.00
201/2/0	4"	TMK-5 LB	150-160.00
201/2/0	4"	TMK-6 MB	150.00
201. or 201	5½"	TMK-1 CM	700-800.00
201. or 201	5½"	TMK-2 FB	500-550.00
201/I	5½"	TMK-2 FB	450-500.00

(continued)

HUM NO.	BASIC SIZE	TRADE MARK	CURRENT VALUE
201/I	5½"	TMK-3 Sty. Bee	375-400.00
201/I	5½"	TMK-4 3-line	310-350.00
201/I	5½"	TMK-5 LB	290-310.00
201/I	5½"	TMK-6 MB	290.00

OLD MAN READING NEWSPAPER
Table Lamp
Hum 202
Closed Number Designation
(See pages 261-262)

SIGNS OF SPRING
Hum 203

Released about 1950, there is a significant mold variation in the 4" basic size, 203/2/0. This size was introduced in the Full Bee (TMK-2) period. It was molded with both feet on the ground and wearing shoes. At some point during this period, it was remodeled so that her right foot is raised above the ground and the foot has no shoe on. The first variation is the more scarce and is valued at about $600-750.00

There is another mold variation worthy of note. It is a version of this figure where there are four fence pickets instead of the usual three and there are more flowers present. The mold number of the example in the photo appears to have been scratched into the figure by hand before firing. Probably a prototype for no more have surfaced.

There is also a variation in mold numbering. When first released, it was in the 201 mold number in only the 5" size. When the smaller 4", 203/2/0, size was released in the Full Bee era, the mold number of the larger was changed to 203/I. The earlier "203" is also found with the decimal designator occasionally. Both sizes have been permanently retired.

Base of the four picket variation showing the unusual split base. Stamped Full Bee, "© W. Goebel", black "Germany". The mold number appears to have been rendered by hand.

SIGNS OF SPRING, Hum 203. This is a very rare and unusual variation. Note the fourth fence post and additional flowers.

SIGNS OF SPRING, Hum 203/1. Three Line Mark (TMK-4), 1948 MID, 5".

276

(continued)

Signs of Spring (cont'd)

HUM NO.	BASIC SIZE	TRADE MARK	CURRENT VALUE
203/2/0	4"	TMK-1 CM	360-430.00
203/2/0	4"	TMK-2 FB	225-325.00
203/2/0	4"	TMK-3 Sty. Bee	175-200.00
203/2/0	4"	TMK-4 3-line	150-175.00
203/2/0	4"	TMK-5 LB	140-150.00
203/2/0	4"	TMK-6 MB	140.00
203 or 203.	5"	TMK-1 CM	400-500.00
203 or 203.	5"	TMK-2 FB	325-375.00
203/I	5"	TMK-2 FB	275-325.00
203/I	5"	TMK-3 Sty. Bee	225-275.00
203/I	5"	TMK-4 3-line	210-230.00
203/I	5"	TMK-5 LB	200-210.00
203/I	5"	TMK-6 MB	200.00

WEARY WANDERER
Hum 204

There is a major variation associated with this figure. The normal figure has eyes painted with no color. The variation has blue eyes. There are only four blue-eyed pieces presently known to be in collectors' hands. These are valued at about $5000.00 each.

This figure was introduced sometime in the early 1950's. There are no other significant variation affecting values.

HUM NO.	BASIC SIZE	TRADE MARK	CURRENT VALUE
204	6"	TMK-1 CM	450-575.00
204	6"	TMK-2 FB	325-380.00
204	6"	TMK-3 Sty. Bee	275-300.00
204	6"	TMK-4 3-line	240-275.00
204	6"	TMK-5 LB	225-240.00
204	6"	TMK-6 MB	225.00

MERRY WANDERER, Hum 204. Left: Incised Full Bee (TMK-2) mark, black "Germany", ©W. Goebel, 5⅞". Right: Stamped Full Bee (TMK-2), black "Germany", © W. Goebel, 5¾".

DEALER or DISPLAY PLAQUES
Hum 205

The following list is of merchant display plaques used by dealers. Each has a large bumblebee perched atop the plaque and a Merry Wanderer figure attached to the right side. All are 5¼" x 4¼" in basic size. Variations are noted at each listing. See also Hum 187.

Hum 205 (German Language) Occurs in the Crown, Full Bee, Stylized Bee and 3-line trademarks. Valued at $1000 to $1200.00

Hum 208 (French Language) Occurs in the Crown, Full Bee and Stylized Bee trademarks. Valued at about $3500 to 5000.00.

Hum 209 (Swedish Language) Occurs in the Crown, Full Bee and Stylized Bee trademarks. Valued at about $3500 to 5000.00. Two distinctly different lettering designs have been found.

Hum 210 (English Language) This is the "Schmid Brothers" display plaques. Made for this distributor, "Schmid Bros., Boston" is found molded in bas relief on the suitcase. There are only four known to exist presently. If found this significant piece would likely bring about $12,000.00

Hum 211 (English Language) There are only two presently known to exist in collectors hands. One in white overglaze, no color and one in full color. This is the only dealer plaque to use the word "Oeslau" as the location of Goebel in Bavaria. Name has since been changed to Rodental, but this is not found on any plaques. (Photo on page 267).

Hum 213 (Spanish Language) Occurs in the Crown, Full Bee and Stylized Bee trademark. Valued at $10,000-12,000.00. (photo on page 267.)

STORE or DISPLAY PLAQUES.
Left: **Hum 205, German language,** incised Crown mark *and* a Stylized Bee mark, 4".
Center: **Hum 208, French language,** Full Bee mark, 3¾".
Right: **Hum 209, Swedish language,** Full Bee mark, 3¾".

Crown	CM	TMK-1	1934-1950
Full Bee	FB	TMK-2	1940-1959
Stylized Bee	Sty Bee	TMK-3	1958-1972
Three Line Mark	3-line	TMK-4	1964-1972
Last Bee Mark	LB	TMK-5	1970-1980
Missing Bee Mark	MB	TMK-6	1979-1991
Hummel Mark (Current)	HM	TMK-7	1991-Present

ANGEL CLOUD
Holy Water Font
Hum 206

Released sometime in the early 1950's, it has been redesigned several times since. It has been in and out of production since but apparently in very limited quantities each time. It has always been in short supply in the older trademarks.

HUM NO.	BASIC SIZE	TRADE MARK	CURRENT VALUE
206	2¼"x4¾"	TMK-1 CM	200-250.00
206	2¼"x4¾"	TMK-2 FB	100-150.00
206	2¼"x4¾"	TMK-3 Sty. Bee	90-100.00
206	2¼"x4¾"	TMK-4 3-line	60-80.00
206	2¼"x4¾"	TMK-5 LB	50.00
206	2¼"x4¾"	TMK-6 MB	50.00

ANGEL CLOUD, Font, Hum 206. Three Line mark, incised 1949 MID, 4¾".

HEAVENLY ANGEL
Holy Water Font
Hum 207

First released sometime in the early 1950's, this piece has the distinction of the highest mold number in the collection that can be found with the Crown mark (TMK-1). There are a number of variations to be found, but none have any significant impact on their collector value.

HUM NO.	BASIC SIZE	TRADE MARK	CURRENT VALUE
207	2"x4¾"	TMK-1 CM	200-250.00
207	2"x4¾"	TMK-2 FB	100-150.00
207	2"x4¾"	TMK-3 Sty. Bee	90-100.00
207	2"x4¾"	TMK-4 3-line	60-80.00
207	2"x4¾"	TMK-5 LB	50.00
207	2"x4¾"	TMK-6 MB	50.00

HEAVENLY ANGEL Font, Hum 207. Three Line mark, incised 1949 MID, 5".

DEALER PLAQUE
Hum 208 through Hum 211 See page 278.

UNKNOWN
Hum 212
Closed Number Designation

This was previously suspected to be another dealer plaque. Then it was thought for a while that this number was intended to be utilized with the letters A through F as mold numbers for a set of musician pieces called Orchestra. It is now known that this was used for a short time merely as an inventory designation for the Band Leader (Hum 129) and several of the musical figurines. The number was not incised on the figures.

NATIVITY SET
Hum 214

In the early 214 sets the Madonna and infant Jesus were molded as one piece. The later ones are found as two separate pieces. Hum 366 the Flying Angel is frequently used with this set. One old model camel and two recently issued new camels are also frequently used with the set but they are not Hummel pieces.

Collectors may note the omission of 214/I in the listing below. It has long been assumed that the mold number was never used because of the possible confusion that might result from the similarity of the "I" and the "1" when incised as a mold number. The existence of a Hum 214/I has now been substantiated. The piece found is in white overglaze and is of two connected geese similar to the geese in the Goose Girl figure. It has the incised *M.I. Hummel* signature.

The number 214 size **NATIVITY SET.**

280

(continued)

HUM NO.	BASIC SIZE	FULL FIGURE	BEE	STYLIZED BEE	THREE LINE	LAST BEE	MISSING BEE
214/A	6½"	MADONNA JESUS	815-1000	140-160	110-140	100-140	100-140
214/A/K		INFANT JESUS (1½"x3¾")	—	45-65	40-45	40-45	35-40
214/B	7½"	JOSEPH	175.00	140-160	130-140	100-105	100-105
214/D	3"	ANGEL SERENADE (Angel Standing)	100-150	75-90	75-90	75-90	75-90
		(Angel Standing)	100-150	75-90	75-95	75-95	75-95
214/E	3¼"	WE CONGRATULATE (See Hum 220)	200-300	170-200	170-200	170-200	170-200
214/F	7½"	SHEPHERD WITH SHEEP	195-225	140-170	130-140	100-110	100-110
214/G	3¾"	SHEPHERD BOY (kneeling)	185-290	170-200	90-105	75-100	75-80
214/H	3¾"	LITTLE TOOTER	125-150	100-125	100-125	100-125	100.00
214/J	5¼"	DONKEY	75-105	60-75	50-65	50-65	50-60
214/K	6½"	COW	75-105	60-70	50-60	50-60	60-60
214/L	8½"	MOOR KING	150.00	140-160	135-140	100-105	100-105
214/M	5¾"	KING (kneeling on one knee)	150.00	140-160	110-115	95-100	95-100
214/N	5½"	KING (kneeling on both knees)	25.00	10-15	10-15	10-15	10-15
214/O	2¼"	LAMB					

In 1988 Goebel began a three-year program to introduce a smaller, third size Nativity Set. They are offered as three or four piece sets as sets in the initial years of the offer and as separate pieces subsequently. They are offered as follows:

1988

214/A/M/0	5¼"	Madonna	75-85.00
214/B/0	6⅛"	Joseph	75-85.99
214/A/K/0	2⅞"	Jesus	25-30.00

1989

366/0	2¾"	Flying Angel	60-65.00
214/J/0	3⅞"	Donkey	30-35.00
214/K/0	2¾"	Ox	30-35.00
214/O/0	1½"	Lamb	10-15.00

1990

214/L/0	6½"	King (standing)	90-100.00
214/M/0	4"	King (on one knee)	80-90.00
214/N/0	4½"	King (on both knees)	80-85.00

1991

214/F/0	5¾"	Shepherd (w/sheep)	90-100.00
214/G/0	4"	Shepherd Boy	70-75.00
214/H/0	3"	Little Tooter	20-25.00

Values quoted above are taken directly from Goebel's Suggested Retail Price List.

UNKNOWN
Hum 215
Closed Number Designation

Not likely to be found. Records indicate it could possibly be a standing child Jesus holding a lamb in his arms.

UNKNOWN
Hum 216
Closed Number Designation

Not likely to be found. No known examples anywhere. Records indicate it might be a Joyful (Hum 53) ashtray if it exists.

BOY WITH TOOTHACHE
Hum 217

This figure, released sometime in the 1950's, has no significant mold or finish variations affecting the normal values. Older models of the figure will have the "WG" after the *M.I. Hummel* incised signature. This mark is illustrated and discussed in the trade mark section at the front of the book.

BOY WITH TOOTHACHE, Hum 217. Three Line mark, incised 1951 MID, 5⅜".

HUM NO.	BASIC SIZE	TRADE MARK	CURRENT VALUE
217	5½"	TMK-2 FB	400-600.00
217	5½"	TMK-3 Sty. Bee	225-275.00
217	5½"	TMK-4 3-line	210-225.00
217	5½"	TMK-5 LB	200-210.00
217	5½"	TMK-6 MB	200.00

BIRTHDAY SERENADE
Hum 218

The most significant variation found is the "reverse mold variation". In the older versions of this double figure piece the girl plays the concertina and the boy plays the flute. In the newer models the instruments are the other way around.

The older, Full Bee (TMK-2) pieces with the "Reverse Mold" were changed beginning in the next trademark period, the Stylized Bee (TMK-3) so you can find the old design in that mark as well. There must have been many of the old design left in stock for you can even find them bearing the Three Line Mark (TMK-4). Note that the boy lost his kerchief when he was given the concertina or accordian.

HUM NO.	BASIC SIZE	TRADE MARK	CURRENT VALUE
218/2/0 (reverse mold)	4¼"	TMK-2 FB	500-550.00
218/2/0 (reverse mold)	4¼"	TMK-3 Sty. Bee	400-450.00
218/2/0	4¼"	TMK-3 Sty. Bee	225-250.00
218/2/0 (reverse mold)	4¼"	TMK-4 3-line	350-400.00
218/2/0	4¼"	TMK-4 3-line	200-225.00
218/2/0	4¼"	TMK-5 LB	160.00

(continued)

Reversed instruments variations, **BIRTHDAY SERENADE,** Hum 218. Left: Full Bee mark, black "Germany", "© W. Goebel", 5⅜". Right: 218/0, Last Bee mark, incised 1952 MID, 5¼".

HUM NO.	BASIC SIZE	TRADE MARK		CURRENT VALUE
218/2/0				160.00
218/0 (reverse mold)	5¼"	TMK-2	FB	600-700.00
218/0 (reverse mold)	5¼"	TMK-3	Sty. Bee	450-550.00
218/0	5¼"	TMK-3	Sty. Bee	275-300.00
218/0 (reverse mold)	5¼"	TMK-4	3-line	400-450.00
218/0	5¼"	TMK-4	3-line	275-300.00
218/0	5¼"	TMK-5	LB	275.00
218/0	5¼"	TMK-6	MB	275.00

Crown	CM	TMK-1	1934-1950
Full Bee	FB	TMK-2	1940-1959
Stylized Bee	Sty Bee	TMK-3	1958-1972
Three Line Mark	3-line	TMK-4	1964-1972
Last Bee Mark	LB	TMK-5	1970-1980
Missing Bee Mark	MB	TMK-6	1979-1991
Hummel Mark (Current)	HM	TMK-7	1991-Present

LITTLE VELMA
Hum 219/2/0

This figure bears a number with the "Closed Number" designation, supposedly meaning a number which never has been and never will be used to designate a *Hummel* figurine. It is a girl sitting on a fence, looking down at a frog on the ground. It was never officially released by the factory, although it has turned up due to a no-longer practical policy of distributing pre-production samples. It was never placed in production due to its similarity to Hum 195 and Hum 201. The owner of the first example of this figure to be uncovered has named it "Little Velma". It was designed in 1952. At least 15-20 examples have been found to date, in the Full Bee (TMK-2) only so far. Collector value $5000-6500.00 depending on condition.

LITTLE VELMA, Hum 219. 219/2/0, Full Bee (TMK-2) with registered trademark symbol, "© W. Goebel", 3¹⁵⁄₁₆".

WE CONGRATULATE
Hum 220

A very similar figure to Hum 214/E (Nativity Set piece) except this figure is on a base and 214/E is not, and the girl has no wreath of flowers in her hair.

Introduced into the line in the 1950's, there is one variation of some significance. At first the piece was produced with a "220/2/0" designator. It was soon dropped leaving only the mold number "220" incised on the base.

WE CONGRATULATE, Hum 220. Three Line Mark (TMK-4), 3⅞".

(continued)

We Congratulate (cont'd)

HUM NO.	BASIC SIZE	TRADE MARK		CURRENT VALUE
220/2/0	4"	TMK-2	FB	200-250.00
220	4"	TMK-3	Sty. Bee	175-200.00
220	4"	TMK-4	3-line	150-175.00
220	4"	TMK-5	LB	145-150.00
220	4"	TMK-6	MB	145.00

HAPPY PASTIME
Candy Box
Hum 221
Closed Number Designation

Previously listed as unknown, it is now known that this is a pre-production sample never released. No known examples outside the company archives.

MADONNA
Wall Plaque
Hum 222

An extremely rare, out of current production piece. It is unique in that there is a metal frame surrounding it. Basic size is 4" x 5". Has been found with several different designs of wire frame around it. Most were originally made with a felt backing. Each may be found with any design of the wire frame or, no frame at all.

HUM NO.	BASIC SIZE	TRADE MARK		CURRENT VALUE
222	4"x5"	TMK-2	FB	700-800.00
222	4"x5"	TMK-3	Sty. Bee	600-700.00

MADONNA, Plaque, Hum 222. No apparent mark other than mold number. Measure 4 x 5. The wire frame is detachable.

TO MARKET
Table Lamp
Hum 223

First introduced into the line in the 1950's, this lamp was temporarily withdrawn from production in 1989 with no reinstatement date given. There are no mold or finish variations significant enough to affect normal values. There is a similar design lamp. See Hum 101.

(continued)

TO MARKET table lamp, Hum 223. Stylized Bee mark (TMK-3), 8¾'', without the light fixture.

HUM NO.	BASIC SIZE	TRADE MARK		CURRENT VALUE
223	9½"	TMK-2	FB	425-475.00
223	9½"	TMK-3	Sty. Bee	375-400.00
223	9½"	TMK-4	3-line	320-340.00
223	9½"	TMK-5	LB	290-300.00
223	9½"	TMK-6	MB	290-300.00

WAYSIDE HARMONY
Table Lamp
Hum 224

First introduced into the line as a redesign of the Hum 111 lamp in the 1950's, this lamp was produced in two sizes. Both were temporarily withdrawn from production in 1989 with no date of reinstatement published. There are no finish or mold variations that have any affect on normal values.

HUM NO.	BASIC SIZE	TRADE MARK		CURRENT VALUE
224/I	7½"	TMK-2	FB	360-400.00
224/I	7½"	TMK-3	Sty. Bee	300-325.00
224/I	7½"	TMK-4	3-line	260-285.00
224/I	7½"	TMK-5	LB	250-260.00
224/I	7½"	TMK-6	MB	250-260.00
224	9½"	TMK-2	FB	500-575.00
224	9½"	TMK-3	Sty. Bee	425-500.00
224/II	9½"	TMK-2	FB	425-475.00
224/II	9½"	TMK-3	Sty. Bee	350-400.00
224/II	9½"	TMK-4	3-line	320-340.00
224/II	9½"	TMK-5	LB	300-325.00
224/II	9½"	TMK-6	MB	290-300.00

(continued)

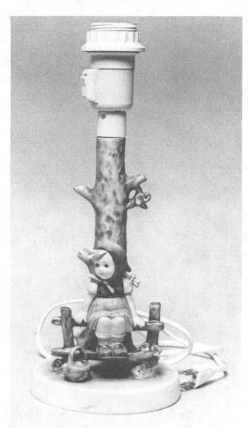

WAYSIDE HARMONY table lamp, Hum 224/II. Missing Bee mark (TMK-6), 9'' without the light fixture.

JUST RESTING table lamp, Hum 225/II. Missing Bee mark (TMK-6), 8⅞'' without the lamp fixture.

JUST RESTING
Table Lamp
Hum 225

First released in the 1950's as a redesign of the Hum 112, it was listed as temporarily withdrawn from production by Goebel in 1989 with no reinstatement date given.

HUM NO.	BASIC SIZE	TRADE MARK		CURRENT VALUE
225/I	7½"	TMK-2	FB	350-400.00
225/I	7½"	TMK-3	Sty. Bee	300-325.00
225/I	7½"	TMK-4	3-line	260-285.00
225/I	7½"	TMK-5	LB	250-260.00
225/I	7½"	TMK-6	MB	250-260.00
225	7½"	TMK-2	FB	500-575.00
225	7½"	TMK-3	Sty. Bee	425-500.00
225/II	9½"	TMK-2	FB	425-475.00
225/II	9½"	TMK-3	Sty. Bee	350-400.00
225/II	9½"	TMK-4	3-line	320-340.00
225/II	9½"	TMK-5	LB	290-300.00
225/II	9½"	TMK-6	MB	290-300.00

THE MAIL IS HERE
Hum 226

First introduced into the line in the 1950's, it was known as "Mail Coach". This name is still favored by many collectors. Incidentally, this figure was preceded by a wall plaque utilizing the same motif (Hum 140).
There are no major variations affecting normal values. It remains in production to date.

THE MAIL IS HERE, Hum 226. This example is an older piece with a Full Bee (TMK-2) trademark in an incised circle. It also has a "by W. Goebel", a black "West Germany" and measures 4½" x 6½".

HUM NO.	BASIC SIZE	TRADE MARK		CURRENT VALUE
226	4¼"x6¼"	TMK-2	FB	700-800.00
226	4¼"x6¼"	TMK-3	Sty. Bee	600-650.00
226	4¼"x6¼"	TMK-4	3-line	525-575.00
226	4¼"x6¼"	TMK-5	LB	505-515.00
226	4¼"x6¼"	TMK-6	MB	505.00

SHE LOVES ME, SHE LOVES ME NOT
Table Lamp
Hum 227

A 7½" lamp base utilizing Hum 174 as part of the design.
It was listed by Goebel in 1989 as temporarily withdrawn from production in 1989 with no reinstatement date given.

HUM NO.	BASIC SIZE	TRADE MARK		CURRENT VALUE
227	7½"	TMK-2	FB	350-400.00
227	7½"	TMK-3	Sty. Bee	300-350.00
227	7½"	TMK-4	3-line	265-290.00
227	7½"	TMK-5	LB	250-260.00
227	7½"	TMK-6	MB	250.00

GOOD FRIENDS
Table Lamp
Hum 228

A 7½" lamp base utilizing Hum 182 as part of the design.
It was listed by Goebel as temporarily withdrawn from production in 1989 with no date for reinstatement given.

HUM NO.	BASIC SIZE	TRADE MARK		CURRENT VALUE
228	7½"	TMK-2	FB	360-390.00
228	7½"	TMK-3	Sty. Bee	300-340.00
228	7½"	TMK-4	3-line	260-290.00
228	7½"	TMK-5	LB	250-260.00
228	7½"	TMK-6	MB	250.00

APPLE TREE GIRL
Table Lamp
Hum 229

A 7½" base utilizing Hum 141 as part of the design.
It was listed as temporarily out of production by Goebel in 1989 with no date of reinstatement given.

HUM NO.	BASIC SIZE	TRADE MARK		CURRENT VALUE
229	7½"	TMK-2	FB	600-750.00
229	7½"	TMK-3	Sty. Bee	300-340.00
229	7½"	TMK-4	3-line	260-290.00
229	7½"	TMK-5	LB	250-260.00
229	7½"	TMK-6	MB	250.00

APPLE TREE BOY
Table Lamp
Hum 230

A 7½" lamp base utilizing Hum 142 as part of the design.
This piece was listed by Goebel as temporarily withdrawn from production in 1989 with no reinstatement date given.

HUM NO.	BASIC SIZE	TRADE MARK		CURRENT VALUE
230	7½"	TMK-2	FB	600-750.0
230	7½"	TMK-3	Sty. Bee	300-340.00
230	7½"	TMK-4	3-line	260-290.00
230	7½"	TMK-5	LB	250-260.00
230	7½"	TMK-6	MB	250.00

BIRTHDAY SERENADE
Table Lamp
Hum 231

This particular lamp was out of production for many years. It utilizes the Hum 218, Birthday Serenade as its design. The old model is found in the Full Bee trademark and reflects the same old mold girl with accordian/boy with flute design. These old mold design lamps measure about 9¾" tall and are fairly scarce. The Hum 231 was reissued in the late 1970's with the instruments reversed. Now the girl plays the flute and the boy, the accordian. The newer pieces are found with the Last Bee (TMK-5) and the Missing Bee (TMK-6) trademarks. See Hum 234.

Goebel has listed this lamp as temporarily withdrawn from production. The date was December 31, 1989 and no reinstatement date was given.

HUM NO.	BASIC SIZE	TRADE MARK	CURRENT VALUE
231	9¾"	TMK-2 FB	1200-1500.00
231	9¾"	TMK-5 LB	450.00
231	9¾"	TMK-6 MB	400.00

BIRTHDAY SERENADE table lamp, Hum 231. Missing Bee mark (TMK-6), measures 8⅞" without the light fixture.

HAPPY DAYS
Table Lamp
Hum 232

The 9¾" Happy Days table lamp was placed in production in the 1950's. It was apparently made in limited numbers in the early days because those with the Full Bee (TMK-2) have always been in short supply. For a while, in the Last Bee (TMK-5) and the Missing Bee (TMK-6) mark they were available, but the factory listed them as temporarily withdrawn from production in late 1989.

HUM NO.	BASIC SIZE	TRADE MARK	CURRENT VALUE
232	9¾"	TMK-2 FB	800-1000.00
232	9¾"	TMK-5 LB	450.00
232	9¾"	TMK-6 MB	400.00

UNKNOWN
Hum 233
Closed Number Designation

Unlikely to be found. There is evidence to suggest that this is a preliminary design for Bird Watcher (Hum 300). No known examples anywhere.

BIRTHDAY SERENADE
Table Lamp
Hum 234

This lamp like the larger Hum 231, was apparently also removed from, or limited in production for a time. Unlike the Hum 231 lamp, however, it can be found in all trademarks beginning with the Full Bee. It was redesigned in the late 1970's with the instruments reversed just as the Hum 231 was. It can be found in the old or new styles in the Full Bee.

HUM NO.	BASIC SIZE	TRADE MARK		CURRENT VALUE
234 (reverse mold)	7¾"	TMK-2	FB	1000-1200.00
234	7¾"	TMK-2	FB	500-750.00
234 (reverse mold)	7¾"	TMK-3	Sty. Bee	500-750.00
234	7¾"	TMK-3	Sty. Bee	350-400.00
234 (reverse mold)	7¾"	TMK-4	3-line	350-450.00
234	7¾"	TMK-4	3-line	325-340.00
234	7¾"	TMK-5	LB	290-300.00
234	7¾"	TMK-6	MB	290-300.00

HAPPY DAYS
Table Lamp
Hum 235

This is a smaller size (7¾") of the Hum 232 lamp. It too was placed in production in the 1950's and removed shortly thereafter. It was reissued in a new design in the late 1970's as was the larger lamp. Unlike the larger lamp, however, this one can be found in all trademarks starting with the Full Bee.

HUM NO.	BASIC SIZE	TRADE MARK		CURRENT VALUE
235	7¾"	TMK-2	FB	500-750.00
235	7¾"	TMK-3	Sty. Bee	400-450.00
235	7¾"	TMK-4	3-line	300-400.00
235	7¾"	TMK-5	LB	280-300.00
235	7¾"	TMK-6	MB	

HAPPY DAYS table lamp, Hum 235. Missing Bee Mark (TMK-6), 1954 MID, measures 7½" without the light fixture.

NO NAME
Closed Number Designation
Hum 236A and Hum 236B

Only one example of each of these is known to exist at this time. The figures are two angels, one at the base of a tree and the other seated on a tree limb. Hum 236A has one angel playing a harp at the base of a tree and the other seated on a tree limb above singing. The Hum 236B has the tree angel blowing a horn and the seated angel playing a lute. No known examples outside the factory archives.

STAR GAZER
Wall Plaque
Hum 237
Closed Number Designation

This piece is a plaque using "Star Gazer" in white overglaze as its design. None known to be in private collection. Factory Archives only.

ANGEL TRIO SET
Angel with Lute, Hum 238/A
Angel with Accordian, Hum 238/B
Angel with Horn, Hum 238/C

These three pieces are usually sold as a set. In current production, they can be found in the current-use Missing Bee (TMK-6), Last Bee (TMK-5) and the 3-line (TMK-4) trademarks. Each is 2-2½" high. They are essentially the same set as the Angel Trio, Hum 38, 39 and 40 but these (Hum 238) are not candleholders.

ANGEL TRIO
Left: Angel with Lute, Hum 238 A, paper sticker with the Last Bee mark, incised 1967 MID, 2⅜".
Center: Angel with Accordian, Hum 238 B, paper sticker with the Last Bee mark, incised 1967 MID, 2⅜".
Right: Angel with Horn, Hum 238 C, paper sticker with the Last Bee mark, 2⅜".

HUM NO.	BASIC SIZE	TRADE MARK		CURRENT VALUE each
238/A,B,C	2-2½"	TMK-4	3-line	55-60.00
238/A,B,C	2-2½"	TMK-5	LB	50-55.00
238/A,B,C	2-2½"	TMK-6	MB	50.00

CHILDREN TRIO
Girl with Nosegay, Hum 239/A
Girl with Doll, Hum 239/B
Boy with Horse, Hum 239/C

These three are usually sold as a set. Placed in production in the 1960's they are essentially the same as the Hum 115, Hum 116 and Hum 117 except that these have no receptacle for holding a candle.

CHILDREN TRIO SET
Left: Hum 239/A
Center: Hum 239/B
Right: Hum 239/C. All three measure 3½'', have 1967 MID's and Last Bee Trademarks on silver paper stickers attached beneath the base.

HUM NO.	BASIC SIZE	TRADE MARK		CURRENT VALUE each
239/A,B,C	3½"	TMK-4	3-line	55-60.00
239/A,B,C	3½"	TMK-5	LB	50-55.00
239/A,B,C	3½"	TMK-6	MB	50.00

LITTLE DRUMMER
Hum 240

Placed into production in the 1950's. This figure is usually found with an incised MID of 1955. There are no variations significant enough to affect normal values for this piece.

HUM NO.	BASIC SIZE	TRADE MARK		CURRENT VALUE
240	4¼"	TMK-2	FB	200-225.00
240	4¼"	TMK-3	Sty. Bee	160-180.00
240	4¼"	TMK-4	3-line	145-160.00
240	4¼"	TMK-5	LB	135-145.00
240	4¼"	TMK-6	MB	135.00

LITTLE DRUMMER, Hum 240. This piece bears the Last Bee (TMK-5) mark, measures 4½'' tall and has an incised 1955 MID.

ANGEL JOYOUS NEWS WITH LUTE
Holy Water Font
Hum 241
Closed Number Designation

The mold number 241 was used by mistake on the next piece listed, "Angel Lights". This design was produced only in prototype and never put into regular production. There is only one presently known to exist outside the factory archives. If sold this unique piece would bring about $10,000.00. It is the Don Stephens Collection, soon to be a part of the Goebel Gallery and *M.I. Hummel* Museum in Rosemont, Illinois.

ANGEL WITH LUTE Font, Hum 241.

ANGEL LIGHTS candle holder, Hum 241. Last Bee mark (TMK-5), incised 1977 MID.

ANGEL LIGHTS
Candle Holder
Hum 241

This was a new release in 1978. It is in the form of an arch which is placed on a plate. A figure sits attached to the top of the arch, with candle receptacles down each side of the arch. The arch is not attached to the plate base. Occurs in the Last Bee trademark only. Has been observed as available at $225-300.00 usually. Suspended from production since January 1, 1990.

ANGEL JOYOUS NEWS WITH TRUMPET
Holy Water Font
Hum 242
Closed Number Designation

This piece was produced as a sample only and never put into the line. It is not likely to ever find its way into a private collection. As far as is known, the only example is in the Goebel archives.

Crown	CM	TMK-1	1934-1950
Full Bee	FB	TMK-2	1940-1959
Stylized Bee	Sty Bee	TMK-3	1958-1972
Three Line Mark	3-line	TMK-4	1964-1972
Last Bee Mark	LB	TMK-5	1970-1980
Missing Bee Mark	MB	TMK-6	1979-1991
Hummel Mark (Current)	HM	TMK-7	1991-Present

MADONNA AND CHILD
Holy Water Font
Hum 243

Even though this piece was apparently not released into the line until the 1960's, it can be found with all trademarks starting with the Full Bee (TMK-2).

There are no significant variations affecting normal values for this font.

HUM NO.	BASIC SIZE	TRADE MARK		CURRENT VALUE
243	3¼"x4"	TMK-2	FB	70-80.00
243	3¼"x4"	TMK-3	Sty. Bee	60-70.00
243	3¼"x4"	TMK-4	3-line	55-60.00
243	3¼"x4"	TMK-5	LB	50-55.00
243	3¼"x4"	TMK-6	MB	50.00

MADONNA AND CHILD Font, Hum 243. Three Line Mark, incised 1955 MID, 4".

UNKNOWN
Hum 244
Open Number Designation

UNKNOWN
Hum 245
Open Number Designation

HOLY FAMILY
Holy Water Font
Hum 246

This font was released into the line in the mid-1950's. There are no significant mold or finish variations affecting normal values. It is usually found with the incised MID of 1955.

HUM NO.	BASIC SIZE	TRADE MARK		CURRENT VALUE
246	3"x4"	TMK-2	FB	70-80.00
246	3"x4"	TMK-3	Sty. Bee	60-70.00
246	3"x4"	TMK-4	3-line	55-60.00
246	3"x4"	TMK-5	LB	50-55.00
246	3"x4"	TMK-6	MB	50.00

HOLY FAMILY, Hum 246. Full Bee Mark, incised 1955 MID, black "Western Germany", 4½".

STANDING MADONNA WITH CHILD
Hum 247
Closed Number Designation

This is a beautiful piece designed in 1961, but apparently rejected by the Siessen Convent. It exists in prototype in the factory archives only.

Photo courtesy *M.I. Hummel* Club

GUARDIAN ANGEL
Holy Water Font
Hum 248

This piece is a redesigned version of Hum 29 which is no longer in production. When placed in the collection it was a 2¼" x 5½" size. The mold number is 248/0. When first produced (Full Bee era), there was a larger version made, the 248/I, but never placed into regular production.

HUM NO.	BASIC SIZE	TRADE MARK		CURRENT VALUE
248/I	2¼"x5½"	TMK-3	Sty. Bee	1000-1500.00
248/0	2¼"x5½"	TMK-3	Sty. Bee	60-70.00
248/0	2¼"x5½"	TMK-4	3-line	55-60.00
248/0	2¼"x5½"	TMK-5	LB	50-55.00
248/0	2¼"x5½"	TMK-6	MB	50.00

GUARDIAN ANGEL Font, Hum 248/0. Three Line Mark, incised 1959 MID, 5⅜".

296

MADONNA and CHILD
Plaque in Relief
Hum 249
Closed Number Designation

Molded as a sample only, this plaque was never put in the line. It is essentially the same design as the Hum 48 Madonna Plaque with the background cut away. No known examples outside the Goebel archives.

LITTLE GOAT HERDER and FEEDING TIME
Bookends
Hum 250/A and Hum 250/B

These were placed in the line in the mid-1960's. If the figurines are removed from the wooden bookend bases, they are indistinguishable from the regular pieces.

They were temporarily withdrawn from production at the end of 1989 with no date for reinstatement given.

LITTLE GOAT HERDER, Hum 25D and **FEEDING TIME** Hum 250B bookends. Left figure measures 4½" and the right, 4¾". Both bear the Missing Bee Mark (TMK-6).

HUM NO.	BASIC SIZE	TRADE MARK		CURRENT VALUE
250/A&B	5½"	TMK-2	FB	400-450.00
250/A&B	5½"	TMK-3	Sty. Bee	300-325.00
250/A&B	5½"	TMK-5	LB	225-300.00
250/A&B	5½"	TMK-6	MB	225-300.00

GOOD FRIEND and SHE LOVES ME, SHE LOVES ME NOT
Bookends
Hum 251/A and Hum 251/B

GOOD FRIENDS, Hum 251 A and **SHE LOVES ME, SHE LOVES ME NOT,** Hum 251 B bookends. Both bear the Stylized Bee mark (TMK-3).

(continued)

297

Good Friends/She Loves Me, She Loves Me Not (cont'd)

These bookends were entered into the line in the mid-1960's. If they are removed from the wooden bookend bases, they are indistinguishable from the regular pieces.

Goebel placed them on a list of pieces that were temporarily withdrawn from production in 1989. There was no reinstatement date given at the time.

HUM NO.	BASIC SIZE	TRADE MARK		CURRENT VALUE
251/A&B	5½"	TMK-2	FB	400-450.00
251/A&B	5½"	TMK-3	Sty. Bee	300-325.00
251/A&B	5½"	TMK-5	LB	225-300.00
251/A&B	5½"	TMK-6	MB	225-300.00

APPLE TREE and APPLE TREE GIRL
Bookends
Hum 252/A and Hum 252/B

These bookends were placed in the collection in the mid-1960's. If the figures are removed from the bookends they are indistinguishable from the regular figurine.

The bookends were temporarily withdrawn from production at the end of 1989 with no stated reintroduction date.

HUM NO.	BASIC SIZE	TRADE MARK		CURRENT VALUE
252/A&B	5¼"	TMK-3	Sty. Bee	300-325.00
252/A&B	5¼"	TMK-5	LB	225-300.00
252/A&B	5¼"	TMK-6	MB	225-300.00

APPLE TREE GIRL and **APPLE TREE BOY** bookends, Hum 252 A and Hum 252 B. Each bears the Stylized Bee mark (TMK-3) and measure 3⅞" tall.

UNKNOWN
Hum 253
Closed Number Designation

Goebel records indicate that this piece was a design much like the girl in Hum 52, Going to Grandma's. There is no evidence that it was ever produced and there are no known examples in the archives or anywhere else.

UNKNOWN
Hum 254
Closed Number Designation

Goebel records indicate that this piece was a design much like the girl figure in Hum 150, Happy Days. There is no evidence that it was ever produced and there are no examples in the archives or anywhere else.

A STITCH IN TIME
Hum 255

First released in the mid-1960's, there are no significant variations that might affect normal values.

In 1990 a smaller size, 3", was added as part of a four figurine series matching mini plates in the same series. When this figure was introduced, the mold number for the larger was changed to 255/0.

A STITCH IN TIME, Hum 255. Three Line Mark (TMK-4), incised 1963 MID, donut base, 5¾".

HUM NO.	BASIC SIZE	TRADE MARK		CURRENT VALUE
255/4/0	5"	TMK-6	MB	85.00
255	6¾"	TMK-3	Sty. Bee	600-750.00
255	6¾"	TMK-4	3-line	275-300.00
255	6¾"	TMK-5	LB	260-275.00
255/0	5¾"	TMK-5	LB	260-270.00
255/0	6¾"	TMK-6	MB	260.00

KNITTING LESSON
Hum 256

Introduced in the mid-1960's Knitting Lesson has no significant variations that might affect normal values. Has incised MID of 1963.

HUM NO.	BASIC SIZE	TRADE MARK		CURRENT VALUE
256	7½"	TMK-3	Sty. Bee	750-1000.00
256	7½"	TMK-4	3-line	500-550.00
256	7½"	TMK-5	LB	475-500.00
256	7½"	TMK-6	MB	475.00

(continued)

KNITTING LESSON, Hum 256. Missing Bee (TMK-6), 1967 MID, 7⅜".

FOR MOTHER
Hum 257

Introduced into the collection in the mid-1960's, this figure has no significant mold or finish variations.

A new smaller size figurine was released as a part of a four piece series with matching mini-plates in 1985. When this was done the mold number for the larger size was changed to 257/0.

HUM NO.	BASIC SIZE	TRADE MARK		CURRENT VALUE
257/2/0	3"	TMK-5	LB	110-120.00
257/2/0	3"	TMK-6	MB	110.00
257	5¼"	TMK-3	Sty. Bee	600-750.00
257	5¼"	TMK-4	3-line	195-225.00
257 or 257/0	5¼"	TMK-5	LB	185-195.00
257/0	5¼"	TMK-6	MB	185.00

FOR MOTHER, Hum 257.
Left: Missing Bee (TMK-6), 1963 MID, 5⅛".
Right: 257 2/0, Missing Bee (TMK-4), 1984 MID, 4".

WHICH HAND?
Hum 258

There are no mold or finish variation that would affect normal values.
Released in the mid-1960's, this figure has no incised MID of 1963.

HUM NO.	BASIC SIZE	TRADE MARK	CURRENT VALUE
258	5¼"	TMK-3 Sty. Bee	600-750.00
258	5¼"	TMK-4 3-line	190-215.00
258	5¼"	TMK-5 LB	180-190.00
258	5¼"	TMK-6 MB	180.00

WHICH HAND, Hum 258. Missing Bee Mark (TMK-6). incised 1963 MID, 5⅜".

NATIVITY SET
(Large)
Hum 260

There was only sketchy information found concerning complete Nativity Sets and little more about the individual pieces in any of the many price lists utilized. Below is a listing of each piece in the Hum 260 Nativity Set. The set has been temporarily withdrawn from production. They are found in 3-line and Last Bee trademarks as well as the Missing Bee mark. The sixteen piece set including the wooden stable is valued at $4000-5000.00.

HUM NO.	BASIC SIZE	FIGURE
260/A	9¾"	MADONNA
260/B	11¾"	JOSEPH
260/C	5¾"	INFANT JESUS
260/D	5¼"	GOODNIGHT (Angel Standing)
260/E	4¼"	ANGEL SERENADE (Kneeling)
260/F	6¼"	WE CONGRATULATE
260/G	11¾"	SHEPHERD

(continued)

Nativity Set (Large) (cont'd)

HUM NO.	BASIC SIZE	FIGURE
260/H	3¾"	SHEEP AND LAMB
260/J	7"	SHEPHERD BOY (Kneeling)
260/K	7½"	LITTLE TOOTER
260/L	7½"	DONKEY
260/M	6"x11"	COW
260/N	12¾"	MOOR KING
260/O	12"	KING (Standing)
260/P	9"	KING (Kneeling)
260/R	3¼"x4"	SHEEP

ANGEL DUET
Hum 251

This figure, essentially is the same design as Hum 193 but does not have a provision for a candle. It is apparently produced in very limited quantities, for they are somewhat difficult to find bearing the older, Three Line mark (TMK-4).

There are no major variations affecting value. There is no reverse mold variations as in the Hum 193 candle holder. There were released in the late 1960's and bear a 1968 incised MID.

HUM NO.	BASIC SIZE	TRADE MARK		CURRENT VALUE
261	5½"	TMK-4	3-line	210-236.00
261	5½"	TMK-5	LB	195-210.00
261	5½"	TMK-6	MB	195.00

ANGEL DUET, Hum 261. Last Bee Mark, incised 1968 MID, 5''.

HEAVENLY LULLABY
Hum 262

First released in the late 1960's, there are no significant mold variations to be found. Each bears an incised MID of 1968.

This figure is the same design as Hum 24 but does not have a provision for a candle. It is apparently produced in very limited quantities, for they are very difficult to locate in older trademarks. Current production piece sells for about $170.00.

HUM NO.	BASIC SIZE	TRADE MARK		CURRENT VALUE
262	3½"x5"	TMK-3	Sty. Bee	210-250.00
262	3½"x5"	TMK-4	3-line	180-210.00
262	3½"x5"	TMK-5	LB	170-180.00
262	3½"x5"	TMK-6	MB	170.00

HEAVENLY LULLABY, Hum 262. 3½'' high this figure bears the Last Bee (TMK-5) trademark and an incised 1968 MID.

MERRY WANDERER
Plaque in Relief
Hum 263

A very rare plaque of the familiar Merry Wanderer motif. There is only one known to be outside the factory collection and in a private collection. As far as can be determined there are no more on the collector market. It is known to bear the Three Line trademark (TMK-4).

ANNUAL PLATES

In 1971 the factory produced its first annual plate. This plate called the Heavenly Angel (Hum 21) design and was released to the Goebel factory workers to commemorate the 100th anniversary of the W. Goebel firm. The plate was subsequently produced without the inscription and was received so well in the United States it was decided that a similar plate would be released annually from then on. The 1971 plate was not released to European dealers.

Since 1971 the firm has released one new design per year, each bearing a traditional Hummel figurine motif. The plates and their current market value are listed on the following pages.

1971 HUMMEL ANNUAL PLATE
Hum 264

There are three versions of this plate. The first is the "normal version". The second differs from the first only in that it has no holes for hanging. It was exported to England where tariff laws in 1971 placed a higher duty on the plate if it had holes than if not. The law states that holes make it a decorative object, subject to a higher duty rate. The third variation is the special original edition produced only for the Goebel firm factory workers. There is an inscription on the back side of the lower rim. It reads in German as follows: "Gewidmet Aller Mitarbeitern Im Jubilaumsjahr. Wirdanken ihnen fur ihre mitarbeit". Roughly translated it is thanks to the workers for their fine service. This is the least common of the three, hence the most sought after.

1972 GOEBEL ANNUAL PLATE
Hum 265

There are three known versions of the 1972 plate. The first is the "normal" one with the regular back stamp and the current Goebel trademark. The second has the same back stamp but bears the 3-line mark instead of the current mark. The third is exactly the same as the second but does not bear the inscription "Hand Painted" and the "2nd" is omitted from the identification of the plate as an annual plate.

Annual Plates: 1971-1973,
Hum 265, 266 & 267.

Annual Plates: 1974-1976,
Hum 267, 268 & 269.

Annual Plates: 1977-1979,
Hum 270, 271, 272.

Annual Plates: 1980-1982,
Hum 273, 274, 275.

(continued)

Annual Plates (cont'd)

Annual Plates: 1983-1985, Hum 276, 277, 278.

Annual Plates: 1986-1988, Hum 279, 283, 284.

Annual Plates: 1989-1990, Hum 287, 288.

Annual Plates: 1991-1992, Hum 288, 286.

Annual Plates (cont'd)

White Overglaze Annual Plates, Left: Hum 271, 1978, **HAPPY PASTIME**, Last Bee trademark incised 1972 MID. Right: Hum 272, **SINGING LESSON**, Last Bee trademark, incised 1972 MID.

DOLL BATH, Hum 289, 1993 Annual Plate.

HUM NO.	SIZE	PLATE DESIGN	YEAR	CURRENT VALUE
264	7½"	Heavenly Angel	1971	450-650.00
265	7½"	Hear Ye, Hear Ye, (TMK-3)	1972	30-50.00
*265	7½"	Hear Ye, Hear Ye, (TMK-4)	1972	45-60.00
266	7½"	Globe Trotter	1973	80-135.00
267	7½"	Goose Girl	1974	40-60.00
**268	7½"	Ride Into Christmas	1975	40-60.00
***269	7½"	Apple Tree Girl	1976	40-60.00
270	7½"	Apple Tree Boy	1977	60-75.00
271	7½"	Happy Pastime	1978	35-50.00
272	7½"	Singing Lesson	1979	20-40.00
273	7½"	School Girl	1980	30-50.00
274	7½"	Umbrella Boy	1981	40-55.00
275	7½"	Umbrella Girl	1982	90-110.00
276	7½"	Postman	1983	150-160.00
277	7½"	Little Helper	1984	60-75.00
278	7½"	Chick Girl	1985	70-90.00
279	7½"	Playmates	1986	110-135.00
283	7½"	Feeding Time	1987	200-235.00
284	7½"	Little Goat Herder	1988	90-115.00
285	7½"	Farm Boy	1989	100-120.00
286	7½"	Shepherd's Boy	1990	140-160.00
287	7½"	Just Resting	1991	130-145.00
288	7½"	Wayside Harmony	1992	140-165.00
289	7½"	Doll Bath	1993	140-155.00

*Made at the same time as the Last Bee marked plated and represents a transition. Not appreciably more valuable.

**Late in 1983 an unusual plate was found in Germany. It was a 1975 Annual Plate but instead of the Ride Into Christmas motif it was a Little Fiddler. No doubt that this was a prototype plate considered for 1975 but obviously not selected. How it managed to find its way out of the factory is anybody's guess. It may have been the only one.

***Somehow a number of the 1976 Annual Plates were inadvertently given the incorrect backstamp "Wildlife Third Edition, Barn Owl" and they were released. How many got out is anybody's guess. It has no value significance.

FUTURE ANNUAL PLATE RELEASES

The 1995 plate will be the final plate issued in this twenty-five plate series.

1994 **Doctor**
1995 **Come Back Soon**

1975 ANNIVERSARY PLATE
Hum 280

This larger plate (10") utilizes the Stormy Weather (Hum 71) design. Presently valued at $100-120.00.

1980 ANNIVERSARY PLATE
Hum 281

This plate is called "Spring Dance" but utilizes only one figure from the Spring Dance piece and the second girl in the plate design is taken from the "Ring Around the Rosie" figurine. It presently sells for $60-80.00.

1985 ANNIVERSARY PLATE
Hum 282

As are the previous Anniversary Plates this last one is 10" in diameter. It uses as its design, the figurine Auf Wiedersehen (Hum 153). It is presently selling at $200-220.00.

Anniversary Plates: Left to right: **STORMY WEATHER** 1975, Hum 280;
SPRING DANCE 1980, Hum 281; **AUF WIEDERSEHN** 1986, Hum 282.

Hum 289 Through Hum 291

"Open Number designation". Number reserved for future release.

FOR FATHER

MEDITATION

FRIENDS FOREVER
Plate Series

This is a four plate series introduced in 1992. The plates are smaller at 7" diameter than the annual plates and also have a decorative border. The first was released with a suggested retail price of $195.00.

1992	Hum 292	MEDITATION
1993	Hum 293	FOR FATHER
1994	Hum 294	SWEET GREETINGS
1995	Hum 295	SURPRISE

OPEN NUMBERS
Hum 296 thru Hum 299
Possible Future Editions

BIRD WATCHER
Hum 300

BIRD WATCHER, Hum 300. Missing Bee mark, incised 1956 MID, 5''.

(continued)

Bird Watcher (cont'd)

First known as "Tenderness", this figure was released in 1979. It was originally designed in the Full Bee (TMK-2) trademark period, there are prototypes in that trademark with an incised MID of 1954.

Far more easy to locate are the regular production pieces bearing the 1956 MID. They start with the Last Bee (TMK-5) and have been in continuous production since.

HUM NO.	BASIC SIZE	TRADE MARK	CURRENT VALUE
300	5"	TMK-2 FB	4000-6000.00
300	5"	TMK-5 LB	205-225.00
300	5"	TMK-6 MB	205.00

CHRISTMAS ANGEL
Hum 301

A new release in 1989, it was originally designed in the Stylized Bee (TMK-3) period, made in prototype with that trademark and given an incised MID of 1957. It was redesigned slightly smaller than the prototype and released with the Missing Bee (TMK-6) and the same 1957 MID. It remains in production.

HUM NO.	BASIC SIZE	TRADE MARK	CURRENT VALUE
301	6¼"	TMK-3 Sty. Bee	4000-6000.00
301	6"	TMK-6 MB	230-250.00

CHRISTMAS ANGEL, Hum 301. Missing Bee mark, incised 1957 MID, 4¾".

CONCENTRATION
Hum 302
Possible Future Edition

This figure was first designed and made in prototype in the Full Bee (TMK-2) era, but regular production has not yet begun. The example in the accompanying photograph has the Full Bee trademark and a 1956 MID.

CONCENTRATION, Hum 302, PFE.

ARITHMETIC LESSON
Hum 303
Possible Future Edition

First designed and made in prototype in the Full Bee (TMK-2) era the figure appears to be a combination of one boy and one girl from Hum 170, School Boys and Hum 177, School Girls. The boy in this figure is also much like the boy in the Dealer Plaque, Hum 460.

THE ARTIST
Hum 304

Placed in regular production about 1970, there is reason to believe it may have been made in extremely limited quantities in the Full Bee (TMK-2) era and somewhat limited in the Stylized Bee (TMK-3) era. The one in the accompanying photograph bears that mark and a 1955 incised MID.

HUM NO.	BASIC SIZE	TRADE MARK		CURRENT VALUE
304	5¼"	TMK-2	FB	4000-5500.00
304	5¼"	TMK-3	Sty. Bee	2000-3000.00
304	5¼"	TMK-4	3-line	240-260.00
304	5¼"	TMK-5	LB	220-240.00
304	5¼"	TMK-6	MB	220.00

THE ARTIST, Hum 304. Left: Missing Bee trademark (TMK-6), incised 1955 MID. Right: Inked-in incised mold number indicating that this is a master model. It bears a stamped Full Bee trademark and "© by W. Goebel, 1955". Note the paint drip on the base. This feature has never made it to the production piece.

THE ARTIST, Hum 304. Three Line Mark, incised 1955 MID, 5¼".

Base of THE ARTIST, showing the inked-in incised mold number indicating that this is a figurine from the Mother Mold, a master model.

310

THE BUILDER
Hum 305

The first prototype of this figure was made in the Full Bee (TMK-2) period and bear that trademark. It was originally introduced into the line in 1963 and remains in production today.

There are no significant mold or finish variations affecting the normal values, but a Full Bee trademarked piece is rare.

THE BUILDER, Hum 305. Three Line Mark, incised 1955 MID, 5⅜".

HUM NO.	BASIC SIZE	TRADE MARK		CURRENT VALUE
305	5½"	TMK-2	FB	4000-5500.00
305	5½"	TMK-3	Sty. Bee	1000-1200.00
305	5½"	TMK-4	3-line	240-260.00
305	5½"	TMK-5	LB	220-240.00
305	5½"	TMK-6	MB	220.00

LITTLE BOOKKEEPER
Hum 306

The first example of this figure was made in the Full Bee (TMK-2) era and those prototypes bear that trademark.

There are no significant mold or finish variations affecting normal values, but a Full Bee trademarked example is rare.

LITTLE BOOKKEEPER, Hum 306. Left: Three Line Mark (TMK-4), 1955 MID. Right: Last Bee (TMK-5) trademark, 1955 MID. Both measure 4½". Shows head position variation.

(continued)

Little Bookkeeper (cont'd)

HUM NO.	BASIC SIZE	TRADE MARK		CURRENT VALUE
306	4¾"	TMK-2	FB	4000-5500.00
306	4¾"	TMK-3	Sty. Bee	1000-1200.00
306	4¾"	TMK-4	3-line	280-300.00
306	4¾"	TMK-5	LB	260-280.00
306	4¾"	TMK-6	MB	260.00

GOOD HUNTING
Hum 307

Introduced in the early 1960's this figure was first made in the Full Bee (TMK-2) era, but the Stylized Bee (TMK-3) trademark and later are the most common.

In older versions of this piece the boy holds the binoculars significantly lower than they are held in the figure made today, but this and any other mold and finish variations have no affect on normal values. The variations merely reflect the normal changes in the evolution of the figurine.

HUM NO.	BASIC SIZE	TRADE MARK		CURRENT VALUE
307	5¼"	TMK-2	FB	4000-5500.00
307	5¼"	TMK-3	Sty. Bee	600-800.00
307	5¼"	TMK-4	3-line	240-260.00
307	5¼"	TMK-5	LB	220-240.00
307	5¼"	TMK-6	MB	220.00

GOOD HUNTING, Hum 307. Left: Three Line Mark (TMK-4), 1955 MID, 5". Right: Missing Bee (TMK-6) mark, 1955 MID, 5⅛".

LITTLE TAILOR
Hum 308

This figure was first produced in the Full Bee (TMK-2) era, but not placed in the line until the 1970's. There are a few of the Full Bee and Stylized Bee (TMK-3) pieces around, but they are rare.

There was a major mold redesign in the Last Bee (TMK-5) era and the old and new may be found in that trademark. See the accompanying photograph for the differences between the two.

LITTLE TAILOR, Hum 308. This photo shows the difference between the old style (left) with an incised 1955 MID and the new (right), 1972 MID. The left measures 5¼'' and the right, 5⅝''. Both bear the Last Bee trademark (TMK-5).

HUM NO.	BASIC SIZE	TRADE MARK		CURRENT VALUE
308	5½"	TMK-2	FB	4000-5500.00
308	5½"	TMK-3	Sty. Bee	2000-2500.00
308	5½"	TMK-4	3-line	240-260.00
308	5½"	TMK-5	LB	220-240.00
308	5½"	TMK-6	MB	220.00

WITH LOVING GREETINGS
Hum 309

When first released in 1983 the suggested retail price was $80.00. It now sells for $175.00 and the basic size is 3½". Take a look at the left hand figure accompanying photograph. When you compare it to the other two, you will see that the prototype is a good bit more complex. This is a good illustration of how a figure evolves from prototype to production. Obviously the paint brush under the boy's arm was judged too vulnerable to breakage and was removed from the production model.

WITH LOVING GREETINGS, Hum 309. Left: Full Bee in an incised circle, "© by W. Goebel", 1955 MID, 3½". This is the blue inkwell with stopper variation. Note brush under left arm. Center: Missing Bee mark, 1955 MID, 3½". Blue inkwell. The brush is now missing. Right: Missing Bee mark, 1955 MID, 3½". Purplish brown inkwell.

With Loving Greetings (cont'd)

When first introduced into the line in 1983, the ink pot was colored blue with turquoise being the color of the writing on the tablet. In late 1987 the color of the ink pot was changed to brown and the color of the writing to blue. This change was made during the Missing Bee (TMK-6) period and can be found with the old or the new color in that trademark.

HUM NO.	BASIC SIZE	TRADE MARK		CURRENT VALUE
309	3½"	TMK-2	FB	4000-5500.00
309	3½"	TMK-5	LB	175-190.00
309	3½"	TMK-6	MB	175.00

SEARCHING ANGEL
Hum 310
Wall Plaque

This piece was first fashioned in the Full Bee (TMK-2) period, but was not released for sale until 1979. They are very rare, but have been found bearing this mark.

SEARCHING ANGEL Plaque. Hum 310. Left: Full Bee mark in an incised circle, incised 1955 MID, 3⅜" x 4¼". Right: Last Bee Mark, incised 1955 MID, 4¼" x 4⅛".

HUM NO.	BASIC SIZE	TRADE MARK		CURRENT VALUE
310	4"x2½"	TMK-2	FB	2500-3500.00
310	4"x2½"	TMK-5	LB	115-125.00
310	4"x2½"	TMK-6	MB	115.00

KISS ME
Hum 311

KISS ME, Hum 311. Left: Three Line Mark (TMK-4), 1955 MID, 6⅛". Right: Missing Bee (TMK-6), 6¼".

(continued)

314

Kiss Me (cont'd)

Kiss Me was first designed and made in the Full Bee (TMK-2) era, but it was not released for sale until the Stylized Bee (TMK-3) period. A few of these Full Bee pieces have made their way into the collector market. They are very rare.

The mold was reworked in the Three Line Mark (TMK-4) period so that the doll no longer wears any socks. They can, therefore be found either way in that trademark.

HUM NO.	BASIC SIZE	TRADE MARK		CURRENT VALUE
311	6"	TMK-2	FB	5000-6000.00
311	6"	TMK-3	Sty. Bee	750-1000.00
311(socks)	6"	TMK-4	3-line	450-550.00
311 (no socks)	6"	TMK-4	3-line	280-300.00
311	6"	TMK-5	LB	260.00
311	6"	TMK-6	MB	260.00

HONEY LOVER
Hum 312

This piece was first found illustrated in the *Golden Anniversary Album* as a Possible Future Edition (PFE) when the book was released in 1984. At that point in time, a few had somehow already made their way into collectors hands. It is now out, having been released as a special *M.I. Hummel* Club exclusive offering. Released at $190.00, it is available to members, only upon after the fifteenth anniversary of their club membership.

HONEY LOVER, Hum 312. Left: This 3⅞" figure has a Full Bee mark and a hand lettered mold number along with the frequently found normal "© by W. Goebel". Additionally there is a painted red "Z" indicating that this particular piece is a prototype. Right: Also a Full Bee marked piece, this 4" figure bears a 1955 incised Mold Induction Date (MID).

HUM NO.	BASIC SIZE	TRADE MARK	CURRENT VALUE
312	3¾"	FB TMK-2	7000-8000.00
312	3¾"	MB TMK-6	350.00
312	3¾"	HM TMK-7	210.00

(continued)

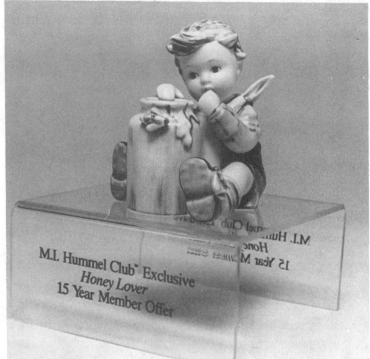

HONEY LOVER, Hum 312/I. Hummel Mark (current use or TMK-7, incised 1955 MID, 3¾". This is an issue exclusively available only to members of the *M.I. Hummel* Club that have attained 15 years of membership.

Photo of the underside of the base of Hum 312/I, **HONEY LOVER** showing the special club backstamp.

SUNNY MORNING
Hum 313
Possible Future Edition

This piece was designed and the first examples made in the mid 1950's, but has not yet been placed in production. This one somehow made it into the collector market.

SUNNY MORNING, Hum 313. Inked in incised 313 mold number, Full Bee trademark in an incised circle, 1955 MID, "© by W. Goebel, 1956", 4¼".

CONFIDENTIALLY
Hum 314

Even though this future was first introduced into the line in 1972, the Last Bee (TMK-5) period, they can be found in the Full Bee (TMK-2), Stylized Bee (TMK-3) and the Three Line (TMK-4) as well.

Apparently they redesigned the figure shortly after releasing it. The new and old styles are evident in the accompanying photograph.

The old and new styles can be found with the Last Bee trademark.

HUM NO.	BASIC SIZE	TRADE MARK		CURRENT VALUE
314	5½"	TMK-2	FB	5000-6000.00
314	5½"	TMK-3	Sty. Bee	1000-1500.00
314	5½"	TMK-4	3-line	500-650.00
314(old)	5½"	TMK-5	LB	400-500.00
314(new)	5½"	TMK-5	LB	260-275.00
314	5½"	TMK-6	MB	260.00

CONFIDENTIALLY, Hum 314, Left: Last Bee mark (TMK-5), incised 1955 MID, 5⅜". Right: Last Bee mark (TMK-5), incised 1972 MID, 5⅞".

MOUNTAINEER
Hum 315

Released during the Stylized Bee (TMK-3) trademark period, it is also found, albeit rare, in with the Full Bee (TMK-2) trademark.

There are no mold or finish variations that would have any effect on the normal values.

MOUNTAINEER, Hum 315. This example is 5" in height, has the Three Line Mark (TMK-4) and bears an incised 1955 MID.

(continued)

Mountaineer (cont'd)

HUM NO.	BASIC SIZE	TRADE MARK		CURRENT VALUE
315	5¼"	TMK-2	FB	5000-6000.00
315	5¼"	TMK-3	Sty. Bee	1000-1200.00
315	5¼"	TMK-4	3-line	210-230.00
315	5¼"	TMK-5	LB	195-210.00
315	5¼"	TMK-6	MB	195.00

RELAXATION
Hum 316
Possible Future Edition

This piece was designed and produced in prototype in the mid-1950's, in the Full Bee (TMK-2) period. They have not yet been put into production, but at least two bearing the Full Bee trademark have somehow made their way into the collector market.

RELAXATION, Hum 316, PFE.

NOT FOR YOU
Hum 317

Even though this figurine was not released for sale until the early 1960's, the Stylized Bee (TMK-3) period, it is also occasionally found bearing the Full Bee (TMK-2) trademark.

There are no mold or finish variations that affect the normal values for the figures with the various trademarks.

HUM NO.	BASIC SIZE	TRADE MARK		CURRENT VALUE
317	6"	TMK-2	FB	4000-5000.00
✳317	6"	TMK-3	Sty. Bee	700-900.00
317	6"	TMK-4	3-line	235-260.00
317	6"	TMK-5	LB	220-235.00
317	6"	TMK-6	MB	220.00

(continued)

NOT FOR YOU, Hum 317. Has an incised Mold Induction Date (MID) of 1955. It is 5⅝'' tall and bears the Missing Bee (TMK-6) trademark.

ART CRITIC
Hum 318

   This figure was first designed and produced in prototype back in the 1950's during the Full Bee (TMK-2) era, but was not released until 1991. At least two of these, marked with the Full Bee trademark, have found their way into the collector market.

   There are no significant mold or finish variation affecting the normal value for the figures bearing the various trademarks.

HUM NO.	BASIC SIZE	TRADE MARK		CURRENT VALUE
318	5¾''	TMK-1	FB	5000-6000.00
318	5¾''	TMK-6	MB	260-275.00

ART CRITIC, Hum 318. Missing Bee mark (TMK-6), incised 1955 MID, 5¼'', first issue backstamp dated 1991.

THE ART CRITIC, Hum 318. Demonstration piece with only the flesh tones and brown base color on the coat painted. Current-use trademark (TMK-7), First Issue backstamp, incised 1955 MID, 5¼''. Valued at about $400.00

DOLL BATH
Hum 319

This figure was first designed and produced during the Full Bee (TMK-2) trademark period, but not released until 1962, during the Stylized Bee (TMK-3) period. It is possible that there are some with the Full Bee trademark out there to be found.

In the 1970's the entire collection underwent a change from the old smooth surface finish to a textured finish. Unlike many of the other figures in the collection, this one made a clean break from the old style finish in the Three Line (TMK-4) trademarked pieces to the new textured finish on the Last Bee (TMK-5) pieces and all thereafter.

HUM NO.	BASIC SIZE	TRADE MARK		CURRENT VALUE
319	5¼"	TMK-2	FB	4000-5000.00
319	5¼"	TMK-3	Sty. Bee	600-800.00
✗319	5¼"	TMK-4	3-line	275-300.00
319	5¼"	TMK-5	LB	260-275.00
319	5¼"	TMK-6	MB	260.00

DOLL BATH, Hum 319. Both bear the Three Line mark (TMK-5). The one on the left has an incised 1956 MID and the other has an MID of 197?. It was impossible to discern what the fourth digit was.

DOLL BATH, Hum 319. Missing Bee mark, incised 1956 MID, 5⅛''.

THE PROFESSOR
Hum 320

First produced in prototype in the mid 1950's during the Full Bee (TMK-2) era, it was not released until 1992. The new ones bear the mold number 320/0, but the Full Bee pieces have the mold number 320, with no size designator and is larger than the production pieces.

There are no significant variations affecting the normal collector values.

HUM NO.	BASIC SIZE	TRADE MARK		CURRENT VALUE
320	5¾"	TMK-2	FB	8000-10,000.00
320/0	4¾"	TMK-5	LB	195-210.00
320/0	4¾"	TMK-6	MB	195.00

(continued)

The Professor (cont'd)

THE PROFESSOR, Hum 320. Hummel mark (current use or TMK-7), incised 1989 MID, 4⅞", first issue backstamp dated 1992.

THE PROFESSOR, Hum 320. This is a master model. Note the red line around the base.

THE PROFESSOR, Hum 320. The base of the Hum 320 master model. Note the inked incised mold number. This is routinely done on pieces made from the mother or master mold.

WASH DAY
Hum 321

When this figurine was first made in the 1950's, the prototypes had the laundry she is holding up much longer and attached to the rest of the laundry down in the basket. This was the Full Bee period. It is not likely, but possible this might be found. The only known examples are in the factory archives and these are marked with the Full Bee (TMK-2) trademark.

In 1989 a new smaller version of this piece was issued as a part of a four piece series with matching mini-plates. They do not have the laundry basket and have an incised mold number of 321 4/0. When they issued this mold number they change the number on the larger pieces to 321/0. You may find it either way on those figures with the Missing Bee (TMK-6) trademark.

WASH DAY, Hum 321. Three Line Mark, incised 1957 MID, 5¾"

(continued)

321

HUM NO.	BASIC SIZE	TRADE MARK		CURRENT VALUE
321/4/0	3"	TMK-6	MB	90-100.00
321	5¾"	TMK-2	FB	5000-6000.00
✳321	5¾"	TMK-3	Sty. Bee	300-350.00
321	5¾"	TMK-4	3-line	275-300.00
321	5¾"	TMK-5	LB	260-275.00
321	5¾"	TMK-6	MB	260.00

LITTLE PHARMACIST
Hum 322

This figurine was first designed and produced in the 1950's and those prototypes bear the Full Bee (TMK-2) trademark. The only known examples are in the factory archives.

There are several variations in the labeling of the medicine bottle at the figure's feet. The version written in German (see photo) has been temporarily withdrawn from production as of December 31, 1984. One of the most difficult to find is the version with "Castor Oil" on the bottle in the Spanish language. When found, it is on the Three Line mark (TMK-4) pieces. It is valued at $3000-5000.00

In 1988 Little Pharmacist was redesigned and all subsequent production of the figure will reflect the following changes: The base has been made more shallow with rounded corners. This renders the figure shorter than its former 6" size to 5¾". The coat is now curved in front at the button line. A breast pocket has been added and the strap (in back) has been made wider and a second button has been added. His bow tie has been straightened and now the eyeglass stems disappear into his hair.

HUM NO.	BASIC SIZE	TRADE MARK		CURRENT VALUE
322	6"	TMK-2	FB	4000-5000.00
✳322	6"	TMK-3	Sty. Bee	750-1000.00
322	6"	TMK-4	3-line	230-250.00
322	6"	TMK-5	LB	220-230.00
322	6"	TMK-6	MB	220.00

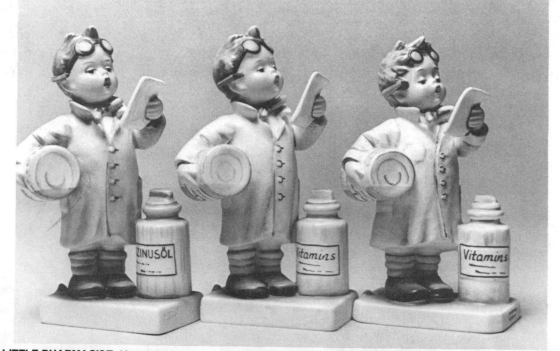

LITTLE PHARMACIST, Hum 322. Left: Last Bee (TMK-5) trademark, 1955 MID, 5¾" the word "REZEPT" is found on the prescription pad in his left hand. Center: Missing Bee (TMK-6) trademark, 1955 MID, 5¾", "RECIPE" is on the pad. Right: The same as the center figure except this one measures 5⅝" and has a different hair style. Other variations are discussed in the accompanying text.

MERRY CHRISTMAS
Hum 323
Wall Plaque

Designed and made in prototype during the 1950's in the Full Bee (TMK-2) period, the plaque was not offered for sale until 1979. It was initially issued bearing the Last Bee (TMK-5) and continues in the line with the present use trademark the Hummel Mark (TMK-7).

HUM NO.	BASIC SIZE	TRADE MARK	CURRENT VALUE
323	4"x5¼"	TMK-2 FB	2500-3500.00
323	4"x5¼"	TMK-5 LB	120-130.00
323	4"x5¼"	TMK-6 MB	120.00

MERRY CHRISTMAS Plaque, Hum 323. Last Bee mark, 3⅛" x 5¼".

AT THE FENCE
Hum 324
Possible Future Edition

This figure was designed and produced in prototype in the 1950's, but has not yet been put into regular production and offered for sale. The one in the picture is marked with the Full Bee (TMK-2) as you can see. Somehow it managed to make it onto the collector market. Notice the line painted around the base. A red line painted so, denotes a painters model, one which is the model by which the Goebel painters try to duplicate when producing the figurines.

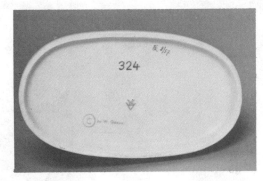

AT THE FENCE, Hum 324, PFE.

HELPING MOTHER
Hum 325
Possible Future Edition

Originally designed and produced in prototype during the 1950's in the Full Bee (TMK-2) trademark era, at least two bearing that trademark are known to be in private collections. Collector value: $7000-9000.00

HELPING MOTHER, Hum 325, PFE.

BEING PUNISHED
Hum 326

The original design and prototype figures was made in the mid-1950's. Those figures have an incised 1955 MID and bear the Full Bee (TMK-2) trademark. Although the piece has not yet been released more than one has made its way onto the collector market. Has reportedly been found with the Stylized Bee (TMK-3) trademark also. Collector value: $6000-7500.00 for either one.

THE RUN-A-WAY
Hum 327

Originally designed and produced in the 1950's, it was not released until 1972.

There exists at least two variations of Hum 327. Significantly they have both been found with the Last Bee (TMK-5) trademark although each variation bears a different mold induction date (MID). The older design (MID 1955) has flowers in the basket, gray jacket, gray hat, and the crook on the cane is turned more sideways. The newer design (MID 1972) has no flowers, a green hat, blue jacket, and the cane is situated with the crook pointing up.

HUM NO.	BASIC SIZE	TRADE MARK		CURRENT VALUE
327	5¼"	TMK-2	FB	4000-5000.00
327	5¼"	TMK-4	3-line	1000-1200.00
327 (old style)	5¼"	TMK-5	LB	750-900.00
327 (new style)	5¼"	TMK-5	LB	225-240.00
327	5¼"	TMK-6	MB	225.00

THE RUN-A-WAY, Hum 327. Left: Last Bee mark (TMK-5), incised 1955 MID, 5⅛". Right: Last Bee Mark (TMk-5), incised 1972 MID, 5½".

325

CARNIVAL
Hum 328

The original design and prototypes were made in the mid-1950's. Those prototypes have a MID of 1955 and bear the Full Bee trademark. When the piece was put into regular production and offered for sale in the 1960's it had the Three Line (TMK-4), but some have been found bearing the Stylized Bee (TMK-3) as well.

There are no major mold or finish variation affecting the normal values.

HUM NO.	BASIC SIZE	TRADE MARK		CURRENT VALUE
328	6"	TMK-2	FB	4000-5000.00
328	6"	TMK-3	Sty. Bee	800-1200.00
328	6"	TMK-4	3-line	215-240.00
328	6"	TMK-5	LB	205-215.00
328	6"	TMK-6	MB	205.00

CARNIVAL, Hum 328. Three Line Mark (TMK-4), incised 1957 MID, 5¾".

OFF TO SCHOOL
Hum 329
Possible Future Edition

This figure was originally designed and made in prototype in the 1950's. None are known to be outside the factory archives. Release date unknown.

Boy and girl walking along. The girl has a book satchel in the crook of her left arm. The boy figure is substantially similar to Hum 82, School Boy.

BAKING DAY
Hum 330

This figure was first made in prototype in the 1950's. These early examples bear the 1955 MID as do they today. It was not released until 1985, during the Missing Bee (TMK-6) period.

There are no significant mold or finish variations affecting normal values.

HUM NO.	BASIC SIZE	TRADE MARK		CURRENT VALUE
330	5¼"	TMK-2	FB	4000-5000.00
330	5¼"	TMK-5	LB	240-250.00
330	5¼"	TMK-6	MB	240.00

(continued)

BAKING DAY, Hum 330. Missing Bee mark, incised 1955 MID, 5¼".

CROSSROADS
Hum 331

This piece was first made and released in the 1950's. It has been reported that there is a variation regarding the position of the trombone. It is not terribly obvious in the photo here but if you look closely, you can see the end of the horn protruding above the boy's head. The reported variation is that the horn is reversed so that it points down instead of up as in the one pictured here. This can't really be regarded as a legitimate variation. It is the result of a mistake in the assembly of the parts at the factory and is likely to be the only one in existence.

In 1990, Goebel issued a special edition of Crossroads to commemorate the demise of the Berlin Wall. Limited to 20,000 worldwide, it is the same figure except the "HALT" sign on the post is placed at the base of the post as if it had fallen. Production of this edition took place during the transition from the Missing Bee (TMK-6) trademark and the Hummel Mark (TMK-7) currently being used. Interestingly, it has been reported that only about 3,500 of the 20,000 were given the Hummel Mark (TMK-7).

The newest variation is another edition created for the U.S. military forces. As with the special "Desert Storm" edition of Hum 50, Volunteers, this one was sold through military base exchange stores only. The edition consists of three pieces. The figure is the regular production model with the sign on the post, but it has an American and German flag beneath the glaze under the base. A second piece is a representation of a piece of the wall with "Berlin Wall" on it in bas-relief. It also has the flags underneath along with the inscription "With esteem and grateful appreciation to the United States Military Forces for the preservation of peace and freedom". That same inscription is found on a brass plate on the front of the third piece, a wooden display base. The Berlin Wall piece is limited to 20,000 worldwide and sequentially hand-numbered beneath the base in the traditional manner of marking limited editions.

HUM NO.	BASIC SIZE	TRADE MARK		CURRENT VALUE
331	6¾"	TMK-2	FB	4000-5000.00
331	6¾"	TMK-3	Sty. Bee	2500-3500.00
331	6¾"	TMK-4	3-line	800-1000.00
331	6¾"	TMK-5	LB	380-400.00
331	6¾"	TMK-6	MB	380-400.00

(continued)

Crossroads (cont'd)

HUM NO.	BASIC SIZE	TRADE MARK		CURRENT VALUE
331 (sign down)	6¾"	TMK-6	MB	700-900.00
331 (sign down)	6¾"	TMK-7	HM	900-1100.00
331 (military edition)	6¾"	TMK-7	HM	600-750.00

CROSSROADS, Hum 331. Left: Last Bee mark (TMK-5), incised 1955 MID, 6⅜". Right: Missing Bee mark (TMK-6), incised 1955 MID, 6⅝". Special Backstamp reading "M.I. Hummel 1990 a Celebration of Freedom". Note the "HALT" sign is now on the ground.

SOLDIER BOY
Hum 332

Originally designed and produced in prototype in the 1950's, this figure was not released for sale to the general public until the early 1960's.

There is a variation on the color of the cap medallion. It is painted red on older pieces and blue on the newer ones. The transition from red to blue took place in the 3-line mark (TMK-4) period and can be found both ways bearing that trademark.

SOLDIER BOY, Hum 332. Left: Three Line Mark (TMK-4), 1957 MID, red cap medallion, 5¾". Right: All is now the same except this one has a blue cap medallion.

HUM NO.	BASIC SIZE	TRADE MARK		CURRENT VALUE
322	6"	TMK-2	FB	4000-5000.00
322	6"	TMK-3	Sty. Bee	800-1000.00
322(red medallion)	6"	TMK-4	3-line	400-500.00
322(blue medallion)	6"	TMK-4	3-line	205-225.00
322	6"	TMK-5	LB	195-205.00
322	6"	TMK-6	MB	195.00

BLESSED EVENT
Hum 333

This figure was designed and produced in prototype in the 1950's, but not released until 1964 during the 3-line (TMK-4) trademark era.

There are no significant variations reported.

There have been no examples found outside the factory archives with the Full Bee (TMK-2) and Stylized Bee (TMK-3) trademarks, but it would not be unreasonable to suspect they may be out there.

HUM NO.	BASIC SIZE	TRADE MARK		CURRENT VALUE
333	5½"	TMK-2	FB	*
333	5½"	TMK-3	Sty. Bee	*
333	5½"	TMK-4	3-line	320-350.00
333	5½"	TMK-5	LB	300-320.00
333	5½"	TMK-6	MB	300.00

*Existence assumed but unsubstantiated.

BLESSED EVENT, Hum 333. Three Line Mark, donut base, 5¼".

HOMEWARD BOUND
Hum 334

HOMEWARD BOUND, Hum 334. Left: Last Bee (TMK-6) mark, 1975 MID, split base, 5½". Right: Last Bee (TMK-6), 1955 MID, donut base.

This figurine was first made in prototype in the mid 1950's, but not released until 1971.

Older models of this design have a support molded in beneath the goat, the newer versions do not have this support.

The transition from the old, molded support model to the newer design took place during the Last Bee (TMK-5) period and can be found either way in that trademark.

HUM NO.	BASIC SIZE	TRADE MARK		CURRENT VALUE
334	5"	TMK-2	FB	4000-5000.00
334	5"	TMK-4	3-line	600-800.00
334 (old style)	5"	TMK-5	LB	375-500.00
334 (new style)	5"	TMK-5	LB	320-340.00
334	5"	TMK-6	MB	320.00

LUCKY BOY
Hum 335
Possible Future Edition

Produced in prototype in the Stylized Bee (TMK-3) period, but not yet released for sale. The example in the accompanying photograph has a red line painted around the base. The red line is used by the factory to denote a figure that is used as a model for the artist to try to duplicate on the production pieces.

LUCKY BOY. Hum 335, PFE.

CLOSE HARMONY
Hum 336

This figure was first produced in prototype in the Full Bee (TMK-2) era, but not released until the early 1960's.

Inexplicably, this piece can be found with the three Mold Induction Dates (MID) of 1955, 1956 or 1957. There is a 1962 MID that is explained by a redesign in that year. What is even more peculiar is those in production currently are yet another redesign, but they bear the 1955 MID. This strange circumstance makes the pieces with the later MID of 1962 more valuable than those with the 1955 MID that are currently in production. It is the only figure in the collection that can be found with four different MID's.

CLOSE HARMONY, Hum 336. Left: Three Line Mark (TMK-4), incised 1957 MID, donut base, 5⅜". Right: three Line Mark (TMK-4), incised 1955 MID, 5¼".

HUM NO.	BASIC SIZE	TRADE MARK		CURRENT VALUE
336	5½"	TMK-2	FB	4000-5000.00
336	5½"	TMK-3	Sty. Bee	1000-1500.00
336	5½"	TMK-4	3-line	600-700.00
336(old)	5½"	TMK-5	LB	350-475.00
336(new)	5½"	TMK-5	LB	260-275.00
336	5½"	TMK-6	MB	260.00

CINDERELLA
Hum 337

CINDERELLA, Hum 337. Left: Full Bee mark in an incised circle, "© by W. Goebel", 4⅝". Note the fourth bird (on the left shoulder). From the collection of Katherine Stephens. Right: Last Bee mark, incised 1958 MID, 4½".

Last Bee 1952 MID, eyes closed.

(continued)

332

Cinderella (cont'd)

Produced first in the Full Bee (TMK-2) era in prototype, this figure was not placed in the collection until 1972 during the Last Bee (TMK-5) period. Any with marks older will bring premium prices.

First versions of this figure have eyes open, newer ones have eyes closed. These variations represent two entirely different molds. Both versions have appeared bearing the Last Bee trademark (TMK-5).

HUM NO.	BASIC SIZE	TRADE MARK		CURRENT VALUE
337	5½"	TMK-2	FB	4000-5000.00
337	5½"	TMK-4	3-line	1500-1700.00
337 (old style)	5½"	TMK-5	LB	900-1200.00
337 (new style)	5½"	TMK-5	LB	260-275.00
337	5½"	TMK-6	MB	260.00

BIRTHDAY CAKE
Candle Holder
Hum 338

Birthday Cake was added to the line in the winter of 1988. It measures 3¾" and has a receptacle for a candle as you can see by the photo here. It has an incised mold induction date of 1956.

There are two versions to be found. The differences are with regard to the texture of the top of the cake surface. It is reported that about the first 2000 were produced with a smooth texture. This was changed to a rough texture ostensibly to correspond to the style of today.

It does exist in the Full Bee (TMK-2) prototype and has recently been turned up in the Stylized Bee (TMK-3) trademark.

HUM NO.	BASIC SIZE	TRADE MARK		CURRENT VALUE
338	3¾"	TMK-2	FB	5000-6000.00
338	3¾"	TMK-3	Sty. Bee	4000-5000.00
338	3¾"	TMK-6	MB	130.00

BIRTHDAY CAKE candle holder, Hum 338. Missing Bee mark, incised 1956 MID, 3⁹⁄₁₆".

BEHAVE
Hum 339
Possible Future Edition

The one in the photo here bears a 1956 Mold Induction Date (MID) indicating that it was designed then or prior, in the Full Bee (TMK-2) era, but this one has the Stylized Bee (TMK-3) trademark. No release date has been disclosed.

 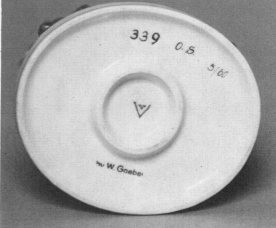

BEHAVE!, Hum 339, PFE.

LETTER TO SANTA CLAUS
Hum 340

The first model (prototype) produced had a tree trunk instead of a milled lumber post for the mailbox. The post was the final design approved for production. It was first released in the early 1970's. It was restyled with a new textured finish that was a general change throughout the collection in the Last Bee Mark (TMK-5) period and can be found either way bearing that trademark. The old pieces sport gray-green pants and the newer ones have red-orange pants.

HUM NO.	BASIC SIZE	TRADE MARK		CURRENT VALUE
340	7"	TMK-2	FB	4000-5000.00
340	7"	TMK-3	Sty. Bee	3500-4000.00
340	7"	TMK-4	3-line	600-750.00
340	7"	TMK-5	LB	305-325.00
340	7"	TMK-6	MB	305.00

LETTER TO SANTA, Hum 340. This particular figurine measures 7⅛", has an incised 1957 MID and bears the Three Mark (TMK-4).

BIRTHDAY PRESENT
Hum 341
Possible Future Edition

Standing girl holding potted plant with both hands.
This future release has been found on the collector market bearing the 3-line (TMK-4) trademark.

MISCHIEF MAKER
Hum 342

First made in prototype in the mid-1950's, this figure was not released for sale until the early 1970's. There are no significant variations affecting normal values.

MISCHIEF MAKER, Hum 342. Has an incised MID of 1960, is 4⅞" tall and bears the Missing Bee (TMK-6) trademark.

HUM NO.	BASIC SIZE	TRADE MARK	CURRENT VALUE
342	4¹⁵⁄₁₆"	TMK-2 FB	4000-5000.00
342	4¹⁵⁄₁₆"	TMK-4 3-line	600-750.00
342	4¹⁵⁄₁₆"	TMK-5 LB	240-250.00
342	4¹⁵⁄₁₆"	TMK-6 MB	240.00

CHRISTMAS SONG
Hum 343

This is one of the six new designs released by Goebel in 1981. There is at least one example of this piece known to exist bearing the Stylized Bee trademark.

All others found so far have later trademarks, but because there were five others designed at the same time and released at the same time that have been found with the Full Bee (TMK-2) trademark it would not be unreasonable to assume there are some out there somewhere.

HUM NO.	BASIC SIZE	TRADE MARK	CURRENT VALUE
343	6¼"	TMK-2 FB	——
343	6¼"	TMK-3 Sty. Bee	2000-3000.00
343	6¼"	TMK-5 LB	195-210.00
343	6¼"	TMK-6 MB	195.00

(continued)

CHRISTMAS SONG, Hum 343. Missing Bee 1957 MID, 6⅜".

FEATHERED FRIENDS
Hum 344

First designed and made in prototype in the mid-1950's, this piece was not released until the early 1970's in the Last Bee (TMK-5) era. Figurines have been found on the collector market, however, that bear the three earlier marks, Full Bee (TMK-2), Stylized Bee (TMK-3) and the 3-line (TMK-4) trademarks.

There are no major mold or finish variations to be found that affect normal collector values.

HUM NO.	BASIC SIZE	TRADE MARK		CURRENT VALUE
344	4¾"	TMK-2	FB	4000-5000.00
344	4¾"	TMK-3	Sty. Bee	2000-3000.00
344	4¾"	TMK-4	3-line	750-1000.00
344	4¾"	TMK-5	LB	240-250.00
344	4¾"	TMK-6	MB	240.00

5⅛". **FEATHERED FRIENDS,** Hum 344. Missing Bee (TMK-6) mark, 1956 MID, 4½".

A FAIR MEASURE
Hum 345

This figure was first made in prototype in the mid 1950's but was not released until the early 1960's.

At least two variations of this figure exist and it is important to note that both have been found bearing the current trademark and different mold induction dates (MID). The older design (MID 1956) shows the boy with his eyes wide open; in the newer design (MID 1972) the boy is looking down so that it appears that he is looking down at his work. See the accompanying photograph. This transition from eyes up to eyes down took place during the Last Bee (TMK-5) and can be found both ways with that trademark.

HUM NO.	BASIC SIZE	TRADE MARK		CURRENT VALUE
346	4¾"	TMK-2	FB	4000-5000.00
346	4¾"	TMK-3	Sty. Bee	2000-3000.00
346	4¾"	TMK-4	3-line	900-1000.00
346 (old style)	4¾"	TMK-5	LB	550-750.00
346 (new style)	4¾"	TMK-5	LB	260-275.00
346	4¾"	TMK-6	MB	260.00

A FAIR MEASURE, Hum 345. Left: Last Bee mark, incised 1956 MID, donut base, 5⅝". Center: Last Bee mark, incised 1972 MID, split base, 5⅝". Right: Missing Bee mark, incised 1972 MID, split base, 5⅝".

THE SMART LITTLE SISTER
Hum 346

The Smart Little Sister was first made in prototype in the 1950's, but not released for sale until the early 1960's. It is nevertheless found with the earlier Full Bee (TMK-3) trademark, albeit rarely. The Stylized Bee (TMK-3) are not so rare, but seem to be available in some limited quantity.

There are no significant variations affecting normal values.

The Smart Little Sister (cont'd)

HUM NO.	BASIC SIZE	TRADE MARK		CURRENT VALUE
346	4¾"	TMK-2	FB	4000-5000.00
346	4¾"	TMK-3	Sty. Bee	1200-1500.00
346	4¾"	TMK-4	3-line	235-270.00
346	4¾"	TMK-5	LB	225-235.00
346	4¾"	TMK-6	MB	225.00

THE SMART LITTLE SISTER, Hum 346. Left: Three Line Mark, incised 1956 MID. Right: Last Bee mark, incised 1956 MID. Both measure 4⅜".

ADVENTURE BOUND
Hum 347

ADVENTURE BOUND, Hum 347. Three Line Mark, incised 1957 MID, 8" long x 7" high.

(continued)

338

Adventure Bound (cont'd)

This large, complicated multi-figure piece was first made in prototype in the mid-1950's, but was not released for sale until 1971-72. It has been made continuously since, but it is produced in limited numbers because it is a difficult and time-consuming piece to make.

There are at least three Full Bee (TMK-2) trademarked pieces known to be in private collections.

There are no significant variations that affect normal collector value.

HUM NO.	BASIC SIZE	TRADE MARK	CURRENT VALUE
347	7¼"x8"	TMK-2 FB	10,000-12,000.00
347	7¼"x8"	TMK-4 3-line	4000-5000.00
347	7¼"x8"	TMK-5 LB	3500-4000.00
347	7¼"x8"	TMK-6 MB	3500.00

RING AROUND THE ROSIE
Hum 348

RING AROUND THE ROSIE, Hum 348 with Full Bee mark (TMK-2) in an incised circle and "© by W. Goebel, Oeslau 1957". There is a painted red "X" beneath the base making it probable that this particular piece is a prototype.

This figure was first molded in 1957, but was not released until 1960. Sizes found in various price lists range from 6¼" to 7¼". The older ones tend to be the larger ones. They all bear a 1957 Mold Induction Date (MID). There are no significant variations affecting normal values.

HUM NO.	BASIC SIZE	TRADE MARK	CURRENT VALUE
348	6¾"	TMK-2 FB	10,000-15,000.00
348	6¾"	TMK-3 Sty. Bee	3200-3500.00
348	6¾"	TMK-4 3-line	2700-2800.00
348	6¾"	TMK-5 LB	2500.00
348	6¾"	TMK-6 MB	2500.00

FLORIST
Hum 349
Possible Future Edition

Standing boy wearing bib apron. He holds a flower in left hand and appears to be examining it closely. There are more flowers growing at his feet.

There is only one example known to be in a private collection. It is a 7½" figure and bears the 3-line (TMK-4) trademark.

ON HOLIDAY
Hum 350

First made in the Stylized Bee (TMK-3) period, this figurine was a new release in 1981. There were apparently a few prototypes made in the Stylized Bee (TMK-3) and the 3-line (TMK-4) trademarks for there have been a few uncovered. The remainder are found in the Last Bee (TMK-5) or later trademarks.

There are no significant mold or finish variations affecting normal collector values.

ON HOLIDAY, Hum 350. Missing Bee (TMK-6), 1965 MID, 4¼".

HUM NO.	BASIC SIZE	TRADE MARK	CURRENT VALUE
350	4¼"	TMK-3 Sty. Bee	2000-3000.00
350	4¼"	TMK-4 3-line	1700-2000.00
350	4¼"	TMK-5 LB	1200-1500.00
350	4¼"	TMK-6 MB	160.00

Crown	CM	TMK-1	1934-1950
Full Bee	FB	TMK-2	1940-1959
Stylized Bee	Sty Bee	TMK-3	1958-1972
Three Line Mark	3-line	TMK-4	1964-1972
Last Bee Mark	LB	TMK-5	1970-1980
Missing Bee Mark	MB	TMK-6	1979-1991
Hummel Mark (Current)	HM	TMK-7	1991-Present

THE BOTANIST
Hum 351

Basic size of this 1982 new design release is 4". There is a very rare example of The Botanist known to exist with the Three Line mark and a 1965 mold induction date. This is apparently a prototype piece and too unusual to place a realistic market value on. There has been another of these prototypes with a 1965 mold induction date (MID) found recently that has the Last Bee (TMK-5) on it. All the newer pieces bear the 1972 MID.

HUM NO.	BASIC SIZE	TRADE MARK		CURRENT VALUE
351	4"	TMK-4	3-line	2000-3000.00
351	4"	TMK-5	LB	1500-1800.00
351	4"	TMK-6	MB	195.00

THE BOTANIST, Hum 351. Missing Bee mark, incised 1972 MID, 4⅝".

SWEET GREETINGS
Hum 352

Sweet Greetings was among the six new designs to be released in 1981. Its basic size is 4⅛". It, like a few others of the new releases, was apparently produced in limited numbers as prototype pieces in the 3-line mark era, for at least one is known to exist that bears that mark. Both the prototype piece and the new release have a mold induction date of 1965.

SWEET GREETINGS, Hum 352. Missing Bee mark, 1964 MID, 4¼".

(continued)

HUM NO.	BASIC SIZE	TRADE MARK		CURRENT VALUE
352	4⅛"	TMK-4	3-line	2000-3000.00
352	4⅛"	TMK-5	LB	1500-1800.00
352	4⅛"	TMK-6	MB	195.00

SPRING DANCE
Hum 353

This figure first appeared in the 1960's. The smaller 353/0 with the 3-line mark is quite rare. This smaller size was released in the Last Bee trademark era.

There are no significant variations that affect normal collector value.

The larger size, 353/I has been temporarily withdrawn from production with no reinstatement date disclosed.

SPRING DANCE, Hum 353. Left: 353/0, Last Bee mark (TMK-5) 1963 MID, 5⅜". Right: 353/I, Three Line mark (TMK-4), 1963 MID, 6¾".

HUM NO.	BASIC SIZE	TRADE MARK		CURRENT VALUE
353/0	4¾"	TMK-4	3-line	2500-3000.00
353/0	4¾"	TMK-5	LB	280-300.00
353/0	4¾"	TMK-6	MB	280.00
353/1	6½"	TMK-4	3-line	600-750.00
353/1	6½"	TMK-5	LB	550.00
353/1	6½"	TMK-6	MB	500.00

HOLY WATER FONTS
Hum 354/A, ANGEL WITH LANTERN
Hum 354/B, ANGEL WITH TRUMPET
Hum 354/C, ANGEL WITH BIRD

Closed Number designation. Three fonts existing in factory prototype, only. Apparently they were never produced.

AUTUMN HARVEST
Hum 355

First produced in prototype in the Stylized Bee (TMK-3) era, this figurine was not released for sale in any quantities until the early 1970's. The earliest production pieces bear the 3-line (TMK-4), but they are apparently in fairly short supply.

They have an incised MID of 1971. There are no significant variations affecting normal collector values.

AUTUMN HARVEST, Hum 355, Left: Three Line Mark, incised 1964 MID, 4⅞''. Right: Missing Bee mark, incised 1964 MID, 5''.

HUM NO.	BASIC SIZE	TRADE MARK	CURRENT VALUE
355	4¾''	TMK-4 3-line	800-1000.00
355	4¾''	TMK-5 LB	195-205.00
355	4¾''	TMK-6 MB	195.00

GAY ADVENTURE
Hum 356

This figure was first produced in prototype in the 1960's and was known as Joyful Adventure at the time. It was released for sale in the early 1970's bearing a 1971 incised MID.

There are no significant variations affecting normal collector values.

HUM NO.	BASIC SIZE	TRADE MARK	CURRENT VALUE
356	4¹⁵⁄₁₆''	TMK-4 3-line	800-1000.00
356	4¹⁵⁄₁₆''	TMK-5 LB	190.00
356	4¹⁵⁄₁₆''	TMK-6 MB	175.00

GAY ADVENTURE, Hum 356. Last Bee (TMK-5), 1971 MID, 4¾''.

GUIDING ANGEL, SHINING LIGHT and TUNEFUL ANGEL
Hum 357, Hum 358 and Hum 359

Originally molded around 1960 with a 1960 MID, these were not released until the early 1970's. Usually sold as a set.

There are no significant variations affecting normal values.

HUM NO.	BASIC SIZE	TRADE MARK		CURRENT VALUE
357	2¾"	TMK-4	3-line	85-95.00
357	2¾"	TMK-5	LB	80-85.00
357	2¾"	TMK-6	MB	80.00
358	2¾"	TMK-4	3-line	80.00
358	2¾"	TMK-5	LB	85-95.00
358	2¾"	TMK-6	MB	80-85.00
359	2¾"	TMK-4	3-line	80.00
359	2¾"	TMK-5	LB	85-95.00
359	2¾"	TMK-6	MB	80-85.00

GUIDING ANGEL, Hum 357. Missing Bee (TMK-6) mark, 1960 MID, 2⅞".
SHINING LIGHT, Hum 358. Missing Bee (TMK-6) mark, 1960 MID, 2¾".
TUNEFUL ANGEL, Hum 359. Missing Bee (TMK-6) mark, 1960 MID, 2⅝".

BOY, GIRL and BOY AND GIRL
Wall Vases
Hum 360/A, Hum 360/B and Hum 360/C

Stylized Bee trademarked wall vases are considered rare. They were first produced around 1955 and discontinued about 1960. Of the three the Boy and Girl (Hum 360/A) seems to be the most easily found. They appear with the Stylized Bee (TMK-3) trademark. Basic size is 4½"x6¼".

All three were reissued with the Last Bee and continued in production in the Missing Bee (TMK-6) Mark Status January 1, 1990. They were temporarily withdrawn from production once again on December 31, 1989 with no reinstatement date disclosed.

HUM NO.	BASIC SIZE	TRADE MARK		CURRENT VALUE
360 A,B&C	4½"x6¼"	TMK-3	Sty. Bee	350-500.00 each
360 A,B&C	4½"x6¼"	TMK-5	LB	150-200.00 each
360 A,B&C	4½"x6¼"	TMK-6	MB	125-140.00 each

(continued)

WALL VASES, Hum 360/A, Hum 360/B, Hum 360/C. All three bear an incised Stylized Bee trademark (TMK-3), "© by W. Goebel", black "Western Germany", incised 1958 MID and measure 5¾".

FAVORITE PET
Hum 361

First made in prototype about 1960, this figure was released for sale in the mid-1960's. There are no significant variations affecting normal collector values.

HUM NO.	BASIC SIZE	TRADE MARK		CURRENT VALUE
361	4¼"	TMK-3	Sty. Bee	800-1000.00
361	4¼"	TMK-4	3-line	275-300.00
361	4¼"	TMK-5	LB	260-275.00
361	4¼"	TMK-6	MB	260.00

FAVORITE PET, Hum 361. Three Line Mark (TMK-4), 1960 MID, donut base, 4¼".

I FORGOT
Hum 362
Possible Future Edition

Made in prototype form in the late 1950's, this figure has not yet been released for sale. Note the line painted around the base on the one in the accompanying photograph. A red painted line such as this denotes an artist's model. It is copied as closely as possible by Goebel artists painting the production figurines.

I FORGOT, Hum 362, PFE.

BIG HOUSECLEANING
Hum 363

The original prototypes of this figure were made during the Stylized Bee (TMK-3) era. The figures have been in continuous production since their release at the end of the Three Line (TMK-4) era. Some were made bearing this trademark, but they are fairly scarce.

There are no significant variations affecting normal value for the figures.

HUM NO.	BASIC SIZE	TRADE MARK	CURRENT VALUE
363	3¹⁵⁄₁₆"	TMK-4 3-line	800-1000.00
✗363	3¹⁵⁄₁₆"	TMK-5 LB	260-275.00
363	3¹⁵⁄₁₆"	TMK-6 MB	260.00

BIG HOUSECLEANING, Hum 363. Missing Bee mark, incised 1980 MID, 4".

SUPREME PROTECTION
Hum 364

This piece is a 9", full color madonna and child and is the first limited edition figurine ever offered to the general public by Goebel. Released in 1984, it was scheduled to be produced during that year only, in commemoration and celebration of the anniversary of Sister M.I. Hummel's 75th birthday. It has a special backstamp identifying it as such. As the first figures began to become available it was discovered that some 3000 to 3500 of them were released with a mistake in the stamp. The *M.I. Hummel* came out as M.J. Hummel. The factory tried at first to correct the mistake by modifying the "J" in the decal to appear as an "I". However, they attempted to change it by cutting the decal and unfortunately the modification didn't come off too well, the result demonstrating quite obviously what they attempted. As a consequence there are the backstamp versions to be found: The correct backstamp; the poorly modified backstamp; and the "M.J. Hummel" incorrect backstamp spelling. This particular backstamp variation is apparently coming into strong demand.

They have been found bearing the 3-line (TMK-4) trademark. These are rare; probably prototype pieces never meant to be sold.

HUM NO.	BASIC SIZE	TRADE MARK		CURRENT VALUE
364	9"	TMK-4	3-line	2500-3500.00
364(regular signature)	9"	TMK-6	MB	250-275.00
364(M.J. variation)	9"	TMK-6	MB	400-500.00
364(M.J. altered version)	9"	TMK-6	MB	500-600.00

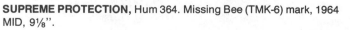

SUPREME PROTECTION, Hum 364. Missing Bee (TMK-6) mark, 1964 MID, 9⅛".

SUPREME PROTECTION, Hum 364. Base photo showing the special inscription.

LITTLEST ANGEL
Hum 365
Possible Future Edition

This beautiful little angel was first made in prototype in the early 1960's and has not yet been put into production. The one in the accompanying photo bears the 3-line (TMK-4) trademark.

THE LITTLEST ANGEL, Hum 365. This particular example bears the Three Line mark and measures 2¾" high.

FLYING ANGEL
Hum 366

This figure is commonly used with the Nativity Sets and has been produced in painted versions as well as white overglaze. The white ones are rare and valued at $200-250.00.

It was first released in the 3-line (TMK-4) trademark period and has remained in production throughout the years. The new smaller version was introduced in 1989.

There are no significant variations affecting normal values.

HUM NO.	BASIC SIZE	TRADE MARK		CURRENT VALUE
366/0	2¾"	TMK-5	LB	85-95.00
366/0	2¾"	TMK-6	MB	85.00
366	3½"	TMK-4	3-line	125-135.00
366	3½"	TMK-5	LB	115-125.00
366	3½"	TMK-6	MB	115.00

FLYING ANGEL, Hum 366.

BUSY STUDENT
Hum 367

First made and released in the mid-1960's, it has been continuously available throughout the years. There are no significant variations that affect normal values.

HUM NO.	BASIC SIZE	TRADE MARK		CURRENT VALUE
367	4¼"	TMK-3	Sty. Bee	600-700.00
367	4¼"	TMK-4	3-line	160-175.00
⨯367	4¼"	TMK-5	LB	150-160.00
367	4¼"	TMK-6	MB	150.00

BUSY STUDENT, Hum 367. Three Line mark (TMK-4), incised 1963 MID, 4¼".

LUTE SONG
Hum 368
Possible Future Edition

Standing girl playing lute. This design is substantially similar to the girl in Close Harmony, Hum 336.

FOLLOW THE LEADER
Hum 369

FOLLOW THE LEADER, Hum 369. Missing Bee mark (TMK-6), 1964 MID, 7".

(continued)

Follow The Leader (cont'd)

This figurine was first made in prototype in the mid-1960's, but not released for sale until the early 1970's. There are no significant variations to affect the normal values.

HUM NO.	BASIC SIZE	TRADE MARK	CURRENT VALUE
369	6¹⁵⁄₁₆"	TMK-4 3-line	1200-1500.00
369	6¹⁵⁄₁₆"	TMK-5 LB	1100-1200.00
369	6¹⁵⁄₁₆"	TMK-6 MB	1100.00

COMPANIONS
Hum 370
Possible Future Edition

This design is much like to Market, Hum 49 except that the girl has been replaced with a boy that is remarkably like the boy of Hum 51, Village Boy.

DADDY'S GIRLS
Hum 371

Daddy's Girls was a new addition to the line in 1989. It measures 4⅞" tall and has an incised mold induction date of 1964 on the underside of the base. Because it was first made in prototype in the 3-line (TMK-4) period there is good reason to suspect there may be one or two out there with that trademark.

They are commonly found in the Missing Bee (TMK-6) are valued at about $210.00. They are in current production.

DADDY'S GIRLS, Hum 371. Missing Bee mark, incised 1964 MID, 4¾".

BLESSED MOTHER
Hum 372
Possible Future Edition

This is a standing Madonna and child.

JUST FISHING
Hum 373

This is a new figure released in early 1985 at a suggested retail price of $85.00. It measures 4¼"x4½". Early Goebel promotional materials referred to this piece as an ash tray. This was in error; probably due to the tray-like base representing the pond. Interestingly it was once more listed as an ashtray in the Goebel price list until the 1993 list where it is listed as a figurine.

It is found in the Missing Bee (TMK-6) trademark and valued at about $205.00. It is in current production.

JUST FISHING, Hum 373. Missing Bee (TMK-6) mark, 1965 MID, measures 4⅛" with the pole.

LOST STOCKING
Hum 374

Made in prototype in the Mid-1960's, this figure was not released for sale until 1965 in the 3-line (TMK-4) trade mark period.

There are no significant variations to affect normal values.

HUM NO.	BASIC SIZE	TRADE MARK		CURRENT VALUE
374	4⅜"	TMK-4	3-line	800-1000.00
374	4⅜"	TMK-5	LB	130-140.00
374	4⅜"	TMK-6	MB	130.00

LOST STOCKING, Hum 374. This piece bears the Last Bee (TMK-5) trademark, measures 4½" and has an incised MID of 1965.

MORNING STROLL
Hum 375
Possible Future Edition

First produced in prototype with the 3-line (TMK-4), this figurine is not yet in production.

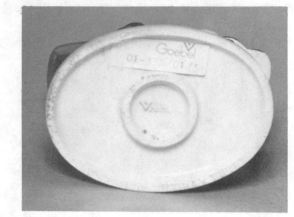

MORNING STROLL, Hum 375, PFE.

LITTLE NURSE
Hum 376

This piece is one of the two new designs to be released in 1982. Although most of them are found with TMK-5 it is known that at least one exists bearing the Last Bee mark (TMK-5) with a 1965 mold induction date. The Last Bee (TMK-5) with a 1965 mold induction date. The Last Bee (TMK-6) or later trademarked pieces have a 1972 MID.

HUM NO.	BASIC SIZE	TRADE MARK	CURRENT VALUE
376	4"	TMK-5 LB	3000-3500.00
376	4"	TMK-6 MB	225-250.00

LITTLE NURSE, Hum 376. Bears the Missing Bee mark (TMK-6), is 4⅛" tall and has an incised 1972 Mold Induction Date.

BASHFUL
Hum 377

This figure was first made in prototype form in the 3-line (TMK-4), but production models in that mark are fairly scarce. Later marks are more easily found.

There are no significant variations found that affect normal values. They are found with a 1966 Mold Induction Date (MID) in the older pieces and sometimes a 1971 MID is found, but the new production figurines do not have an incised MID.

HUM NO.	BASIC SIZE	TRADE MARK		CURRENT VALUE
377	4¾"	TMK-4	3-line	800-1000.00
377	4¾"	TMK-5	LB	180-200.00
377	4¾"	TMK-6	MB	180.00

BASHFUL, Hum 377. Last Bee mark, incised 1966 MID, 4⅝".

EASTER GREETINGS, Hum 378. Last Bee mark, incised 1971 MID, 5".

EASTER GREETINGS
Hum 378

The original prototypes of Easter Greeting were made during the 3-line (TMK-4) period of production, but regular production figurine bearing this mark are scarce. They have an incised MID of 1971.

There are no significant mold or finish variations affecting normal collector values.

HUM NO.	BASIC SIZE	TRADE MARK		CURRENT VALUE
378	5½"	TMK-4	3-line	800-1000.00
378	5½"	TMK-5	LB	195-210.00
378	5½"	TMK-6	MB	195.00

DON'T BE SHY
Hum 379
Possible Future Edition

Little girl with kerchief on head. She is feeding bird perched on fence post.

DAISIES DON'T TELL
Hum 380

This is the Goebel Collectors' Club Special Edition offered exclusively to club members in 1981. As with all the others it could be purchased by current members with redemption cards for $80.00 in the U.S. and $95.00 in Canada. As of May 31, 1985 it was no longer available on the secondary market. It is available only in the Missing Bee (TMK-6) trademark and valued at $150-160.00.

The mold induction date is 1972. There is at least one known to exist bearing the 3-line mark (TMK-4) and one MID of 1966. This latter piece is exceedingly rare and a realistic collector value cannot be assigned.

DAISIES DON'T TELL, Hum 380. Missing Bee mark, incised 1972 MID, 5".

FLOWER VENDOR
Hum 381

This figurine was released in the early 1970's at the end of the Stylized Bee (TMK-3) and 3-line (TMK-4) era, but can only be found in the latter. Those are fairly scarce.

There are no significant variations affecting values.

HUM NO.	BASIC SIZE	TRADE MARK	CURRENT VALUE
✗ 381	5½"	TMK-4 3-line	800-1000.00
381	5½"	TMK-5 LB	220.00
381	5½"	TMK-6 MB	220.00

FLOWER VENDOR, Hum 381.
Last Bee (TMK-5) mark, 1971 MID, 5⅛".

FLOWER VENDOR, Hum 381. Demonstration piece with only the facial features painted. The flesh tones are applied before the face details in demonstrations. In early demonstrations it was not always done as in this case. Last Bee trademark (TMK-5), incised 1971 MID, donut base, 5¼". Valued at about $450-500.00.

VISITING AN INVALID
Hum 382

This figurine was released first in the 3-line (TMK-4) era, but they are scarce and hard to find with that trademark. There are not significant variations to report.

HUM NO.	BASIC SIZE	TRADE MARK	CURRENT VALUE
382	4¹⁵⁄₁₆"	TMK-4 3-line	800-1000.00
382	4¹⁵⁄₁₆"	TMK-5 LB	195-210.00
382	4¹⁵⁄₁₆"	TMK-6 MB	195.00

VISITING AN INVALID, Hum 382. Last Bee mark, incised 1971 MID, 4⅞"

GOING HOME
Hum 383

This new piece for 1985 was released at a suggested retail price os $125.00. Basic size is 5". The first examples were apparently made in the prototype phase in the previous trademark, the Last Bee (TMK-5) for one bearing that trademark has recently surfaced.

There are no significant variations that influence collector values.

HUM NO.	BASIC SIZE	TRADE MARK	CURRENT VALUE
383	5"	TMK-5 LB	3000-3500.00
383	5"	TMK-6 MB	280.00

GOING HOME, Hum 383. Missing Bee (TMK-6). 1972 MID, donut base, 4¹⁵⁄₁₆".

EASTER TIME
Hum 384

Occasionally called "Easter Playmates" this figure was first produced in prototype form in the 3-line (TMK-4). It was first released for sale in the very end of that period so they are fairly scarce in that trademark. There are no significant variations that affect collector value.

HUM NO.	BASIC SIZE	TRADE MARK		CURRENT VALUE
384	3¹⁵⁄₁₆"	TMK-4	3-line	800-1000.00
384	3¹⁵⁄₁₆"	TMK-5	LB	240-250.00
384	3¹⁵⁄₁₆"	TMK-6	MB	240.00

EASTER TIME, Hum 384. Last Bee trademark, incised 1971 MID, 4".

CHICKEN LICKEN
Hum 385

This one of the twenty five pieces first released in 1971-72 with the 3-line mark. It has a mold induction date (MID) of 1971 and has been in production since. In 1990 Goebel released a smaller size, 3¼", with the incised mold number 385/4/0. The recommended retail price at release was $85.00.

There are no significant variations affecting collector value.

HUM NO.	BASIC SIZE	TRADE MARK		CURRENT VALUE
385/4/0	3¼"	TMK-5	LB	90-100.00
385/4/0	3¼"	TMK-6	MB	90.00
385	4¾"	TMK-4	3-line	800-1000.00
385	4¾"	TMK-5	LB	260-275.00
385	4¾"	TMK-6	MB	260.00

CHICKEN LICKEN, Hum 385. Last Bee mark, incised 1971 MID, 4¹¹⁄₁₆".

ON SECRET PATH
Hum 386

This is one of the twenty five pieces first released in 1971-72 in the 3-line (TMK-4) trademark. It has a mold induction date (MID) of 1971 and has been in production since introduced.

There are no significant variations affecting the collector value.

HUM NO.	BASIC SIZE	TRADE MARK		CURRENT VALUE
386	5⅜"	TMK-4	3-line	800-1000.00
386	5⅜"	TMK-5	LB	225-240.00
386	5⅜"	TMK-6	MB	225.00

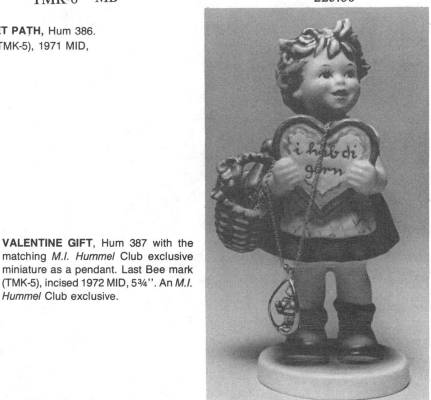

ON SECRET PATH, Hum 386. Last Bee (TMK-5), 1971 MID, 3⅜".

VALENTINE GIFT, Hum 387 with the matching *M.I. Hummel* Club exclusive miniature as a pendant. Last Bee mark (TMK-5), incised 1972 MID, 5¾". An *M.I. Hummel* Club exclusive.

VALENTINE GIFT
Hum 387

This rather special figure was the first special edition figurine available only to memebers of the Goebel Collectors Club (now the *M.I. Hummel* Club), an organization sponsored by and a division of the Goebel firm. It was originally released in 1977 at $45.00 with a redemption card obtained through membership in the club. The size is 5¾". The most commonly found piece bears the Last Bee mark (TMK-5) and sells at $400-600.00. Older pieces (TMK-4) have brought as much as $2000.00 As of May 31, 1984 it was no longer available except on the secondary market.

Crown	CM	TMK-1	1934-1950
Full Bee	FB	TMK-2	1940-1959
Stylized Bee	Sty Bee	TMK-3	1958-1972
Three Line Mark	3-line	TMK-4	1964-1972
Last Bee Mark	LB	TMK-5	1970-1980
Missing Bee Mark	MB	TMK-6	1979-1991
Hummel Mark (Current)	HM	TMK-7	1991-Present

LITTLE BAND
Candle Holder
Hum 388

This is a three figure piece utilizing Hum 389, 390, and 391 on one base and is provided with a candle receptacle. It was released in the 3-line (TMK-4) period and was in continuous production until the company placed it on a list of figurines that were temporarily withdrawn from production on December 31, 1990. They disclosed no reinstatement date. See photo on next page.

HUM NO.	BASIC SIZE	TRADE MARK		CURRENT VALUE
✗388	3"x4¾"	TMK-4	3-line	235-260.00
✗388	3"x4¾"	TMK-5	LB	220-235.00
388	3"x4¾"	TMK-6	MB	220.00

LITTLE BAND music box, Candle Holder Hum 388/M, Three Line mark (TMK-4), 1968 MID.

LITTLE BAND music box and candle holder, Hum 388 M.

LITTLE BAND
Candle Holder and Music Box
Hum 388/M

This is the same piece as Hum 388 but is mounted on a wooden base with a music box movement inside. When it plays, the Little Band figure rotates.

There are no significant variations affecting collector values.

The company placed this figure on a list of pieces taken out of production temporarily on December 31, 1990. There was no reinstatement date disclosed.

HUM NO.	BASIC SIZE	TRADE MARK		CURRENT VALUE
388/M	4¾"x5"	TMK-4	3-line	325-350.00
388/M	4¾"x5"	TMK-5	LB	300-325.00
388/M	4¾"x5"	TMK-6	MB	300.00

(continued)

Little Band (cont'd)

LITTLE BAND Candle Holder, Hum 388.

CHILDREN TRIO
Hum 389 Girl with Sheet Music
Hum 390 Boy with Accordian
Hum 391 Girl with Horn

These three pieces are the same figures used on Hum 388, 388/M, 392 and 392/M. They are on current suggested price lists as available in a set of three or separately.

There are no significant variations affecting collector values for the various trademarked pieces.

CHILDREN TRIO
Hum 389, **Girl With Sheet Music**, Last Bee (TMK-5) mark, 2⅝".
Hum 390, **Boy With Accordian**, Three Line Mark (TMK-4), 2¾".
Hum 391, **Girl With Horn**, Last Bee (TMK-5) mark, 1968 MID, 2¾".

HUM NO.	BASIC SIZE	TRADE MARK		CURRENT VALUE
389	2½"-2¾"	TMK-3	Sty. Bee	90-100.00
389	2½"-2¾"	TMK-4	3-line	80-90.00
389	2½"-2¾"	TMK-5	LB	75-80.00

(continued)

Children Trio (cont'd)

HUM NO.	BASIC SIZE	TRADE MARK		CURRENT VALUE
389	2½"-2¾"	TMK-6	MB	75.00
390	2½"-2¾"	TMK-3	Sty. Bee	90-100.00
390	2½"-2¾"	TMK-4	3-line	80-90.00
390	2½"-2¾"	TMK-5	LB	75.00-80.00
390	2½"-2¾"	TMK-6	MB	75.00
391	2½"-2¾"	TMK-3	Sty. Bee	90-100.00
391	2½"-2¾"	TMK-4	3-line	80-90.00
391	2½"-2¾"	TMK-5	LB	75-80.00
391	2½"-2¾"	TMK-6	MB	75.00

LITTLE BAND
Hum 392

The same as Hum 388 except that this piece has no provision for a candle. Little Band is listed as having been temporarily withdrawn from current production status with no reinstatement date given.

There are no significant variations affecting collector value.

HUM NO.	BASIC SIZE	TRADE MARK		CURRENT VALUE
392	4¾"x3"	TMK-4	3-line	235-260.00
392	4¾"x3"	TMK-5	LB	220-235.00
392	4¾"x3"	TMK-6	MB	220.00

LITTLE BAND music box, Hum 392/M Three Line mark (TMK-4), 1968 MID. Two of three styles of bases found.

LITTLE BAND, Hum 392. Last Bee (TMK-5) mark, 3"x 4 13/16".

LITTLE BAND
Music Box
Hum 389/M

The same piece as Hum 392 but is placed atop a base with a music box movement inside. When it plays the piece revolves.

There are no significant mold or finish variations affecting values.

HUM NO.	BASIC SIZE	TRADE MARK		CURRENT VALUE
392/M	4¼"x5"	TMK-4	3-line	325-350.00
392/M	4¼"x5"	TMK-5	LB	300-325.00
392/M	4¼"x5"	TMK-6	MB	300-325.00

DOVE
Holy Water Font
Hum 393
Possible Future Edition

The Design of this font includes a flying dove and a banner with the inscription " + KOMM + HEILIGER + GEIST +". This translates in English "Come Holy Spirit". No known examples outside Goebel archives.

TIMID LITTLE SISTER
Hum 394

This two figure piece was a new design released with five others in 1981. It has been found with the Last Bee trademark (TMK-5). Both the older vintage pieces and the commonly found current-use trademarked pieces bear the 1972 mold induction date. When released in 1981 the price was $190.00.

There are no significant variations that affect collector value.

HUM NO.	BASIC SIZE	TRADE MARK	CURRENT VALUE
394	7"	TMK-5 LB	3000-3500.00
394	7"	TMK-6 MB	390-400.00

TIMID LITTLE SISTER,. Hum 394. Missing Bee mark, 1972 MID, 6¾" Base is split lateral beneath.

SHEPHERD BOY
Hum 395
Possible Future Edition

This piece is of a boy and lamb. They are standing by a fence. A bird is perched on a fence post. No known examples outside factory archives.

RIDE INTO CHRISTMAS
Hum 396

This figurine remains quite popular and is in great demand by collectors. Perhaps this is why the company released a smaller version in 1982. The release of the smaller piece necessitated a change in the mold number of the larger one from 396 to 396/1.

The larger size bears a Mold Induction Date (MID) of 1971 and the smaller has a 1981 MID.

There are no significant production variations that affect collector values for this piece.

HUM NO.	BASIC SIZE	TRADE MARK		CURRENT VALUE
396/2/0	4¼"	TMK-5	LB	135-165.00
396/2/0	4¼"	TMK-6	MB	135.00
396	5¾"	TMK-4	3-line	1600-2200.00
✶396	5¾"	TMK-5	LB	250-315.00
396	5¾"	TMK-6	MB	220.00

RIDE INTO CHRISTMAS, Hum 396. Demonstration piece with only the flesh tones on the face painted. Missing Bee trademark, incised 1971 MID, 6''. Valued at about $700-800.00.

RIDE INTO CHRISTMAS, Hum 396/I. Missing Bee mark, 1971 MID, 6''.

THE POET
Hum 397
Possible Future Edition

Standing child reciting from book held in left hand. No known examples outside company archives.

SPRING BOUQUET
Hum 398
Possible Future Edition

Girl picking flowers. She holds bouquet in left arm. No known examples outside the company archives.

VALENTINE JOY

This is the fourth special edition offered exclusively to the members of the Goebel Collector's Club. Issued in 1980-81 they bear a 1979 mold induction date and measure 5⅝" and were available for $95.00 with the club redemption card. Although it is known that there are existing examples with the Last Bee trademark (TMK-5) the piece is normally found with the Missing Bee (TMK-6). Available only on the secondary market.

HUM NO.	BASIC SIZE	TRADE MARK		CURRENT VALUE
399	5¾"	TMK-5	LB	$10,000.00
399	5¾"	TMk-6	MB	200-250.00

VALENTINE JOY, Hum 399. Left: Last Bee mark, incised 1973 MID, split base, 6¼". Note the grass and bird on the base. Old style. Right: Missing Bee mark, incised 1979 MID, 5¾".

WELL DONE!
Hum 400
Possible Future Edition

Two standing boys. One, wearing shorts, pats the other, in long pants, on shoulder. No known examples outside the company archives.

FORTY WINKS
Hum 401
Possible Future Edition

Seated girl with small boy next to her. He is asleep with his head on her right shoulder. No known examples outside the company archives.

TRUE FRIENDSHIP
Hum 402
Possible Future Edition

Seated girl eating porridge from bowl held in her left hand. Her right hand holds a spoonful and a bird is perched on her right forearm.

AN APPLE A DAY
Hum 403

An Apple A Day was released in 1988. It is 6½" tall and carries an incised 1974 mold induction date. The price at the time of release was $195.00

The fact that the design was copyrighted in the Last Bee (TMK-5) trademark era makes it possible that they exist, at least as prototypes, with that trademark. There are no known examples in private collections.

There are no significant variations that affect collector value.

Presently available only in the Hummel Mark (TMK-7), it is listed in the 1993 Goebel Suggested Retail Price List at $260.00.

AN APPLE A DAY, Hum 403. Missing Bee mark, incised 1974 MID, 6½''.

SAD SONG
Hum 404
Possible Future Edition

Standing boy singing. He looks as if he is about to cry. Holds sheet music at back with right hand. No known examples outside the company archives.

SING WITH ME
Hum 405

First released in 1985. The basic size is 5". The one in the accompanying photo measures slightly bigger at 5⅛" tall. A mold induction date of 1974 is found incised on the underside of the base. Found in the Missing Bee (TMK-6) and the Hummel mark (TMK-7).

There are no significant variations that affect collector value.

HUM NO.	BASIC SIZE	TRADE MARK	CURRENT VALUE
405	5"	TMK-6 MB	280.00

SING WITH ME, Hum 405. Missing Bee mark (TMK-6), incised 1974 MID, 5''.

PLEASANT JOURNEY
Hum 406

Released in 1987, this new piece has a basic size of 6½" long by 6¼" high. This piece, like the Chapel Time clock is limited to those produced in 1987. They will not be produced again in the 20th Century. The release price was $500.00 and is valued at about $1750-2000.00. It is found only with the Missing Bee (TMK-6) trademark. There are no variations affecting the value.

PLEASANT JOURNEY, Hum 406. Missing Bee mark, incised 1976 MID, 7⅜" long x 6⅜" high. Century Collection, 1987.

FLUTE SONG
Hum 407
Possible Future Edition

Seated boy playing flute for lamp standing in front of him. The boy is seated on what appears to be a stump.

SMILING THROUGH
Hum 408

This is the ninth redemption piece available only to members of the Goebel Collectors' Club. It was released in 1985 at $125.00 with redemption card. The mold number incised on the bottom of this figurine is actually 408/0. The reason for this is that a larger model was molded in 1976, but never released. It was made as a sample only and resides in the factory archives now. This larger version was 6" while the one released to club members is only 4¾". As of May 31, 1987 they are available only on the secondary market and are found only in the Missing Bee (TMK-6) trademark. Collector value: $175-200.00.

There are no significant variations that affect value.

(continued)

Smiling Through (cont'd)

SMILING THROUGH, Hum 408/0. Missing Bee mark (TMK-6), incised 1983 MID, 4¾".

COFFEE BREAK, Hum 409. Missing Bee mark (TMK-6), incised 1976 MID, 3¹⁵⁄₁₆".

COFFEE BREAK
Hum 409

This is the ninth special edition piece available to members of the Goebel Collector's Club exclusively. It was available to them, with redemption card until May 31, 1986. The issue price for Coffee Break was $90.00. Now available only on the secondary market, in the Missing Bee (TMK-6) only. It is valued at $100-125.00.

TRUANT
Hum 410
Possible Future Edition

Walking boy with book satchel on his back. He carries a T-square in his right hand.

DO I DARE?
Hum 411
Possible Future Edition

Standing girl holding flower in her left hand and basket in the crook of her right arm.

THE LITTLE ARCHITECT
Hum 410

New for 1993, this figure has a basic size of 6" and bears the mold number 410/I. The price is the suggested retail price list is $290.00.

OPEN NUMBER
Hum 411
Possible Future Edition

BATH TIME
Hum 412

This figure was released for sale in 1990 during the Missing Bee (TMK-6) trademark era. It is found in that trademark and the current-use trademark, the Hummel mark (TMK-7).

There are no significant variations that affect the collector value, $350.00.

WHISTLER'S DUET, Hum 413. Hummel Mark (current use or TMK-7) incised 1979 MID, 4'', first issue backstamp dated 1992.

BATH TIME, Hum 412. Missing Bee, 1978 MID, 6⅛''.

WHISTLER'S DUET
Hum 413

This figure was released in late 1991 and is found only in the Hummel mark (TMK-7). It is listed with the basic size of 4⅜'' and a price of $250.00 in the 1993 suggested retail price list from Goebel.

There are no significant variations that affect the collector value.

IN TUNE
Hum 414

This figure is one of six new designs released by Goebel in 1981. Its basic size is 4'' and is a matching figurine to the 1981 Annual Bell.

It was released during the Missing Bee (TMK-6) era and is found in that mark and in the current-use trademark, the Hummel mark (TMK-7). It is valued at $2500-3000.00 in the Last Bee trademark and is $250.00 in the current suggested retail price list.

There are no significant variations that affect the collector value.

IN TUNE, Hum 414. Missing Bee (TMK-6) 1979 MID, 4".

THOUGHTFUL, Hum 415, Missing Bee mark (TMK-6), incised 1980 MID, 4½".

THOUGHTFUL
Hum 415

This is another of the six new designs released by Goebel in 1981. Its basic size is 4½" and is a matching piece to the 1980 Annual Bell. Thoughtful has a 1980 mold induction date (MID) and has been found only with the (Missing Bee or TMK-6) and the Hummel mark (TMK-7). Those pieces bearing the Missing Bee trademark are valued at $205-220.00.

There are no important variations that affect that value.

JUBILEE
Hum 416

Beginning in January of 1985 this very special figurine was made available to collectors and limited to the number of them sold during 1985 only. The figure has a special backstamp reading "50 Years, *M.I. Hummel* Figurines, 1935-1985, The Love Lives On". It is in celebration of the Golden Anniversary of Hummel figurines. It is 6¼" high and the factory recommended retail price was $200.00.

There are at least two of these found with "75" instead of the "50" that is on the Golden Anniversary figure. The speculation is that this piece was originally designed to celebrate the 75th anniversary or perhaps *M.I. Hummel's* birthday. Whatever the reason, they exist and their value would be in the mid to high five figure range.

Another unusual variation is one where the circle where the "50" appears is a shiny gold gilt. This particular piece, the only one known to be in a private collection, bears a Last Bee (TMK-5) trademark. Apparently Goebel had what appeared to be a good idea for the golden anniversary, but they applied the gilt it didn't come out to their satisfaction after being fired and they scrapped the idea. This is a unique piece and there is no way to realistically assign a value to it.

The normal Jubilees are found only with the Missing Bee (TMK-6) and are valued at $200.00 on the collector market.

JUBILEE, Hum 416. Missing Bee (TMK-6), 1980 MID, 6¼".

JUBILEE, Hum 416. This is the figurine with the unique gold gilt "50" discussed in the accompanying text.

JUBILEE, Hum 416. Shows the special inscription backstamp beneath the base.

WHERE DID YOU GET THAT?
Hum 417
Possible Future Edition

Standing boy and girl. Boy holds his hat in both hands. It has three apples in it. Girl dangles doll in left hand.

Crown	CM	TMK-1	1934-1950
Full Bee	FB	TMK-2	1940-1959
Stylized Bee	Sty Bee	TMK-3	1958-1972
Three Line Mark	3-line	TMK-4	1964-1972
Last Bee Mark	LB	TMK-5	1970-1980
Missing Bee Mark	MB	TMK-6	1979-1991
Hummel Mark (Current)	HM	TMK-7	1991-Present

WHAT'S NEW
Hum 418

Added to the line in 1990, What's New? is 5¼" tall. The suggested retail price was $200.00. It can be found with the Missing Bee (TMK-6) and the current use Hummel mark (TMK-7).

There are no variations that affect the collector value.

Found only in the Missing Bee (TMK-7). The collector value for the Missing Bee trademarked pieces is $260-275.00.

WHAT'S NEW?, Hum 418. Missing Bee mark, 1981 MID, 5''.

GOOD LUCK!
Hum 419
Possible Future Edition

Standing boy with his left hand in his pocket. He holds an umbrella in his right arm.

IS IT RAINING?
Hum 420

The figure was added to the line in 1989. The one in the accompanying photo measures 6" tall. It has a mold induction date of 1981 and the retail price at release was $175.00. March 1993 retail in price list is $240.00.

It is found bearing only the Missing Bee (TMK-6) trademark and the current-use trademark, the Hummel mark (TMK-7).

There are no significant variations to affect the collector value of $240-250.00.

IS IT RAINING?, Hum 420. Missing Bee (TMK-6) mark, 1981 MID, 6''.

IT'S COLD
Hum 421

This is the sixth in a series of special offers made exclusively to members of the Goebel Collectors' Club. It is available only from them initially, requiring a special redemption card issued to members. Each of these special editions have shown themselves to be good candidates for fairly rapid appreciation in collector value. The figurine bears a 1981 MID and was sold with redemption card for $80.00.

There are no significant variations that affect the collector value of this figurine.

It is found only bearing the Missing Bee (TMK-6) trademark and valued at $160-175.00.

IT'S COLD, Hum 421. Missing Bee mark (TMK-7), incised 1981 MID, 5⅛".

WHAT NOW?, Hum 422 with the matching *M.I. Hummel* exclusive miniature as a pendant. Missing Bee mark, incised 1981 MID, 5½". An *M.I. Hummel* Club exclusive.

WHAT NOW?
Hum 422

This is the seventh special edition issued for members of the Goebel Collectors' Club. The usual redemption card was required for purchase of this figurine at $90.00. What Now? stands 5¼" high. Available only on the secondary market as of May 31, 1985, it is valued at $170-180.00.

There are no variations that affect this collector value.

HORSE TRAINER
Hum 423

Horse Trainer was added to the line in 1990 at 4½" and a suggested retail price of $155.00. It can be found with the Missing Bee (TMK-6) and the current use Hummel mark (TMK-7). The collector value is presently $200-215.00 for the figures with the Last Bee trademark. There are no variations that affect this value.

HORSE TRAINER, Hum 423. Missing Bee, 1981 MID, 4 ⅝".

SLEEP TIGHT, Hum 424. Missing Bee mark, 1981 MID 4¾".

SLEEP TIGHT
Hum 424

A 1990 release, this piece can be found with the Missing Bee (TMK-6) and the current use Hummel mark (TMK-7). At 4½" Sleep Tight has a collector value range of $200-215.00 for the pieces bearing the Missing Bee trademark.

PLEASANT MOMENT
Hum 425
Possible Future Edition

Two seated girls. One holds flowers in left hand. The other reaches down with right hand toward a yellow butterfly.

PAY ATTENTION
Hum 426
Possible Future Edition

Girl sitting on fence. She holds flowers and basket and is looking away from a crowing black bird perched on the fence post behind her.

372

WHERE ARE YOU?
Hum 427
Possible Future Edition

Boy sitting on fence. He holds bouquet of flowers. There is a bird perched on a fence post.

I WON'T HURT YOU
Hum 428
Possible Future Edition

Boy with hiking staff in left hand. He is looking down at a ladybug in his right hand.

HELLO WORLD
Hum 429

Released in 1989 as a special edition available to members of the Goebel Collectors' Club with redemption cards of which the expiration date was May 31, 1990. There are already two variations to be found. 1989 is the year of the club's transition from the Goebel Collectors' Club to the *M.I. Hummel* Club. Apparently a few of these went out with the old special edition backstamp before it was discovered. All those subsequently released will bear the *M.I. Hummel* Club backstamp. The piece stands 5½" high.

They can be found with either club inscription and also in either the Missing Bee (TMK-6) trademark or the current-use trademark, the Hummel mark (TMK-7). The collector value for either variation and either trademark is the same at $130-150.00.

HELLO WORLD, Hum 429. Missing Bee mark, incised 1983 MID, 5⅝".   IN D—MAJOR, Hum 430. Missing Bee (TMK-6) mark, 1981 MID, 4⅛".

IN D MAJOR
Hum 430

This 1988 release is listed at 4⅜" tall. The one in the photo here measures 4⅛". It carries a 1981 mold induction date incised beneath the base. It was released at $135.00.

There are no significant variations to affect the value. Found with the Missing Bee (TMK-6) trademark and the current-use trademark, the Hummel mark (TMK-7) only. The value for the Missing Bee figure is $180-200.00.

THE SURPRISE
Hum 431

This figure, introduced in 1989, is the twelfth special edition for members of the Goebel Collectors' Club (now *M.I. Hummel* Club) only. The expiration date on the redemption card is May 31, 1990. The Surprise bears the incised mold induction date of 1981 as well as the same date in decal beneath the current trademark. This figure is the first to also bear the little bumblebee. It is to appear on all future special editions for club members. It is 5⅜" high. It is found only with the Missing Bee (TMK-6) and is valued at $130-150.00.
There are no significant variations.

THE SURPRISE, Hum 431. Missing Bee mark, incised 1981 Mid, 5½".   **KNIT ONE, PURL ONE**, Hum 432. Missing Bee (TMK-6), 1982 MID 6".

KNIT ONE, PURL ONE
Hum 432

This figure was a new addition to the line in 1981. It was made to go with the 1982 Annual Bell of the same motif. Note that it has no base.

It is found only with the Missing Bee (TMK-6) trademark and the current-use trademark, the Hummel mark (TMK-7). The collector value for the Missing Bee trademarked figurine is $105-115.00. There are no significant variations to affect this value.

SING ALONG
Hum 433

Newly released in 1987 at $145.00 it measures 4⅜" tall and bears an incised mold induction date of 1982.

It can be found only in the Missing Bee (TMK-6) trademark and the current-use trademark, the Hummel mark (TMK-7). There are no variation to affect the collector value of $260-275.00.

SING ALONG, Hum 433. Missing Bee mark, incised 1982 MID, 4¼".

FRIEND OR FOE
Hum 434

This 4" figure was released in 1991 at $195.00 suggested retail. It bears an incised 1982 mold induction date (MID). It is found only in the Missing Bee (TMK-6) and the current-use trademark, the Hummel mark (TMK-7). There are no variations to affect the collector value of the normal production pieces. They are valued at $195-205.00.

FRIEND OR FOE, Hum 434. Demonstration piece with only the flesh tones and dress painted. Current use trademark, incised 1982 MID, 3⅞". Valued at about $300.00.

FRIEND OR FOE, Hum 434. Missing Bee trademark, incised 1982 MID, 3¾". Has the first issue backstamp dated 1991.

DELICIOUS
Hum 435
Possible Future Edition

Standing child about to eat red candy held in left hand.

AN EMERGENCY
Hum 436

Boy with bandage on his head. He is about to push the button on the doctor's gate.

THE TUBA PLAYER
Hum 437

This figure was released in the winter of 1988. It is listed as 6¼", but the one in the photo here actually measures 6⅛" high. It carries a 1988 mold induction date and the Missing Bee (TMK-6) trademark. They continue in production in the current-use trademark, the Hummel mark (TMK-7).

There are no variations to affect the value of the Missing Bee pieces. They are valued at $240-250.00.

(continued)

THE TUBA PLAYER, Hum 437. Missing Bee mark, 1983 MID, 6⅛''.

SOUNDS OF THE MANDOLIN, Hum 438. Missing Bee mark (TMK-6) incised 1984 MID, measures 3⅝''.

SOUNDS OF THE MANDOLIN
Hum 438

This 3¾" figure was released in 1987 as one of three musical angel pieces. The other two are Song of Praise, Hum 454 and The Accompanist, Hum 453.

The figurine was originally placed in the line bearing the Missing Bee (TMK-6) trademark and they continue in production today with the current-use trademark, the Hummel mark (TMK-7).

The collector value for the Missing Bee pieces is $110-120.00. There are no variations to affect that value.

A GENTLE GLOW
Candle Holder
Hum 439

Newly released in 1987 this piece is a small standing child. The candle receptacle appears to be resting on greenery that the child holds up with both hands.

The figurine is found only in the Missing Bee (TMK-6) and the current-use trademark, the Hummel mark (TMK-7). There are no variation to affect the collector value of the pieces. The Missing Bee trademarked figures are valued at $190-200.00.

A GENTLE GLOW, candle holder, Hum 439. Missing Bee (TMK-6), 5¼''.

BIRTHDAY CANDLE
Candle Holder
Hum 440

This 5½" candleholders is the tenth special edition available to members of the Goebel Collectors' Club only. It bears the following inscription on the base: "EXCLUSIVE SPECIAL EDITION NO. 10 FOR MEMBERS OF THE GOEBEL COLLECTORS' CLUB". It was released at $95.00 with the redemption card cut-off date of May 31, 1988. It was released in conjunction with the Tenth Anniversary Celebration of the founding of the club.

It is found in the Missing Bee (TMK-6) only and is valued at $130-150.00. There are no variations affecting value.

BIRTHDAY CANDLE candle holder, Hum 440. Missing Bee mark (TMK-6), incised 1983 MID, 5¼".

CALL TO WORSHIP clock, Hum 441. Missing Bee mark (TMK-6), incised 1988 MID, 13". Century Collection, 1988.

CALL TO WORSHIP
Clock
Hum 441

This is only the second clock ever made from a Hummel design. It stands 13" tall and has a musical movement that chimes every hour. There are two tunes to choose from. You can choose either at random by moving a switch beneath. The tunes are Ave Maria or the Westminster Chimes. It is the second offering in what Goebel calls the Century Collection. These are pieces produced in the Twentieth Century limited in production to one year only. This is signified on the base with the addition of the Roman numeral XX. The suggested retail price in the 1988 year of production was $600.00.

They can be found in the Missing Bee trademark only. They are valued at $800-1000.00. There are no variations that affect that value.

CHAPEL TIME
Clock
Hum 442

This is the first clock to be put into production and released by Goebel. It was limited to one year of production (1986) and will not be made again in this century. As part of the artist's mark and date on the bottom is the Roman numeral XX meaning the Twentieth Century. The base also bears the current-use Missing Bee (TMK-6) trademark and a blue *M.I. Hummel* signature with the inscription "The Love Lives On".

There are several variations, mostly having to do with the windows in the chapel building. So far, the most commonly found version is that with all windows closed and painted, except for the four in the belfry. The rarest, as of this writing, is a version with all windows closed and painted. According to Goebel this version was a pre-production run numbering 800-1000. It has been reported that a few of these have been found with the two small round windows in the gables open. A third version has the gable and the belfry windows all open. There are other variations with regard to the base and size of the hole in the bottom (to replace battery), but these are not presently considered significant.

The clock is 11½" tall. The following is a breakdown of the values of the three variations:
Belfry windows and gable windows open........$2500-2800.00
Belfry windows and gable windows painted.....$1200-1500.00
Belfry windows open, gable windows painted...$2000-2500.00

CHAPEL TIME clock, Hum 442. Missing Bee mark (TMK-6), incised 1983 MID 11⅛".

COUNTRY SONG
Clock
Hum 443
Possible Future Edition

Boy blowing horn. He is seated on a flower covered mound. Blue flowers are used instead of numbers on the clock face.

UNKNOWN
Hum 444 and Hum 445
Possible Future Editions

A PERSONAL MESSAGE
Hum 446
Possible Future Edition

This is a girl on her knees using a large pen to write on paper. There is an ink well to her left. This piece looks somewhat like Hum 309, "With Loving Greetings".

MORNING CONCERT
Hum 447

This is the eleventh special edition piece made and offered exclusively for members of the Goebel Collectors' Club (now *M.I. Hummel* Club). They were available to members until the expiration date of May 31, 1989. Morning Concert has a mold induction date of 1984 incised beneath the base and the special edition club backstamp in decal underglaze. It stands 5" tall and was available to members for $98.00.

It is available only in the Missing Bee (TMK-6) and is valued at $110-125.00. There are no significant variations.

MORNING CONCERT, Hum 447. No apparent marks other than an incised 1984 MID. It is from the Missing Bee mark period. It is an *M.I. Hummel* Club exclusive offer.

CHILDREN'S PRAYER
Hum 448
Possible Future Edition

Boy and girl standing, looking up at roadside shrine of Jesus on the Cross.

THE LITTLE PAIR
Hum 449

In 1990 the *M.I. Hummel* Club began offering special figures to those members who had passed certain year milestones of membership. This particular piece is made available to only those members who have attained or surpassed their tenth year of membership. Each bears a special backstamp commemorating the occasion. The 10th year club exclusive is available to qualified members for $200.00.

They are found only in the Missing Bee (TMK-6) and the current-use trademark, the Hummel mark (TMK-7).

THE LITTLE PAIR, Hum 449. Missing Bee mark, incised 1985 MID, 5½". Exclusively available only to members of the *M.I. Hummel* Club who have attained 10 years of membership.

WILL IT STING?
Hum 450
Possible Future Edition

This is a figure of a girl looking at a bee perched on a plant at her feet.

JUST DOZING
Hum 451
Possible Future Edition

This piece is a boy asleep holding a doll.

FLYING HIGH
Hum 452

This is the first in a series of hanging ornaments. It is not, however, the first Hummel hanging ornament; the first being the Flying Angel, Hum 366, commonly used with the Nativity Sets. Flying High was introduced in late 1987 as the 1988 (first edition) ornament at $75.00. It measures 3½" x 4⅛".

There are three variations with regard to additional marks. When first released there were no additional markings. The second variation is the appearance of a decal reading "First Edition" beneath the skirt. The third is the appearance of the "First Edition" mark and "1988" painted on the back of the gown.

The value of the regular, dated version is $100-125.00 and the undated and the unmarked variation is $125-150.00. They are found only with the Missing Bee (TMK-6) trademark and the current-use trademark, the Hummel mark (TMK-7).

FLYING HIGH, Hum 452. 1988 Christmas ornament, Missing Bee (TMK-6) mark, no other apparent markings. This is one of the early undated ornaments.

THE ACCOMPANIST, Hum 453. Missing Bee mark (TMK-6), incised 1984 MID, 3¼".

THE ACCOMPANIST
Hum 453

This piece along with Hum 454, Song of Praise and Hum 438, Sounds of the Mandolin, were introduced in 1987 as a trio of angel musicians. It was released at $39.00. The figurine measures 3¼" high and has an incised mold induction date of 1984.

It is not found with any earlier trademark than the Missing Bee (TMK-6) and is valued at $90-100.00 in that mark.

SONG OF PRAISE
Hum 454

This piece is one of three angel musician figures introduced in 1987. The others are the preceding Hum 453 and Hum 438, The Accompanist. It stands 3" high.

It is not found with any earlier trademark than the Missing Bee (TMK-6) and is valued at $90-100.00 in that mark.

SONG OF PRAISE, Hum 454, Missing Bee Mark, 1984 MID, 2⅞".

THE GUARDIAN
Hum 455

A 1991 release, The Guardian 3½" figure. The suggested retail price at the time of release was $145.00. It bears an incised MID of 1984 and for those made in 1991, there is the "First Issue" backstamp dated 1991. They are not found with any earlier trade mark than the Missing Bee (TMK-6). Collector value: $155-165.00.

THE GUARDIAN, Hum 455. Missing Bee mark, 1985 MID 2¾'', first issue backstamp dated 1991.

UNKNOWN
Hum 456

Open number for possible future edition.

SOUND THE TRUMPET
Hum 457

This was a new introduction to the line in 1987. It measures 2¾" high and has an incised mold induction date of 1984. It was introduced at $45.00.

It is not found with a trademark any earlier than the Missing Bee (TMK-6) and is valued at $90-100.00 in that mark.

SOUND THE TRUMPET, Hum 457. Missing Bee mark, 1984 MID, 2 ¹³⁄₁₆''·

382

STORYBOOK TIME
Hum 458

This piece was introduced as new for 1992 in the Fall 1991 issue of *INSIGHTS*, the *M.I. Hummel* Club newsletter, with the name "Story Time". Inexplicably, all references to the piece have subsequently referred to it as "Storybook Time". It is listed as 5" tall and the release price was $330.00.

It is found only in the current-use trademark, the Hummel mark (TMK-7). It is listed in the current Goebel suggested retail price list at $360.00.

IN THE MEADOW, Hum 459. Missing Bee (TMK-6) mark, 1985 MID, 4".

STORYBOOK TIME, Hum 458. Hummel mark 19 current use or TMK-7), incised 1985 MID, 5⅛", first issue backstamp dated 1992.

IN THE MEADOW
Hum 459

This was released in 1987 as one of five 1987 releases. The size is 4" and the release price was $110.00. It has an incised mold induction date of 1985 beneath the base.

It is found only with the current-use trademark, the Hummel mark (TMK-7). It is listed in the Goebel suggested retail price list at $180.00.

TALLY
Retail Dealer Plaque
Hum 460

This dealer plaque was introduced in 1986. It was thought that it was to replace the Hum 187 Merry Wanderer dealer plaque, but in 1990 the Merry Wanderer style was reissued. When Tally was first introduced there was apparently a shortage with dealers limited to only one each, but shortly thereafter the shortage was alleviated. The boy on the plaque is, as you can see, very similar to the center figure in School Boys, Hum 170. The base of the plaque bears an incised mold induction date of 1984.

There are no structural or color variations presently known, but there are variations in the language used on the front of the plaque. There is German as in the photo accompanying, Swedish, French, Spanish, Dutch, a version for British dealers and of course one for the American market for a total of seven. The plaque was released at $85.00 in the U.S. and is presently valued at about $150-200.00. The British version is valued at $500.00.

The foreign language plaques are valued as follows:

Dutch	800-1000.00
French	1000-1800.00
German	700-800.00
Italian	1200-1500.00
Spanish	1200-1500.00
Swedish	800-1000.00

The retail dealer plaque, **TALLY**, Hum 460. Left to right the languages are: Italian, Swedish and Dutch.

The retail dealer plaque **TALLY,** Hum 460. Left to right the countries are: United States, Great Britain, Germany, France, Spain.

UNKNOWN
Hum 461 and Hum 462
Possible Future Editions

MY WISH IS SMALL
Hum 463

This is a *M.I. Hummel* Club exclusive offering for the 1992-93 club year. Available only in the current-use trademark, the Hummel mark (TMK-7). It is available exclusively to members with redemption cards at $170.00. It is available to members with redemption cards at $170.00. It is 5½" tall.

MY WISH IS SMALL, Hum 463/0. An *M.I. Hummel* members only exclusive offering. It is 5½" tall, bears the current use trademark (TMK-7), the special club backstamp and an incised 1985 MID.

UNKNOWN
Hum 464 through Hum 466
Possible Future Editions

THE KINDERGARTNER
Hum 467

A new release for 1987 this figure stands 5" high. The release price was $100.00. The actual measurement of the figurine in the photo here is 5⅜" and it bears a mold induction date of 1986 incised beneath the base.

It is not found with a trademark any earlier than the Missing Bee (TMK-6) and is valued at $180.00 in that mark.

THE KINDERGARTNER, Hum 467. Missing Bee (TMK-6), 1985 MID, 5⅜".

HARMONY IN FOUR PARTS
Hum 471

This is the 1989 addition to the Century Collection. These pieces are limited to the production year in the Twentieth Century and will not be produced again in this century. They each bear a special backstamp indicating this. The stamp is 1989 underlined with the Roman numeral XX beneath. This is in the center of a circle made up of the *M.I. Hummel* signature and the words "CENTURY COLLECTION". It measures 9" wide and 10" high. The mold induction date is 1987. The lamp post was originally made of the same fine earthenware that Hummel pieces are rendered in, but it was soon noted that the post was very easily broken. To alleviate this problem Goebel began using a metal post instead. Although there is not presently any difference in the value of these, it is reasonable to project that the earthenware post version may become the more desirable to serious collectors thereby making it more valuable. Only time will tell. Hum 471 was released at $850.00.

It is not found in any earlier trademarks than the Missing Bee (TMK-6) mark and is valued at $1000-1250. in that mark.

HARMONY IN FOUR PARTS, Hum 471. Missing Bee mark, incised 1987 MID, 9⅛" long x 9¹⁵⁄₁₆" high, Century Collection dated 1989.

ON OUR WAY
Hum 472

This unusual piece was introduced as new for 1992 in the Fall, 1991 issue of *INSIGHTS*, the *M.I. Hummel* Club newsletter. It is the Century Collection piece for 1992. The number available is limited by the number produced during the one year of production. They bear a special identifying backstamp and are accompanied by a certificate of authenticity. Size is 6½" x 5½" x 8" and the release price was $950.00.

It is available only in the current-use trademark, the Hummel mark (TMK-7) and is still listed at $950.00 in the 1993 Goebel suggested retail price list.

ON OUR WAY, Hum 472. Hummel Mark (current use of TMK-7), incised 1987 MID, 8", Century Collection, 1992.

UNKNOWN
Hum 473 and Hum 474

Open numbers for possible future editions.

MAKE A WISH
Hum 475

This was a new release in 1989. The basic size is 4¼" and bears a 1987 incised MID.

There are no significant variations. These cannot be found with a trademark any earlier than the Missing Bee (TMK-6) and are valued at $175.00 in that mark.

MAKE A WISH, Hum 475. This example stands 4½", has the Missing Bee (TMK-6) trademark and a 1987 Mold Induction Date (MID).

WINTER SONG, Hum 476, Missing Bee trademark, incised 1987 MID, 4".

WINTER SONG
Hum 476

This was a 1987 release. It stands 4½" tall and was priced at $45.00 when introduced. It bears an incised mold induction date of 1987 and appears with a trademark no earlier than the Missing Bee (TMK-6) and is valued at $100-120.00 in that mark.

A BUDDING MAESTRO
Hum 477

This figure measures 3⅞" tall. It was released in 1987 at $45.00 and is found in trademarks no earlier than the Missing Bee (TMK-6) mark. It is valued at $95-115.00 in that mark. There are no significant variations.

A BUDDING MAESTRO, Hum 477. Missing Bee mark, incised 1987 MID, 3¹⁵⁄₁₆".

I'M HERE, Hum 478. Missing Bee (TMK-6) mark, 3⅛".

I'M HERE
Hum 478

I'm Here was released in 1988 as a new addition to the line. The figure in the photo measures 3" and is listed in price lists as 2¾". It carries a 1987 incised mold induction date.

It is not found in trademarks any earlier than the Missing Bee (TMK-6) and is valued at $95-115.00 in that mark. There are no significant variations.

I BROUGHT YOU A GIFT
Hum 479

Beginning June 1, 1989 the 4" bisque plaque with the Merry Wanderer motif that was given to every new member of the Goebel Collectors' Club is officially retired. At the same date the club became officially the *M.I. Hummel* Club and a new membership premium, I Brought You a Gift, was introduced. At the time of transition each renewing member was given one. In addition each new member will receive one. It is 4" high and has the incised mold induction date of 1987 on the underside of the base. There are two variations to be found with regard to the club special edition backstamp. If you will look at the accompanying photograph of the base you will note one old club name beneath the bumblebee. This is found on the early examples. Newer ones have the *M.I. Hummel* Club name on them.

They are found with the Last Bee (TMK-6) trademark and the current-use trade mark, the Hummel mark (TMK-7) and are valued at $75.00 in either mark presently.

(continued)

I BROUGHT YOU A GIFT, Hum 479. *M.I. Hummel* Club, exclusive members only offering. It is 4" tall, bears the Missing Bee trademark (TMK-6), the club backstamp and an incised 1987 MID.

Left: **I BROUGHT YOU A GIFT,** Hum 479, Missing Bee mark, incised 1987 MID, 4".
Right: **LUCKY FELLOW,** Hum 560, Hummel Mark (current use or TMK-7), 5⅝".

Photo of the base of I BROUGHT YOU A GIFT showing the old "Goebel Collectors Club" name.

HOSANNA
Hum 480

Released in 1989, this figure stands 4" tall. It has a 1987 mold induction date incised under the base. The suggested retail price at the time of the release was $68.00.

It is not found in any trademarks earlier than the Missing Bee (TMK-6) and is valued at $75.00 in that mark.

HOSANNA, Hum 480. Missing Bee (TMK-6) mark, 1987 MID, 4".

LOVE FROM ABOVE
1989 Christmas Ornament
Hum 481

This is the second edition in the hanging ornament series, 1989, that began with the 1988 Flying High, Hum 452. It bears the Missing Bee (TMK-6) trademark and was released at $75.00. It is now valued at about $100.00 in that mark.

LOVE FROM ABOVE, Hum 481. 1989 Christmas ornament, Missing Bee (TMK-6) mark, 1987 MID, 3¼".

ONE FOR YOU, ONE FOR ME, Hum 482. No apparent markings of any sort, 3³⁄₁₆".

ONE FOR YOU, ONE FOR ME
Hum 482

This piece was a new released in 1988. It is 3⅛" high and carries a 1987 incised mold induction date. It was originally priced at $50.00.

It is not found with any earlier trademark than than the Missing Bee (TMK-6) and is valued at $95-115.00 in that mark.

I'LL PROTECT HIM
Hum 483

New in 1989 this figure stands 3¾" high. It bears an incised mold induction date of 1987 on the underside of the base.

It is not found with any earlier trademark than the Missing Bee (TMK-6) and is valued at $75-90.00 in that mark.

I'LL PROTECT HIM, Hum 483, Missing Bee (TMK-6) mark, 1987 MID, 3¾".

PEACE ON EARTH
1990 Christmas Ornament
Hum 484

The third in an annual released of *M.I. Hummel* Christmas ornaments, this one was released at $80.00 suggested retail. The size is 4".

It is found only in the Missing Bee (TMK-6) trademark and is valued at about $100.00 in that mark.

PEACE ON EARTH, Hum 484. 1990 Christmas ornament, Missing Bee (TMK-6) mark, 1987 MID, 4⅛".

A GIFT FROM A FRIEND, Hum 485. Hummel mark (current use or TMK-7), incised 1988 MID, 5". An *M.I. Hummel* Club exclusive offer.

A GIFT FROM A FRIEND
Hum 485

This little 4⅜" fellow was offered exclusively to members of the *M.I. Hummel* club in the club year 1991-92. Its availability to members at $160.00 was subject to the cut-off date of May 31, 1993.

It is found with the current-use trademark, the Hummel mark (TMK-6) only. There are no significant variations. It is valued still selling at $160.00.

I WONDER
Hum 486

This was a club exclusive offered to a member of the *M.I. Hummel* Club only, during the club of the year of June 1, 1990 to May 31, 1991. They were offered at $140.00. The size is listed as 5¼" and it bears the Bumble Bee club backstamp.

It is found in both the Missing Bee (TMK-6) and the current use trademark, the Hummel mark (TMK-7). They are still valued at $140.00 with the older mark being slightly higher than the new.

I WONDER, Hum 486. Missing Bee (TMK-6), incised 1988 MID, 5¼".

I WONDER, Hum 486. Demonstration piece with only flesh tones painted. Current use trademark (TMK-7), *M.I. Hummel* Club special backstamp, incised 1988 MID, 5⅛". Valued at about $300-400.00.

LET'S TELL THE WORLD
Hum 487

Released in 1990 as part of the Century Collection, Let's Tell the World is 10½". The production number was limited to the number produced during 1990 and the edition is listed as closed in the 1992 Goebel price list with no price so presumably they are no longer available. The actual number of them produced is not presently known. Each piece bears a special backstamp commemorating the 55th Anniversary of *M.I. Hummel* figurines. Released at $875.00.

They are available only in the Missing Bee (TMK-6) trademark and are valued at $900.00.

LET'S TELL THE WORLD, Hum 487. Missing Bee mark, 1988 MID, 8"x10⁷⁄₁₆" high, Century Collection dated 1990, 1935-1990 55 Years of *M.I. Hummel* Figurines.

OPEN NUMBERS
Hum 488 through Hum 492

These are mold numbers for which there is no known design for a figure at present. They will probably be used for any new designs developed in the future.

TWO HANDS, ONE TREAT
Hum 493

This special 4" figure is an *M.I. Hummel* Club exclusive. It was made available as a renewal premium, a gift, to those members renewing their membership in the club year 1991-92. The club placed a $65.00 valuation on the piece at that time.

They are found with the current-use trademark, the Hummel mark (TMK-7) only. They are presently valued at about the same.

TWO HANDS, ONE TREAT, Hum 493. Hummel mark (current use mark or TMK-7), incised 1988 MID, 4".

OPEN NUMBER
Hum 494
Possible Future Edition

EVENING PRAYER
Hum 495

Introduced as "New for '92" in the fall, 1991 issue of the *M.I. Hummel* Club newsletter this figure is listed at 3¾" tall and the release price was $95.00.

It has an incised 1988 Mold Induction Date (MID) and is found only in the current-use trademark The Hummel mark (TMK-7). It is valued at $105-120.00.

EVENING PRAYER, Hum 495. Hummel mark (current use or TMK-7), incised 1988 MID, 3⅞", first issue backstamp dated 1992.

UNKNOWN
Hum 488 through Hum 499

Open numbers for possible future editions.

FLOWERS FOR MOTHER
Mother's Day Plate
Hum 500
Possible Future Edition

This plate was listed in the index of the *M.I. Hummel* - The Golden Anniversary Album. Little else is known at this time. It was not illustrated.

DOLL PARTS
Hum 501 through Hum 511

These mold numbers were utilized to identify the heads, arms and legs of the eight porcelain dolls released by Goebel starting in 1984. There were eight different heads and the left and right hands were the same on each doll. That accounts for the ten mold numbers used.

DOLL PARTS
Hum 512 through Hum 519

These are the mold numbers used to identify the parts of the dolls by the Danbury Mint (see page 117). There were eight dolls in all.

OPEN NUMBERS
Hum 520 through Hum 529

LAND IN SIGHT
Hum 530

This large, complicated piece is very special. Land in Sight is a sequentially numbered, limited edition of 30,000 world wide, released in 1992 to commemorate Columbus' discovery of America. It is 9⅛" x 8⅜" x 5⅞". The special backstamp reads: "1492 - The Quincentennial of America's Discovery". There is also a medallion accompanying it. The release price was $1,600.00.

The only trademark to be found on all this piece is the current-use Hummel mark (TMK-7). It is still valued at about the same.

LAND IN SIGHT, Hum 530. Hummel mark (current use mark or TMK-7), incised 1988 MID, 9" long x9⅛" high, #1,112 of 30,000. The medallion that accompanies the figure is hanging from the mast. It is not attached.

OPEN NUMBERS
Hum 531 through Hum 533
A NAP
Hum 534

This piece was introduced as new for 1991 in the Fall issue of the *M.I. Hummel* Club newsletter, *INSIGHTS*. It is listed as 2¼" in size and released at $100.00.

It is found with the Hummel mark (TMK-7) only and is listed in the 1993 suggested retail price list at $110.00.

A NAP, Hum 534, Missing Bee (TMK-6) mark, 1988 MID, paper First Issue sticker, 2½".

OPEN NUMBERS
Hum 535 through Hum 540

SWEET AS CAN BE
Hum 541

This is a 4" basic size figure that was offered in a special "Preview Edition" exclusively to members of the *M.I. Hummel* Club for the 1993-94 club year. They will be given the standard club exclusive backstamp for the year. It will be put into regular production with the regular trademark afterward.

Goebel placed a value of $125.00 on the figure in the spring of 1993.

SWEET AS CAN BE, Hum 541. 1993/94 club exclusive "Preview Edition".

OPEN NUMBERS
Hum 542 through 547

FLOWER GIRL
Hum 548

This is a special figure available only to members of the *M.I. Hummel* Club and then only upon or after the fifth anniversary of their membership. It is 4½" high and bears a special backstamp to indicate its unique status.

The figure is available to members presently, in the Hummel mark (TMK-7) at $130.00. They began making them in the previous trademark era, that of the Missing Bee (TMK-6). These are valued at about the same today.

FLOWER GIRL, Hum 548. Missing Bee mark, incised 1989 MID, 4½".
An *M.I. Hummel* Club exclusive offer.

A SWEET OFFERING
Hum 549

This is an *M.I. Hummel* Club exclusive for members only. Free to members renewing their membership, it carries the mold number "549/3/0", and has a basic size of 3½". Goebel valued the piece at $80.00 in the spring of 1993.

A SWEET OFFERING, Hum 549 3/0. 1993/94 club renewal gift, 3½''.

OPEN NUMBERS
Hum 550 through Hum 552

SCAMP
Hum 553

This was a new figure in 1992. It has a basic size of 3½" and is found only in the current-use, Hummel mark (TMK-7) at $105.00. Has an incised Mold Induction Date (MID) of 1989.

There are no significant variations.

SCAMP, Hum 553. Hummel mark (current use or TMK-7), incised 1989 MID, 3⅝'', first issue backstamp dated 1992.

CHEEKY FELLOW
Hum 554

This figure was offered in a special "Preview Edition" exclusively to the members of the *M.I. Hummel* Club for the 1992-93 club year. They were given the standard club exclusive backstamp for that year period. The figure will then become a regular production piece and will no longer have the special marking. Goebel placed a value of $120.00 on the figure in the spring of 1992. It is valued at about the same presently.

Left: **CHEEKY FELLOW,** Hum 554, Hummel mark (current-use or TMK-7), incised 1989 MID, 4³⁄₁₆".
Right: **MY WISH IS SMALL,** Hum 463/0, Hummel mark (current-use or TMK-7), incised 1985 MID, 5½".

CHEEKY FELLOW, Hum 554. Incised 1989 MID, 4⅛".

OPEN NUMBER
Hum 555

ONE PLUS ONE
Hum 556

When this figure was first made available it was in a limited form. Released in 1993, they were not made available through normal channels, but rather only at authorized dealer promotions that were billed as a "District Manager Promotion" in the United States and a "Canadian Artist" promotion in Canada. They were made available for purchase by anyone interested, on a first-come, first-served basis. These pieces bear a special marking on the base to indicate they were part of the promotion with the regular markings. They were sold for $115.00 at these events.

OPEN NUMBERS
Hum 557 through Hum 559

LUCKY FELLOW
Hum 560

This is the figure given free to members who renewed their membership in the club year 1992-93. It has a basic size of 3½" and Goebel valued it at $75.00 in the summer of 1992. It is presently valued at about the same.

LUCKY FELLOW, Hum 560. An *M.I. Hummel* Club members only exclusive offering. It is 3⅝" tall, bears the current use trademark (TMK-7), the special club backstamp and an incised 1989 MID.

GRANDMA'S GIRL
Hum 561

In 1993, the day after the First Annual *M.I. Hummel* Club Convention there was a special meeting held for local chapter members from all over the United States and Canada. Each member attending (650) was given either a Hum 561, Grandma's Girl or a Hum 562, Grampa's Boy. On the side of the bases of each was the inscription "1993 - *M.I. Hummel* Club Convention". Each was also signed by Goebel's Master Sculptor Gerhard Skrobek.

The regular piece is in the 1993 suggested retail price list at $135.00 and the Missing Bee piece is valued at about the same. The convention edition is valued at about $200-300.00.

GRANDMA'S GIRL, Hum 561. Missing Bee mark, 1989 MID incised, 4". Has the first issue backstamp dated 1991.

GRANDMA'S GIRL, Hum 561 showing the convention inscription.

GRANDPA'S BOY
Hum 562

There was a special meeting only for local chapter members after the First Annual *M.I. Hummel* Club Convention in 1993. Each member (650) was given either a Grandma's Girl, Hum 561 or a Grandpa's Boy, Hum 562. On the side of the base of each was the inscription "1993 - *M.I. Hummel* Club Convention". Goebel's Master Sculptor Gerhard Skrobek had signed each of them also.

The regular production pieces is listed in the 1993 suggested retail price list at $135.00. The Last Bee (TMK-6) pieces are valued at about the same. The convention edition is valued at about $200-300.00.

GRANDPA'S BOY, Hum 562. Missing Bee mark, 1989 MID incised, 4¼". Has the first issue backstamp dated 1991.

GRANDPA'S BOY, Hum 562 showing the convention inscription.

OPEN NUMBERS
Hum 563 through Hum 568

A FREE FLIGHT
Hum 569

This figure was released in late 1992. Its basic size is 4¾". It is not found in any trade marks earlier than the Missing Bee (TMK-6). There are no significant variations. It continues in production today.

A FREE FLIGHT, Hum 569. Hummel mark (TMk-7), 4¾".

OPEN NUMBER
Hum 570

ANGELIC GUIDE
1991 Christmas Ornament
Hum 571

It is not found in any earlier trademark than the Missing Bee (TMK-6) and is valued at about $100.00 in that mark.

ANGELIC GUIDE, Hum 571. 1991 Christmas ornament, Missing Bee (TMK-6) mark, 1989 MID, 3½".

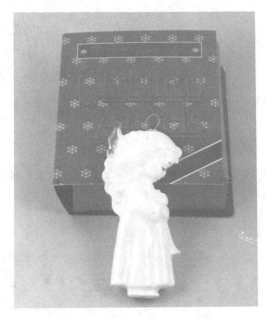

Christmas Angel CELESTIAL MUSICIAN, Hum 578 with its box, 3".

ANGELS OF CHRISTMAS
Christmas Ornament Series
Hum 575 through Hum 582, Hum 585 and Hum 586

This was a series of ornaments made by Goebel in 1990 for the Danbury Mint for mail order distribution. They were made in full color for Danbury. Please refer to page 117.

In 1992 Goebel made them available as the "Christmas Angels", but the finish is different. These small ornaments appear to have been made from the same molds as the Danbury mint pieces, but they are rendered in white overglaze with only their eyes and lips painted in color in the same fashion as the "Expressions of Youth" series. The wing tips are flashed in 14K gold. They are listed at $25.00 each in the 1993 Goebel Suggested Retail Price List. They are listed following:

See next page.

Photo courtesy M.I. Hummel Club.

Hum 575	Heavenly Angel	3"
Hum 576	Festival Harmony with Mandolin	3"
Hum 577	Festival Harmony with Flute	3"
Hum 578	Celestial Musician	3"
Hum 579	Song of Praise	2½"
Hum 580	Angel With Lute	2½"
Hum 581	Prayer of Thanks	3"
Hum 582	Gentle Song	3"
Hum 585	Angel in Cloud	2½"
Hum 586	Angel with Trumpet	2½"

OPEN NUMBERS
Hum 583 and Hum 584
Hum 587 through Hum 599

WE WISH YOU THE BEST
Hum 600

It is not found in any trademark earlier than the Missing Bee (TMK-6) and is valued at $1400.00 in that mark. The value for those examples bearing the current-use trade mark, the Hummel mark (TMK-7) is $1300.00.

WE WISH YOU THE BEST, Hum 600. Missing Bee mark, incised 1989
MID, 9⅝" wide x 9¼" high, Century Collection dated 1991.

OPEN NUMBERS
Hum 601 through Hum 615

402

PARADE OF LIGHTS
Hum 616

This 6" figurine, released in 1993, seems to be a cousin of Carnival, Hum 328. It is in the 1993 suggested retail price list at $235.00.

PARADE OF LIGHTS, Hum 616. Hummel mark (TMK-7), 6''.

OPEN NUMBERS
Hum 617 through Hum 621

LIGHT UP THE NIGHT
1992 Christmas Ornament
Hum 622

This is another in the annual series of ornaments. It appears in the 1993 suggested price list at $100.00.

LIGHT UP THE NIGHT, Hum 622. 1992 Christmas ornament, Hummel mark (TMK-7), 1990 MID, 3¼''.

HERALD ON HIGH, Hum 623. 1993 Christmas ornament.

HERALD ON HIGH
1993 Christmas Ornament
Hum 623

This is another in the annual series of ornaments. It appears in the 1993 suggested retail price list at $155.00.

OPEN NUMBERS
Hum 624 and Hum 625

I DIDN'T DO IT
Hum 626

This basic size 5½" figure is the *M.I. Hummel* Club exclusively offering for the club year 1993-94. It is available to members with redemption cards at $175.00. It has the special club exclusive backstamp.

I DIDN'T DO IT, Hum 626. 1993/94 club exclusive, 5⅝". The thing he holds behind himself is an archery bow.

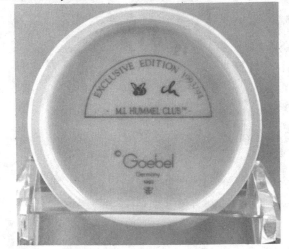

Base of the Hum 626 showing the *M.I. Hummel* Club special backstamp.

OPEN NUMBERS
Hum 627 through Hum 634

Crown	CM	TMK-1	1934-1950
Full Bee	FB	TMK-2	1940-1959
Stylized Bee	Sty Bee	TMK-3	1958-1972
Three Line Mark	3-line	TMK-4	1964-1972
Last Bee Mark	LB	TMK-5	1970-1980
Missing Bee Mark	MB	TMK-6	1979-1991
Hummel Mark (Current)	HM	TMK-7	1991-Present

WELCOME SPRING
Hum 635

This is the 1993 Century Collection piece. It is limited to the number produced in that one year this century. It is marked so on the base and comes with a certificate of authenticity.

The release price was $1,085.00 in the suggested retail price list from Goebel.

WELCOME SPRING, Hum 635. Hummel mark (TMK-7), 12¼", 1993 Century Collection piece.

OPEN NUMBERS
Hum 636 through Hum 645

CELESTIAL MUSICIAN
Christmas Tree Ornament
Hum 646

A new release in 1993 as the first in a new series of ornaments. This is essentially the same design as the Hum 188, Celestial Musician figurine without a base. It's basic size is 2⅞" and is in the 1993 suggested retail price list at $90.00

CELESTIAL MUSICIAN, Hum 646. 1993 Annual Christmas Ornament.

OPEN NUMBERS
Hum 647 through Hum 668

FRIENDS TOGETHER
Hum 662

This figurine was released in the summer of 1993 in two basic sizes. The smaller of the two, Hum 662/0 at 4", will be the regular production figures. It will bear a special "Commemorative Edition" backstamp and sold through regular channels. The larger size, Hum 662/1, 6", is a limited edition. This is the first of three cooperative fund-raising efforts between Goebel and the U.S. Committee for UNICEF, the United Nations Children's Fund. The art from which the figurine is taken is from work done by Sister Maria Innocentia Hummel in connection with her convent at Siessen and their African missionary work during the 1930's. The figurines were not released to the public until September 3, 1993, but were available exclusively to members of the *M.I. Hummel* Club on a first come, first served basis for roughly one month prior to the general release. These were not marked with the special club exclusive backstamp and are not considered club pieces.

The 6" size will be limited in production to 25,000 world-wide. That seems a large number at first, but considering the millions of collectors, the number is small. Each will be hand numbered with the special markings as in the accompanying illustration.

The suggested retail price for the 4" size at release was $260.00. The release price for the limited edition, 6" size, was $475.00 with $25.00 of that amount being contributed to UNICEF.

KITCHEN MOLDS
Hum 669 through Hum 674

These mold numbers are used to identify the kitchen mold sold the Danbury Mint. Please refer to page 117.

CANDLE HOLDERS
Hum 676 through Hum 679

These mold numbers are used to identify four candle holders sold by the Danbury Mint. Please refer to page 117.

OPEN NUMBERS
Hum 680 through Hum 689

SMILING THROUGH
Wall Plaque
Hum 690

This is the second special editions produced exclusively for members of the Goebel Collectors Club. It was available through membership in the club only. Members received a redemption certificate upon receipt of their annual dues and they could purchase the piece through dealers who are official representatives of the club for $55.00. It appears bearing the Last Bee trademark (TMK-5) only. 5¾" round. It is presently valued at about $65-75.00. As of May 31, 1984 it was no longer available as a redemption piece.

SMILING THROUGH plaque, Hum 690 in the optional frame. Last Bee mark, 5¾" diameter. *M.I. Hummel* Club exclusive.

OPEN NUMBERS
Hum 691 through Hum 699

1978 ANNUAL BELL
Hum 700

This is the first edition of a bell which the factory has begun producing, one each year. This first bell utilized the "Let's Sing", Hum 110, motif. It is a first of its kind and like the first edition Annual Plate it experienced quite a rapid rise in value for a while. It was first released at $50.00 and is presently bringing about $40.00.

1979 ANNUAL BELL
Hum 701

This is the second edition bell released in 1979. It utilized the Hum 65 "Farewell" design motif. The suggested retail release price was $70.00. Now selling for about $20.00.

1980 ANNUAL BELL
Hum 702

The third edition in the series of annual bells. This bell utilizes the design motif of a boy seated, reading from a large book in his lap. It is somewhat similar to Hum 3 or 8, The Girl Bookworm. The design is named "Thoughtful". Issue price: $85.00. Now selling for about $30.00.

1981 ANNUAL BELL
Hum 703

The fourth bell in the series uses the design from Hum 414, In Tune. Released at $115 it is now selling for about $40-45.00.

Annual Bells: 1978 1979 1980 1981 1982

1982 ANNUAL BELL
Hum 704

This fifth bell in the series matches the design of Hum 174, She Loves Me, She Loves Me Not. Released at $85 and now selling at $65-70.00.

1983 ANNUAL BELL
Hum 705

This is the sixth bell in the series. The design is called Knit One. The release price was $90 and it is presently widely advertised at about $55-60.00.

1984 ANNUAL BELL
Hum 706

The seventh bell in the annual series derives its design from the figurine Mountaineer. The release price was $90.00 and it is presently selling at about $70.00.

Annual Bells: 1983, 1984, 1985, 1986, 1987

1985 ANNUAL BELL
Hum 707

The eighth bell in the series matches the design of the figurine Girl with Sheet Music. The release price was $90.00 and it is presently advertised for sale at $60.00.

1986 ANNUAL BELL
Hum 708

The ninth bell in the series. Uses the figurine Sing Along, Hum 433 as its design. Release price: $100.00. It is presently selling at $95-100.00.

1987 ANNUAL BELL
Hum 709

The tenth bell in the series. Uses With Loving Greetings, Hum 309 as its design. Release price. $110.00 It is presently selling at $140.00.

1988 ANNUAL BELL
Hum 710

The eleventh bell in the series. Uses Busy Student, Hum 367 as its design. Release price: $120.00. It is presently selling at about $105.00.

1989 ANNUAL BELL
Hum 711

The twelfth bell in the series. Uses Latest News, Hum 184 as its design. It was released at a suggested retail price of $135.00. A few of these Hum 711 bells were produced with the mold number 710 incised before the mistake was discovered. The present collector value is $110-115.00.

1990 ANNUAL BELL
Hum 712

This is the thirteenth bell in the series. It uses What's New? as its design. The release price was $140.00 and is presently selling at about $150.00.

Annual Bells: 1988, 1989, 1990, 1991, 1992

1991 ANNUAL BELL
Hum 713

The fourteenth bell in the series. It uses Favorite Pet as its design. It is presently selling at $130-140.00.

1992 ANNUAL BELL
Hum 714

The fifteenth bell in the series uses Whistler's Duet as its design motif. Released at $165.00 it is now widely advertised for $115-120.00. This was the final edition in the series.

ANNIVERSARY BELL
Hum 730

Although this has been seen it will probably not come to be. It is listed in the index of the book M.I. HUMMEL — GOLDEN ANNIVERSARY ALBUM, but was not illustrated. The original intention was to release it as a companion piece for a plate in the Anniversary Plate Series, but since the series was cancelled so went the bell.

CELEBRATION PLATE SERIES

A series of four 6" plates made available exclusively to members of the Goebel Collectors' Club (now the *M.I. Hummel* Club) starting in 1986 and issued one a year.

MOLD	YEAR	DESIGN	TRADE MARK	COLLECTOR VALUE
735	1986	Valentine Gift	MB TMK-6	$120.00
736	1988	Daisies Don't Tell	MB TMK-6	$120.00
737	1987	Valentine Joy	MB TMK-6	$120.00
738	1989	It's Cold	MB TMK-6	$120.00

CELEBRATION PLATE SERIES: It's Cold, Daisies Don't Tell, Valentine Joy, Valentine Gift.

OPEN NUMBERS
Hum 739 and Hum 740

LITTLE MUSIC MAKERS
Mini-Plate Series

This is a four plate series of 4" diameter plates. At the same time as the plates were issued a smaller figurine in matching motif was issued. The plates were limited in number to the amount produced during each year of the release. They are all found with the Missing Bee (TMK-6) trademark. There is no explanation for the non-sequential mold number/year of release situation.

MOLD	YEAR	DESIGN	COLLECTOR VALUE
741	1985	Serenade	$25-40.00
742	1987	Band Leader	$40-55.00
743	1986	Soloist	$35-50.00
744	1984	Little Fiddler	$25-40.00

LITTLE MUSIC MAKERS Plate Series. Plates are accompanied by the corresponding figurines. Serenade, Band Leader, Soloist, Little Fiddler.

LITTLE HOMEMAKERS
Mini-Plate Series

This four piece mini-plate series was begun in 1988. The plates are 4" in diameter and there was a small matching figure issued each year along with them. Each was limited to the number of each produced in the year of issue. All but the last one in the series bear the Last Bee (TMK-6) trademark. The last one, produced in 1991, is found with the current-use trademark, the Hummel mark (TMK-7).

MOLD	YEAR	DESIGN	COLLECTOR VALUE
745	1988	Little Sweeper	$35-50.00
746	1989	Wash Day	$40-50.00
747	1990	Stitch in Time	$35-45.00
748	1991	Chicken Licken	$60-70.00

LITTLE HOMEMAKERS Plate Series. Plates are accompanied by the corresponding figurines. Little Sweeper, Wash Day, Stitch in Time, Chicken Licken.

CHRISTMAS BELL SERIES

This four bell series began with the 1989 offering and ended with the 1992 bell. They were rendered in a soft blue and each has a clapper fashioned in the shape of a pine cone. They are 3¼" in height.

The only significant variation to be found is with regard to color. Some 250-300 of the 1990 bell, Ride into Christmas were made in greenish yellow color and given to company representatives as a Christmas present from Goebel

MOLD	YEAR	DESIGN	COLLECTOR VALUE
775	1989	Ride Into Christmas	50.00
776	1990	Letter To Santa Claus	
777	1991	Hear Ye, Hear Ye	50.00
778	1992	Harmony in Four Parts	
			50.00

CHRISTMAS BELLS, Left to right: 1989, Hum 775, Ride Into Christmas; 1991, Hum 777, Hear Ye, Hear Ye; 1992, Hum 778, Harmony in Four Parts.

1990 CHRISTMAS BELLS. The one on the right is the reverse side of the regular 1990 bell, Letter to Santa Claus, in a soft pastel blue color. The bell on the left is rendered in a greenish yellow color in a limited edition of 295.

413

CHRISTMAS BELL SERIES

A new four bell series was initiated with the 1993 issue. This really is a continuation of the original series as the base of the bells is the same.

MOLD	YEAR	DESIGN	COLLECTOR VALUE
779	1993	Celestial Musician	50.00

CELESTIAL MUSICIAN bell showing the location of the markings in the bells.

CELESTIAL MUSICIAN, Hum 779. The 1993 Christmas Bell.

APPENDIX A
PHOTOGRAPHING YOUR COLLECTION

There are two very good reasons for taking good photographs of your collection. The most important is to have a record of what you had in the unfortunate event of a theft, fire or any other disaster that may result in the loss or destruction of your collection. Insurance companies are loathe to take your word that you had a Hum 1, Puppy Love worth ten times the normal value just because its head was tilted in a different direction. A photograph would prove it. In the case of theft you have little chance of identifying your collection in the event of a recovery in some instances. Law enforcement authorities often recover stolen property that can't be identified as to owner. If you have photographs and documentation such as detailed descriptions of marks etc., they can help you positively identify what is yours. The second reason for this section is to help you also, but me as well. I get hundreds of photos each year, most of which are useless. You send me the photograph(s) with your questions and all I can see is what looks like a scarecrow out in the middle of a four acre field or a fuzzy Feathered Friends figurine due to its being out of focus. Can't help you much there. So, ready for your photography lesson?

This will be simple and fun for most of you. It won't make you America's next Ansel Adams, but it will make you a better photographer of figurines. You experts and pros can move on to the next section now.

THE CAMERA

The two most common cameras most of us use today are the 35mm single lens reflex (SLR) and the very common automatic "point and shoot" cameras that use the mini negative disc or regular 35mm film. The method for taking the picture differs slightly with the type so we will go through the basic set-up to get your figurines ready to shoot and then describe the method for each of the camera types.

SETTING

I employ a light blue or gray paper background normally that starts flat on a table top and is rolled up behind the figurine forming a curved background so there is no horizontal line to distract from the figure. You probably won't want to get that elaborate so go out and get a sheet of poster board. I recommend a light gray, pale blue or a beige for a neutral background. Cut it in half, putting one piece flat on the table top and the other propped up somehow behind it as in the diagram. The diagram is overly simple and out of scale, but illustrates the idea.

If this too is more than you want to try, a simple table top or any flat surface will suffice. Try to avoid any with a patterned surface.

LIGHTING

There are two types of light, natural or available light and artificial.

Natural Light - The simplest and best light is natural light outdoors, on an overcast day or in the shade on a bright sunshiny day. This eliminates harsh shadows. You can get almost the same light indoors if you shoot your picture at a large window that is admitting much light but not letting direct sunlight in.

Artificial Light - If you wish to shoot inside under artificial light you can do so in a bright, well-lighted room. You must be careful, however, about the type of light you have. Fluorescent lighting will produce pictures with a decidedly greenish cast. Incadescent lighting, ordinary light bulbs, will cause your pictures to come out with a yellowish or red cast. This is true when using ordinary, daylight color film designed for use outdoors or with a flash. Most modern photo processing labs can filter this color distortion out, but you must tell them about the type of light you used beforehand.

Using a flash is the third possibility, but under ordinary circumstances produces a severe, flat picture with harsh shadows.

If you can devise a way of filtering the flash, diffusing it or bouncing it, results are generally much more satisfying. The best use of flash is for "fill light" when shooting outdoors. It fills in shadows, eliminating them if done right.

CHOICE OF FILM

Film comes in different speeds (ASA ratings). The higher the ASA the faster the speed. The faster the speed, the less light needed to take a good photograph. There is a trade-off, however. The faster the speed the grainier the picture. This should not be of concern to you unless you are going to enlarge the picture or submit it for publication. I recommend that you use film with an ASA or 100 or 200, but if you have a poor light situation the ASA 400 would give you satisfactory pictures. Those of you with the modern automatic cameras shouldn't need to worry about switching these ASA's because your camera will automatically adjust to the ASA. Be sure to read your manual about this (You *did* read your manual didn't you?). Those of you with the more complicated SLR's know what to do.

GENERAL TECHNIQUES

First, you have a choice of methods. It you are shooting the pictures for insurance inventory purposes you may choose to make a gang shot; that is shooting of two or three or more, or shooting your display cabinets or shelves (if there is a glass door, be sure to open it first). The latter is less desirable because you lose the detail you may need for identification later. If you don't wish to shoot each individual piece, then shoot them in groups of no more than three or four and try to match sizes as best you can.

When you take your pictures get in as close as you can, filling the frame with the figures. Try to hold the camera as low and level with the pieces as you can unless this causes a hand or some other part of the figure to obscure or cast a shadow on a face or other important feature. Sometimes adjusting the position of the figure can alleviate this problem. Remember, you want to show it at its best. If your camera is capable of close-up photography or there is a close-up lens attachment for it, take shots of the underside of the base of each piece or at least of the most valuable ones. These close-up attachments are usually quite inexpensive and come in sets of three lens.

TECHNIQUE FOR AUTOMATIC CAMERAS

Most of the automatic cameras of today come with a fixed focus lens or an automatic focus feature. Some even have a "macro" feature allowing you to get a little closer than normal to your subject. This feature allows a little nicer close-up portraiture, but is not of much use for our purposes here. Most automatic cameras will not allow you to get any closer than three feet from your subject. Any closer and everything will be out of focus. The field of view at three feet will be about 20" x 24". If you put one 6" figurine in the middle of that, take the picture and process it, you will get a photo about 4" x 5" in size and the figurine will be less than 1¼" tall, a lonesome trifling tidbit in the center (Remember the Scarecrow in the forty acre field?). It would be of little use in identification. A few of these cameras have close-up attachments available so check your manual to see if yours is one of them. If not then you will at best, only be able to make group pictures. You might want to experiment with one roll of film. Some of the automatic cameras will do much more than others and some will do better than the manual indicates. If your experiment is a failure, I suggest you prevail upon a friend or relative who has a better camera to help you out. Better yet, go out and buy one. The single lens reflex cameras are not near as complicated to use as they appear.

TECHNIQUE FOR THE SINGLE LENS REFLEX (SLR) CAMERA

Chances are many of you who have SLR's have never tried to do macro work. That is what small object photography is called. If you have perfected that art, you have permission to skip the rest of this section.

Macrophotography is a big word for a relatively simple technique, the results of which can be quite rewarding. In fact many of the photos in this book were shot with a Honeywell Pentax SLR with a standard 55mm lends that I bought many years ago. Many of you will probably have much newer and better cameras than mine. Your camera should do as well as mine which will focus down to about 13" from the subject with a 5" x 7" field of view and with a set of inexpensive close-up lens (less than $20.00), you can get spectacular close-ups. Remember though, the more magnification you get, the less depth of field is available. I may have lost some of you there. Depth of field is simply the area in front of the camera that will photograph with acceptable sharpness. Said another way, it is the difference between the nearest and the furthest point of acceptable sharpness in the scene to be photographed.

Focusing and Depth of Field - The depth of field you will be concerned with here is a function of the f-stop selected for the photograph and to a lesser extent, the distance from the lens to the subject. Simply put, the higher the f-stop selected, the more depth of field you have. It varies with the lens but the depth of field on my camera at f-16 is about 3" when it is focused as close as possible. When I focus on a figurine I try to focus about midway into its depth. This is entirely sufficient to keeping all parts of the figurine in focus in most cases. You may be able to do a little better or a little worse depending on your lens. Although you will likely be working as close to the subject as you can get, you should know that the further you get from the subject, the more the depth of field.

Shutter Speeds and f-stops - We have already noted that you will want to use a high f-stop number, f-11 or higher. Well the higher the f-stop, the smaller the aperture (the hole through which the reflected light passes on its way to the film). The smaller that hole is the longer it takes enough light reflected from your subject to form a good image on the film. So it follows that the smaller the hole the longer the shutter must remain open. Since we want enough depth of field so that all the figurine is in focus we'll have to trade off for time. That means the shutter speed will be too slow for you to hand hold your camera. That is why you will need to buy or borrow a tripod. Some folks are clever enough to jury-rig one. It would also be a good idea to have a cable release to insure that you do not shake the camera when tripping the shutter. They are inexpensive and available anywhere good cameras are sold.

Shooting the Picture - Here is a typical set-up in sufficient light to take your pictures:

Film speed . . . . . . ASA 100 to 200

Shutter speed . . . . 1/8 to 1/30

f-stop . . . . f-11 to f-16

Focal distance . 14" to 18" approx.
As close as you can or need to be.

You will likely need to experiment a little until you are happy with the results. There are 12 print rolls of film available if you don't wish to waste film. The best way to find the ideal set-up for your light conditions is to shoot at different f-stops, leaving everything else constant, and place a piece of paper with your subject with the setting written on it or do the same thing varying any setting you want. You then will have a set of photos from which to pick the best and have the best camera setting right there in the picture.

SOME LAST NOTES ON PHOTOGRAPHING YOUR COLLECTION

Now you have your photograph(s). First, especially if this is an insurance inventory, you should have two sets of photographs. One set for you to keep at home to work with when you need to and the other in a safe deposit box or a separate location in case of fire or other happenstance resulting in the loss of your photographs. Second, you should have a written record either on the back of the photos or separate from them, of the date of purchase, the amount of the purchase, where or from whom you obtained it, the size, the trademark and every other mark to be found on the piece. This data along with the photo can leave no doubt as to ownership. This is especially true when, as in the case of Hummel, each piece is hand painted therefore slightly different from any other like piece; same as people. One last comment: If you are photographing the piece to send to me - give me the same information.

APPENDIX B

CURRENT PRICE LIST

This listing is taken from the Suggested Retail Price List issued by the Goebel company. Dated March 1, 1993, it is the published suggested retail price for the figures and other items which bear the trademark presently being used by the company. The appearance of a particular piece on this list is not necessarily an indication that it is available from dealers. Few dealers have the wherewithal to pick their stock and even fewer have the ability to stock every piece in every size in any depth at all.

NAME	MOLD NUMBER	APPROX. SIZE	RETAIL PRICE	NAME	MOLD NUMBER	APPROX. SIZE	RETAIL PRICE
A Budding Maestro	477	4"	95.00	Bashful	377	4¾"	180.00
Accompanist, The	453	3¼"	90.00	Bath Time	412	6⅛"	350.00
A Fair Measure	345	5½"	260.00	Begging His Share	9	5½"	220.00
A Free Flight	569	4¾"	185.00	Be Patient	197/2/0	4¼"	175.00
A Gentle Glow	439	5¼"	190.00	Be Patient	197/I	6¼"	260.00
A Nap	534	2½"	110.00	Big Housecleaning	363	4"	260.00
Accordian Boy	185	5"	180.00	Bird Duet	169	4"	130.00
Adoration	23/I	6¼"	325.00	Bird Watcher	300	5¼"	205.00
Adoration	23/III	9"	510.00	Birthday Cake	338	3½"	130.00
Adventure Bound	347	7½"x8¼"	3500.00	Birthday Serenade	218/2/0	4¼"	160.00
An Apple A Day	403	6⅜"	260.00	Birthday Serenade	218/0	5½"	270.00
Angel Duet	261	5"	195.00	Blessed Child	78/I/83	2½"	TW
Angel Serenade	214/D/I	3"	80.00	Blessed Child	78/II/83	3½"	TW
Angel Serenade	260/E	4¼"	TW	Blessed Child	78/III/83	5¼"	TW
Angel Serenade with Lamb	83	5½"	195.00	Blessed Event	333	5½"	300.00
Angel with Accordian	238/B	2"	50.00	Book Worm	8	4"	195.00
Angel with Lute	238/A	2"	50.00	Book Worm	3/I	5½"	270.00
Angel with Trumpet	238/C	2"	50.00	Book Worm	3/II	8"	TW
Angelic Song	144	4"	135.00	Boots	143/0	5½"	180.00
Apple Tree Boy	142/3/0	4"	130.00	Boots	143/I	6½"	300.00
Apple Tree Boy	142/I	6"	245.00	Botanist, The	351	4½"	195.00
Apple Tree Boy	142/V	10"	1080.00	Boy With Accordian	390	2¼"	75.00
Apple Tree Boy	142/X	33"	TW	Boy With Horse	239/C	3½"	50.00
Apple Tree Girl	141/3/0	4"	130.00	Boy With Toothache	217	5½"	200.00
Apple Tree Girl	141/I	6"	245.00	Brother	95	5½"	180.00
Apple Tree Girl	141/V	10"	1080.00	Builder, The	305	5½"	220.00
Apple Tree Girl	141/X	33"	TW	Busy Student	367	4¼"	150.00
Art Critic	318	5½"	260.00	Carnival	328	6"	205.00
Artist, The	304	5½"	220.00	Celestial Musician	188/4/0	3⅛"	90.00
Auf Wiedersehen	153/0	5"	220.00	Celestial Musician	188/0	5¼"	195.00
Auf Wiedersehen	153/I	7"	270.00	Celestial Musician	188/I	7"	TW
Autumn Harvest	355	4¾"	195.00	Chick Girl	57/2/0	3¼"	135.00
Baker	128	4¾"	175.00	Chick Girl	57/0	3½"	155.00
Baking Day	330	5¼"	240.00	Chick Girl	57/I	4¼"	250.00
Band Leader	129/4/0	3"	90.00	Chicken Licken	385/4	3⅛"	90.00
Band Leader	129	5"	180.00	Chicken Licken	385	4¼"	260.00
Barnyard Hero	195/2/0	4"	150.00	Chimney Sweep	12/2/0	4"	110.00
Barnyard Hero	195/I	5½"	290.00	Chimney Sweep	12/I	5½"	195.00
				Christ Child	18	6"x2"	TW

NAME	MOLD NUMBER	APPROX. SIZE	RETAIL PRICE	NAME	MOLD NUMBER	APPROX. SIZE	RETAIL PRICE
Christmas Angel	301	6¼"	230.00	Goose Girl	47/0	4¾"	205.00
Christmas Song	343	6½"	195.00	Goose Girl	47/II	7½"	TW
Cinderella	337	4½"	260.00	Grandma's Girl	561	4"	135.00
Close Harmony	336	5½"	260.00	Grandpa's Boy	562	4⅛"	135.00
Confidentially	314	5½"	260.00	Guardian, The	455	2¾"	155.00
Congratulations	17	6"	180.00	Guiding Angel	357	2¾"	80.00
Coquettes	179	5"	260.00	Happiness	86	4¾"	120.00
Crossroads (Original)	331	6¾"	380.00	Happy Birthday	176/0	5½"	195.00
Culprits	56/A	6¼"	265.00	Happy Birthday	176/I	6"	270.00
Daddy's Girls	371	4¾"	220.00	Happy Days	150/2/0	4¼"	160.00
Doctor	127	4¾"	145.00	Happy Days	150/0	5¼"	270.00
Doll Bath	319	5"	260.00	Happy Days	150/I	6¼"	430.00
Doll Mother	67	4¾"	190.00	Happy Pastime	69	3½"	145.00
Duet	130	5"	250.00	Happy Traveller	109/0	5"	130.00
Easter Greetings	378	5¼"	195.00	Hear Ye! Hear Ye!	15/2/0	4"	135.00
Easter Time	384	4"	240.00	Hear Ye! Hear Ye!	15/0	5"	180.00
Evening Prayer	495	4"	105.00	Hear Ye! Hear Ye!	15/I	6"	225.00
Eventide	99	4¾"x4¼"	315.00	Hear Ye! Hear Ye!	15/II	7"	TW
¶Farewell	65	4¾"	240.00	Heavenly Angel	21/0	4¾"	110.00
Farm Boy	66	5"	205.00	Heavenly Angel	21/0/1/2	6"	190.00
Favorite Pet	361	4¼"	260.00	Heavenly Angel	21/I	6¾"	230.00
Feathered Friends	344	4¾"	240.00	Heavenly Angel	21/II	8¾"	TW
Feeding Time	199/0	4¼"	175.00	Heavenly Lullaby	262	5"x3½"	170.00
Feeding Time	199/I	5½"	240.00	Hello	124/0	6¼'	195.00
Festival Harmony, w/Flute	173/0	8"	280.00	Holy Child	70	6¾"	TW
				Home From Market	198/2/0	4¾"	130.00
Festival Harmony, w/Mandolin	172/0	8"	280.00	Home From Market	198/I	5½"	195.00
Flower Vendor	381	5¼"	220.00	Homeward Bound	334	5¼"	320.00
Follow The Leader	369	7"	1100.00	Horse Trainer	423	4½"	200.00
For Father	87	5½"	195.00	Hosanna	480	3⅞"	90.00
For Mother	257/2/0	4"	110.00	I'll Protect Him	483	3¼"	75.00
For Mother	257	5"	185.00	I'm Here	478	3⅛"	95.00
Forest Shrine	183	9"	495.00	In D Major	430	4¼"	180.00
Friend or Foe?	434	3⅞"	195.00	In The Meadow	459	4"	180.00
Friends	136/I	5"	195.00	In Tune	414	4"	250.00
Friends	136/V	10¾"	1080.00	Is It Raining?	420	6⅛"	240.00
Gay Adventure	356	5"	175.00	Joyful	53	4"	110.00
Girl With Doll	239/B	3½"	50.00	Joyous News	27/III	4¼"x4¾"	195.00
Girl With Nosegay	239/A	3½"	50.00	Just Fishing	373	4¼"	205.00
Girl With Sheet Music	389	2¼"	75.00	Just Resting	112/3/0	4"	135.00
Girl With Trumpet	391	2¼"	75.00	Just Resting	112/I	5"	250.00
Going Home	383	4¾"	280.00	Kindergartner, The	467	5¼"	180.00
Going To Grandma's	52/0	4¾"	250.00	Kiss Me	311	6"	260.00
Good Friends	182	5"	175.00	Knit One, Purl One	432	3"	105.00
Good Hunting	307	5"	220.00	Knitting Lesson	256	7½"	475.00
Good Night	214/C/I	3½"	80.00	Land in Sight (limited edition)	530	9⅛"x9⅜"x5⅞"	1600.00
Good Night	260/D	5¼"	TW	Latest News	184	5"	260.00
Good Shepherd	42	6¼"	220.00				
Goose Girl	47/3/0	4"	155.00				

TW: Temporarily withdrawn from production with no stated reinstatement date.

NAME	MOLD NUMBER	APPROX. SIZE	RETAIL PRICE	NAME	MOLD NUMBER	APPROX. SIZE	RETAIL PRICE
Let's Sing	110/0	3"	115.00	Mother's Darling	175	5½"	195.00
Let's Sing	110/I	4"	155.00	Mother's Helper	133	5"	175.00
Letter To Santa Claus	340	7¼"	305.00	Mountaineer	315	5"	195.00
Little Architect, The	410/I	6"	290.00	Not For You!	317	6"	220.00
Little Bookkeeper	306	4¾"	260.00	One For You, One For Me	482	3⅛"	95.00
Little Cellist	89/I	6"	195.00	++One Plus One	556	4"	115.00
Little Cellist	89/II	7½"	TW	On Holiday	350	4¼"	160.00
Little Drummer	240	4¼"	135.00	On Secret Path	386	5¼"	225.00
Little Fiddler	2/4/0	3"	90.00	Out of Danger	56/B	6¼"	265.00
Little Fiddler	4	4¾"	185.00	Parade of Lights	616	6"	235.00
Little Fiddler	2/0	6"	205.00	Photographer, The	178	5"	260.00
Little Fiddler	2/I	7½"	TW	Playmates	58/2/0	3¼"	135.00
Little Fiddler	2/II	10¾"	TW	Playmates	58/0	4"	155.00
Little Fiddler	2/III	12¼"	TW	Playmates	58/I	4¼"	250.00
Little Gabriel	32	5"	125.00	Postman	119/2/0	4½"	125.00
Little Gardener	74	4"	110.00	Postman	119	5"	180.00
Little Goat Herder	200/0	4¾"	175.00	Prayer Before Battle	20	4¼"	155.00
Little Goat Herder	200/I	5½"	220.00	Professor, The	320	4⅜"	195.00
Little Guardian	145	4"	135.00	Retreat To Safety	201/2/0	4"	150.00
Little Helper	73	4¼"	110.00	Retreat To Safety	201/I	5½"	275.00
Little Hiker	16/2/0	4½"	110.00	Ride Into Christmas	396/2/0	4¼"	220.00
Little Hiker	16/I	6"	200.00	Ride Into Christmas	396/I	5¾"	390.00
Little Nurse	376	4"	225.00	Ring Around The Rosie	348	6¾"	2500.00
Little Pharmacist	322/E	6"	220.00	Run-a-way, The	327	5¼"	225.00
Little Scholar	80	5½"	195.00	St. George	55	6¾"	300.00
Little Shopper	96	5½"	130.00	Scamp	553	3½"	105.00
Little Sweeper	171/4/0	3⅛"	90.00	School Boy	82/2/0	4"	130.00
Little Sweeper	171/0	4¼"	120.00	School Boy	82/0	5"	415.00
Little Tailor	308	5½"	220.00	School Boy	82/II	7½"	415.00
Little Thrifty	118	5"	130.00	School Boys	170/I	7½"	1100.00
Little Tooter	214/H	3"	95.00	School Girl	81/2/0	4¼"	130.00
Little Tooter	214/H	4"	110.00	School Girl	81/0	5"	175.00
Little Tooter	260/K	5½"	TW	School Girls	177/I	7½"	1100.00
+Lost Sheep	68/2/0	4¼"	125.00	Sensitive Hunter	6/2/0	4"	135.00
+Lost Sheep	68/0	5½"	180.00	Sensitive Hunter	6/0	4¾"	175.00
Lost Stocking	374	4¼"	130.00	Sensitive Hunter	6/I	5½"	230.00
Mail Is Here, The	226	6"x4½"	505.00	Serenade	85/4/0	3"	90.00
Make A Wish	475	4½"	175.00	Serenade	85/0	4¾"	120.00
March Winds	43	5"	145.00	Serenade	85/II	7½"	410.00
Max And Moritz	123	5"	205.00	She Loves Me, She Loves Me Not	174	4½"	170.00
Meditation	13/2/0	4½"	130.00	Shepherd's Boy	64	5½"	200.00
Meditation	13/0	5½"	205.00	Shining Light	358	2¾"	80.00
Meditation	13/V	13¾"	TW	Sing Along	433	4⅜"	260.00
Merry Wanderer	11/2/0	4¼"	125.00	Sing With Me	405	4¾"	280.00
Merry Wanderer	11/0	4¾"	175.00	Sister	98/2/0	4¾"	130.00
Merry Wanderer	7/0	6¼"	245.00	Sister	98/0	5½"	180.00
Merry Wanderer	7/I	9½"	TW	Skier	59	5"	195.00
Merry Wanderer	7/II	9½"	TW	Sleep Tight	424	4½"	200.00
Merry Wanderer	7/X	33"	TW				
Mischief Maker	342	5"	240.00				

TW: Temporarily withdrawn from production with no stated reinstatement date.

420

NAME	MOLD NUMBER	APPROX. SIZE	RETAIL PRICE	NAME	MOLD NUMBER	APPROX. SIZE	RETAIL PRICE
Smart Little Sister, The	346	4¾"	225.00	Which Hand?	258	5½"	180.00
Soldier Boy	332	6"	195.00	Whistler's Duet	413	4⅜"	250.00
Soloist	135/4/0	3"	90.00	Whitsuntide	163	7"	290.00
Soloist	135	4¾"	120.00	Winter Song	476	4¼"	100.00
Song of Praise	454	3"	90.00	With Loving Greetings	309	3½"	175.00
Sounds of Mandolin	438	3¾"	110.00	Worship	84/0	5"	145.00
Sound the Trumpet	457	3"	90.00	Worship	84/V	12¾"	TW
Spring Dance	353/0	5¼"	280.00				
Star Gazer	132	4¾"	195.00				
Stitch In Time	255/4/0	3¼"	85.00				
Stitch In Time	255/I	6¾"	260.00				
Stormy Weather	71/2/0	4¾"	270.00				
Stormy Weather	71/I	6¼"	415.00				
Storybook Time	458	5⅛"	360.00				
Street Singer	131	5"	170.00				
Surprise	94/3/0	4"	140.00				
Sweet Greetings	352	4¼"	195.00				
Sweet Music	186	5"	180.00				
Telling Her Secret	196/0	5"	270.00				
Thoughtful	415	4¼"	205.00				
Timid Little Sister	394	6¾"	390.00				
To Market	49/3/0	4"	150.00				
To Market	49/0	5½"	250.00				
Trumpet Boy	97	4¾"	120.00				
Tuba Player	437	6⅛"	240.00				
Tuneful Angel	359	2¾"	80.00				
Umbrella Boy	152/A/0	4¾"	530.00				
Umbrella Boy	152/A/II	8"	1300.00				
Umbrella Girl	152/B/0	4¾"	530.00				
Umbrella Girl	152/B/II	8"	1300.00				
Village Boy	51/3/0	4"	110.00				
Village Boy	51/2/0	5"	125.00				
Village Boy	51/0	6"	220.00				
Visiting an Invalid	382	5"	195.00				
Volunteers	50/2/0	5"	205.00				
Volunteers	50/0	5½"	270.00				
Waiter	154/0	6"	195.00				
Waiter	154/I	7"	260.00				
Wash Day	321/4/0	3⅛"	90.00				
Wash Day	321	6"	260.00				
Watchful Angel	194/I	6¾"	290.00				
Wayside Devotion	28/II	7½"	395.00				
Wayside Devotion	28/III	8¼"	520.00				
Wayside Harmony	111/3/0	4"	135.00				
Wayside Harmony	111/I	5"	245.00				
Weary Wanderer	204	6"	225.00				
We Congratulate	214/E/I	3½"	150.00				
We Congratulate	220	4"	145.00				
We Congratulate	260/F	6¼"	TW				
What's New?	418	5¼"	260.00				

ANNUAL SERIES

Bells

1992 Whistler's Duet (FINAL EDITION)	714	6"	160.00
1978 through 1992 Closed			

Christmas Bells

1993 Celestial Musician	779	3¼"	50.00
1992 Harmony In Four Parts	778	3¼"	50.00
1989 through 1992 Closed			

Miniature Ornaments

1993 Celestial Musician	646	2⅞"	90.00

Ornaments

1993 Herald on High (FINAL EDITION)	623	4½"	155.00
1992 Light Up the Night	622	3⅜"	100.00
1988 through 1992 Closed			

Plates

1993 Herald on High	623	4½"	155.00
1992 Waysid Harmony	288	7½"	210.00
1971 through 1992 Closed			

Friends Forever Plates

1993 For Father	293	7"	195.00
1992 Meditation	292	7⅛"	210.00

ASHTRAYS

Boy With Bird	166	3½"x6¼"	TW
Happy Pastime	62	3½"x6¼"	TW
Let's Sing	114	3½"x6¼"	TW
Singing Lesson	34	3½"x6¼"	TW

TW: Temporarily withdrawn from production with no stated reinstatement date.

NAME	MOLD NUMBER	APPROX. SIZE	RETAIL PRICE
BOOKENDS			
Apple Tree Boy & Girl	252/A&B	5"	TW
Bookworms	14/A&B	5½"	TW
Good Friends & She Loves Me, She Loves Me Not	251/A&B	5"	TW
Little Goat Herder & Feeding Time	250/A&B	5½"	TW
CANDLE HOLDERS			
Angel Duet	193	5"	200.00
Angelic Sleep	25	3½"x5"	TW
Angel Lights with Plate	241/B	10¼"x8¼"	235.00
Angel Lights w/out Plate	241	10¼"x8¼"	TW
Angel w/Lute	I/38/0	2"	40.00
Boy With Horse	117	3½"	50.00
Candlelight	192	6¾"	210.00
Girl With Fir Tree	116	3½"	50.00
Girl With Nosegay	115	3½"	50.00
Herald Angels	37	4"x2¼"	TW
Little Band	388/M	4¾"x2¼"	TW
Lullaby	24/I	5"x3½"	TW
CANDY BOXES			
Chick Girl	III/57	6¼"	TW
Happy Pastime	III/69	6"	TW
Joyful	III/53	6¼"	TW
Let's Sing	III/110	6"	TW
Playmates	III/58	6¼"	TW
Singing Lesson	III/63	6"	TW
CENTURY COLLECTION			
″1993 Welcome Spring	635	12¼"	1085.00
§1992 On Our Way	472	6½"x5½"x8"	950.00
1986 through 1992 Closed			
CHRISTMAS ANGELS			
Angel In Cloud	585	2½"	1085.00
Angel With Lute	580	2½"	25.00
Angel With Trumpet	586	2½"	25.00
Celestial Musician	578	3"	25.00
Festival Harmony With Flute	577	3"	25.00
Festival Harmony With Mandolin	576	3"	25.00
Gentle Song	582	3"	25.00
Heavenly Angel	575	3"	25.00
Prayer of Thanks	581	3"	25.00
Song of Praise	579	2½"	25.00

NAME	MOLD NUMBER	APPROX. SIZE	RETAIL PRICE
FIGURINE MINIATURES			
Accordian Boy	—	⅞"	105.00
Apple Tree Boy	—	⅞"	130.00
Baker	—	⅞"	105.00
Busy Student	—	⅞"	105.00
Cinderella	—	⅞"	105.00
Doll Bath	—	⅞"	105.00
Goose Girl	—	⅞"	130.00
Little Fiddler	—	⅞"	105.00
Little Sweeper	—	⅞"	105.00
Merry Wanderer	—	⅞"	130.00
Postman	—	⅞"	105.00
School Boy	—	⅞"	120.00
Serenade	—	⅞"	105.00
Stormy Weather	—	⅞"	130.00
Visiting An Invalid	—	⅞"	115.00
Waiter	—	⅞"	115.00
Wayside Harmony	—	⅞"	140.00
We Congratulate	—	⅞"	130.00
Displays for the Miniatures			
+Barvarian Church	—	—	60.00
+Bavarian Cottage	—	4"	64.00
+Bavarian Marketsquare w/Bridge	—	4¼"	110.00
+Bavarian Village	—	5"	100.00
+Countryside School	—	4¾"	100.00
+Display Plaque	3¼"x1 15/16"	130.00	
+Marketsquare Flower Stand	—	1¾"	35.00
+Roadside Shrine	—	4"	60.00
+Snow-Covered Mountain	—	—	100.00
+Trees	—	—	40.00
Vignettes with Solitaire Domes (Limited Editions)			
Bakery Day w/Baker & Waiter	—		225.00
The Flower Market w/Cinderella	—	135.00	
Winterfest w/Ride Into Christmas	—		195.00
FONTS			
Angel Cloud	206	4¾"	50.00
Angel Duet	146	4¾"	50.00
Angel Facing Left	91/A	4¾"	40.00
Angel Facing Right	91/B	4¾"	40.00
Angel Shrine	147	5"	50.00
Angel Sitting	22/0	3½"	40.00

TW: Temporarily withdrawn from production with no stated reinstatement date.

NAME	MOLD NUMBER	APPROX. SIZE	RETAIL PRICE
FONTS			
Angel With Bird	167	4¾"	50.00
Child Jesus	26/0	5"	40.00
Child With Flowers	36/0	4"	40.00
Good Shepherd	35/0	4¾"	40.00
Guardian Angel	248/0	5½"	50.00
Heavenly Angel	207	4¾"	50.00
Holy Family	246	4¾"	50.00
Madonna & Child	243	4"	50.00
White Angel	75	3½"	40.00
Worship	164	4¾"	50.00
LAMP BASES			
Apple Tree Boy	230	7½"	TW
Apple Tree Girl	229	7½"	TW
Birthday Serenade	234	7¾"	TW
Birthday Serenade	231	9¾"	TW
Culprits	44/A	9½"	TW
Good Friends	228	7½"	TW
Happy Days	235	7¾"	TW
Happy Days	232	9¾"	TW
Just Resting	225/I	7½"	TW
Out of Danger	44/B	9½"	TW
She Loves Me, She Loves Me Not	227	7½"	TW
To Market	223	9½"	TW
Wayside Harmony	224/I	7½"	TW
Wayside Harmony	224/II	9½"	TW
MADONNAS			
Flower Madonna, Color	10/I/11	8¼"	390.00
Flower Madonna, White	10/I/W	8¼"	165.00
Madonna Holding Child, Color	151/II	12"	675.00
Madonna Holding Child, White	151/W	12"	320.00
Madonna w/Halo, Color	45/I/6	12"	115.00
Madonna w/Halo, White	45/I/W	12"	70.00
Madonna w/o Halo, Color	46/I/6	11¼"	TW
Madonna w/o Halo, White	46/I/W	11¼"	TW

NAME	MOLD NUMBER	APPROX. SIZE	RETAIL PRICE
MUSIC BOXES			
Chick Girl	—	6¼"x4½"	TW
In Tune	—	6¼"x4½"	TW
Little Band w/Candle		4¾"x5"	TW
Little Band w/o Candle		4¾"x5"	TW
Ride Into Christmas	—	6¼"x4½"	TW
Umbrella Girl	—	6¼"x4½"	TW
NATIVITY FIGURINES			
Madonna	214/A/M/O	5¼"	120.00
St. Joseph	214/B/O	6⅛"	120.00
Infant Jesus	214/A/K/O	2⅞"x1⅛"	40.00
Flying Angel	366/0	3⅛"	85.00
King Kneeling	214/M/O	4¼"	130.00
King Kneeling w/Box	214/N/O	4⅛"	125.00
King, Moorish	214/L/O	6⅜"	140.00
Little Tooter	214/14/O	3⅛"	95.00
Shepherd Kneeling	214/G/O	4"	110.00
Shepherd Standing	214/F/0	5½"	145.00
Small Camel Standing	—	6½"	160.00
Small Camel Lying	—	3¼"x7½"	160.00
Small Camel Kneeling	—	4"x7¼"	160.00
Donkey	214/J/O	4"	50.00
Lamb	214/O/0	1½"x1"	17.00
Ox	214/K/0	2¾"x5"	50.00
Madonna	214/A/M/I	6½"	160.00
St. Joseph	214/B/I	7½"	160.00
Infant Jesus	214/A/K/I	3½"x1½"	60.00
Angel Serenade	214/D/I	3"	80.00
Flying Angel	366/I	3½"	115.00
Good Night	214/C/I	3½"	80.00
King, Moorish	214/L/I	8¼"	170.00
King Kneeling	214/M/I	5½"	160.00
King Kneeling w/Box	214/N/I	5½"	150.00
Little Tooter	214/H/I	4"	110.00
We Congratulate	214/E/I	3½"	150.00
Shepherd w/Sheep-1 pc.	214/F/I	7"	165.00
Shepherd Boy	214/G/I	4¾"	120.00
Camel Standing	—	11½"	205.00
Camel Kneeling	—	9"	205.00
Camel Lying	—	8"	205.00
Donkey	214/J/I	5"	65.00
Lamb	214/O/I	2"x1½"	20.00
Ox	214/K/I	6¼"x3½"	65.00
Madonna	260/A	9¾"	TW
St. Joseph	260/B	11¾"	TW
Infant Jesus	260/C	5¾"	TW
Good Night	260/D	5¼"	TW
Angel Serenade	260/E	4¼"	TW

TW: Temporarily withdrawn from production with no stated reinstatement date.

NAME	MOLD NUMBER	APPROX. SIZE	RETAIL PRICE
King, Moorish	260/N	12¾"	TW
King, Kneeling	260/P	9"	TW
King, Standing	260/O	12"	TW
Little Tooter	260/K	5½"	TW
We Congratulate	260/F	6¼"	TW
Shepherd, Standing	260/G	11¾"	TW
Shepherd Boy, Kneeling	260/J	7"	TW
Sheep (Standing) w/Lamb	260/H	3¾"	TW
Sheep (Lying)	260/R	3½"x4"	TW
Donkey	260/L	7½"	TW
Ox	260/M	6"x11"	TW

NATIVITY SETS

NAME	MOLD NUMBER	APPROX. SIZE	RETAIL PRICE
Holy Family, 3 Pcs. Color	214/A/M/O,B/O,A/K/O	—	270.00
Holy Family, 3 Pcs. Color	214/A/M/I,B/I,A/K/I	—	380.00
12 piece set figurines only, Color	214/A/M/I,B/I,A/K/I,F/I,G/I,J/I,K/I,L/I,M/I,N/I,O/I,366/I		
16 piece set figurines only, Color	214/A/M/I,B/I,A/K/I C/I,D/I,E/I,F/I,G/I,H/I,J/I,K/I,L/I,M/I,N/I,O/I,366/I		
17 piece set, Large Color Nativity set with wooden stable	260/A-R	—	TW

WALL PLAQUES

NAME	MOLD NUMBER	APPROX. SIZE	RETAIL PRICE
Ba Bee Ring-Boy	30/A	4¾"x5"	85.00
Ba Bee Ring-Girl	30/B	4¾"x5"	85.00
Child In Bed	137	2½"x2¾"	60.00
Flitting Butterfly	139	2½"x2½"	60.00
Little Fiddler	93	5"x5½"	TW
Madonna	48/0	3"x4"	TW
Merry Christmas	323	5¼"	120.00
Quartet	134	6"x6"	TW
Retreat To Safety	126	4¾"x4¾"	TW
Searching Angel	310	4⅛"x3⅜"	115.00
Swaying Lullaby	165	5¼"x5¼"	TW
Standing Boy	168	5¾"x5¾"	TW
The Mail Is Here	140	4¼"x6¼"	TW
Tuneful Goodnight	180	5"x5¾"	TW
Vacation Time	125	4"x4¾"	TW

WALL VASES

NAME	MOLD NUMBER	APPROX. SIZE	RETAIL PRICE
Boy	360/B	4½"x6¼"	TW
Boy & Girl	360/A	4½"x6¼"	TW
Girl	360/C	4½"x6¼"	TW

M.I. HUMMEL CLUB® Exclusive Collectibles

Anniversary Figurines (prices effective June 1, 1993)

NAME	MOLD NUMBER	APPROX. SIZE	RETAIL PRICE
Flower Girl (5 Year Figurine)	548	4⅜"	130.00
The Little Pair (10 Year Figurine)	449	4½"	200.00
Honey Lover (15 Year Figurine)	312	3⅞"	210.00

Club Figurines

NAME	MOLD NUMBER	APPROX. SIZE	RETAIL PRICE
*1993/94-I Didn't Do It	626	5½"	175.00
*1993/94 Sweet As Can Be	541	4"	125.00
**1992/93-My Wish Is Small	463/0	5¼"	170.00
**1992/93-Cheeky Fellow (preview edition)	554	4"	125.00
***1991/92-Gift From A Friend	485	4⅜"	160.00
***1991/92-Miniature Morning Concert w/Display 1977 through 1990 Expired	27054	4¾"	175.00

Celebration Plate Series

1986 through 1990

Expired

SIZES INDICATED ARE ONLY APPROXIMATE
PRICES SUBJECT TO CHANGE WITHOUT NOTICE

TW Temporarily Withdrawn

*** Redemption card available to members who join prior to June 1992

** Redemption card available to members who join prior to June 1993

* Redemption card available to members who join prior to June 1994

§ Edition Complete

" Production in the 20th Century limited to 1993

+ Retired in 1992

¶ Retires in 1993

' Not an "M.I. Hummel" figurine

++ Only available at District Manager events

TW: Temporarily withdrawn from production with no stated reinstatement date.

INDEX

A Free Gift When You Join!

The M.I. Hummel Club®

Join the M.I. Hummel Club and start a year full of fun and excitement in a special way! The *M.I. Hummel®* figurine, *I Brought You A Gift*, is free with your membership to the M.I. Hummel Club. Created for new members only, this prized figurine is just the first of so many benefits you'll receive as a Club member.

There are the Club Exclusives: Limited-edition figurines offered for two years only, never to be issued again and available solely to club members. You'll also enjoy an informative, thought-provoking quarterly magazine, and the opportunity to join a Local Chapter and meet new friends. And each year, the Club offers fabulous trips to Europe with a "members-only" tour of the Goebel factory, where you'll learn all about the intricate production process and meet our master artists busy at their craft.

So whether you're a seasoned collector or someone who just discovered *M.I. Hummel* figurines, come and join in the many enjoyable benefits of M.I. Hummel Club membership.

I Brought You A Gift
(Hum 479) 3 3/4"

Some of our special benefits include:

- *I Brought You A Gift*, the FREE M.I. Hummel Club exclusive figurine for new Club members only. A retail value of US $85 CDN $105
- Membership and Redemption Cards, your only way of obtaining Club Exclusive figurines.
- INSIGHTS, the quarterly magazine filled with behind-the-scenes updates, fascinating articles, helpful hints, and more.
- A handsome binder to keep your issues of INSIGHTS, complete with divider pages, which includes the history of *M.I. Hummel* figurines, a special mention of valued member services, and your own collector's log.
- Exciting Club travel opportunities, including a "Members-Only" tour of the Goebel factory in Germany, where *M.I. Hummel* treasures are made.
- Local Chapters of the M.I. Hummel Club, to make new friends and to share your interest in *M.I. Hummel* figurines.
- Schedule of in-store promotions featuring artists and other *M.I. Hummel* representatives in your area.
- Club services, such as the Research Department and Collectors' Market to match buyers and sellers of *M.I. Hummel* collectibles.

(See Next Page)

Join the Club!
Here's how...

For exclusive membership privileges, simply complete the attached application and mail it along with your personal check or money order, payable to the M.I. Hummel Club. One year's membership fee is US $45.00 and CDN $60.00. Prices are subject to change. Mastercard, Visa, and American Express are also gladly accepted.

Or call the Club at:
1-800-666-CLUB (2582)
to join today.
Have you enclosed your check or money order?
US $45.00 • Canada $60.00

Cut Here - Cut Here

M.I. Hummel Club New Member Application
Goebel Plaza, P.O. Box 11, Pennington, New Jersey 08534-0011

Please enroll me as a new member.

NAME, FIRST	(PLEASE PRINT)	MIDDLE INITIAL	LAST

STREET ADDRESS			APARTMENT NUMBER

US CITY		STATE	ZIP+4

CANADA CITY		PROVINCE	POSTAL CODE

Enclosed, please find my payment for: (check one)
☐ U.S. $45.00
☐ CDN $60.00
☐ Enclosed is my check or money order made payable to:
   M.I. HUMMEL CLUB
Please charge my: ☐ MASTERCARD   ☐ VISA
                  ☐ AMERICAN EXPRESS

AREA CODE	PHONE NUMBER

I understand that within 6 to 8 weeks, you will send me my membership card, redemption cards and membership package with the *M.I. Hummel figurine, I Brought You A Gift,* and binder.

MEMBERSHIP FEES SUBJECT TO CHANGE WITHOUT NOTICE

CARD NUMBER _____   EXPIRATION DATE _____

SIGNATURE _____   DATE _____